D1544868

GOVERNING CAPITALIST ECONOMIES

Governing Capitalist Economies

Performance and Control of Economic Sectors

EDITED BY

J. Rogers Hollingsworth

Philippe C. Schmitter

Wolfgang Streeck

New York   Oxford

OXFORD UNIVERSITY PRESS

1994

338.9
G7212

al)

Oxford University Press

Oxford   New York   Toronto
Delhi   Bombay   Calcutta   Madras   Karachi
Kuala Lumpur   Singapore   Hong Kong   Tokyo
Nairobi   Dar es Salaam   Cape Town
Melbourne   Auckland   Madrid

and associated companies in
Berlin   Ibadan

Copyright © 1994 by Oxford University Press, Inc.

Published by Oxford University Press, Inc.,
200 Madison Avenue, New York, New York 10016

Oxford is a registered trademark of Oxford University Press

All rights reserved. No part of this publication may be reproduced,
stored in a retrieval system, or transmitted, in any form or by any means,
electronic, mechanical, photocopying, recording, or otherwise,
without prior permission of Oxford University Press.

Library of Congress Cataloging-in-Publication Data
Governing capitalist economies: performance and control of economic sectors /
edited by J. Rogers Hollingsworth, Philippe C. Schmitter, Wolfgang Streeck.
p. cm.   Includes bibliographical references and index.
ISBN 0-19-507968-X
1. Industry and state — Congresses.   2. Capitalism — Congresses.
3. Comparative economics — Congresses.   I. Hollingsworth, J. Rogers
(Joseph Rogers), 1932– .   II Schmitter, Philippe C.
III. Streeck, Wolfgang, 1946– .
HD3611.G677   1994
338.9 — dc20   93-6603

2   4   6   8   9   7   5   3   1

Printed in the United States of America
on acid-free paper

For Robert Boyer
great scholar
stimulating teacher
loyal friend
and
wonderful citizen

University Libraries
Carnegie Mellon University
Pittsburgh PA 15213-3890

ACKNOWLEDGMENTS

THIS project is an effort to bring together specialists from different disciplines and from different areas of the world to study the governance of advanced capitalist economies. It seeks to focus on global problems, while at the same time trying to understand differences and similarities in industrial sectors both within and across countries located in several broad cultural areas: Western and Northern Europe, North America, and East Asia.

We wish to acknowledge generous support from several organizations for helping us to move beyond the study of capitalism in a single culture area. Early on, the project received financial support from the American Council of Learned Societies—Social Science Research Council Joint Committee on Western Europe. Throughout the project, we also received financial support from the Ford Foundation, and toward the end of the project we had additional assistance from the Japan Foundation.

Our research group met for the first time in the spring of 1988 at the Johnson Foundation's Conference Center—"Wingspread"—in Racine, Wisconsin. A second meeting was held in June of the following year at the Rockefeller Foundation's conference center, Villa Serbelloni, in Bellagio, Italy. At both meetings, we discussed drafts of the following papers and conducted extensive discussions about many of the problems raised in this volume. We are very grateful to both of these organizations for the use of their facilities—each being one of the world's best conference centers for scholarly research.

We are obliged to a number of sympathetic commentators who attended one or both group meetings. These include Masahiko Aoki, John L. Campbell, Michael Gerlach, Gerhard Lehmbruch, Richard Nelson, Yoshitaka Okada, Walter Powell, Joel Rogers, and Marc Schneiberg. We especially acknowledge Robert Boyer of Paris, who not only attended both conferences and made valuable written comments about each paper but also made several trips to the United States to work with the editors on this project. Jerald Hage and Ellen Jane Hollingsworth generously read each paper and made useful comments at a timely point in the project. Many colleagues on several continents offered valuable advice, but we especially wish to thank Bo Gustafson, Charles Sabel, Fritz Scharpf, Volker Schneider, Oliver Williamson, and Jonathan Zeitlin.

CONTENTS

GOVERNING CAPITALIST ECONOMIES

CHAPTER 1

Capitalism, Sectors, Institutions,
and Performance

J. Rogers Hollingsworth, Philippe C. Schmitter,
and Wolfgang Streeck

CAPITALISM is an economic system defined by free markets and private property in the means of production. Whereas the latter (private property) gives rise to a relationship of employment between capital and labor that involves the exercise of managerial prerogative through hierarchical authority, the former (free markets) constitutes a social space for voluntary contract and competitive conflict. All forms of capitalism share these fundamental characteristics. At the same time, even in the most capitalist of economies, economic action is shaped, not just by markets and private property relations, but also by a wide range of other institutions. Markets and property rights are always embedded in, and modified by, local institutional contexts of a noneconomic, social kind. While private property rights and free market exchanges make for the common elements of capitalism as an economic system, the social and political institutions surrounding them are the sources of differences among empirical capitalist economies.

Central among the questions addressed in this book is how important these differences are and will continue to be. For most of the modern period, but especially in the decades after World War II, it has been both intuitively plausible and pragmatically acceptable to emphasize the *unity of capitalism* over the *diversity of capitalist societies*. Marxists, of course, have always been prominent members of the "one capitalism" camp. They did not deny the existence of differences between national economies, between workers in different occupations, or between capitalists in different sectors, but regarded them as either irrelevant or the expression of different stages of "capitalist development." Some societies had advanced further in the general capitalist trajectory than others; the late-comers would catch up institutionally in a matter of time.

Convergence theory, whether implicit or explicit, was never a monopoly of the opponents of capitalism. The discipline of economics was originally very concerned with social institutions and their consequences for economic outcomes, but the ascendant neoclassical synthesis, in its quest for "rigor" and "information

3

economy," focused its range of inquiry on markets and, occasionally, organizational hierarchies. Other social institutions were seen as interfering with the idealized realization of these two and, hence, were treated only as sources of deplorable deviation from efficiency and productivity. Under the optimistic assumptions of neoclassical functionalism, these institutional interferences were not expected to survive. Ultimately, they would have to give way to the competitive pressures for "economizing." This would inexorably lead to the convergence of different capitalists toward a market-driven corporate model of "industrialism" that happened conspicuously to resemble the leading economy of the time, the United States. In the 1950s and 1960s, hardly anyone disagreed with the assumption that the more traditional and, therefore, backward economies like Japan, Germany, or Europe as a whole would have to adopt American patterns of industrial organization, procurement of finance, management, division of labor at the point of production, industrial relations, skill formation, and the like.

Ironically (and retrospectively), convergence theory was most appealing at a time when national economies were still relatively isolated from each other. As this changed with accelerating globalization of exchanges in the 1970s and 1980s, the differences among existing capitalist systems became much more visible and more relevant. For example, while most Americans in the 1960s knew very little about Japanese industrial relations or industrial policy, today the subject is a major concern of media coverage and everyday conversations. Moreover, the sociopolitical environment within which economic activity is embedded is now commonly and insistently perceived to be related to differences in the economic performances among countries.

Furthermore, certainty about the direction of "capitalist development" has declined, and not just on the Left. As the American economy suffers from obvious and deeply rooted deficiencies, many observers have looked to others, particularly the Japanese and German experiences, as models of what capitalism may look like in the future in terms of management techniques, public policies, and industrial relations. For some, the very idea of a convergence in the trajectories of nationalist economies has lost credibility. The differences among local capitalists seem not only persistent but also more important and interesting than do the similarities.

In this volume, capitalism in advanced industrial societies is compared according to four themes.

1. The Notion of Capitalism as an Institutional Order

The common premise throughout this book is that economic action is a special case of social action and, therefore, needs to be coordinated or governed by institutional arrangements. Coordination problems arise with respect to the setting of prices, the determination of the quantity of production, the raising of capital, the standardization of products, the provision of consumers with information, the regulation of product quality, the determination of the amount and type of labor to be employed, the definition of the terms of its compensation, etc.

Coordination is accomplished through a set of institutions that together form the economy's system of governance. A governance system is defined as the *totality of institutional arrangements—including rules and rule-making agents—that regulate transactions inside and across the boundaries of an economic system.* Alternative concepts used in this volume are "socioeconomic regime," or "industrial order."

Contemporary mainstream economics postulates essentially two mechanisms of governance: *markets and corporate hierarchies.* Markets are arenas in which individual or corporate actors holding separate property rights in different resources voluntarily engage in free, legally enforceable contractual exchanges. Markets are the place for buying and selling, with prices providing more or less distorted information for the allocation of goods and services. Corporate hierarchies, by contrast, are institutions that permit some actors to wield authority over others on the basis of property rights vested in a formal organization to which both categories of actors belong. In the limited institutional repertory envisaged by mainstream economics, corporate hierarchies are the preferred, and in fact the only "economic," alternative to markets.

Markets and hierarchies tend to be appropriate arrangements for coordinating exchanges among actors if these reflect a sequential or serial type of interdependence—in other words, if the output of one unit is the input of the other. They are capable of structuring exchanges among actors engaged in dissimilar activities (and potentially conflictual), for example, producers and processors, financiers and manufacturers, labor and capital. Oliver Williamson's early work was devoted to identifying the specific subsets of transactions—uncertainty in outcome, the frequency of transactions, and asset specificity—all of which, he argued, require extensive monitoring. In these circumstances, Williamson argued that markets perform suboptimally and, as a result, corporate hierarchies are more likely to emerge as the optimal mechanism of governance (Williamson, 1975, 1985).

Corporate hierarchies often result from strategies of vertical integration. This can provide a means for coping with problematic interdependence among actors by minimizing uncertainty in relations among suppliers, distributors, and other complementary actors. For example, steel companies may merge with producers of iron one or with transportation companies; food processing companies may move into food distribution, or vice versa; oil companies may become producers of chemicals. Corporate hierarchy can also result when a company expands to cover multiple products within the same industry—for instance, the history of IBM; or when organizations in the same industry merge to achieve economies of scale and increase profits.

Economic theory has reluctantly recognized a third mechanism of governance: the modern *state.* Wherever possible, it has been analytically and prescriptively assigned a different role from the other two mechanisms. The state is accorded a legitimate function in the definition of property rights, the enforcement of contracts, and the setting of general rules of competition. In short, the state creates and maintains those minimal conditions without which markets and hierarchies would not be possible. In all but the most libertarian conceptions, the state is also accepted as a provider of last resort of collective goods that neither markets nor corporate hierarchies can provide efficiently or reliably on their own, such as fresh air, a stable currency, general education, and protection against fires, crime, worker rebelliousness, political insurgency, foreign armies, and so forth.

The self-appointed function of neoclassical economics vis-à-vis the state is to ensure that the agents of the state do not succumb to their (presumably) inherent tendency to expand their role beyond those goods and services that are necessary for the compensation of market-*cum*-hierarchy failures and for the proper operation of the other two (inherently) legitimate mechanisms of governance.[1] This is because the state is generally suspected of allocative inefficiency—unlike markets and hierarchies that are presumed to be efficient unless proven otherwise.[2]

In reality, of course, states have assumed a much wider range of roles due both to their unparalleled capacity for supplying authoritative, "public" regulation of transactions among economic actors, and to the unrestrained demand for their intervention by a set of aroused and disadvantaged "publics." Both are accomplished by a specialized set of bureaucratic agencies backed ultimately by the potential resort to legitimate force. Whether by supply or demand, the state may influence the price of products, determine the quantity of production, supply capital, dictate product standards, regulate product quality, and set wages. It may also own and operate entire sectors of an economy, or just strategic enterprises "of national interest" with them. Variation in the role of states from sector to sector, across countries, and over time is an important issue on the research agenda concerning economic governance, despite the fact that most empirical and historical state activities exceed what is considered desirable or even legitimate by most economists.

Another mechanism of economic coordination consists of *informal networks* (Alter and Hage, 1993; Campbell, Hollingsworth, and Lindberg, 1991; Marsden, 1990; Nielsen, 1988; Jarillo, 1988; Contractor and Lorange, 1988; Schopler, 1987; Powell, 1987; Granovetter, 1985; Pfeffer and Nowak, 1976). It has also been called the clan (Hollingsworth and Lindberg, 1985; Ouchi, 1980) or the community (Streeck and Schmitter, 1985). Generally speaking, informal networks are loosely joined sets of individuals or organizations in which transactions are conducted on the basis of mutual trust and confidence sustained by stable, preferential, particularistic, mutually obligated, and legally nonenforceable relationships. They may be kept together either by value consensus or resource dependency—that is, through "culture" and "community"—or through dominant units imposing dependence on others. In either case, they coordinate economic action in ways clearly different from markets, hierarchies, and states.

Economic theorists have, in different ways, tried to come to terms with the observation that where there are well-developed and stable networks capable of mediating and regulating complex economic transactions, economic actors often prefer them over both markets and hierarchies (Williamson, 1985; Aoki, 1987, 1988; Eccles, 1981; Streeck, 1981; Hollingsworth, 1991). Where networks are available, vertical integration is less likely to occur, presumably because networks are more responsive to environmental fluctuations. In other words, they are more "flexible" than hierarchies. Moreover, network structures seem to be well suited for environments in which economic actors have fairly high trust among each other. For example, the approximately twenty-eight firms that make up the Mitsubishi group in Japan form a network engaged in preferential trading that has no formal hierarchical structure. Mitsubishi is not a conglomerate, for there is no central board or holding company. Nor is it a cartel; the member firms engage in different lines of business. The companies within the Mitsubishi group have established and have managed to sustain long-term, stable trading relations on the basis of personalistic and particularistic ties (Dore, 1983), which, in the world of neoclassical economics, should only serve to distort the market and result in suboptimal allocation. The discovery in the 1980s of the competitive superiority of Japanese companies over firms in institutionally simpler environments has resulted in a number of attempts to theorize the efficiency features of network-like informal relations. One example consists of modifications in transaction cost economics to include notions of "soft contracting," as distinct from the hard or explicit contracting (Aoki, 1988; Lazarson, 1988; Streeck, 1991; Hollingsworth, 1991; Håkansson and Laage-Hellman, 1984; Williamson, 1985).

Still another mechanism of coordination that has recently attracted wide attention is the *association*—or, where they are strongly institutionalized, "private interest government" (Streeck and Schmitter, 1985). Associations are collective organizations formed among specific categories of actors in identical, similar, or adjacent market positions that define and promote public (or "categorical") goods. They do so in three ways: (1) by organizing and enforcing cooperative behavior among their members, (2) by engaging in collective contracts with other associations, and (3) by mobilizing and/or influencing public policy to their own and their members' advantage.[3] Associations have been formed by both worker and business interests. For example, trade associations have been important in the governance of economic sectors, not only in Europe and Japan but also in the United States (Schneiberg and Hollingsworth, 1989). They seem to have thrived especially in competitive and decentralized sectors, and in more mature phases of the product life cycle (e.g., in textiles, pharmaceuticals, and semiconductors). In all modern economies, companies have associated with each other to collect information about production levels and prices, to conduct joint research and development, to promote standardization, to engage in technology transfer and vocational training, to channel communication and influence to state agencies, to formulate codes of conduct, to negotiate with labor, and even to decide on prices, production goals, and investment strategies. Ironically, workers have generally been less well organized, but the literature on unions and collective bargaining is far more voluminous than that on business associations. Among other things, unions have been found to be involved—(admittedly, with different degrees of success)—in wage setting, regulation of working conditions and job specifications, determination of working hours, management of employment levels, and indeed the regulation of investment or the setting of product prices.

Markets, hierarchies, states, networks, and associations represent distinctive modes of governance. All are likely to be present to varying degrees in any given economy or economic sector. The object of comparative empirical research on institutional arrangements for coordinating economic activity is to determine the relative importance of the various modes of governance in different contexts, to describe how they are articulated with one another, and to assess the extent and direction of change in regimes over time.

For example, in managing relations with their suppliers, manufacturing firms may try to ensure stable and reliable provision at sufficient quality and acceptable prices through the "hard contracting" mechanisms of market relations, through vertical integration in corporate hierarchies, through authoritative regulation by state agencies, through "soft contracting" based on informal network relations, through long-term agreements with supplier associations, or through any combination of these. In addition, corporations and economies have to find adequate institutional arrangements to procure capital, labor, and knowledge; to generate the necessary skills in their work force; and to develop satisfactory relations between producers and wholesalers, and between retailers and customers. Understanding the determinants, the choices, and the dynamics of different modes of governance for addressing these problems is an important task of an empirically oriented political economy, and it is to the accomplishment of that task that this volume seeks to make a contribution.

2. The Importance of Sectors as Sites of Political Economy

This book explores the idea that modes of economic *governance* may differ not only by countries—reflecting different institutional legacies and distributions of national political power—but also by *sectors*, in accordance with specific economic and technological conditions. There is no generally accepted definition of the boundaries of a sector. For the purposes of this book, a sector is simply a population of firms producing a specified range of potentially or actually competing products. The sector, thus defined, interacts with a number of environments in procuring key resources such as capital (from investment houses, banks, private investors, etc.), labor (from households and unions), raw materials (from producers and distributors), and intermediate products (from industries "upstream" in the product chain), and in disposing of its final outputs (through transport providers and retailers to customers). Mechanisms of governance are required to coordinate transactions inside as well as across sector boundaries.

Capitalism can no longer be studied as a whole, but must be broken down into its parts. Instead of evolving, as both liberals and Marxists had presumed, toward a single, unified, and perfectly competitive market in which all factors of production would flow to their marginally most efficient use without spatial or functional barriers, capitalism seems to give rise to significant, persistent, and perhaps even growing variation in the conditions under which resources and rewards are distributed. Both to capture the diversity of capitalism and to render it manageable, *it seems useful to focus on the sector as the key unit for comparative analysis.* A number of changes in technology, market structure, and public policy seem to have converged to make this mesolevel (e.g., the intermediate location between the microlevel of the firm and the macrolevel of the whole economy) increasingly salient. One of the purposes of this book is to explore why this may be the case.

In seeking to establish a theoretical basis for the "sectoral economy," there are two avenues of inspiration, which represent two different sources for the historical development of sectors. On the one hand, sectors are one of the two nexuses—the other being the community or locality—where exchanges among producers and among producers, suppliers, and consumers can be *socially constructed* (Streeck and Schmitter, 1985). On the other hand, sectors provide one of the principal frameworks within which public policies can be *effectively administered*—the other being the issue arena. Sectors can be initiated and sustained from below through the independent actions of capitalists and their trading partners and interlocutors, or they can be created from above through the imposition of boundaries and rules by public authorities. Needless to say, both self-organization and public policy can interact and combine to produce a sector—an outcome that is especially likely when capitalists find it difficult or impossible to stabilize their exchanges on a voluntary basis and end up appealing to the state or some other outsider for help.

Attention to the mesolevel of sectors (which in different countries can also be called by other names such as industries, industry groups, branches of production, products, product groups, etc.) immediately makes the student sensitive to something that has seemingly escaped the attention of most economists: namely, that not all sectors are organized as markets. Instead, once one looks around in any deliberate and systematic way, an astonishing variety of "mechanisms" or "arrangements" for regulating transactions and exchanges become highly visible, whether inside and across the boundaries of any one sector. The "Organized Capitalism"/"Neo-corporatist" perspective highlights the prospective role of interest associations, but the French *École de la Régulation* reminds us that "the process of fitting production and social demand" necessarily involves a wide and diverse range of governing institutions, not just those setting wages and norms of production. Technology must be generated and assimilated; financial resources must be mobilized and distributed; standards must be established and enforced; products must be announced and reliably delivered; aggregate demand must be generated and sustained.[4] Markets, hierarchies, and networks may accomplish some of these tasks. Associations are but one of several mechanisms available to resolve the others. The distinctive mix of all of them becomes what we call "the mode of regulation."

3. The Relationship Between Social Institutions and Economic Performance

Throughout this volume, we make the argument that governance regimes matter. Local or regional social-institutional contexts can significantly affect the *competitive performance* of national sectors in international markets. Sectoral regimes within nation-states are in turn influenced and transformed by international competitive pressures, which may well constitute one of the most important and independent sources of institutional change in the contemporary world of high interdependent national capitalisms.

More specifically, the contributors to this volume share the view that an institutional perspective on the economy should address questions of efficiency and performance, even if social scientists normally try either to avoid those subjects or to leave them to economists. The social institutions that emerge historically to coordinate economic transactions need not always be "efficient" in a strictly economic sense. There is no reason to accept the implicit or explicit functionalism that typically goes with the economistic perspective on institutions. In contrast to Williamson (1975, 1985), North (1990) even argues that most institutional forms of coordination have not been efficient. But this does not mean that pressures for "economizing" are not real or that they have no impact on the selection of coordination regimes. The important reservation is that different modes of sectoral governance and modes of national regulations may have different capacities for conforming to these pressures, and they may emerge with solutions that are different but equally competitive.

The scholar focusing on sectoral industrial orders at the present time cannot fail to notice that the continuous and rapid integration of world markets has resulted in unprecedented competition, not just among firms, but among the entire complexes of social, institutional, and political substructures in which firms are embedded. The fact that sectors in some countries have been more successful than in others in responding to growing world market pressures in the 1970s and 1980s inevitably gives rise to the research question whether this can be related to different mixes of markets, hierarchies, informal networks, associative self-regulation, and state intervention in the management and control of transactions inside and across sectoral boundaries. In such circumstances, comparing social institutions in terms of their economic performance—their "efficiency"—is no longer merely an academic concern: *It is rather the reality of international "capitalist development" that increasingly puts entire local and national socioeconomic systems to competitive tests.* As economic theory finds it increasingly difficult to account for cross-national variations in competitiveness, comparative institutional analysis may hold the key for understanding how different *industrial orders obstruct or facilitate the efforts of industries to survive in world markets.* To understand sectoral institutional regimes, we must be sensitive not only to how an array of performance criteria (e.g., efficiency, quality, market share, egalitarian concerns, etc.) shape institutional arrangements but also how institutional arrangements shape sectoral performance.

4. The Problem of "Convergence"

Paradoxically, just as the globalization of the economy has drawn renewed attention to the persistence of national specificities, it has also given rise to other, more sophisticated versions of convergence theory. The decade of the 1970s, in particular, was when technological, economic, and other "determinisms" declined in fashion and national cultures and politics were rediscovered as repositories of lasting and significant differences between capitalist economies and societies. This reflected *both* the breaking up of the postwar international economic regime in which the pervasive influence of the United States on other countries could be mistaken for developmental trends driving all capitalist societies in a similar direction *and* the vastly divergent performances of national economies following the "oil shock" of 1973. But the ensuing period was also a time in which the nation-state began to undergo dramatic changes *in its role* vis-à-vis both the domestic and the international economy. In either respect, economic internationalization confronted even the largest and most powerful nation-states with a devaluation of their most precious resource—*sovereignty*, that is, the ability to make autonomous *and* effectively binding decisions on behalf of a *territorial society demarcated by state borders*. With this progressive erosion of sovereignty, the future of nation-states and of national political arrangements *as barriers against institutional convergence* became increasingly doubtful.

This decline in national economic sovereignty in the 1970s and 1980s has yet to be empirically measured or theoretically understood. Among its most visible manifestations has been the loss of what could be called "Keynesian capacity," or the ability to manage employment levels through reflationary fiscal and monetary policies by national governments. One reason for this is that, with the growing interpenetration of "national" economies, the external contribution to each "domestic" product has increased to a level where it can no longer be treated as a mere addition to an essentially closed economic circuit whose territorial domain is coterminous with the jurisdiction of a national government. Another related factor is the unprecedented mobility of capital, which can be traced back to the emergence of offshore banking in the 1950s. This has culminated in a liberalized financial market that is beyond the control of any individual state and not yet within the control of an effective international organization. Generally speaking, increasing external interdependence in these and other domains seem to have irreversibly weakened the control of national political institutions over their respective economies. Not only the *external* but also the *internal* sovereignty of the national state has been undermined. This more than anything else may be behind the ongoing worldwide redefinition of the "proper" role of the state in economic matters, pushing many nations in the common direction of deregulation and privatization.

Convergence theory no longer focuses on the problem of whether there is movement toward some "mixed economy" between capitalism and socialism. Rather, it confronts the problem of whether convergence may be resulting from a process of economic globalization that removes formerly "national" economies from the influence of national institutions, but does not submit them to control by new, global regulatory institutions. If this form of convergence is occurring, the outcome could be the transformation of local, particular capitalisms with all their varied mechanisms of governance into a single bi-regulated supranational capitalism with much less requisite variety. It might be emancipated from the tutelage of national politicians and state agents, and liberated from the influence of social pressures and class conflicts that have in the past interfered with untrammelled market allocation and managerial prerogative of corporate hierarchies, but it could also be exposed to uncertainties and turbulences of unprecedented magnitudes. It remains to be seen whether this process is occurring at the regional level—that is, the twelve capitalisms of the European Community moving toward their single internal market. If this type of process occurs at either the continental or global level, persistent differences in national capitalisms should recede in importance, surviving only as a matter of local consumer taste or as a symbol of cultural style.

A number of observers believe that many sectors are rapidly losing their distinctive character. For example, it has often been pointed out that the German banking sector differs historically from its British and American counterparts because of its closely institutionalized and legally supported links to domestic manufacturing industry—links that, in turn, are widely regarded as a major reason for the long-term investment capacity and the resulting high international competitiveness of German manufacturing firms. However, as financial markets become truly integrated-*cum*-deregulated on a global scale, German banks may more and more find it difficult to reconcile their interests as business enterprises with their functions as instruments of national industrial policy. Unlike the relatively closed and regulated national capital markets of the past, competition may be too sharp, clienteles too diverse, and transactions too dispersed to support special, long-term, *Hausbank*-style attention to a selected national constituency, especially if that constituency is itself internationalizing its operations, organizations, and credit sources. The globalization of "financial services," by stripping national banking sectors of their role as national industrial policy instruments, may contribute significantly toward ending those sectoral differences among countries that have for so long survived all predictions of imminent "convergence."

At the same time that it reduces the significance of nations as units of choice and analysis, globalization may increase the importance of sectors. If the sectors of a given "national" economy cease to be unified by their sovereign authority and assimilated by their common nationality, each could begin to resemble its counterparts in other countries. It may well then be the case that the major remaining differences in the functioning and social embedding of modes of governance will reside in those globally integrated sectors. Secure from external institutional intervention, transactions within such sectors may be governed according to the logic—the *Eigengesetzlichkeit*—of their specific productive structures and of the constraints imposed by their particular technologies. Sectors may begin to converge toward a "best practice," as imposed by international competition irrespective of their politico-spatial location. Alternatively, they may concentrate in those places of the world where the historical heritage of governance arrangements is, for whatever reason, most sympathetic to their needs.

There is also another scenario we must consider. Firms may well be so embedded into a configuration of social institutions that the governance of sectors will continue to be distinctive to the particular society in which they are located. Hence, there would be no convergence in sectoral governance, and entire sectors in some societies would diverge from the best practice. Under such circumstances, sectors that had once been very successful may well succumb in the long run to international competitiveness. It is hoped that the case studies that follow will yield insights about the convergence and divergence in the governance of sectors. Whatever the case, sectors seem likely to become increasingly important subjects and objects for the comparative study of capitalism in a postnational age of economic globalization.

The Case Studies

This book is the first result of the collective effort of a study group on "comparative capitalism." As implied above, it strives theoretically to integrate several bodies of literature focusing on the coordination of economic actors: the transaction cost economics literature that focuses on the transactions of different economic actors; the various literatures that address the efforts of actors to engage in collective action—for example, the efforts of labor to develop unions, employers to develop trade associations, etc.; the corporatist literature that has focused on the emergence of private-interest governments; and a vast sociological and political economy literature that focuses on how the performance of firms is shaped by the socioeconomic environment in which they are embedded.

At an early stage, the group decided to begin its work with a *comparative inventory of governance mechanisms at the sectoral level*. We chose this empirical and taxonomic approach to provide a rich factual base that could encompass as much as possible the wide variety of coordination regimes existing in modern capitalist economies. But the group also resolved to avoid a merely descriptive exercise by addressing the analytical problem of the relationship between institutional structures and economic competitiveness. Moreover, recognizing that the dynamics of economic institutions change over time, our participants accepted the need to ground their work historically. In particular, the degree and variety of *performance pressures* faced by various governance mechanisms clearly depends, among other things, on the historical development of the markets in which they are embedded: their extension and scope, their predictability, the kind of competition they generate, the degree of strategic choice they leave to participants, and the kind of institutional capacities on which they place a premium.

It was against this background that the group selected as its first project *the comparison of sectoral regimes from the viewpoint of their economic performance in the 1970s and 1980s* and to try in turn to trace the dynamic effects of performance pressures and competitive outcomes on such regimes in the present. Nine sectors were chosen as research sites. Most of them are in manufacturing, the one exception being the securities industry. All but one, the dairy industry, are highly competitive internationally. The choice of sectors was constrained by the need to connect with ongoing research—internationally comparative research needs a long lead time—and to find participants who were sympathetic to the project's general approach. As a result, the number and selection of countries that are compared for each sector differ widely, which should be acceptable since the

Table 1.1. Sectors and countries

	Austria	Canada	Germany	France	Japan	Sweden	U.K.	U.S.
Printed circuit board					×		×	
Steel					×			×
Shipbuilding			×		×	×		
Machine tools			×					×
Chemicals			×				×	
Automobiles			×	×			×	
Dairy	×		×				×	
Consumer electronics				×			×	
Securities		×					×	×
Total	1	1	5	2	3	1	6	3

project does not primarily aim either at understanding particular countries or at surveying the universe of sectors, but tries to shed light on the general relationship between institutional structures and economic performance.

As Table 1.1 shows, the chapters cover a total of eight countries. The United Kingdom is included in six sector studies, and Germany in five. Japan and the United States follow with three sectors each. The sectoral studies of shipbuilding (Stråth), automobiles (Dankbaar), dairying (Traxler and Unger), and securities (Coleman) each compare three countries. The remaining five chapters focus on two countries each.

The sequence of sectoral analyses begins with three chapters that include Japan: Sako's research on the printed circuit board industry, the paper by O'Brien on steel, and Stråth's chapter on shipbuilding. The latter also covers Germany, and this applies to the following four papers as well: Herrigel on machine tools, Grant and Paterson on chemicals, Dankbaar on automobiles, and Traxler and Unger on dairying. The papers on chemicals, automobiles, and dairying include the United Kingdom, and so do the last two empirical papers, Cawson on consumer electronics and Coleman on securities. The concluding chapter is an effort to draw generalizations from the empirical material.

Notes

1. In other words, neoclassical economics could be described either as an academically institutionalized lobby for the "private sector" in search of profit-making opportunities, or as a highly developed rhetorical technique for convincing state agents to turn their profitable activities over to "the market." There is, therefore, no limit to the state tasks that economists have suggested for "privatization"; the list certainly includes each and every one of those mentioned in the text. In this respect, Ronald Coase, the Nobel

Laureate for Economics in 1991, in the question and answer period following his Nobel Prize address in Stockholm, referred to neoclassical economics as a form of theology.
2. Which, arguably, is not possible inside the paradigm. If markets or hierarchies are found to produce suboptimal results, a neoclassical economist's instinct would be to assume that this was due to too little, not too much, of one or the other, and he or she would suggest that the solution is to reduce rather than increase the influence of other social institutions, such as state agencies. Because there will always be many state agencies and other forms of collective institutions, the pure recipe cannot really be tested.
3. Both the importance and distinctiveness of associations as a source of social order, and the properties of association as distinct from communities, markets, and states, have been pointed out by Streeck and Schmitter (1985).
4. For a useful, general overview of this approach in English, see Boyer, 1987; Aglietta, 1982; Boyer and Mistral, 1983; and Andre and Delorme, 1983.

References

Aglietta, M. (1982). *Regulation et Crise du Capitalisme* (2d ed.). Paris: Calman-Levy.
Alter, Catherine and Jerald Hage. (1993). *Organizations Working Together: Coordination in Interorganizational Networks*. Newbury Park, Calif.: Sage.
Andre, C., and Robert Delorme. (1983). *L'Etat et L'Economie*. Paris: Seuil.
Aoki, Masahiko. (1987). "The Japanese Firm in Transition." In Kozo Yamamura and Yasukichi Yasuba (eds.), *The Political Economy of Japan*: Vol. 1 (pp. 263–88). Stanford, Calif.: Stanford University Press.
Aoki, Masahiko. (1988). *Information, Incentives and Bargaining in the Japanese Economy*. Cambridge: Cambridge University Press.
Boyer, Robert, and J. Mistral. (1983). *Accumulation, Inflation, Crises* (2d ed.). Paris: PUF.
Boyer, Robert. (1987). "Technical Change and the Theory of 'Regulation.'" (Mimeograph, Couverture Orange, CEPREMAP, No. 8707.)
Campbell, John, J., Rogers Hollingsworth, and Leon Lindberg. (1991). *The Governance of the American Economy*. Cambridge and New York: Cambridge University Press.
Contractor, Farok, J., and Peter Lorange. (1988). *Cooperative Strategies in International Business*. Lexington, Mass.: Lexington Books.
Dore, Ronald. (1983). "Goodwill and the Spirit of Market Capitalism." *The British Journal of Sociology*, 34, 459–82.
Eccles, Robert. (1981, December). "The Quasifirm in the Construction Industry." *Journal of Economic Behavior and Organization*, 2, 355–57.
Fagerberg, J. (1984). "The 'Regulation School' and the Classics: Modes of Accumulation and Modes of Regulation in a Classical Model of Economic Growth." (Mimeograph, Couverture Orange, CEPREMAP, No. 8426.)
Granovetter, Mark. (1985). "Economic Action and Social Structure: The Problem of Embeddedness." *American Journal of Sociology*, 91, 481–510.
Håkansson, Håkan, and Jens Laage-Hellman. (1984). "Developing a Network Rand D Strategy." *Journal of Productivity Innovation Management*, 4, 224–37.
Hollingsworth, J. Rogers. (1991, March). "Die Logik der Koordination des verabeitenden Gewerbes in Amerika." *Kolner Zeitschrift fur Soziologie und Sozial Psychologie*, 43, 18–43.
Hollingsworth, J. Rogers, and Leon Lindberg. (1985). "The Role of Markets, Clans, Hierarchies, and Associative Behavior." In Wolfgang Streeck and Philippe Schmitter (eds.), *Private Interest Government: Beyond Market and State* (pp. 221–54). London and Beverly Hills, Calif.: Sage Publications.

Jarillo, J. Carlos. (1988). "On Strategic Networks." *Strategic Management Journal*, 9, 31–41.

Lazarson, Mark H. (1988). "Organizational Growth of Small Firms: An Outcome of Markets and Hierarchies." *American Sociological Review*, 53, 330–42.

Marsden, Peter V. (1990). "Network Data and Measurement." *Annual Review of Sociology*, 16, 435–63.

Nielsen, Richard P. (1988). "Cooperative Strategy." *Strategic Management Journal*, 9, 475–92.

North, Douglass C. (1990). *Institutions, Institutional Change and Economic Performance*. New York: Cambridge University Press.

Ouchi, William G. (1980). "Markets, Bureaucracies, and Clans." *Administrative Science Quarterly*, 25(1), 129–41.

Pfeffer, Jeffrey, and Philip Nowak. (1976). "Joint Ventures and Interorganizational Dependence." *Administrative Science Quarterly*, 21, 398–418.

Powell, Walter W. (1987). "Hybrid Organizational Arrangements: New Form or Transitional Development?" *California Management Review*, 30, 1, 67–87.

Schneiberg, Marc, and J. Rogers Hollingsworth. (1989). "Transaction Cost Economics and Trade Associations." In Oliver Williamson and Masahiko Aoki (eds.), *The Firm as a Nexus of Treaties* (pp. 199–232). London and Beverly Hills, Calif.: Sage Publications.

Schopler, Janice H. (1987). "Interorganizational Groups: Origins, Structure, and Outcomes." *Academy of Management Review*, 12, 702–13.

Streeck, Wolfgang, and Philippe C. Schmitter. (1985). "Community, Market, State and Associations? The Prospective Contribution of Interest Governance to Social Order" In Wolfgang Streeck and Philippe C. Schmitter (eds.), *Private Interest Government: Beyond Market and State* (pp. 1–29). Beverly Hills, Calif.: Sage Publications.

Streeck, Wolfgang. (1981). "Organizational Consequences of Neo-Corporatist Manageability of Industrial Relations." *British Journal of Industrial Relations*, 19, 149–69.

Streeck, Wolfgang. (1991). "On the Institutional Conditions of Diversified Quality Production." In Egon Matzner and Wolfgang Streeck (eds.), *Beyond Keynesianism: The Socio-Economics of Production and Full Employment* (pp. 21–61). Aldershot, UK: Edward Elgar.

Williamson, Oliver E. (1975). *Market and Hierarchies: Analysis and Antitrust Implications*. New York: Free Press.

Williamson, Oliver E. (1985). *The Economic Institutions of Capitalism*. New York: Free Press.

CHAPTER 2

Neither Markets nor Hierarchies

A Comparative Study of the Printed Circuit
Board Industry in Britain and Japan

Mari Sako

W HY have different nations come to adopt different governance structures to organize the production of similar goods and services? And how have different institutional arrangements for production and transactions affected the economic performance of industrial sectors and national economies? This paper attempts to address these issues by making a comparison of British and Japanese practices in a narrowly defined sector, namely the printed circuit board (PCB) industry.

Historically, institutional arrangements for coordinating production and transactions may in part be determined by technological development, which determines, *inter alia*, the scope for specialization and the resulting division of labor. They may also be attributable to organizational innovation, which may be a result of conscious managerial strategies, which in turn are affected by a country's cultural traditions and value preferences. Of course, the extent to which a country can learn from the experience of other more industrially developed nations and the role of historical accidents must also be taken into account.

In a more ahistorical theoretical setting, the relative efficacy of vertical integration and the market mechanism in manufacturing, as argued by Oliver Williamson (1975), depends much on the conception of the market. Given that Adam Smith's "invisible hand" mechanism is no more than an ideal type, particularly in the manufacturing sector, it becomes necessary to identify what are in practice the alternative coordinating systems facilitating the exchange of goods in the marketplace.

Williamson's original formulation of markets versus hierarchies is too polarized a contrast, and was subsequently modified by his concept of "obligational contracting" (Wachter and Williamson, 1978). The latter, an intermediate form of coordinating production, has also been labeled variously as "quasi-integration" (Blois, 1972), "quasi-vertical integration" (Monteverde and Teece, 1982), "quasi-firm" (Eccles, 1981), and "quasi-disintegration" (Aoki,

1984). The prefix *quasi* indicates that the governance structure is neither complete integration into a single firm, nor market exchange between two independent firms. Other authors, in referring to similar coordinating mechanisms, use such phrases as "visible handshaking" (Aoki, 1984)—a twisting of Okun's "invisible handshake" (Okun, 1981:89), "invisible link" (Yoshino and Lifson, 1986), *Chukan soshiki* or intermediate forms of organization (Imai, Itami, and Koike, 1985), "relational contracting" (Dore, 1983; Macneil, 1985, 1987), "flexible specialization" (Piore and Sabel, 1984), and "networks" (Powell, 1990).

What constitute linkages—coordinating mechanisms—in the marketplace may range from "tangible" institutional arrangements such as interfirm shareholding (Aoki, 1984; Okimoto, 1986; Richardson, 1972), customers' ownership of tools at the supplier's (Monteverde and Teece, 1982), and legally established trade associations (Streeck and Schmitter, 1985), to more "intangible" arrangements such as informal personal networks (Granovetter, 1985; Okimoto, 1986: 41–42; Yoshino and Lifson, 1986) based on friendship, trust, and exchange of obligations. The implication of certain authors is that some nations are more suited to relying on a particular institutional arrangement (governance) than others because of their value preferences. Thus, for example, a society with high trust may require less vertical integration than another with low trust in order to achieve the same degree of control (Arrow, as quoted by Williamson, 1985:405–6).

At first sight, it is not at all obvious why intermediate forms of governance such as informal networks should contribute to competitiveness. Considerations for friendship and returning favors or fulfilling obligations may well make the terms of trade in interfirm relations deviate from competitive conditions. So grave is this concern to remain allocatively efficient that some economists associate any moral consideration with inefficient practices (Baumol, 1975). By moral considerations, they mean cozy, paternalistic, or family-like feelings that, they assume, most certainly lead to organizational slack, lack of effort, mediocrity, and other factors associated with economic backwardness. By contrast, other economists argue that, as the price system is never perfect in conveying all aspects of the goods being exchanged, moral considerations become essential complements to the smooth workings of the market (Arrow, 1975). The moral considerations in question here are honesty, keeping promises, and even altruism and other community feelings toward fellow human beings, which stamp out self-interested crookedness and cheating—including the "opportunism" assumed to be ever-present by Williamson—in a civilized society.

This chapter is structured as follows. The opening section presents a conceptual framework defining the modes of governance to be employed for empirical classification. Here, an industrial sector is conceptualized as containing a mix of different institutional arrangements, including vertically integrated hierarchies, trade associations, and a market where customers and suppliers trade. The market is governed according to whether transactions rely on social relations that exist or become established between trading partners. The two extremes of possible coordinating mechanisms are labeled Arm's-length

Contractual Relations (ACR) and Obligational Contractual Relations (OCR). The second section provides some background information on the structure and the significance of the printed circuit board industry in each country's industrial economy. The third section, the empirical core of the chapter, analyzes relationships between PCB suppliers and their customer companies, and relationships among PCB suppliers. It is shown that although variations exist within the Japanese and British sectors, the norm in Japanese trading links in the marketplace is of the OCR type, whereas the British norm is of the ACR type.

Section four provides some explanations for the British–Japanese differences identified empirically. They are in terms of corporate structures, supporting institutions in financial and labor markets, and business ideology. The last section examines the implications of the ACR–OCR difference for corporate performance and industrial competitiveness. Both ACR and OCR have their respective advantages and disadvantages in achieving competitiveness. But particularly in sectors where interfirm coordination over quality and design is important, obligational relations are a necessary prerequisite. The Japanese PCB sector (and by implication the broader manufacturing sector) performs well because obligational relations enable suppliers to respond effectively to (1) fierce competition in oligopolistic final markets, (2) cost-reduction targets set by customer companies, and (3) rivalry among suppliers ranked according to their performance in a suppliers' association.

The Conceptual Framework

Let us accept the use of the term "governance" to refer to the process of coordination and regulation of transactions. Then what distinguishes the study of governance from the study of industrial structures is as follows. While the latter is satisfied with discovering the degree of industrial concentration and vertical integration within a sector, the former must go further to identify what institutions and norms facilitate the coordination of transactions and productive activities within and among sectors.

Within a defined industrial sector, a distinction may be made between competitor and customer-supplier relations. The former may be governed by a range of different institutional arrangements, including trade associations and more informal networks or communities in industrial district. These different governance modes conduce to a different mix of cooperation and competition.

The latter, bilateral relations between customers and suppliers, may take place within a vertically integrated corporation, or in the market. As a framework of empirical analysis, the two extremes of the spectrum of governance modes in such "vertical" relations, whether they are within or across the firm's boundary, may be labeled ACR (Arm's-length Contractual Relations) and OCR (Obligational Contractual Relations). ACR refers to economic exchange in which contractual obligations are clear-cut and discrete. By contrast, OCR involves a more diffuse relationship, which is characterized by a longer time span for reciprocity and heavier mutual dependence in trading than is the case for ACR. What underpins a long-time horizon and heavy dependence as an acceptable, and even preferred, state of affairs in OCR is the existence of "goodwill trust." Goodwill trust is a sure feeling that a particular trading partner would not take unfair advantage of one's circumstances; in short, it is a faith in the absence of opportunistic behavior.[1]

The dimension of society-wide morality that makes people more comfortable with ACR- or OCR-type relations is that of universalism and particularism (Parsons, 1951). At the universalistic extreme, the identity of trading partners does not matter as long as the required goods are produced and delivered; in this sense, trading partners are "faceless." Suppliers who can deliver the same goods are interchangeable for the buyer, while there is the same duty by the supplier to fulfill commitment whoever is the purchaser. For example, one has the same duty not to pass false coin, or not to forge quality assurance certificates, onto anyone. By contrast, under particularism, more subtle obligations are involved; trading partners are not all treated as equal, but given priority. For instance, one passes on information about impending shortages to some customers, but not others. One decides who should have their orders filled first when material supplies break down. Such prioritization is according to the strength of the trading relation with the company to which one is obligated, while a relationship becomes strengthened as "goodwill trust," and possibly affective sentiments, develop over time between trading partners.

The ultimate objective in focusing on the ACR–OCR contrast is to understand the exact coordinating mechanisms through which high-quality, low-cost production may be achieved. ACR may be sought to avoid the potential pitfalls of slack effort due to patronage, favoritism, or sheltering from the impersonal and invigorating forces of the market. By contrast, OCR, by relying on "goodwill trust," may elicit the right kind of incentives to produce fine-quality goods at low cost. But just as equally likely, OCR may confirm the worst fears of those more comfortable with ACR—namely that absence of material sanctions may work toward more slack-effort exertion. Thus, we cannot simply seek a causal link between governance modes and economic peformance, as there are other important environmental conditions—economic and technological—that affect the outcome. The pertinent question to ask, therefore, is *not* what governance structure fosters sound economic performance, but what governance mode, under what circumstances, is linked to sound economic performance.

The Printed Circuit Board Industry in Britain and Japan: Technology, Market Size, and Industry Structures

Before printed circuit boards (PCBs) were invented in the late 1940s as a result of exchange of technical information between the British and American military services, electronic components used to be hand-wired to turret lugs staked into terminal boards. Printed circuits provided a system of making electrical interconnections without wires, by imprinting a circuitry normally obtained by etching away a copper-coated laminate made of insulating materials such as glass epoxy. The circuitry has become finer and technically more demanding over time, with a thousandth of an inch (0.025 mm) being critical in some cases;

hence, the design and production of the artwork is often carried out with the aid of a computer. The manufacturing process involves an odd mixture of a mechanical engineering process of drilling and chemical processes of plating and etching on the one hand (imparting the image of traditional heavy industries with noise, dust, and fumes) and on the other hand the imaging process that requires a dust-free environment associated with "clean rooms in high-tech electronics."

The use of PCBs in a wide range of manufactured goods makes the industry more significant to national manufacturing competitiveness than the value of its production, about $20 billion in 1988, indicates. The PCB industry has been chosen for study not only for this reason but also because they are all "bespoke" products—there are no such things as standardized PCBs that can be procured "off-the-shelf." Coordination in production and transaction is potentially more rife with problems in the case of customized rather than standardized components.

The PCB industries in Britain and Japan both face similar international competitive pressures, for many of the final equipment industries they serve—particularly automobiles and electronics—are global. However, some major differences in characteristics exist between the British and the Japanese PCB industries. First, the size of the Japanese PCB market ($5.8 billion in 1988) is over ten times as large as the British market ($509 million). Second, a greater proportion of Japanese than British PCBs are for consumer electronics (see Table 2.1), which tend to have larger batch sizes than PCBs for nonconsumer goods. Third, the Japanese PCB market is relatively closed, with a low import penetration ratio of just less than 2 percent and an export–output ratio of 2 percent embodied mainly in final equipment export. This compares with the British export ratio of 14 percent and import penetration of 25 percent, high but well below the 60 percent or so for the British electronics industry as a whole.

Despite these differences, there are also some apparent similarities, particularly in industrial structures. First, the industry in both countries is fragmented with a large number of small and medium-sized firms. This partly reflects the relatively low entry cost into the industry in the past, when all drilling and punching operations could be done manually, and the only other

Table 2.1. Markets Served by PCB Manufacturers, 1985

Market Segment	Britain (%)	Japan (%)
Consumer electronics	5.0	36.8
Automobiles	2.8	1.3
Telecommunications	28.0	7.4
Data processing	34.0	45.4
Industrial electronics	28.0	9.2
Total	100.0	100.0

SOURCE: *Electronics Manufacture in Japan and South Korea.* Report of a study tour sponsored by the Printed Circuit Association and the Department of Trade and Industry, UK, October 1987.

piece of equipment required was a number of sinks for plating and etching. Stories of PCB operations starting out in a shed (using fish tanks in one instance in the UK) abound in both Britain and Japan. These were either completely new businesses or diversified operations set up by entrepreneurs who already had a foothold in one of the processes of PCB manufacturing, such as drilling, plating, etching, or photography.

Based on best estimates made by respective national trade associations, the British PCB industry consists of about 100 major companies (including vertically integrated ones, although there may be as many as 400 if small companies are included), employing 16,000 workers. The Japanese PCB industry is said to employ 25,000 workers at as many as 800 companies, although 200 companies capture the major part of total output. Thus, the average company size, with roughly £3 million sales turnover and thirty employees in Japan, and less than £1 million turnover and fourty employees in Britain, is quite small. Despite this similarity, we should not forget that partly because the Japanese market is ten times as large as the British market, the largest independent Japanese PCB manufacturer, with a turnover of £256 million (at 3 = ¥230) and 1800 employees, compares with the largest British producer, at £26 million turnover and 500 employees (in 1988).

Another apparent British–Japanese similarity is the extent of vertical integration. Although difficult to estimate accurately, about a quarter of the Japanese PCB market and 30 percent of the British PCB market are said to be supplied by vertically integrated electronics companies. What is different between the two countries is the direction of change in the extent of integration in the recent past. The dynamic adjustment in the degree of vertical integration in each nation may best be understood as a contrasting response to the same factor, namely the ever-increasing investment expenditure necessary to keep up with technological advances.

In Britain, the proportion of the vertically integrated segment of the PCB market might have been as high at 50 percent in the early to mid-1980s. But by the late 1980s, major British corporations such as Plessey and STC decided to sell off their in-house PCB manufacturing facilities, in accordance with a business strategy to concentrate on their so-called core business. The need to prioritize areas for investment was one factor behind such strategy. As a consequence, independent specialist PCB companies, and not in-house facilities, are expected to invest in the most up-to-date technology.

In Japan, by contrast, there are a significant number of diversified vertically integrated corporations, such as Fujitsu and NEC, whose in-house PCB plants remain technology leaders producing not only for in-house use but also for sale in the free market. Unlike in Britain, there is no tendency for them to hive off their PCB operations. Moreover, there are some new entrants into the PCB industry, who wish to participate financially in existing specialist PCB manufacturers, or set up joint venture companies with them. These entrants used to be raw material suppliers who wanted to secure markets for their products. But more recently, there are large corporations in maturing industries, such as steel and textiles, that have excess labor and are looking for new industries in which to enter. A joint venture between a spinning company and a specialist PCB company is an example of a good match between one partner with financial clout but no technical expertise in PCBs and the other with technical expertise but without sufficient funds for new investment.

From the above, it is evident that the performance of British and Japanese PCB companies may be affected by numerous factors, some lying within and others outside the PCB industry.

Empirical Analysis

Having outlined the industrial structure of the PCB industry, this section will describe, on the basis of sample case study evidence as well as other evidence,[2] how the mix of various modes of governance differ in (1) relations between independent PCB suppliers and their customer companies and (2) relations among PCB manufacturers in Britain and Japan.

Vertical Relations: The ACR–OCR Spectrum

The first striking difference between Japanese and British PCB manufacturers is the relatively heavy dependence of Japanese suppliers on fewer customers. In the sample of companies interviewed, the percentage of total annual sales turnover attributable to orders placed by the largest customer ("transactional dependence" for short) ranged from 6% to 25% in Britain, and from 15% to 85% in Japan.

Variations existing within each country's industry reflect differences in individual companies' corporate strategy, and the type of market niches identified by them. For example, in Britain, a supplier specializing in quick turnaround (i.e., short lead time) prototype boards had low dependence, whereas those with relatively high dependence had their market niche in PCBs requiring high-volume, long-run production. By the same token, part of the reason why dependence is generally higher in Japan than in Britain is due to a greater proportionate demand for high-volume PCBs mainly by Japanese consumer electronics manufacturers.

In Japan, the proliferation of subcontractors (some totally dependent on a single customer) has been caused by the rapid economic growth in the postwar period (although the basis for it had been laid down before and during World War II; See Minato, 1987; also Nakamura, 1981:15). Large companies sought to secure as much production capacity as possible, not only in the urban areas in which they were located but also in the rural areas, by extending their subcontracting network (Chuo University Economic Research Centre, 1976). High transactional dependence of subcontractors, it can be argued, resulted from rapid demand growth outstripping feasible capacity expansion.

Over time, a more uncertain growth in demand has led some suppliers to reduce their transactional dependence. It was the 1973 oil price shock and subsequent recessions that led Japanese customer companies to encourage their highly dependent subcontractors to diversify their customer base as steadily growing orders could no longer be guaranteed from their existing clientele. In response, some Japanese PCB suppliers have steadily lowered their transactional dependence, but to levels still considered high in Britain. The British discomfort with high transactional dependence is related to an assumption often made by customer companies about "captive" PCB suppliers, that they are also monopoly suppliers, whether they are owned by a parent company to produce solely for in-house use or are independent suppliers dominated by a single customer. Customer companies, however monopolistic they might be in their own markets, wish to buy their components in competitive markets. The disadvantage of trading with captive suppliers is twofold: Customers cannot play one noncaptive supplier against another to extract cheap prices out of one, and captive suppliers have little incentive (owing to a lack of fear of losing orders) or opportunity to gather information on efficient production techniques.

At the same time, British suppliers themselves are keen to ensure themselves against possible loss of orders by diversifying customer outlets. Moreover, they believe in the beneficial consequences, not only of being kept on their toes for fear of losing orders, but also of maximizing access to transaction-borne market and technical information attainable only from particular customers. Such a belief is similarly held in Japan. But in general, a greater proportion of suppliers and customer in Britain are convinced of this market-stimulus argument for low transactional dependence than in Japan, where many believe it possible to have market stimulus and high dependence at the same time.

Another reason behind the British preference for low transactional dependence may be a cultural one, an inclination for individualism applied to corporate entities as units. In a society that values individual autonomy, dependence is demeaning and irksome. Moreover, high dependence risks exposure to the danger of intervention and lack of self-control. Thus, there appears to be a genuine sense in which British PCB manufacturers dislike intervention in their "domestic" affairs (e.g., production scheduling, factory layout) by their customers. This preference for self-control is reinforced by the institutional bias given by the British financial structure, which requires that a company stay profitable in the short run. And to ensure short-run profitability, no British manager of a supplier firm wishes the company's performance to be swayed by the decisions on orders taken by managers of another company.

This last factor, together with the conditioning due to differing economic growth experiences, accounts for the difference in what is thought by PCB suppliers to be the ideal transactional dependence: In Japan, the predominant ideal was to have three major customers each taking up a third of the business, whereas 15 percent to 20 percent were quoted as the maximum threshold dependence by British suppliers. The gap reflects the difference in the working assumption, in Japan that the relation will continue, and in Britain that it might be broken at any time.

Heavy transactional dependence and long-term commitments in sub-contracting relationships go hand in hand. In Japan, many of the PCB manufacturers said that they have been trading continuously with their major customers for the last fifteen to twenty years, even before they started manufacturing PCBs in some cases. In Britain, there may also have been long-term trading relationships between some of the PCB manufacturers and their customers. Nevertheless, these PCB suppliers have still had to quote annually for contracts, some of which they lost to other suppliers. Thus commitment is rarely made by British customer companies to continuous ordering, beyond a period of twelve months.

One facet of the British–Japanese difference in their preference for long-term or short-term contracts is the different usage of one-off contracts. In Britain, the business of quick turnaround PCBs is thought to be highly profitable; not only are there companies specializing in this area of the market, but other PCB manufacturers indulge in it to make quick profits (they can earn a premium of up to 250 percent), often at the risk of messing up the production scheduling and delaying the delivery of regular orders.

In Japan by contrast, spot contracts are generally disliked. A prototpe PCB order is accepted by the manufacturers only if they expect to obtain orders for the regular production run following it. For regular customers, the norm is not to charge any premium at all for the price of prototype PCBs or of those requiring shorter than normal lead times. In effect, prototype and short lead time orders are offered as a service to regular customers and are loss makers in themselves. As an example of prioritization, one company is said to refuse all spot contracts unless the potential customer is known to the company's regular materials suppliers who personally ask that the job be done. Thus only spot contracts in a particularistic setting are taken up.

Besides heavier dependence and longer-term commitment of Japanese suppliers, they also engage, on average, in more intense communication with customers than do British suppliers. Consequently, despite a smaller number of customers per Japanese supplier, the Japanese PCB companies do not necessarily expand less per capita resources in sales (as measured by the ratio of sales personnel to total employees) than do British suppliers. For example, many Japanese PCB suppliers said that their sales people visit their major customers on a daily basis, sometimes several times a day, to see not only the purchasing manager but also inspection or design personnel. Visiting the customer's development department is an essential part of the sales person's activity to pick up early information on possible future orders. There is apparently always something to discuss every day, and even if there is no specfic business to conduct, it is necessary to drop by to sustain the relationship. There might just be a new purchase order form or an artwork produced a few hours earlier to be picked up rather than mailed. If so, the sales person can check the form or the artwork there and then and discuss any unclear points with the buyer. Such communication is facilitated by many of the Japanese PCB manufacturers having several regional sales offices located near their major customers.

In Britain, the sales–purchasing interaction in the PCB industry is less intense. But because of the customized nature of PCBs requiring tighter coordination, intercompany communication appears more frequent than it might be in some other sectors of the British industry. For example, one supplier who places great importance on customer liaison employs four sales engineers who spend much of their time with the customers, picking up an artwork rather than it being sent by mail, explaining face-to-face what is wrong with a particular customer's photography, and promising to be at the customer's office within twenty-four hours should there be anything wrong with the PCBs delivered.

Besides the sales–purchasing interaction, there are in both countries multilevel customer–supplier contacts among quality, design, production, and technical personnel of the two companies. Clearly, bad communication between departments within the customer company can cause difficulty in customer–supplier relationships, resulting in production of misspecified goods or delay in delivery. Complaints on this type were made by some of the British PCB suppliers, but not by any of the Japanese suppliers.

To summarize, on average, Japanese PCB suppliers conform to the OCR pattern of trading with their customers, whereas British PCB suppliers prefer to adopt ACR-type relations. This is also reflected in greater density of customer–supplier communication in Japan than in Britain.

Relations Among PCB Supplier Companies

SUPPLIERS' ASSOCIATIONS AND CONFERENCES. Besides the bilateral customer–supplier relations as described above, there are, in both Britain and Japan, supplier networks formed at the initiative of a customer company. The nature of such supplier networks differs vastly between the two countries, partly because of different degrees of transactional dependence of suppliers involved.

In Japan, a sense of community in the supplier network is promoted by the formation of a suppliers' association at the initiative of the customer company—for example, Toyota's Kyohokai or Matsushita's Kyoeikai. Such an association is a privileged group of selected suppliers who satisfy a number of criteria set by the customer company. The association exists for the purpose of facilitating intense communication between the customer company and its primary suppliers, providing a regular forum for technology transfer and disclosure of confidential business plans to the trusted few. Primary suppliers themselves may have their own association of subcontractors. Provided that high trust relations prevail, such hierarchical supplier networks have a considerable advantage in saving on information costs and reducing future uncertainty.

The electronics industry in Japan is said to have a looser form of supplier network than in the automobile industry. There is indeed evidence that the membership is more stable in Toyota's association than in Matsushita's association. Nevertheless, the network of suppliers and subcontractors that companies such as Matsushita, Hitachi, and NEC have built up over time is substantial. Except in a few cases, the customer companies have no financial stake in these suppliers, which indicates that other more effective means of control besides shareholding exists in Japanese corporate groupings. One such means is the unitary perspective created by the ideology of coprosperity and coexistence (*kyoei kyozon*) between the customer company and its suppliers, manifested in the sharing of bad times as well as good times, and enhanced by regular social events such as golf tournaments and end-of-year parties.

The manufacturing of PCBs tends to be regarded as the task of independent specialist suppliers, and is therefore a sector with relatively low transactional dependence in Japan, compared with other areas such as electronic assembly. Despite this, there are some Japanese PCB companies that identify themselves as belonging to the groupings headed by their largest customers. Even if PCB suppliers feel that their customer companies may not have the in-house expertise to instruct them in a hands-on fashion on how to improve particular production processes, they still find the quarterly or biannual suppliers' association meetings—when confidential future production plans are disclosed by the customer—invaluable in planning their own production schedules.

In Britain, because customer companies and suppliers are much less mutually dependent, customers are less willing to disclose business plans even bilaterally, never mind to a group of suppliers. However, the recent practice of some British electronics companies and Japanese multinationals located in Britain of holding annual supplier conferences indicates that customer companies are coming to realize the benefit of creating a core supplier base that is more stable than in the past.

SUBCONTRACTING NETWORKS WITHIN THE PCB INDUSTRY. Supplier networks in Japan, whether they are in the electronics, automobile, or garment-making industries, are typically hierarchical, and are headed by a patron customer company, as described in the previous subsection. In such hierarchical authority relations, it is not clear how much information exchange actually occurs among suppliers who belong to the same suppliers' association and who may be direct competitors. By contrast, when the will to associate comes internally among a group of companies in the same industry and not imposed from the top, a spirit of mutual help exists that facilitates freer information flows. The Japanese economy is full of such horizontal associations, particularly in industries such as textiles, with a geographical concentration of producers.

An example of a subcontracting network in the PCB industry, which combines both the hierarchical and horizontal types of trading relationships, is the case of Eastern Company. It heads a cooperative association of ten PCB companies, all located in a rural area of Nagano Prefecture. This association was formally established in 1981 under the Law Promoting Small and Medium Sized Subcontracting Firms, which has the purpose of supporting plans by groups of weak and dependent subcontractors to develop themselves into more independent firms. Among the activities of this particular Nagano association is a recent attempt to engage in joint research on new automated technology, for which an application for a subsidy has been made to the Ministry of International Trade and Industry (MTI). It has also jointly purchased certain materials common to all members, such as etching chemicals, to benefit from lower prices derived from bulk buying.

Beneath what appears to be no more than a local cooperative association is a community. The ten member companies coexist in an interdependent fashion. One member specializes in gold plating only and two in NC (numerical control) drilling only; they act as subcontractors to other members.[3] The other seven association members manufacture entire PCBs, but there is also much interfirm trading among them. For instance, Eastern uses two of them to produce whole PCBs at a slightly lower cost than possible if internally produced. One of them used to be a plating subcontractor, which started manufacturing PCBs at the request of and under the technical guidance of Eastern; it is now partly owned by Eastern with joint directorship. Another member company was set up by an ex-Eastern employee who quit the company because he wanted to become independent.

The member companies' felt need to upgrade the overall technical standard of the ten companies jointly without producing dropouts derives from the possibility that a company might at any time call upon any other company to complete a customer's order on time. Helped by spin-offs and joint directorships in some cases, free and open exchange of information on production techniques and management among member companies is encouraged. Besides much socializing among directors of the companies, there are monthly association meetings at which general information on each company's commercial trends is exchanged, and topical subjects such as how to halt sliding prices are debated. There are also regular technical study groups at which speakers from the engineering department of a nearby university or from material suppliers are invited to address member company employees.

Subcontracting networks of the kind just described exist in Japan not only in the PCB industry but also in other sectors. They are more akin to a grouping of small firms in an industrial district with its own subculture, which Piore and Sabel (1984) and others (e.g., Trigilia, 1986) have described, and are to be distinguished from vertical suppliers' associations. Informal networks do not exist to the same extent in Britain today.

TRADE ASSOCIATIONS IN THE PCB INDUSTRY. Moving away from the communitarian arrangement in a geographically concentrated area involving only a handful of firms, the next governance structure for analysis is the trade association for the PCB industry at the national level. The Japanese association (Japan Printed Circuit Association, or JPCA) and its British counterpart (Printed Circuit Association, or PCA) have similar aims of promoting the interests of those engaged in the PCB industry, but as described below, they differ in several respects, in particular in the extent of control over members' behavior.

The Japan Printed Circuit Association began in 1962, when a handful of PCB companies got together to form an association. As the PCB industry expanded, JPCA become a non-profit-making legal entity (*shadan hojin*) under a MITI regulation in 1976. By 1987, JPCA had 387 members; included are both independent specialist PCB manufacturers, PCB manufacturing divisions of vertically integrated corporations, and some suppliers of materials and equipment.

As the sole trade association for the PCB industry in Japan, JPCA derives its power not just from being a monopolistic association, but more importantly from being a body to which the central government, and more specifically the sponsoring ministry, MITI, delegates the responsibility for framing and administering public programs. In the PCB industry, these include the Structural Improvement Program (*kozo kaizen keikaku*) and the Program on Modernization of Small and Medium-sized Enterprises (*chusho kigyo kindaika keikaku*) based on the 1963 Law to Promote the Modernization of Small and Medium-sized Enterprises.

Broadly speaking, the objectives of both programs are to "rationalize" and "modernize" the PCB industry by improving product quality, encouraging the diffusion of new process technologies, specifying an optimal scale of production, improving the welfare of employees, and protecting the environment from pollution. For each objective, the programs specify detailed targets as part of the plans. For example, the technology improvement targets consist of exactly how many NC drilling machines, automatic etching lines, CAD (computer-aided design) systems, and so forth, each worth so much, ought to be installed in the PCB industry as a whole. Implementation of these plans is administered by the trade association, which itself plays a major role in assessing the appropriateness of the targets.

The consequences of this explicit delegation of public administrative responsibility to the JPCA are as follows:

1. JPCA collects detailed data on member companies' production, management, investment, and financial statements on an annual basis under the supervision of the Information Technology Section of MITI. The survey is conducted with the overt purpose of collecting basic data necessary for formulating policies for improvement, and the results are published in a report available to all members, policymakers, and the general public. The response rate for the survey has been relatively high, at just over 80 percent.

2. JPCA also has the potential capacity to control its members' behavior, by resorting to informal yet effective policing. One manifestation of this was the way JPCA attempted to put a stop to the plunge in PCB prices due to the yen appreciation. The association formed in 1987 a committee to consider how to tackle the problem of the ultrastrong yen. As a result of committee deliberations, not only did JPCA write a petition for "improving trading relations" to the major customer companies but it also urged members to exercise "self-control" over their prices, while asking members to report to JPCA any instances of PCB manufacturers undercutting others.

The Printed Circuit Association (PCA) in Britain originally started out as a section of the Electronic Components Industry Federation (ECIF). It became an independent body in January 1984, while remaining officially affiliated to ECIF. Besides PCA, a trade association, there are also learned societies—for example, the Institute of Metal Finishing PC Group, and the Institute of Interconnection Technology (IIT). The latter was formed in late 1987 by merging the preexisting Institute of Circuit Technology and the Northern UK Circuit Group. Late 1987 also marked the linking of the PCA and the IIT into the Printed Circuit Industry Federation (PCIF), which hopes to overcome the Institute of Metal Finishing's reluctance to join. The federation intends also to invite other bodies such as CEMA (Circuit Equipment and Materials Association) and SMART (Surface Mount and Related Technology) to join, and eventually to merge the PCA and the IIT into a single organization. The federation is therefore in a considerable state of flux.

The PCA has about 120 members; these include, besides PCB manufacturers, materials and equipment suppliers. The association is also actively recruiting companies that are customers of PCB manufacturers, such as final electronic equipment manufacturers and electronic assembly houses. When questioned whether such extension of eligibility to membership might lead to a dilution of the effectiveness of guarding the core members' interests, the PCA replied that the benefit of learning together for better quality and greater market share—of "enhancing coprosperity," a phrase actually employed by the PCA—is greater than the cost arising from a potential conflict of commercial interests. It appears that the PCA is trying to combine the objectives of both JPCA and Japanese suppliers' associations.

The PCA has a number of activities, including the annual conference, technical and commercial workshops, a monthly newsletter, and a market data survey. The difficulty the PCA is facing in getting members to participate in this survey highlights a difference between the PCA and the JPCA. The survey asks about sales, prices, bill-to-book ratios, and so forth. The survey results are copyrighted by the association and are disclosed only to those who participate. Useful though it would be for the PCA to grasp the state of the British PCB market statistically, it has yet to persuade its self-interested members that it would also be to their benefit. The newsletter has carried various exhortations for members to participate, but the number of respondents has never been much more than twenty, which makes the quality of the data collected unrepresentative of the industry as a whole. The November 1988 issue of the newsletter sought ideas from members on how to increase voluntary participation in the survey, short of fining nonparticipants, which would render the exercise involuntary. The difficulty the PCA is facing in enforcing its wish to collect a reliable set of market data over time stems from the following:

1. The PCA is a relatively new organization with not many established rules and practices as yet. Many potential members are thinking of joining only if it has proved to be competent and effective.

2. British PCB manufacturers, like companies in other sectors in Britain, have existed with less of a guild tradition than their Japanese counterparts. They are individualistic companies with less communitarian obligations to the industry as a whole than their Japanese counterparts and therefore are reluctant to engage in any activity not directly benefitting their business. Even if they are assured of the confidentiality of the market data, they are less reluctant to return the survey questionnaire, either because they feel that disclosing sensitive information to direct competitors may harm their business prospects, or because they do not see any direct benefit to them.[4]

3. The PCA is not a body that is conferred responsibility by the government to administer any state-run programs. The British government has not, until

very recently, had a policy toward small and medium-sized companies, and even today it is restricted to provision of advice and short-term finance. There is no sector-specific assistance, in spite of past experiments with corporatism. This policy stance reflects the fact that the British government generally holds the well-entrenched view of business conspiracy that Adam Smith entertained.[5] Businessmen running the PCA as a loosely organized interest group in a pluralistic political setting would also not dream of controlling the members' behavior, nor of establishing a strong linkage with the central government's sponsoring ministries.

To summarize, PCA is very much a loose association of independent firms that have joined it voluntarily. PCA's power of enforcement over its membership is minimal. By contrast, JPCA plays a significant role in sectoral governance, as it has come to exercise tight control over its membership by virtue of having privileged access to the central government (MITI in particular as the sponsoring ministry). Thus, JPCA has the characteristics of what Streeck and Schmitter called Private Interest Governments (Streeck and Schmitter, 1985). This British–Japanese difference in the role of trade associations is not peculiar to the PCB industry, but is reflected in other sectors as well.

Why Variations Exist Between Britain and Japan

Having described in some detail the essential features of governance modes in the British and Japanese PCB industries (as summarized in Table 2.2), this section addresses the question of why there is variation in governance arrangements in the two countries. The explanations provided below are mainly in terms of national economywide institutions and business ideologies.

Existing Institutional Models of Corporate Interlinkages

One reason why ACR is predominant in Britain and OCR is predominant in Japan is the existence of corporate groupings in Japan, and the absence of such an institution in Britain. Two types of grouping ought to be distinguished in present-day Japan. The first type, known in Japan as *kigyo shudan*, or simply *gurupu* (group), is a horizontal corporate grouping of large companies. Each grouping has a city bank, a trading company, and a number of manufacturing

Table 2.2. Summary of British–Japanese Differences in the Mix of Governance Modes

	Britain	Japan
Transactional dependence	6%–25%	15%–85%
Projected length of trading	Duration of current contract	Beyond current contracts
Intensity of communication	Less frequent	Frequent and multifaceted
Subcontracting within the PCB industry	Very little	Common
Trade associations	Loose, voluntary Remote access to the state	Tight, communitarian Privileged access to the state

firms engaged in all major industrial sectors. Multilateral interfirm shareholdings exist within the grouping, while group company presidents meet on a regular basis. Although much trading takes place across the group boundary, trading within a corporate grouping—be it between the bank and its clients, or between industrial buyers and suppliers—is likely to be on preferential terms.

To the extent that trading practices by *kigyo shudan* companies provide a powerful model and norm for independent companies, the corporate grouping as an institution is relevant to the PCB industry. However, independent PCB manufacturers are too small, and are themselves not part of any corporate grouping dominated by large companies. Thus, it is the second type of grouping, the *keiretsu*, which is directly relevant here. A *keiretsu* group may involve one of the large *kigyo shudan* manufacturing companies, such as NEC in the Sumitomo group, or a more independent manufacturer such as Sony or Toyota, which heads a multilayer of suppliers, all rather heavily dependent on a single patron company. Thus, a *keiretsu* group is a hierarchical ordering by a large firm of smaller supplier firms, in many cases without direct shareholding links.

The *keiretsu* grouping as an institution explains why some Japanese PCB suppliers are comfortable in their heavy dependence on a single customer. It also reinforces the general acceptance by smaller firms of the legitimacy of a large manufacturer's authority over its smaller suppliers. In Britain, by contrast, no PCB supplier thinks of itself as part of the GEC group or the Rover group unless there is a direct parent–subsidiary link. Moreover, trading relations between large British electronics or automobile companies and their smaller PCB suppliers are often predicated on the assumption of an equal balance of power, and rarely on hierarchical authority.

Long-term versus Short-term Perspective:
Finance or Something Else?

The long-term perspective, which is one feature of OCR-type relations, is more widely apparent in the Japanese PCB industry than in the British one. For instance, the Japanese trade association, JPCA, conducted a survey of PCB manufacturers, final equipment manufacturers, and process machinery and raw material suppliers in order to get some idea as to the long-term "vision" of where the PCB industry was heading. Survey results were compiled as a 500-page report in 1987 (JPCA, 1987b). No such exercise has ever been conducted in Britain, where each firm presumably wants to keep its view on the future to itself, if ever it is inclined to make long-term projections.

At the level of the corporation, some British companies point to the short-term orientation of the City, and the necessity to ensure quarterly profitability in order to keep up their stock prices. By contrast, Japanese companies are said to be able to afford a long-term perspective because of their greater reliance on bank loans and less on equity finance (Dore, 1987, chapter 6; Corbett, 1987). The relevance of this view to the PCB manufacturers is as follows. Since only a handful of PCB companies are publicly quoted in both countries, stock prices are not a matter of concern for the majority of private companies. What is at issue instead is twofold: the company objective and the availability of long-term finance.

As far as company objectives are concerned, the majority of British PCB companies have a preference for earning target profits, which they are generally unwilling to sacrifice for growth. In contrast, Japanese PCB companies often have a strong objective for growth, even with very low margins, which motivates them to invest even in a downturn. The precariousness of such a strategy is highlighted in the attitude of British PCB companies, which generally face a shortage of long-term finance, and therefore must rely on internal earnings for investment. In Japan, a longer-term investment plan is possible as funds are abundant, either from government financial institutions offering low-interest loans or from commercial banks at which customer companies may act as guarantors or even from some companies in mature industries eager to set up joint ventures in the PCB industry.

Employment Systems and Industrial Relations

Long-term commitments made by customer companies to their core suppliers have a similar historical origin as the so-called lifetime employment system as practiced by large Japanese corporations. In both cases, investment in the form of technology transfer to smaller suppliers or in the form of training core employees was deemed necessary when there were shortages of technologically capable subcontractors or skilled workers whose expertise could be brought in by paying the rate for the job. The deliberately constructed outcome of stable relations in order to appropriate the fruit of past investment has made both the Japanese labor-management relations and subcontracting relations appear more cooperative.

The industrial relations system in Japan is relevant to the governance mode in the PCB industry in another sense. As is well known, pay differentials by firm size are larger in Japan than in Britain (see Tables 2.3 and 2.4). Given that enterprise unions exist in large Japanese corporations in order to ensure the same terms and conditions of employment for core employees of all establishments within a company, such wage differentials cannot be exploited

Table 2.3. Pay Differentials by Establishment Size, 1985 (Manufacturing only)

Establishment Size	Japan (¥000)	Britain (£)
−99	2550 (52.6)[a]	7232 (75.9)
100–999	3544 (73.1)	8069 (84.7)
1000+	4847 (100.0)	9528 (100.0)

SOURCES: MITI *Kogyo Tokei Hyo* (Industrial Census); Business Monior, *Census of Production*, Summary Volume PA1002.

Figures in parentheses indicate differentials as percentage of the 1000 + size levels.

Table 2.4. Pay Differentials by Enterprise Size and Type of Workers (Manufacturing only)

Enterprise size	Japan (1986)		Britain (1985)	
	Manual Workers	Nonmanual Workers	Manual Workers	Nonmanual Workers
−99	78.7%	82.2%	82.1%	89.9%
100–999	84.0%	86.7%	84.6%	93.0%
1000+	¥290,800	¥345,400	£8136.8	£10,622.4

SOURCES: Business Monitor *Census of Production: Rodo Tokei Yoran* (Handbook of Labor Statistics), 1988.
Percentages as proportion of the 1000+ size pay level. Japanese figures are monthly pay for male regular workers only. British figures refer to annual income.

unless establishments are organized as separate corporations. Hence, there is an advantage for a large customer company to subcontract the manufacture of PCBs to separate companies, where lower pay and longer hours of work normally apply. This factor partially accounts for the greater degree of vertical disintegration in the Japanese PCB industry.

Moreover, employment security and relatively good pay in the Japanese employment system can only be given to the core labor force. The future viability of the Japanese employment system depends not only on the numerical flexibility provided by the existence of temporary, largely female, part-time and subcontract workers, but also on extending the frontier of the "lifetime employment zone" to loosely defined corporate groupings (Inagami, 1988). In other words, while much of the lifetime employment career has hitherto been spent within one company, there are increasing instances of "seconding," or permanently transferring, those hired for lifetime employment to group companies, affiliates and subsidiaries, and to subcontractors within the *keiretsu* group.

The acceptance by some Japanese PCB manufacturers of a few employees in their mid-fifties from their main customers is at least in part to repay the accumulated obligation of receiving invaluable technical guidance. There is a clear quid pro quo here. The supplier bears the burden of the customer company's wish to ease the retirement process of its unwanted employees while the customer provides training for the supplier's younger employees at the customer's site or transfers its own technologists for instruction, often without fully charging for such service.

BUSINESS IDEOLOGY. Finally, the type of ideology held by business people clearly affects the governance mode. Japanese business is very much a community, in which actors have a heightened sense of interdependence and a preference for particularistic relationships. Owing to the predominance of particularistic relations in business, prosperity is believed to be attainable not through the workings of the "invisible hand" in markets, but through conscious cooperation within and between firms.

In Britain, by contrast, the more individualistic orientation of the British people and their preference for universalistic morality gave way to easy acceptance of the invisible-hand ideology, namely that the pursuit of self-interest in the economic and political sphere by everyone leads to good outcome for all. As part of this ideology, impersonalized open competition is seen to be fair. It may be that the relatively slow growth of the British economy reinforced the perception of conflict, rather than commonality, of interests, which can best be resolved by not relying on particularistic structures which offend the British sense of fairness. Moreover, the slower pace of growth allowed adequate time for new methods to spread via the market mechanism, without large companies taking a lead in transferring technology to smaller firms, as happened in Japan. This buttresses the view that it is the market, rather than human agency, which is the arbiter of resource allocation.

To summarize this section, many of the British–Japanese differences in the mix of governance modes in the PCB industry can be explained in terms of differences in industrial growth experience, corporate objectives, financial institutions, and employment systems. A difficulty lies in assessing the degree of importance of culture—in the narrow sense of people's value preferences and behavioral dispositions—in trading relationships between companies. But to the extent that companies are set up and run by individuals and to the extent that the majority of business people appear to work within their national institutions, the modal trading practices in Britain must at least be consistent with a British preference for individualism, clearly defined rights and obligations, autonomy or minimum dependence, and separation of work from leisure or family life. Similarly, the Japanese custom and practice in business transactions is in line with that country's disposition for dutifulness, interdependence, exchange of diffuse obligations, and high trust among people within the same group.

Implications for Competitiveness

Given the aforementioned British–Japanese differences in the mix of governance modes in the PCB industry, what are their implications for the competitiveness of individual companies and the industrial sector? This last section examines the issue of competitiveness in a dynamic setting, in which wealth creation through productivity-improving changes is just as important as efficient allocation of resources.

No single indicator of competitiveness can enable one to compare the British and Japanese scenes, but a number of indicators may be examined, including productivity, profitability, and price. At the level of the PCB industry sector as a whole, on average, labor productivity is clearly higher, but profitability lower, in Japan than in Britain in recent years.[6] On PCB prices, the strong yen in the mid-1980s could have made Japanese costs increase much faster than British costs, but there is no evidence that average Japanese prices have become higher than British prices. It is argued below that the reasons for the British–Japanese difference in the bundle of performance indicators is partly due to the differential choice of ACR–OCT patterns of trading within the PCB industry and partly due to structures and conditions external to the sector. In theory, the ACR and OCR patterns of trading have the following advantages and disadvantages in adjusting to changing needs and circumstances. Enhancing competitiveness under each governance mode amounts to creating conditions that enhance the advantages and restrain the disadvantages.

	ACR PATTERN	OCR PATTERN
ADVANTAGES	Flexibility to change trading partners as prices dictate or whenever contracts expire.	Intense communication, based on trust, enabling good quality, prompt delivery, and joint problem-solving efforts.
DISADVANTAGES	Minimal information exchange; potential for misunderstanding in design or quality specifications.	Rigidity in changing order levels and trading partners.

Thus, a priori, the ACR pattern of trading may be suitable for exchange of standardized goods, as there is little scope for misunderstanding over design or quality specification. Allocative efficiency is then achieved by flexibly changing trading partners as prices dictate. OCR trading has an advantage in facilitating good coordination over design, delivery, and problem solving, which matters more in markets for customized rather than standardized goods. The question is how to minimize the corresponding disadvantage of rigidity in OCR arising out of a bias toward sustaining the existing relationship. The answer seems to lie in some mechanism that effectively translates the market signals into incentives for suppliers to make continuous productivity-enhancing ("X-efficiency") improvements.

As an illustration, let us assume realistically a market structure for the PCB industry in which a large enough number of suppliers compete for customers' orders. At times of excess capacity in the PCB industry, there is a downward pressure on prices as lower demand induces more PCB manufacturers to change from average cost to marginal cost pricing to remain in business. Customer companies in such circumstances behave differently in order to minimize their costs. In ACR-type relations, the customer's response would be to switch suppliers from existing suppliers to new ones offering cheaper prices; how and how long new suppliers can afford to sustain an undercut price is none of the customer's business. In contrast, in OCR-type relations, the customer chooses the "voice" option (Hirschman, 1970) so as to bring about a market-conforming outcome. If the threat of exit by the customer is effective, the supplier has a sufficient incentive to exert greater effort to think of ways to reduce costs and hence prices. Since it is within the customer company's consideration not to drive its supplier to the point of bankruptcy, the supplier is given a grace period during which it can eventually lower prices.

At the other extreme when there is excess demand for PCBs, the ACR scenario would be for prices to be bid up rapidly as PCB suppliers bank on obtaining premium prices for shorter lead-time delivery or for customers to secure delivery at all. In this circumstance, neither customers' "voice" nor "exit" is potent. Prices are bid up less in OCR-type relations, however, as customer companies take it for granted that they receive preferential treatment, with minimum premium pay, for being long-term regular customers.

The upshot of ACR–OCR differences on competitiveness is that ACR traders, mainly in British industry, have an incentive always to seek the most competitive bidder. But the resulting transaction costs may be high, particularly for customized goods, such as PCBs, for which the price does not convey all the information necessary to one's trading partners.[7] This factor tends to lower the overall productivity. Moreover, British PCB companies feel the need to target a relatively high rate of profit over sales, as an insurance against uncertain and unstable future orders placed by uncommitted customers.

It is of course an empirical question whether the allocative inefficiency in OCR trading is more or less outweighed by X-efficiency over time. In the case of the Japanese PCB industry, it is argued below that X-efficiency gains outweigh allocative inefficiencies because (1) the final markets that PCB suppliers serve are fiercely competitive, (2) the PCB industry is also highly competitive with relatively low barriers to entry, and (3) their customers have devised an incentive structure of rank-ordering that ensures that the survival of PCB suppliers depends on making constant productivity-enhancing improvements.

It is expected that in times of excess capacity, some PCB manufacturers engage in "buying-in" tactics, quoting prices well below cost. However, the extent to which the existence of low price quotations is sufficient for customers to switch from their existing suppliers differed between Britain and Japan. In Britain, only a 15 percent price differential was said to be sufficient in the case of one PCB company for one of its customers to switch from it to another supplier with a lower quotation. In Japan, a price differential as large as 40 percent did not, in one instance, shake the commitment that locked the buyer into an existing relation.[8]

The major reason for the seemingly more rigid and inefficient pricing strategy of Japanese companies lies in a different pricing convention. For long-run repeat orders, prices are generally renegotiated once a year in Britain, at which cost increases at the supplier level (whether in materials or in labor) are passed on and paid for by the customer. Cost increases in Japan are either partially or wholly absorbed by the supplier, as PCB prices, particularly in the consumer end of the electronics industry, never rise and can only fall over time. The harsh reality of fierce competition among final equipment manufacturers even before the post-1985 appreciation in the yen led to a "request" by customers every six months to reduce prices (*cosuto down*) either across the board for all or for specific part numbers. As a result of such "requests," a 40 percent differential between the price of an existing supplier and the price quoted by a new potential supplier can be narrowed in no time.

Why and how do Japanese PCB suppliers comply with such "requests" for price reduction? The *how* is the easier part of the question to answer. Some engage in internal cost-cutting exercises through the conventional Quality Circle and individual suggestion systems. The other method is Value Analysis or Value Engineering, which involves making suggestions to customers on modifications in PCB design, the use of cheaper chemicals, and so forth, so as to lower the cost of producing PCBs. Cost savings from supplier-initiated changes are typically shared by customer and supplier. However, in recent years, limits to the above methods were reflected in price reductions eating into profit margins, which on average fell from 2.4 percent (of sales) in 1985, to -0.2 percent in 1986 and -1.2 percent in 1987 (JPCA, 1987a).

The *why* part of the above, question has ambiguous implications. On the one hand, heavy dependence of PCB suppliers on a few customers tips the power balance in the customers' favor; in this situation, PCB manufacturers cannot afford to refuse cost-reduction requests as there is always the potential threat of withdrawing a large order. Given the large number of small subcontractors, competition among them in Japan can be cutthroat, and a loss of orders once and for all is serious owing to a bias toward long-term commitments in trading. On the other hand, the willingness of some PCB suppliers to incur short-term deficits, admittedly greater in a national crisis than if pressured by some incompetent customer firms, appears to be based on trust, on expectations that their customers would not simply exploit them to the point of bankruptcy. In fact, large customer companies are said to be well aware of the possible social outcry that would result from causing a subcontractor to go bankrupt as a consequence of withdrawing an order or squeezing cheap prices. This type of behavior may be interpreted as risk-sharing over time, in which the customer and the supplier share both good times and bad times, helping each other in times of need.

A complementary force enhancing X-efficiency in Japanese OCR-type relationships lies in the institutionalized competition existing among core suppliers, which are ranked according to quality and delivery performance by the customer company. The customer publicizes the monthly assessed ranking list—for instance, by displaying it on a purchasing department bulletin board that can be seen by visiting suppliers. Here, competition is based not on any absolute criteria, but on relative ranking. Suppliers who climb up the ladder are assured an increasing level of desirable orders, while those who slide down face diminishing levels of orders. This incentive structure provides another momentum for continuous improvements by suppliers, aside from the more moralized basis for maintaining X-efficiency. That is to say, the customer's insistence on high standards of quality and timely delivery is met by a keen response by suppliers, as these, are the essential indicators of being worthy of trust—the factor on which the trading relation is based. Because of such a moral incentive, what is popularly known as just-in-time delivery with low stock-holding is more likely to succeed in OCR- than in ACR-type relations.

Summary and Conclusions

This chapter examined the mix of governance modes in the PCB industry, which were classified into Arm's-length Contractual Relations (ACR) and Obligational Contractual Relations (OCR). It was shown empirically that interfirm relations in the British PCB industry were more of the ACR-type, and Japanese relations more of the OCR-type. The Japanese PCB industry also has a trade association that has more control over its membership behavior than its British counterpart. Reasons for the British–Japanese variations in the mix of governance modes were identified as differences in economic growth experience, corporate objectives, financial institutions, employment and industrial relations systems, and business ideology.

In assessing competitiveness, Japanese PCB companies were found to have performed better than their British counterparts in terms of productivity and in keeping prices down in the face of the strong yen. The performance indicator in which British PCB companies excelled on average was profitability.

The issue of how governance modes affect sectoral competitiveness is not straightforward, for it cannot be asserted as a general theory that the OCR pattern of trading is better- or worse-performing than the ACR pattern. A monopolistic industry structure may well remove incentives for dominant firms with OCR-type relations to remain or become competitive. Fierce competition among final goods producers and the existence of a myriad of small sub-contractors who face low entry costs in the Japanese economy help to ensure that OCR-type trading relations result in competitiveness. Because of less atomistic final goods markets in Britain, relying on OCR-type relations in the British industry may not elicit the same kind of incentives for greater effort (X-efficiency) as in Japan.

Companies with ACR-type relations are more prone to resort to "exit" than to "voice" in adapting to changing circumstances, thus ensuring quick price and quantity adjustments to ensure allocative efficiency. At the same time, ACR suppliers have an incentive to ensure against order fluctuations by having relatively high target profits. The "voice" option preferred by OCR companies, by contrast, gives a basis for risk-sharing over time, creating a stable environment favorable for long-term investment planning.

Notes

The research reported in this paper was funded mainly by a grant (reference F0023 2298) from the Economic and Social Research Council, UK. I am grateful to Professor Ron Dore, who was co-investigator for the research, for providing both helpful insights and encouragement. An earlier version of this paper was presented at a conference in Bellagio, Italy in 1989 for a project "Comparing Capitalist Economies: Variations in the Governance of Sectors" directed by Rogers Hollingsworth, Philippe Schmitter, and Wolfgang Streeck. I am grateful to them and other participants in the project for comments. I also benefitted much from discussions with Masahiko Aoki, Richard Samuels, and with the participants of an MIT seminar that Richart Samuels organized: Michael Smitka, Hugh Whittaker, and Stephen Wood.

1. See Sako (1991, 1992) for more details on the concept of trust in buyer-supplier relations.

2. Findings in this and subsequent sections are based on semistructured interviews during 1986–89 with ten Japanese and ten British PCB suppliers of varying sizes, and a number of custome companies—six in Japan and four in Britain—with which some of the sample suppliers traded, mainly in the electronics industry. The other major sources of information have been the trade associations.

3. Such vertical disintegration is a widespread feature of the Japanese PCB industry. According to an annual survey by the Japan Printed Circuit Association, Japanese PCB manufacturers used on average 24 subcontractors each; and the production stages most frequently subcontracted out were the production of whole PCBs, followed by drilling holes and plating (JPCA, 1987a).

4. In this respect, British PCB manufacturers are similar to American machine tool companies, for which the industry is no more than the sum of individual firms within it. By contrast, Japanese PCB suppliers are more like German machine tool builders who are more disposed to feel obligated to contribute to the accumulation of public goods in the community (see Herrigel, 1988).

5. "People of the same trade seldom meet together, even for merriment or diversion, but the conversation ends in a conspiracy against the public, or in some contrivance to raise prices" (Smith, 1925:130).

6. In the absence of data for the best measure of productivity in Britain, namely value added per worker, sales turnover per worker of £42,000 in Britain in 1989 compares with that of £83,500 (£ = ¥230) in Japan in 1987. The Japanese figure is an average of nonconsumer PCB companies that responded to the JPCA survey, while the British figure is an average of the largest 40 UK companies, whose company accounts were analyzed by Mike Hannon Marketing, UK. Even allowing for the greater use of subcontractors by Japanese than by British PCB suppliers, the gap between the Japanese and British productivity levels in the rato of 2:1 is unlikely to be eliminated. The profitability data (profit before taxation as percentage of sales turnover) from JPCA and Mike Hannon Marketing are as follows (owing to differences in company accounting conventions, the figures provide only rough indications):

YEAR	JAPAN	BRITAIN
1982	2.8	3.8
1983	1.5	6.0
1984	3.3	5.5
1985	2.4	7.3
1986	−0.2	0.0
1987	−1.2	4.5

7. In reality, price-fixing is a highly nebulous operation, so that a supplier may quote widely varied prices for a similar specification according to how badly it wants to secure the order. There is evidence in Britain that price quotation exercises conducted by the PCA, which specify not only design and materials but also lead time, invariably produce a variety of quoted prices with a highest—to—lowest ratio of between 4:1 to 7:1.

8. Shimada (1987) notes, in his discussion on the causes of U.S.–Japanese trade frictions, which is highly relevant to the ongoing Structural Impediments Initiative talks, that such stickiness in trading among Japanese companies explains much of the closed nature of Japanese domestic markets to foreign producers.

References

Aoki, Masahiko (ed.). (1984). *The Economic Analysis of the Japanese Firm*. Amsterdam: North-Holland.

Aoki, Masahiko. (1988). *Information, Incentives, and Bargaining in the Japanese Economy*. New York: Cambridge University Press.

Arrow, Kenneth J. (1975). "Gifts and Exchanges." In Edmund S. Phelps (ed.), *Altruism, Morality, and Economic Theory*. New York: Russell Sage Foundation.

Asanuma, Banri. (1989). "Manufacturer-Supplier Relationship in Japan and the Concept of Relation-Specific Skills." *Journal of the Japanese and International Economies*, 3, 1–30.

Baumol, William J. (1975) "Business Responsibility and Economic Behaviour." In E.S. Phelps (ed.), Altruism, *Morality, and Economic Theory*. New York: Russell Sage Foundation.

Blois, K.J. (1972). "Vertical Quasi-Integration." *Journal of Industrial Economics*, 20(3), 253–72.

Chuo University Economic Research Centre. (1976). *Chusho Kigyo no Kaiso Kozo* (The Hierarchical Structure of Small and Medium-sized Enterprises). Tokyo: Chuo University Press.

Corbett, Jenny. (1987). "International Perspectives on Financing: Evidence from Japan." *Oxford Review of Economic Policy*, 3(4), 30–55.

Dore, Ronald. (1983). "Goodwill and the Spirit of Market Capitalism." *British Journal of Sociology*, 34(4), 459–82.

Dore, Ronald. (1987) *Taking Japan Seriously*. London: Athlone Press.

Eccles, Robert. (1981). "The Quasi-Firm in the Construction Industry". *Journal of Economic Behaviour and Organisation*, 2, 335–57.

Granovette, Mark. (1985). "Economic Action and Social Structure: The Problem of Embeddedness." *American Journal of Sociology*, 91(3), 481–510.

Herrigel, Gary. (1993). "Industry as a Form of Order: A Comparison of the Historical Development of the Machine Tool Industries in the United States and Germany" (pp. 97–128, this volume).

Hirschman, Albert. (1970) *Exit, Voice and Loyalty*. Cambridge, Mass.: Harvard University Press.

Hirschmeier, Johannes, and Tsunehiko Yui. (1981). *The Development of Japanese Business 1600–1980*. London: George Allen & Unwin.

Imai, Kenichi., Hiroyuki Itami, and Kazue Koike. (1985) *Naibu Soshiki no Keizaigaku* (The Economics of Internal Organization). Tokyo: Toyo Keizai Shimposha.

Inagami, Takesh. (1988). *Japanese Workplace Industrial Relations* (Japanese Industrial Relations Series no. 14). Tokyo: The Japan Institute of Labor.

JPCA. (1987). *Purinto Haisenban Kogyo no Genjo* (The Current State of the Printed Circuit Board Industry). Tokyo: Japan Printed Circuit Association.

JPCA. (1987). *Purinto Kairo Kogyo no Chu-Choki Tenbo* (Medium to Long-Term Prospects of the PCB Industry). Tokyo: Japan Printed Circuit Association.

Leibenstein, Harvey. (1987). *Inside the Firm: The Inefficiencies of Hierarchy* Cambridge, Mass: Harvard University Press.

Macneil, Ian R. (1985) "Relational Contract: What We Do and Do Not Know." *Winconsin Law Review*, 3, 483–525.

Macneil, Ian R. (1987). "Relational Contract Theory as Sociology: A Reply to Professors Lindenberg and de Vos." *Zeitschrift für die gesamte Staatswissenschaft* (Journal of Institutional and Theoretical Economics), 143, 272–90.

Minato, Tetsuya. (1987). "Ryotaisenkan ni okeru nihongata shitauke seisan shisutemu no hensei katei" (Historical Background of the Japanese Inter-Firms Production System: 1920–1945). *Aoyama Kokusai Seikei Ronshu* (Aoyama International Political and Economic Journal), 7, 87–118.

Monteverde, Kirk, and David Teece. (1982). "Appropriable Rents and Quasi-Vertical Integration." *Journal of Law and Economics*, 25, 321–28.

Nakamura, Takafusa. (1981). *The Postwar Japanese Economy: Its Development and Structure*. Tokyo: University of Tokyo Press.

Okimoto, Daniel. (1986). "Regime Characteristics of Japanese Industrial Policy." In Hugh Patrick (ed.), *Japan's High Technology Industries*. Seatle: University of Washington Press.

Okumura, Hiroski. (1987). *Shin Nihon no Rokudai Kigyo Shudan* (Six Largest Corporate Groupings in Japan). Tokyo: Daiyamondo-sha.

Okun, Arthur M. (1981). *Prices & Quantities: A Macroeconomic Analysis*. Oxford: Basil Blackwell.

Parsons, Talcott. (1951). *The Social System*. London: Routledge & Kegan Paul.

Phelps, Edmund S. (ed.). (1975). *Altruism, Morality and Economic Theory*. New York: Russell Sage Foundation.

Piore, Michael J. and Charles F. Sabel. (1984). *The Second Industrial Divide*. New York: Basic Books.

Powell, Walter W. (1990). "Neither Market nor Hierarchy: Network Forms of Organization." In B.M. Staw and L.L. Cummings (eds.), *Research in Organization Behaviour*, Vol. 12. Greenwich, Conn.: JAI Press.

Richardson, George B. (1972). "The Organisation of Industry." *Economic Journal*, 82, 327.

Sako, Mari. (1991). "The Role of Trust' in Japanese Buyer-Supplier Relationships." In a special issue of *Ricerche Economiche*, M. Aoki and G. Brunello (eds.), Vol. XLV, Nos. 2, 3, pp. 375–99.

Sako, Mari. (1992). *Prices, Quality and Trust: Inter-firm Relations in Britain and Japan*. Cambridge: Cambridge University Press.

Shimada, Katsumi. (1987). "Boeki masatsu to torihiki kanko" (Trade Frictions and Trading Custom and Practice). *Kyotogakuen University Review*, 16(2), 24–76.

Smith, Adam. (1925) *The Wealth of Nations* (4th, ed.). Edwin Cannan (ed.). London: Methuen & Co. (Original work published 1776)

Streeck, Wolfgave, and Phillpe C. Schmitter. (eds.). (1985). *Private Interest Government: Beyond Market and State*. Beverley Hills and London: Sage Publications.

Trigilia, Carlo. (1986). "Small-Firm Development and Political Subcultures in Italy." *European Sociological Review*, 2(3), 161–175.

Wachter, Michael L., and Olive E. Williamson. (1978). "Obligational Markets and the Mechanics of Inflation." *The Bell Journal of Economics*, 9(2), 549–71.

Williamson, Oliver E. (1975). *Markets and Hierarchies*. New York: Free Press.

Williamson, Oliver E. (1979). "Transaction-Cost Economics: The Governance of Contractual Relations." *Journal of Law and Economics*, 22(2), 3–61.

Williamson, Oliver E. (1985). *The Economic Institutions of Capitalism*. New York: Free Press.

Womack, James P., et al. (1990). *The Machine That Changed the World*. New York: Rowson Associates.

Yoshino, Michael. Y., and Thomas B. Lifson. (1986). *The Invisible Link: Japan's Sogo Shosha and the Organisation of Trade*. Cambridge, Mass.: MIT Press.

CHAPTER 3

Governance Systems in Steel

The American and Japanese Experience

Patricia O'Brien

THE systems of industrial governance in Japan and the United States differ in stark and important ways. In Japan, which is known for its "enterprise capitalism," a complex web of relationships governs transactions among economic actors. In the United States, decisions governing the production of goods and services are made largely within separate, independent corporate entities. This chapter examines how the systems of governance in Japan and the United States affected the ability of each country's postwar steel industry to take advantage of market opportunities. The study focuses on the arrangements in each nation by which steel companies resolved three areas of potential conflicts: capacity, technological innovation, and pricing. My argument is, first, that the different systems of governance used by Japan and the United States to manage these factors in part explain the different economic outcomes of each steel industry. Second, Japan's system, which encouraged the steel industry to develop explicit, cooperative strategies to manage its industrywide economic problems, was more conductive to global competitiveness in the industry.

Included in this chapter is a brief overview of the systems of industrial governance in Japan and the United States. Following that is a short discussion of the economic characteristics of steelmaking. The body of the chapter consists of a detailed explication of the evolution of each country's steel industry with a focus on how each system of governance affected individual companies' investment decisions. The chapter concludes with a brief consideration of the future of the steel industry in both nations.

Two Systems of Industrial Governance

The salient aspect of Japan's system of industrial governance—that is, the process by which activities among economic actors are coordinated or managed—is the plethora of nonmarket relationships existing among enterprises (Badaracco, 1991; Miyazaki, 1976; Okumura, 1982). Political or social institutional relationships exist in all market economies, but in Japan these are so pronounced that, in reflecting back on his experiences, General Douglas MacArthur, who was

Supreme Commander of the Allied Powers in the Pacific during World War II, once remarked of Japan that "the world has never seen so abnormal an economic system" (Cohen, 1958:195–96). More recently, two economists described Japanese firms as enmeshed in a "thick and complex skein of relations matched in no other country" (Caves and Uekusa, 1976:495).

Japan's intraindustry relationships or affiliations cut across many different types of enterprises. The oldest, and arguably biggest, industrial networks are those Japanese groups—*keiretsu*—that descend from the *zaibatsu*, the giant, powerful combines that dominated prewar Japan. These enterprise groups, whose origins date back to the seventeenth century, link together a large number of firms from a broad range of industries and coordinate their activities. Mitsubishi, for example, encompasses more than 150 legally separate companies ranging from heavy industries like autos and steel to chemicals, glass, paper, electronics, insurance, and real estate. Although these group relationships are generally loose, they include interlocking equity ownership and sources for capital financing, as well as ready sources of information, ideas, products, and services.

A second form of *keiretsu* is the enterprise group composed of suppliers and contractors linked together in a tight, organized hierarchy around a large, dominant manufacturing company, such as Toyota or Matsushita. These networks are characterized by substantial cross-ownership, a heavy dependence by suppliers on the core company, and a powerful exchange of information and technology. As in the *zaibatsu*-descendant *keiretsu*, the presidents of the affiliated companies meet regularly.

A third type of institutional arrangement prevalent in Japan is the group or affiliation of producers of the same goods or services. At times, these horizontal relationships are formal, such as when they take the form of officially sanctioned cartels or trade associations. At other times, interfirm relationships are merely informal ad hoc arrangements among like producers.

Japan's business–government relationship is a fourth medium through which activities are coordinated within markets. In the postwar decades, the Japanese goernment assumed the role of the developmental state and, through its leading agencies—the Ministry of International Trade and Industry (MITI), the Ministry of Finance, and the Economic Planning Agency—intervened in sectoral markets to shape and accelerate the drive toward industrialization (Johnson, 1982; McCraw and O'Brien, 1986).

In the United States, on the other hand, the prevailing norm governing the production of goods and services is that critical decisions are within the jurisdiction of independent and legally separate corporate entities. In controversial areas in which public and private interests may clash—such as consumer safety or environmental protection—the autonomy of companies may be constrained or impeded by government regulations. But in general, American firms are "industrial citadels" with separate spheres of managerial authority circumscribed by fairly sharp boundaries (Badaracco, 1991:2–4). It is common for American corporations to strive to minimize their dependence on outsiders. As a result, firms have integrated extensively both backward, into raw material and component parts production, and forward, into marketing and distribution. Thus, American companies led the world in developing the large, modern industrial enterprise (Chandler, 1990).

The American pattern of industrial governance was shaped in large part by the distinctly American institution of antitrust. American industries attempted to form cartels in the late nineteenth century, but these efforts were suppressed by the Sherman Antitrust Act of 1890. Intraindustry relationships were further circumscribed by the passage in 1914 of both the Clayton Antitrust Act and the Federal Trade Commission Act. The Clayton Antitrust Act specifically condemned a number of common business practices including discriminatory pricing, exclusive or tying contracts, and interlocking directorates and shareholding. Meanwhile, the Federal Trade Commission Act set up and empowered a new federal agency with investigatory and enforcement authority against those relationships that were deemed "unfair methods of competition" (Henderson, 1924; Thorelli, 1955).

Today, many of the interlocking relationships and negotiations that exist in Japan are explicitly prohibited under American antitrust law. The laws prohibit interfirm agreements that coordinate price, production, or investment as well as mergers that significantly increase industrial concentration. The assumption behind these laws is that, in a free market, the risk and uncertainty about other companies' behavior will direct firms toward innovation, low prices, and efficient operating procedures. Consequently, American antitrust policy has sought to make arm's-length market transactions the primary means of resource allocation.

Of course, neither the Japanese nor the American system of industrial governance is a pure, or ideal, type. Interfirm behavior in Japan and the United States is never *exclusively* market or nonmarket determined. Both countries are capitalist economies and, in both, companies exhibit tendencies to behave as rivals as well as cohorts. Japanese industries are characterized by fierce interfirm rivalry. Moreover, Japan has maintained an antimonopoly law, bestowed upon it by the Allied Powers following World War II, as well as a Japan Fair Trade Commission (FTC) to administer it. In America, price signaling and joint ventures are integral parts of business strategy. Nevertheless, there remains a systematic difference in the patterns of industrial governance in the two countries. In America, arm's-length transactions remain an abiding shibboleth of society, whereas in Japan, companies are embedded in a complex web of nonmarket relationships.

The Economic Characteristics of Steelmaking

To understand the governance systems that prevailed in the steel industry, it is first necessary to understand the particular economics of steelmaking. The steel manufacturing process is generally composed of three discrete steps.[1] First, the raw materials—iron ore, coke, and limestone—are combined in a blast furnace and heated to reduce the ore to liquid pig iron. Second, the pig iron is oxidized in a steel furnace to remove most of the carbon, as well as other elements such as silicon or phosphorus. The second process yields raw steel. Third, the raw steel is put through a series of intermediate steps, such as being poured into a mold and solidified in a casting called an *ingot*.[2] The steel ingot is reheated (in soaking pits) and then converted into manageable semifinished shapes (blooms, billets, or slabs). The semifinished shapes are cooled and, finally, rolled and shaped into finished products.

"Integrated" steel companies engage in all three steps of the process just described. All over the world, steel companies discovered that they could increase their efficiency by consolidating the three stages of the steelmaking process within one plant. In fact, the typical American firm is integrated all the way back to mining and preparing its own raw materials.

From its beginning in the mid-nineteenth century up to the present, steel has been a capital-intensive industry. Its high capital requirement translates into a large fixed-cost component. Consequently, the industry became characterized by substantial economies of scale in manufacturing. If a company operated at a high volume of capacity — "full and steady" around the clock — the fixed cost per unit was minimized. As volume fell, however, the fixed cost per unit rose. Thus, efficiency in steelmaking depends in large part on running plants as full and fast as possible.

With integrated production and high capital costs, large steel companies were clearly more economical than small ones. During the post–World War II decades, blast-furnance technology improved enormously and made large-scale furnaces, which were formerly unwieldy, even more efficient. The optimal yield of a blast furnace increased gradually from 300,000 tons of pig iron a year to 3 million tons. Similarly, a hot strip mill, which is used to roll slabs into sheets, could produce 3 million or 4 million tons annually. By the mid-1970s, the minimum efficient scale for an integrated plant was between 6 million and 7 million tons of steel capacity a year (Crandall, 1981:11; Mueller and Kawahito, 1978:6).

One other critical factor in the economics of the steel industry is the nature of its demand. Because steel is a basic product consumed mainly by other industrial producers, its demand is essentially derived from that of other industries. A society's demand for steel depends largely on its rate of capital formation (construction and equipment investments) and its consumption of consumer durables (autos and appliances). Since steel is durable, customers can choose to postpone replacing steel products, by extending the life of a dilapidated machine, for example. As a result, steel demand is tightly linked to general economic trends and is highly susceptible to cyclical fluctuations. A cyclical fluctuating demand can make it difficult to run steel plants full and steady. In addition, steel demand is relatively price inelastic. That is, as steel prices decrease, total steel consumption increases proportionately less (TNEC, 1940:13914–79; Stocking, 1954:28–29).

The response of steelmakers all over the world to these economic conditions has been to attempt to insulate themselves from the periodic threat of overcapacity and large losses. Through formal and informal cartels, price signaling, and implicit price leadership, steel companies have demonstrated a long history of trying to stabilize output and control prices (Stocking and Watkins, 1947: 171–215; Webb, 1980).

The Japanese Steel Industry

The Early Postwar Years

When World War II ended in August 1945, Japan's steel industry was in ruins. In Japan's fourteen years of war, from 1931 to 1945, steel output had risen from 2.1 million to 8.5 million tons, the highest in Japan's history.[3] But by 1946, Japan produced a mere 0.6 million tons of crude steel, and less than 30 percent of its iron and steelmaking facilities were in operation. Moreover, prospects for the industry's recovery were grim. To begin with, the steel industry was essentially the product of Japan's wartime mobilization. Although Japan's modern iron and steel industry started in 1897 when the government built the integrated Yawata Iron Works, the industry had remained small, fragmented, and struggling. Until 1925, Japan had imported more steel than it produced. In 1931, when Japan went to war with Manchuria, the government, fearing that the weak steel industry could not adequately serve Japan's military demand, assumed responsibility for mobilization. For the next fourteen years, the Japanese government coordinated raw material procurement, distribution, financing, and pricing in steel. Peace ended the heavy war-related demand by the military for steel and munitions, the industry's only output. At that point, Japan's civilian economy, which was crippled by severe inflation and shortages of food, energy, and foreign exchange, appeared unable to generate sufficient civilian demand for steel to replace the military demand.

Second, Japan's steel plants and equipment were obsolete, debilitated, or both. For more than a dozen years, the equipment had been used unremittingly but maintained minimally so that most steelmaking equipment needed to be repaired or replaced. Moreover, because demand after the war had shifted from military goods to sheets, strips, and hoops needed by capital-goods industries in peacetime, firms needed to replace obsolete rolling mills with newer and better equipment. As Japan's equipment manufacturers were also not operating, new steel furnaces and mills would have to be imported from Europe or the United States. This is turn would require a supply of foreign currency, which Japan lacked.

Finally, Japan faced a severe raw material and energy shortage. At the conclusion of the war, China, Manchuria, and Korea, Japan's chief sources of raw materials, were closed to Japanese trade. Cut off from their suppliers in Southeast Asia, Japanese steel companies were forced to turn to Western supplies, which, being farther away, were much more costly to transport. The prospect of obtaining raw materials and equipment abroad seemed hopeless since Japan had exhausted its foreign exchange during the war.

These economic factors—low demand, obsolete equipment, and expensive raw materials—did more than just prevent most steel works from operating. When combined with Japan's spiraling inflation, they also ensured that Japan's steel companies would have manufacturing costs that were the highest in the world. In the immediate postwar years, Japanese steel costs were 50 percent to 100 percent higher than those of similar products manufactured in America and Britain (Kawahito, 1972:34; Shinohara, 1982:24). High manufacturing costs, naturally, precluded Japanese steelmakers from exporting in all but extreme cases of market shortages.

In sum, market conditions for the Japanese steel industry following the end of the war were dismal. John Foster Dulles, who represented the United States at one of the early peace treaty negotiations, reportedly observed that "suicide was not an illogical step for anyone concerned about Japan's economic future" (McDiarmid, 1966:136). In 1947, Japan's real gross national product was slightly more than 50 percent of its 1937 level, and domestic steel demand was the lowest since 1916. Japan had forty-three iron and steelmaking companies, most of which operated small, highly specialized plants. Only four of these companies were even integrated, and together they operated only one plant that approached the minimum efficient scale in steelmaking. Many Western analysts, observing the unusual circumstances that had produced the wartime industry, speculated that the heyday of Japan's steel industry was past (Zimmerman, 1951:685).

Judging from market conditions, one would not have expected Japanese firms to invest in capital-intensive and natural-resource-dependent industries. Instead, one would have expected the available capital to have been channeled into the then-existing labor-intensive industries such as textiles, cigarette lighters, and Christmas tree ornaments. But market forces alone do not fully explain the evolution of Japan's postwar industry structure. Contrary to the expectations of Western analysts, Japan's leading steel companies embarked on major programs of renovation and expansion. By 1955, pig iron capacity had doubled, open-hearth capacity had increased 30 percent, and capacity for hot- and cold-rolled strips had increased sevenfold. Moreover, the industry's investment trajectory took it far beyond reconstruction to make it the largest and lowest-cost steel industry in the world. To understand what happened and why, one must understand the system of industrial governance that prevailed in the Japanese economy.

The Business–Government Relationship

In the postwar years the objective of the Japanese government was to rebuild the country's devastated economy. To accomplish this, Japan needed a large volume of exports from which it would earn the foreign exchange necessary to import food, raw materials, equipment, and technology. To build a trade balance that could support the country's huge import requirements, Japan required key export industries, preferably in high value-added products. In the government's view, if left to conventional market forces, high value-added industries might never develop, or at least not as rapidly as desired by the government. Thus, MITI targeted four potential export industries for growth. One of these was steel.[4]

Steel was targeted as a priority for two reasons. First, world steel demand was already strong and was expected to become even stronger as national economies recovered and converted to peacetime consumption. A large demand for steel exports combined with their high degree of value-added suggested that steel could contribute more to Japan's foreign currency earnings than other manufactured items such as low value-added textiles, which remained Japan's primary export product until 1951. Second, as the "rice of industry," steel was considered essential for Japan's own domestic economic development (Johnson, 1982:268). A steel industry would enable Japan to rebuild its demolished cities and transportation system and provide the basic input for rebuilding other industries such as shipbuilding, automobiles, and machinery.

The first problem confronting the steel industry was that if Japan's market was open to imports, lower-priced foreign steel would flood the country, thus preventing Japan's high-cost steelmakers from operating. Consequently, MITI's first method of governing—or of maintaining order in the industry—was simply to exclude all foreign steel from Japan. Until the mid-1960s, therefore, steel imports were generally prohibited.

The second problem the industry faced was that high fixed costs and cyclical demand made steel a risky investment. Companies faced the possibility of getting trapped in a vicious circle of overcapacity, price-cutting, low margins, and large losses. MITI reduced the risk of overcapacity and large losses by strictly controlling the amount of new capacity built in Japan. In the early postwar years, MITI could influence managers' decisions by exerting its control over scarce foreign exchange, required by steelmakers for importing coal, iron ore, scrap steel, and technological licenses, as well as by its power to administer low-interest capital. During the early 1950s, steel companies submitted capital expansion plans to MITI's Heavy Industries Bureau for review. If MITI approved the plan, the company was granted low-interest loans from Japanese banks. If MITI found a company's plan inconsistent with its own plan for the industry, government officials met with company management to negotiate a mutually acceptable level of investment.

By protecting the domestic market and controlling, or governing, capacity, MITI balanced domestic supply with projected domestic and export demand. Thus, steel companies were assured a full and steady throughput, which minimized the per unit fixed cost. As one analyst has asserted, by targeting the industry and coordinating supply in this way, MITI reduced the risk to "close to nil unless Japan itself went under" (Johnson, 1982:207).

Through this early capital-allocation program, MITI also influenced the steel industry's efficiency by shaping its industry structure. Although thirty two of Japan's forty-three steelmakers received financing in 1951, about 72 percent of this funding, equal to $227 million, was channeled to the four major steel companies. Three integrated steelmakers—Yawata, Fuji, and NKK—received 58 percent of the funding, with Yawata, Japan's largest steel company, individually absorbing more than 25 percent of the loans. MITI concentrated the industry's expansion in Japan's four largest companies to enable them to take advantage of the economies of scale in steelmaking. By circumventing the market mechanism and accelerating the development of an oligopolistic structure in steel, MITI increased the efficiency of Japan's largest steelmakers.

By the late 1950s, MITI's power was vastly reduced from that of the previous decade because, although the agency still controlled foreign exchange allocations, little low-cost capital was available for steelmakers. Steel companies obtained private capital from equity markets and Japanese banks on the basis of the steelmakers' potential earning power. Nevertheless, MITI continued to try to use its power over foreign exchange allocations to guide the amount of capacity that entered the market.

Since MITI believed that the route to minimizing long-run steel costs and securing world market share was to invest continually in more efficient means of production, it linked the right to build new capacity to a combination of past market share and demonstrated efficiency. For any firm to "win" the right to build new capacity, it had to show that it had the most modern equipment available. This system encouraged firms to "scrap and build" functioning equipment and replace it with state-of-the-art technology as a prerequisite for growth.

Although the major steel companies generally agreed with MITI's efforts to maintain an orderly industry, the business–government relationship was one of constant negotiation. Frequently, MITI's intervention met with some resistance from steelmakers. In the early years, when MITI concentrated resources in the largest firms, small and medium-sized steel companies challenged the Ministry, charging it with "attaching undue importance to big makers" (Japan's Iron and Steel Industry, 1953-1954:73). In 1951, Kawasaki Steel, an open-hearth steelmaker and Japan's fourth largest steel company, embarked on a long and notorious battle with MITI. In that year, Kawasaki Steel applied to MITI for funds to build a large, greenfield integrated steel plant.[5] Supported by Japan's major banks, MITI vehemently opposed Kawasaki Steel's plans, arguing that added capacity was unnecessary and would result in "excess competition." For over one and one-half years, Kawasaki Steel battled MITI, focusing national media attention on the subject of steel capacity. Finally, at the end of 1952, MITI approved Kawasaki Steel's proposal. Long after Kawasaki Steel built the Chiba Works, industry managers talked of Kawasaki Steel's management's defiance of MITI's steel policies (Lynn, 1982:109; Yonekura, 1984:8–15).

In the mid-1960s, MITI's power was again challenged, this time by Sumitomo Metal, Japan's fifth largest steelmaker. A fiercely independent and aggressive steel producer, Sumitomo Metal continued to invest in new capacity during the recession of 1963–1965 in what appeared to be a flagrant disregard for the industry's moratorium on new capacity construction.[6] In 1965, Sumitomo Metal challenged MITI's production limits by continuing to compete for domestic market share. MITI tried to order Sumitomo's compliance by threatening to limit the company's coking coal imports to exactly the amount the company would need to produce the restricted quantity of output. This heavy-handed intervention, unusual for MITI, was counterproductive. It provoked strong opposition from industry, the press, and eventually even other steel companies, which, while they opposed Sumitomo Metal's defection, also opposed greater government intervention. The underlying conflicts that surfaced in the Sumitomo Metal incident abated in the strong market resurgence of 1967 and were never really resolved (Johnson, 1982:268–71; Sengo Sangyushi eno Shogen, 1977: 57–76; Sumitomo Annual Report, 1966:1). The notorious Kawasaki and

Sumitomo Metal incidents demonstrate the tenuous nature of the Japanese government's system of industrial governance. MITI exercised its influence not through legislated policies but rather through constant persuasion and the application of informal pressure. MITI had little legal authority and, after 1956, few sanctions through which to control manager's decisions. In the late 1950s, MITI proposed a constitutional amendment that would allow it to increase and administer government loans in exchange for authority to guide the investment decisions of large firms, but this proposal was met by unequivocal opposition from large, medium, and small steelmakers alike. Unwilling to relinquish their autonomy, firms objected to the bureaucratic control of private industry (Kodo, 1967:99).

Neither MITI nor any other government agency could compel Japanese steel companies to adopt unwanted business policies. Instead, government bureaucrats met regularly with steel company managers and, over time, persuaded them to participate voluntarily in market stabilization measures. Japanese steel executives cooperated because, like executives in capital-intensive industries in other countries, they recognized their mutual interdependence and mutual interest in market stability.

By the 1960s, when MITI's power over capital was greatly lessened, its role in steel was primarily hortatory. But by then, horizontal relationships among steel companies had replaced the business–government relationship as the primary source of industrial governance.

Intraindustry Relationships

According to Japanese steel managers, an intense spirit of competition prevailed among steel companies from the early postwar years, when the Occupation authorities divided and privatized the government-owned and government-operated steel company, through the 1980s. Yet throughout the postwar decades, presidents of major steel companies met regularly with one another. While there is no formal record of the industrywide meetings, a Japanese newspaper account described a typical 1980 meeting as follows (quoted in Yamamura, 1982:83):

> The Iron-Steel Building in Nihonbashi, Tokyo. Around noon every Monday, elderly gentlemen arrive in black cars.... They go to Room 704, on the entrance of which is a sign reading, "The Regular Monday Club Meeting." The members consist of the senior executives of eight major steel producers. They sit at a rectangular table around the section chief of the Ministry of International Trade and Industry, who is seated at the head of the table. Ogawa, who heads the Iron and Steel Section of the Basic Industries Bureau of MITI, presides over the meeting. On his left is Vice President Ohashi of [Nippon Steel] and on his right is senior Director Yamaguchi of [NKK].... During lunch few speak.... After coffee, the members listen to Ogawa's presentation. The meeting ends after about an hour. The official name of the Monday Club is the General Session of the Market Policies Committee. It was organized in 1958....

The precise effects of these or other industrywide meetings are at best elusive. But, according to Japanese steel managers, starting in 1958 the companies began to replace the government by developing their own system for coordinating new capacity investments. Although the companies had at times objected to MITI's intervention in private, entrepreneurial decisions, they shared MITI's perspective on the need for capacity coordination.

Under the industry's system of *jishu chosei*, "voluntary-adjustment" or "self-regulation," managers of the leading steel companies met regularly to coordinate capacity investment plans. Like the government's system of controlling capacity, the industry allocated capacity rights according to a combination of past market share and efficiency. Thus, the *jishu chosei* system encouraged firms to invest continually in the most efficient technology available. Through this system, the companies attempted to maintain an orderly, stable rate of capacity growth that matched the growth in domestic and export demand for steel. When, for example, steel demand declined in late 1964, steel executives agreed to limit investments to those projects already under construction. When the economy worsened in the next year, managers agreed to a moratorium on all new steel capacity. Only investments for modernizations were permitted.

Jishu chosei meetings were intensely heated, described by managers as "boxing matches" among the firms. While the industry was not required to have government officials—from either MITI or Japan's FTC—present, MITI officials were sometimes invited to arbitrate disagreements. Industry representatives would also meet regularly with MITI to coordinate the industry's projections with the economic plans of the government. At *jishu chosei* meetings, the larger companies tended to argue strongly for market stability and implicit cartels while the smaller firms advocated free market competition. Occasionally, as in the Sumitomo Metal incident in 1965, the industry's entreaties would fail to win a firm's compliance, and a firm would disregard the industry's agreement and expand its capacity. Nevertheless, all major firms regularly attended the meetings and most abided by the capacity limits.

Steelmakers also used horizontal relationships to coordinate steel prices. Despite the attempt of the government and the industry to coordinate capacity decisions, business cycles in the global or domestic market caused temporary conditions of overcapacity and price-cutting. In the early postwar period, competition often included relentless price wars. In 1952, for example, when faced with a worldwide recession and new entrants to the global market, the industry found its demand projections overly optimistic and, in response, domestic steel prices fell by 20 percent. In this market, steel company profits would fall and, according to MITI, "unless something was done, some makers would be forced to take substantial losses" (Japan's Iron and Steel Industry, 1953/1954:91).

In the early 1950s, the industry petitioned the Japanese Diet (the legislature) to allow recession and rationalization cartels to be formed during downcycles in the economy. A constitutional amendment was passed in 1953 allowing some industries—with MITI's authorization—to maintain domestic prices above market levels during crises. Although steel prices were generally set by the marketplace, relief was available through cooperative pricing agreements during downturns.

The striking aspect of Japan's intraindustry relationships is not that the steel industry sought to control capacity or prices, because many other steel industries in the world have sought that, but rather that the Japanese government, through MITI, created an environment in which the industry could stabilize market fluctuations. Whereas some governments, such as in the United States, perceive overcapacity and price-cutting as normal risks inherent in the market sytem, the Japanese government, at least at times, judged them to be obstacles that could hinder the stable, orderly growth of an industry. By sanctioning implicit capacity and price cartels, the Japanese government socialized the risk of the steel companies' investments. Companies could invest aggressively, confident that during economic downturns relief was available.

Corporate Strategy and Performance

At first glance, the history of the Japanese steel industry reveals aggressive company management strategies that centered on continuous investments in modern manufacturing equipment and facilities. No overall government policies *compelled* these successful business policies. Steel managers appear to have allocated resources to maximize the long-run viability of their firms. On closer examination, however, it becomes clear that the particular pattern of investment decisions followed by Japanese steel executives were not followed in any major market economy other than Japan. In the first place, the expansion strategies of the Japanese steel companies reflected an enormous gamble that was based on an unusual optimism about the continued stability and growth of the global steel market. Year after year, the companies relentlessly expanded their production capacity despite a domestic supply that exceeded domestic demand and persistent cyclical recessions. Second, Japanese steel firms invested in plant rationalizations that required sacrificing short-term profits for uncertain gains in long-run productivity. These decisions, which differed radically from those followed by American steel companies during the same period, made sense within Japan's system of industrial governance.

Japanese steel companies in concert with the government adjusted the risk inherent in steelmaking and in doing so actually altered one of the fundamental dynamics of traditional capitalism. In this environment in which firms were protected from large losses and directed away from short-term profit maxi-mization, steel companies expanded aggressively and raced to outrationalize each other. Firms emerged from recessions with optimistic plans and responded to the government's economic programs with correspondingly large demand projections. Although by 1953, the industry was as big as it had ever been, the companies continued to expand in a stable, orderly manner through the 1970s. Output rose from 8.5 million tons in 1953 to 150 million tons in 1975. This relentless optimism, in an industry with high fixed costs and cyclical demand, made sense in a market in which risk was socialized and firms were sheltered from some of the deleterious effects of market forces.

Japanese steel companies did not simply invest in incremental capacity.

Rather, the industry's history reflects a distinctive pattern of continued rationli-zations of new and old facilities. For example, Japanese firms, like American ones, invested heavily in open-hearth furnace capacity from 1950 to 1960. By the mid-1950s, every open-hearth furnace had been replaced or significantly rebuilt since the end of the war. Yet when, by the 1960s, it became clear that the basic oxygen furnace was the superior technology, Japanese companies replaced their open-hearth furnaces with basic oxygen technology. For some firms, like Kawasaki, this required dismantling functioning equipment that was less than ten years old. Other firms, such as Yawata, which had rebuilt every one of its open-hearth furnaces by then, simply scrapped twenty years of accumulated investments. By the late 1970s, Japan's major steel companies had replaced *every* one of their open-hearth furnaces.

At times, the companies went to astounding lengths to modernize. In the 1970s, NKK, Japan's second largest steelmaker, actually razed its 5.5-million-ton facility and built an entirely new 6-million-ton, ultramodern facility. NKK spent the equivalent of $5 billion to reclaim 7 million square meters of land from the sea, construct an island site, and build an integrated greenfield facility. To accomplish its goal of modernization, NKK scrapped over twenty years of accumulated investment in its Keihin Steel Works to build a facility that added almost no new capacity to the company.

In a mere two decades, Japan's steel industry was transformed from a collection of small, backward producers to the most modern and technologically sophisticated producers in the world. In 1943, at the height of the industry's mobilization for war, Japan produced 8.5 million tons of steel, less than 10 percent of U.S. output. By the late 1970s, Japan had matched the United States in steel output, as both countries were now producing about 115 million tons annually. Moreover, Japanese steel producers had attained an estimated cost advantage of between $66 and $120 per ton (equal to 30 percent of total costs) over American and European producers (Barnett, 1977; Bradford, 1977; CWPS, 1977; FTC, 1977; Mueller and Kawahito, 1978). Not surprisingly, Japanese steel firms led the world in steel exports.

According to most analytical studies, Japan's cost advantage stemmed from the industry's extremely modern facilities and its full exploitation of economies of scale (Crandall, 1981:72; Mueller and Kawahito, 1978:6). The differences in scale are particularly striking: By the mid-1970s, the average capacity of an integrated plant in Japan had reached 7.4 million tons, while the average size of an integrated American plant was only 2.9 million tons—less than half as large (see Table 3.1). Japan's ten largest plants could produce 10.6 million tons of steel annually, while the ten top U.S. plants could only produce 5.9 million tons. No less than 71 percent of Japan's entire national capacity was represented by these ten plants, compared to only 37 percent for America. The simple fact was that Japan's steel plants averaged more than twice the size of America's plants.

Japan also led the world in technology and manufacturing processes. In 1975, Japan's steel was manufactured in a mere 69 blast furnaces, half of which measured 2000 cubic meters or more. The United States produced the same

Table 3.1. Crude Steel Capacity, 1977–1978 (millions of net tons)

Japan		United States	
Plant location (company)		Plant location (company)	
Fukuyama (NKK)	17.6	Indiana Harbor, IN (Inland)	8.5
Mizushima (Kawasaki Steel)	14.0	Gary, IN (US Steel)	8.0
Chiba (Kawasaki Steel)	10.0	Sparrows Pt., MD (Bethlehem Steel)	7.0
Kimitsu (Nippon Steel)	10.5	Great Lakes, MI (National Steel)	6.6
Wakayama (Sumitomo Steel)	10.2	E. Chicago, IN (Jones & Laughlin)	5.5
Kashima (Sumitomo Steel)	9.9	Burns Harbor, IN (Bethlehem Steel)	5.3
Yawata (Nippon Steel)	9.7	S. Chicago, IL (US Steel)	5.2
Oita (Nippon Steel)	9.3	Fairless, PA (US Steel)	4.4
Nagoya (Nippon Steel)	8.3	Cleveland, OH (Republic Steel)	4.4
Kakogawa (Kobe Steel)	7.1	Wierton, WV (National Steel)	4.0
Total	106.6		58.9

SOURCE: Japan data from IISS, *Steel Industry in Brief: Japan* (1977); U.S. data from IISS Commentary: *Steel Plants USA, 1960–1980.*

amount of steel in 300 furnaces, only five of which measured 2000 cubic meters or more. Japanese companies were also more advance in adopting the large hot strip mills, the second facility exhibiting large economies of scale. In the early 1970s, Japan's hot strip mills averaged 2 million tons of output annually while American plants averaged 1.26 million tons. Likewise, Japanese firms installed continuous casting machines long before American producers. In 1976, some 35 percent of Japan's crude steel output was continually cast, compared to 10.5 percent of U.S. output (IISS, 1983:26–43).

Of course, Japanese companies developed these competitive advantages through a complicated set of circumstances. Low wages and a possibly favorable exchange rate were conducive to the development of an export industry. Moreover, an explosively growing gross national product (GNP) created a burgeoning demand for steel. Strict capital controls limited the opportunities for Japanese investors and restricted entry by preventing capital inflows. The Korean War helped to stimulate demand for steel in the early years just as high prices for scrap steel in the world market made the basic oxygen furnace an even more attractive investment. These market forces presented Japan with opportunities; in fact, they were the identical opportunities faced by many other newly industrializing countries. But Japan, *unlike* any other nation, fully exploited these market opportunities and transformed its small, backward steel industry into the most advanced in the world.

The central argument presented here is that the bold corporate strategies that created the Japanese miracle in steel resulted from a unique combination of cooperative industrial governance systems and intense interfirm rivalry, within a protected arena. This unusual and, at first glance, paradoxical combination of market forces and concerted actions worked in tandem to yield, on one hand, the benefits of rivalry and, on the other hand, to shelter firms from the inherent risks attending the huge investments typical of steel.

The United States Steel Industry

The Postwar Years

In 1945, the United States was the preeminent steel-producing nation in the world, responsible for over one half of all global steel production. The country had 95 million tons of steelmaking capacity, the majority of which was owned by fifteen large, integrated companies. Soon after the industry's beginning, in the mid-nineteenth century, major U.S. steel companies, led by dynamic entrepreneurs like Andrew Carnegie, caught up with and surpassed the established, and previously dominant, British iron and steel firms. From the turn of the century, American steelmakers possessed clear productivity advantages associated with superior scale and technology. By the early 1950s, the average capacity of American steel plants was 2.8 million tons, compared to 1.1 million tons for plants in Britain and France, and 0.8 million tons for plants in Japan (Cockerill, 1974:38; Barnett and Schorsch 1983:18). Moreover, the industry benefited from a huge domestic market, a proprietary supply of raw materials, and access to the world's largest capital market.

Yet for American steelmakers, the future market seemed uncertain. Indeed, when Japan surrendered in August 1945, the industry had found itself with thousands of cancelled contracts and tens of thousands of redundant workers. Since steel products were central to the country's successful transition from a war to a peacetime economy, the end of the war brought a huge new demand for steel. But industry economists, fixed on the low level of steel consumption that characterized the 1930s, regarded the postwar steel demand growth as a temporary aberration. Believing that the postwar boom would inevitably subside, they feared that with capacity additions, steel plants could never run full and steady. Instead, their companies would be left with overcapacity and heavy losses. Also, changes in industrial design and societal preferences threatened to bring a surge of new materials into markets that were formerly the exclusive domain of basic steel. By the late 1950s, prestressed concrete in construction, copper and plastics in pipes, aluminum in containers, and lightweight steel in autos threatened to take market share away from integrated steelmakers.

Other changes, too, presented the industry with potential opportunities as well as new competition. First, although the chemical process of steelmaking had barely changed since the industry's beginning, several technological innovations improved manufacturing efficiencies. The chief innovation came during the late 1950s when European researchers discovered a more efficient method of refining pig iron into top-quality steel using a basic oxygen process. By blowing a jet of high-purity oxygen through the top of the furnace rather than the bottom as previous designs did, the basic oxygen furnace (BOF) refined iron in less than an hour, compared to seven or eight hours for the open-hearth furnace. In addition to reducing the heat time, the BOF used half the quantity of scrap and less labor than did the open-hearth furnace. This technological breakthrough in the steelmaking furnace would relegate the open-hearth furnace to obscurity within two decades.

Moreover, during the postwar decades, blast furnace technology improved enormously and increased the efficiency of large-scale furnaces. Combined with numerous process improvements in technology, this accelerated the upward trend in the size of steel plants and equipment. Finally, continuous casting technology, which was developed in the 1960s, eliminated the ingot stage of the manufacturing process. In continuous casting, the molten steel is poured into a trough from which it flows into water-cooled molds and then directly into semifinished shapes. By eliminating the ingot pouring, cooling, reheating, and rolling, this innovation minimized steel waste and yielded savings in energy consumption and labor.

After World War II, the world market for iron ore began changing. Fearing that the U.S. industry was rapidly depleting its domestic ore supply, the owners of American mines—who were mainly U.S. steel companies—increased iron ore prices sharply. This set off a search for new raw material deposits in North and South America and Australia, as well as experiments with new manufacturing processes that depended less on high-quality ore. When new sources were eventually found, American steel companies lost their historic advantage in cheap, high-quality Lake Superior ore.

Lastly, as the governments of war-torn countries—Germany, France, and Japan—targeted steel as a strategic industry and rebuilt their facilities, the American steel industry faced new competition. With the help of the Economic Cooperation Association (ECA), a supranational organization for countries receiving aid from the U.S. Economic Recovery Program, the European steel industries were rebuilding in a planned, orderly fashion that suggested a strict rationalization of their industry structures. American producers immediately perceived that, as in the prewar years, they might again be forced to compete with a strong European cartel (*Iron Age*, 1949:120). This time, however, cartelization could lead foreign producers to have a genuine cost advantage that would not only prohibit American steel from selling in European markets but also make U.S. producers vulnerable to competition from cheap imports at home.

By the early 1960s, U.S. steel executives were aware of these developments (*Fortune*, 1960:123–27; 1966:130–37). Yet, for most of three decades, the industry responded and adjusted only minimally to these changes. It can be argued that one of the reasons the industry responded as it did was that its industrial governance system—in which firms made independent, autonomous decisions—trapped firms in conservative, risk-minimizing practices that precluded effective adjustment strategies. Market forces may have dictated that, in the end, American companies simply could not maintain their superiority. But the industry could have adjusted by closing inefficient capacity, investing in productivity improvements, and concentrating production in efficient facilities to fully exploit the economies of scale. Instead, the industry adjusted through a slow, painful, and costly process of lagging competitiveness, falling sales, staggering losses, and company failures. Given the American system of industrial governance, no other method of adjustment may have been feasible.

Business, Government, and Labor Relations

The American business–government relationship in steel reveals a pattern of adversarial and conflict-ridden encounters. Intent on preserving the country's competitive ideal—which posited that a society's resources were optimally allocated in a free market composed of many firms selling products through fierce price competition—the U.S. government attempted to protect the public against the potential dangers that huge corporations represented. Over time the American steel industry's governance system reflected the interaction of the industry's economics and these ideals and values, which were embedded in the American political system.

Ever since the Bureau of Corporations began investigating the U.S. Steel Corporation in 1905, the American steel industry has been on a collision course with the government. U.S. Steel was one of the first corporations subject to a congressional committee investigation (in 1911) and, later that year, it became the target of the most prolonged antitrust suit in American history. In every decade of the twentieth century, the steel industry has been investigated by the U.S. Department of Justice for some form of questionable competitive practice. Steel has also had a colorful and controversial history with the White House, stretching from President Theodore Roosevelt's "entente" relationship with Judge Elbert Gary, chairman of U.S. Steel, through William Howard Taft's endorsement of an antitrust suit against U.S. Steel and Franklin D. Roosevelt's denunciation of the industry as a "concealed cartel system"; there were also President Truman's attempt to seize the steel mills and John F. Kennedy's and Lyndon Johnson's confrontations with the industry over pricing (Hoopes, 1963; Kolko, 1963; Urofsky, 1969).

In 1946, the steel industry entered an acrimonious dispute with the government over the proper level of national steel capacity. Government planners, relying on studies of aggregate demand and supply prepared by public-sector economists during the war, anticipated a large, new steel demand. Anxious to avoid a steel shortage because it could become a bottleneck to the entire nation's economic growth, public policymakers urged the steel industry to expand.

But steel industry executives argued that existing U.S. capacity—which exceeded 92 million tons annually—could amply provide for the country's future domestic needs. The industry argued that the postwar growth was temporary, the result of pent-up wartime demand and was about to end. From 1945 to 1960, this fundamental dispute between American business and government festered. Industry executives, obsessed with the high fixed-cost nature of their business and the consequent risks to their companies, continued to resist entreaties to invest in capacity expansion. The federal government, now supported by a majority of public opinion, continued to urge expansion and to hint darkly that the industry's primary interest was in maintaining excessively high prices and profits.

The central problem for the industry was the age-old nightmare of over-capacity. As Walter Tower, the president of the American Iron and Steel Institute, remarked in 1947:

> [in] all this talk of great shortages and pent-up demands, there is much that recalls the experience of 27 years ago. It was then that the idea of "accumulated shortages" gained popular acceptance. Then, too, we heard about a steel-starved world. Some prophets of that day saw visions of at least "ten years of unbroken and unparalleled prosperity" for the steel industry. The very next year your furnaces operated at 35 percent of capacity.... (Tower, 1947:635)

The extreme cyclicality and uncertainty of demand, combined with the American governance system in which risk remained privatized, pushed American producers toward strategies of extreme caution.

Both sides in the capacity-expansion debate had legitimate arguments. Goverment planners were correct to anticipate vigorous growth in demand while industry executives were, quite rationally, unwilling to assume the private risk associated with an uncertain future demand. Amid talk of a "steel-starved world" following World War I, American steel companies had expanded only to find themselves operating at a dismal 34.5 percent of capacity in 1921. When some steelmakers again invested in the late 1920s, their new plants opened in a market that supported only 19.5 percent of capacity.

When geopolitical considerations intervened, the U.S. government temporarily suspended this system of governance. For example, in the spring of 1950, when America was on the brink of both the Cold War and the Korean War, the government instituted a series of economic programs designed to subsidize, and thereby induce, new capital investment in steel. As in World War II, the Congress passed an accelerated-depreciation tax provision for defense-related plants, including steel mills. Under this program, the Department of Defense provided "certificates of necessity" to approved projects, which would allow them to be depreciated over five years rather than the usual twenty. In a related program, the Reconstruction Finance Corporation, a government agency, provided low-cost loans to holders of such certificates (Tiffany, 1988:90–96).

Steel company executives also had a bitterly hostile relationship with organized labor. Throughout the early postwar years, labor's powerful union, the United Steelworkers of America, succeeded in securing escalating wage increases. The industry conceded to the wage demands, however, only after major strikes—in 1949, 1952, 1956, and 1959. These strikes proved deleterious to the industry and wrought havoc with the "full and steady" prerequisite for low-cost production. Moreover, the industry's poor relationship with labor inevitably resulted in the federal government intervening to arbitrate disputes. For example, in one of the most notorious steel–labor disputes, President Truman in 1952 attempted to seize and nationalize the steel industry[7] (Marcus, 1977; Westin, 1958).

The business, government, and labor relationship in American steel reveals two distinct patterns. First, business, government, and labor were in an essentially adversarial relationship, one in which there was no neutral, nonhostile method for resolving problems (Tiffany, 1988). The prevailing methods used to resolve conflicts—strikes, attempted seizures, antitrust suits, congressional investigations, and public denunciations—reflect the extent to which American business, government, and labor perceived themselves as autonomous actors without pressing common interests. And the problems of cyclical demand and overcapacity were considered exclusively private matters and not public-sector concerns.

Second, and more importantly, the ideals and values of the American political system led policymakers to view the industry's problems, which were inherent in all capital-intensive industries subject to cyclical demand, as not only natural but also desirable. Supported by economic theory, American policymakers believed that risk and rivalry would yield a Schumpeterian process of "creative destruction" and, ultimately, a more technologically and socially efficient industry. Thus, the country's prevailing systems of governance in steel compelled firms to assume privately all of the risks of their strategic decisions. While the industry's lagging competitiveness would have profound implications not only for the steel companies but also for labor and the rest of the economy, the country simply had no system of governance through which firms could respond collectively to the economic threats and opportunities they faced.

Intraindustry Relationships

The modern American steel industry's governance system is rooted in the industry's beginning—in the 1860s—after experiments with heat led to the discovery and commercialization of a process for manufacturing affordable steel. As the rapid expansion of the U.S. economy following the Civil War set off a huge demand for metal products, the new industry grew rapidly. By 1880, America was producing over a million tons of crude steel and, by 1900, its output had surpassed 10 million tons.

As the early steelmakers discovered the importance of steady, continuous volume, they launched a fierce competitive race in steel. The farsighted Andrew Carnegie, who had spent 12 years working for the railroads—the country's first high-scale-economy industry—was particularly influential in ushering in this race (Livesay, 1975; Wall, 1970). Just as the railroads ran big, full trains very fast, Carnegie ordered workers to push the steel furnaces relentlessly to push out the maximum amount of steel regardless of the rated capacity or the wear and tear on the furnace. By "hard driving," as the practice was known, plants minimized the unit cost of production.

Once Carnegie had captured the cost advantages of scale and speed, he slashed prices. He underbid and undercut other railmakers, thus forcing them over and over again to meet his price. The price of steel rails in nineteenth-century America fell from $158.50 a ton in 1868, to $68.75 in 1875, to $42.25 in 1878 (Temin, 1964:283–84). To earn profits in a market with falling prices, companies had no choice but to emulate Carnegie's business practices. Fierce price competition also became the prevailing way of doing business in product markets in which there was no dominant entrepreneur. In tin plate, wire nails, hoops and pipes, producers fought for volume through vicious price wars.

To some extent, then, the American steel industry's beginning resembled the competitive market ideal. The country's rapid growth created a huge demand for steel product, and the new technology offered entrepreneurs seemingly boundless opportunities to meet this demand. By 1889, there were 749 iron and steel establishments, 304 blast furnace establishments, and 445 steelworks and rolling mills in operation (U.S. Bureau of the Census, 1914:640–41). And, as in the model of pure competition, these firms competed fiercely on price for a place in the growing American steel market.

During the 1870s and 1880s, however, some steelmakers began to question the industry's merciless ways of doing business. While the early industrialists recognized that cutthroat competition was a natural response to the capital intensity and cyclical demand in steelmaking, they also came to believe that a fundamental market stability was necessary to ensure that firms enjoyed financial solvency and growth.

Therefore, like manufacturers in other capital-intensive industries, steelmakers began to experiment with alternative forms of governance to control the conditions of cutthroat competition. At first, the industry tried informal arrangements—"gentlemen's agreements" and pools—that were not sanctioned by American law. These informal arrangements met with only limited success. When they failed, steelmakers turned to horizontal consolidations—mergers of firms engaged in manufacturing the same products—as an alternative. As a wave of horizontal combinations spread through the American economy in the 1890s, over 500 metal producers were consolidated into new combinations, or "trusts."

There were several advantages to horizontal consolidations in steel. First, by combining previously separate entities, one steelmaker could now control a greater proportion of the industry's output. Thus, horizontal consolidation was a tighter form of cooperation, one that did not rely on the voluntary compliance of several autonomous enterprises. Second, through horizontal consolidations, steelmakers expanded their capacity and capabilities. Finally, steelmakers discovered that by rationalizing the new and old entities into one large production center, they could increase the overall efficiency of the enterprise.

At the same time, steelmakers had discovered that the optimal way to assure their plants a steady, continuous flow of materials was for each firm—and ideally each plant—to engage in all three stages of the steelmaking process (Chandler, 1977:258–72). Thus, American steelmakers began to grow through vertical integration—by acquiring or merging with enterprises engaged in earlier or later stages of production. Vertical integration was also a defensive strategy to keep other producers from destroying or dominating a market.

The industry's consolidation culminated in 1901 when the Wall Street financier J.P. Morgan oversaw a merger of twelve newly consolidated steel companies to form the United States Steel Corporation. This giant corporation was the result of both horizontal and vertical integration, since Morgan had merged consolidations of finishing mills—American Hoop and National Tube, for example—and integrated producers—Federal Steel and Carnegie Steel. The formation of U.S. Steel was also in part a defensive move for Morgan who, as a major investor in Federal Steel and National Tube, wanted to prevent an all-out price war between the efficient Carnegie Steel Company and the newly organized and overcapitalized consolidations such as Federal Steel. Capitalized at $1.4 billion, U.S. Steel possessed nearly half the country's steelmaking capacity and two-thirds of its production.

Between 1870 and 1901, the industry's economics and the American legal environment—which prohibited cartels—had converged to shape the structure and competitive practices of the steel industry. As formal price agreements were prohibited by law and informal price agreements had failed to quell the industry's cutthroat competition, companies turned to structural solutions—namely horizontal consolidations—to stabilize prices. They also discovered that growth through horizontal and vertical consolidations enabled them to increase their efficiency by expanding capacity and capabilities, rationalizing facilities, and ensuring a constant flow of materials through the steelworks. By the turn of the century, it was clear that American steel would be dominated by a relatively few large, integrated companies. The fundamental economics of steelmaking, combined with a particular set of historical circumstances, transformed the industry from one with hundreds of separate iron, steel, and rolling establishments to one in which capacity was concentrated in a relatively few companies (Lamoreaux, 1985).

Although the industry's structure would continue to evolve as the smaller firms built market share, the fundamental transformation from an atomistic industry structure to an oligopoly turned out to be permanent. The majority of American steelmaking capacity remained concentrated in a handful of large companies through changes in both product markets and geographic markets, through exponential growth during two world wars, and through several recessions and the longest economic depression in American history.

The oligopolistic structure, however, could not prevent price competition in steel during periods of weak demand. The interdependence of steel firms combined with the price inelasticity of demand implied that a price cut by one steelmaker was likely to injure all producers. That is, though low prices would temporarily divert sales to the price cutter, other firms would quickly match the price and, since overall demand would not increase proportionately, the industry would sell roughly the same quantity of steel, simply at lower prices and profits for all.

One method of industrial governance, that of explicit cooperation among companies in the same industry, was strictly prohibited by America's antitrust law. Ever since the federal government ended the infamous "Gary dinners" in 1911, at which the industry is said to have discussed prices and other areas of competition (*United States v. U.S. Steel Corporation*, 1915:160; Robinson, 1926), the government prevented the industry from using collective measures to protect itself from market uncertainties. Consequently, under the leadership of Elbert

H. Gary, chairman of U.S. Steel's board of directors from 1901 until his death in 1927, the industry established a tacit system for eliminating price competition that prevailed throughout most of the rest of the century. First, U.S. Steel published its prices in the industry's leading trade journal and announced that it would try to adhere to them regardless of fluctuations in demand. Second, the corporation announced that all of its subsidiaries, regardless of their location, would sell at the corporation's published mill price—which excluded freight— plus a freight charge roughly equal to the railroad freight *from Pittsburgh* to the customer's destination. By requiring that all subsidiaries charge the "Pittsburgh Plus price," Gary eliminated price competition among U.S. Steel's subsidiaries. U.S. Steel's published prices, which remained relatively high during downturns and relatively low during booms, were followed by all major American steel producers.[8]

Although U.S. Steel's price umbrella benefitted other steelmakers, not all firms were at first convinced that the Pittsburgh Plus system served their interests. But as companies gained experience as the benefactors of U.S. Steel's "friendly competition" and then—during a brief period during 1909—were subject to the corporation's unfriendly competition, they came to recognize their mutual interdependence and mutual interest in a high price (Cotter, 1921:227; Stevens, 1922:398). Thus, since explicit horizontal agreements were prohibited by law, the industry adopted tacit governance mechanism, such as price leadership and market signaling, to maintain uniform and relatively stable prices.

Of course, absolute price uniformity was impossible without legally enforced sactions against defectors. Small steelmakers occasionally cut prices to attract orders, a practice that was broadly condemned and that frequently prompted industrywide discussions of potential legal remedies to prevent this "unfair competition" and "short-sighted selling." One competitor, writing in *Iron Age* in 1928, expressed his opinion of "unskilled amateurs who break the rules to win":

> The individual who refuses to cooperate with his competitors, and who insists upon ruthless price cutting as a means of obtaining business, is worse than a criminal. He is a fool. He not only pulls down his competitors; he pulls down himself and his whole trade. He scuttles the ship in which he himself is afloat. (*Iron Age*, November 8, 1928:1181)

Thus, by the end of World War II, the governance system is American steel was firmly established. Most steelmakers understood their interdependence and the utter futility of open price cuts or other market-destabilizing behavior. At the same time, the federal government strictly prohibited companies from searching for explicitly joint solutions to limit competition or stabilize the market. The government perceived its own role as one of preserving the market mechanism rather than one of facilitating the industry's adaptation to particular economic or competitive conditions. Therefore, firms in the steel oligopoly managed their interdependence and maintained a high degree of market stability through a system of tacit, implicitly coordinated, risk-minimizing strategies.

Company Strategies and Performance

The postwar capacity-expansion debate was resolved when, in the spring of 1950, the federal government instituted economic policies that induced steelmakers to expand. The government's programs—which were essentially low-cost loans—transformed the economics of steel expansion. In response to the government's incentives, the steel industry embarked on its largest growth program of the twentieth century. Major producers and new entrepreneurs alike flocked to the government with proposals for new steel plants. By the end of January 1951, Washington had granted certificates of necessity for nearly 16 million tons of new capacity. By the end of that first year, there were twelve new blast furnaces under construction and even a new greenfield plant, U.S. Steel's Fairless Works. From 1951 to 1960, the industry increased overall national steel capacity from 100 million tons to 148 million—a 48 percent leap in only ten years.

Unfortunately for the American industry as a whole, this focus on tonnage expansion was misguided. To begin with, after 1955, growth in American steel consumption was relatively flat (FTC, 1977). As American steel capacity increased faster than consumption, capacity utilization in plants steadily declined. Between 1958 and 1982, American steel capacity was underutilized every year except for three. Moreover, since steel consumption in Japan and Canada as well as the EEC (European Economic Community) was growing rapidly, steel companies there were more likely to operate with a full and steady throughput.

Second, as many foreign steel manufacturers had rebuilt their demolished plants, they were well positioned to compete with American producers. Japanese steel, in particular, was produced in large, modern plants with state-of-the-art technology. On the other hand, most American capacity was in old, unrefurbished plants. When, in 1959, a disastrous 116-day strike paralyzed the U.S. Steel industry, cheap imports surged into the domestic market. From 1959 onward, the United States was a net importer of steel.

By the 1960s, the industry was in an exceedingly vulnerable position. Substitute products and a receding market base had slowed the growth of American steel consumption. The discovery of new sources of iron ore in Australia, Canada, and South America combined with a significant decrease in ocean freight rates eroded American steel's raw material advantage. Perhaps most importantly, American steelmakers simply watched as foreign producers responded to their own booming domestic markets. Not surprisingly, foreign steelmakers acted by investing in new technology and taking advantage of ever-increasing economies of scale. Moreover, some producers—like those in Japan—were assisted by industrial governance systems that ensured the industry a full and steady throughput.

American steel industry executives did launch a series of modest modernization programs. Companies tried to retrofit new technology onto the industry's old facilities. In some cases, open-hearth furnaces were replaced with more efficient basic oxygen furnace technology. In response to price competition from imports, companies attempted to rationlize the flow of materials and manufacturing processes. However, these investments were not enough.

By 1970, it was evident to steel executives that their industry had fallen into a deadly trap: a vicious cycle of rising imports, falling volume, escalating costs, and falling profits. Concluding that in this market no individual steel company could cope effectively with the problems besetting the industry, American steel managers turned to political solutions: They began to seek protection against foreign imports.

How all this happened is, naturally, complex. American steel companies faced a market with declining demand, competition from cheap imports, rising capital and labor costs, and extreme overcapacity. Moreover, compared to many other countries, GNP growth was relatively slow and the dollar, serving as the world's reserve currency, may have been overvalued. In light of these factors, it is not surprising that rates of return in steel fell and alternative investments looked more attractive, yet the cost-benefit calculations that led companies to retreat and eventually to diversify into other industries assumed sustained conditions of overcapacity and price-cutting from imports. If by coordinating production and closures, some American steel plants could have assumed "full and steady" throughput and been protected from low-priced imports, the return from investments in new technology may have looked quite different.

The key fact is that under the customary ways of doing business in the United States, each firm faced a highly uncertain market. Consequently, in steel, as in other high-fixed-cost industries, managers became preoccupied with trying to avoid losses by stabilizing price and volume. Since horizontal relationships to limit output or maintain prices were illegal under American antitrust law, the most the industry could do collectively was to maintain prices through implicit price leadership schemes. But individually, each company could try to protect itself from excessive losses by steadfastly avoiding increases in fixed costs.

Thus, in the very brief time between the early 1950s and the middle 1970s, the American steel industry fell from the largest and most technologically advanced in the world to a condition in which it could not even maintain its domestic market share. Steel imports into the United States rose from 1 percent of domestic consumption in 1950 to 14 percent in 1976 and to 22 percent by 1982. In fact, without the protectionist measures the industry had secured from the American government, imports in 1982 would very likely have been larger. By the late 1970s, the American steel crisis had reached such proportions that the industry's net income had fallen to zero and more than 50 percent of the industry's capacity was idle. As 200 steel plants were shut down and more than five steel companies closed or initiated bankruptcy proceedings, 45 percent of America's steelworkers were laid off, causing the worst unemployment since the Great Depression in steel-producing regions of the country. With losses accumulating year after year, America's major steel companies began to diversify—investing their remaining capital in other industries such as oil, chemicals, and fabricated metal products. As the chairman of U.S. Steel, David M. Roderick, commented, the entire process amounted to a "state of accelerating self-liquidation" (Miller, 1984:33).

Under the system of governance that prevailed in American steel, where risk is assumed by each firm privately, the companies' caution is hardly surprising. Over time, American steel companies simply ceased to invest aggressively in new technology or production processes, at least compared with the Japanese practices of the postwar decades. Instead, managers' attention became fixed on minimizing losses, or maximizing short-term profits. In the American system, there was simply no countervailing force that would have motivated a rational manager, in possession of adequately functioning equipment, voluntarily to raise short-run fixed costs by scrapping old plants and investing in new technology. Such a strategy would have seemed suicidal. Yet, as we have seen, this very strategy provided the fundamental basis for the Japanese miracle in steel.

Conclusion and a Look Forward

The economic characteristics of the modern steel industry created market uncertainties that influenced the strategies of steel producers. High capital requirements combined with a cyclical demand made the industry highly vulnerable to cutthroat competition. Because steel demand is also relatively price inelastic, fierce price competition can injure many firms in the industry.

As a result, steelmakers long recognized their interdependence and developed governance systems to manage these industrywide uncertainties. But the governance systems that evolved in different countries depended on a number of factors, including national objectives and the national economic and legal framework. Thus, it is not surprising that governance mechanisms in steel differed from nation to nation.

This chapter argues that the different systems of governance that evolved in Japan and the United States contributed to the ability of each country's steel industry to take advantage of market opportunities in the post–World War II decades. Additionally, the findings suggest that Japan's system was more conducive in facilitating global competition in steel.

The Japanese system of industrial governance in steel aimed to maintain a full and steady throughput in all Japanese steel companies. In the 1950s, capacity was coordinated by the Japanese government through MITI, which derived its power first from controlling low-cost capital and, later, from controlling foreign exchange allocations. By the 1960s, Japanese steel capacity was coordinated entirely by the steel oligopoly itself. Understanding the importance of stability and the dangers of overcapacity, Japanese steel firms negotiated each year's level of capacity expansion.

The system of industrial governance that emerged in Japan radically altered the market conditions in steel. With a protected domestic market, steel firms were assured a monopoly over domestic demand. Second, because capacity expansion was controlled, or governed, the risk of excess capacity was lessened. Domestic supply was equilibrated with projected domestic and export demand, and firms were therefore assured a high and steady throughput that minimized fixed costs. Consequently, the Japanese system of industrial governance lowered the risk of investment.

The governance mechanism that prevailed in the American steel industry at the end of World War II also evolved as a response to the problems of destructive price competition. The American system, however, traced its origins back to the turn of the century when American producers possessed clear advantages in scale and technology. American steelmakers' competitive advantages, together with the American liberal tradition, resulted in the government acting more as a constraint than as a facilitator of the steel industry's method of maintaining stability. That is, the governance mechanisms open to American steelmakers were strictly circumscribed by the ideals and values represented in the nation's competition policies.

This system, in which risk was privatized and firms made autonomous decisions, was adequate during years of growing steel demand and minimal foreign competition in the U.S. market. As global conditions changed, however, uncertainty increased and the old, deeply rooted governance mechanisms proved inadequate in facilitating investment in the American integrated steel sector.

In the long run, of course, the American steel industry's governance mechanisms will change to accommodate the new global conditions, but for at least two decades, the industry's performance was constrained by the governance system in which risk was assumed by each firm privately.

By the early 1980s, the global market had again changed. The Japanese steel industry faced a stagnant domestic market and rising barriers to their export trade. Moreover, the 50 percent revaluation of the yen against the dollar, which began in late 1985, turned Japan into a high-cost steel producer and created competition from new entrants such as Korea and Taiwan, whose exchange rates were linked to the dollar. Finally, integrated steel producers all over the world faced price competiton in the mid-1970s when technological innovations and changes in scrap steel prices gave rise to a new segment of American producers called "minimills."

As Japanese steel output fell, the companies launched radical restructuring programs. Capacity was shut down and steelworkers were laid off or "transferred" to other companies within the enterprise group. Steel firms began to diversify their product lines, often into completely unrelated businesses. Nippon Kokan, Japan's second largest steelmaker, started a food company that raised and produced meat products, bought a 50 percent interest in National Steel Company—America's sixth-largest steel producer—and bought Great Western Silicon, a manufacturer of silicon used in semiconductors, from General Electric. From 1982 to 1988, Japanese steel firms cut total costs per ton by 38 percent. Despite these adjustments, the Japanese steel industry lost the equivalent of $2 billion in 1986.

At the same time, the American steel industry, helped by the devalued dollar and import restraints, began to revive. After savage layoffs and a loss of one-third of the country's capacity, the surviving companies emerged with some hope for their futures. As an example, USX, which was formerly U.S. Steel, had reduced its work force by 75 percent since 1981, while, for the same period, the industry as a whole had reduced its costs of production by 30 percent.

Nevertheless, it would be entirely wrong to conclude that the Japanese and American steel industries had reversed positions. The story is very much unfinished, and it is far too early for mature historical judgment. What we know with certainty is that the American method of adjustment, in which firms made separate, autonomous decisions, cost the steel industry over $11 billion in losses during the 1980s. In Japan, on the other hand, steel companies are working together, as well as with the government and labor, to restructure the industry. These different industrial governance systems, which resulted in privatized risk in America and socialized risk in Japan, will continue to influence the ability of each nation's steel industry to respond to global market forces.

Notes

1. The Steel manufacturing process composed of three steps pertains only to integrated steelmaking. Since the 1970s, integrated producers in America and Japan have lost market share to a new segment of the industry, called "minimills." Responsible for about 20 percent of the American steel market in 1989, minimills manufacture primarily light steel products, traditionally low-end-of-the-market steel products. Minimills rely mainly on scrap steel, which they then melt in electric furnaces and shape and roll into products exactly as integrated producers do. Operating without blast furnaces, with virtually no investment in raw materials and transportation facilities and with a limited range of products, minimills are unencumbered by high capital costs and, consequently, can operate efficiently with as little as 250,000 tons of capacity per year. Although minimills are responsible for an increasing amount of market share, they do not have the technical capability to replace the integrated sector completely. (Barnett and Crandall, 1986; Miller, 1984).

2. In the 1960s, the third stage of the manufacturing process was simplified by the invention of *continuous casting*. In continuous casting, the molten steel could be poured into a trough from which it flowed into water-cooled molds and then directly into semifinished shapes, which eliminated the need for ingot pouring, cooling, reheating, and rolling.

3. Japan's steel output has been converted from metric tons to net tons for comparability with American steel output.

4. The other industries targeted in 1950 were coal, shipbuilding, and chemical fertilizers.

5. "Greenfield" refers to an entirely new plant rather than a renovated or "rounded out" plant.

6. Sumitomo Metal's independence was reflected by the company's distinction of being the only Japanese steel producer that, by the late 1960s, had consistently refused to appoint a retiring government bureaucrat to its board of directors. In 1969, Sumitomo's president gave in and invited the retiring MITI vice-minister to join the board. According to some, the company had learned that it needed "the bureaucratic skills of a MITI insider" (Johnson, 1982:271).

7. The U.S. Supreme Court ruled the seizure unconstitutional and returned the steel mills to their legal owners.

8. There are several explanations for U.S. Steel's price strategy. Gary, himself, is said to have believed that the price umbrella would encourage the rest of the industry to follow and, in that way, the destructive policies of cutthroat competition would be ended (Tarbell, 1925). By not extracting excess profits from the market during shortages, U.S. Steel's policy may have dissuaded new firms from entering the market and destabilizing the industry (Baumol, Panzar, and Willig, 1982). Finally, it is frequently argued that fear of antitrust prosecution contributed to U.S. Steel's decision against maximizing short-run profits (McCraw and Reinhart, 1989).

References

Aoki, Masahiko. (1984). "Aspects of the Japanese Firm." In Masahiko Aoki (ed.), *The Economic Analysis of the Japanese Firm* (pp. 3–43). New York: Elsevier Science Publishing Company.

Badaracco, Joseph, L. (1991). *The Knowledge Link: How Firms Compete Through Strategic Alliances.* Boston: Harvard Business School Press.

Barnett, Donald F. (1977, October 15). "International Competitiveness in Steel and Dynamic Advantages." Working Paper. Washington, D.C.: American Iron and Steel Institute.

Barnett, Donald F., and Robert W. Crandall. (1986). *Up From the Ashes: The Rise of the Steel Minimill in the United States.* Washington, D.C.: Brookings Institution.

Barnett, Donald F., and Louis Schorsch. (1983). *Steel: Upheaval in a Basic Industry.* Cambridge, Mass. Ballinger.

Baumol, William J., John C. Panzar, and Robert D. Willig. (1982). *Contestable Markets and the Theory of Industry Structure.* New York: Harcourt Brace Jovanovich.

Bradford, Charles. (1977). "The Japanese Steel Industry: A Comparison with Its United States Counterpart." New York: Merrill Lynch, Pierce, Fenner & Smith Inc.

Caves, Richard E., and Masu Uekusa. (1976). "Industrial Organization." In Hugh Patrick and Henry Rosovsky (ed.), *Asia's New Giant: How the Japanese Economy Works* (pp. 459–523). Washington D.C.: Brookings Institution.

Chandler, Alfred D. Jr. (1977). *The Visible Hand: The Managerial Revolution in American Business.* Cambridge, Mass.: Harvard University Press.

Chandler, Alfred D. Jr. (1990). *Scale and Scope.* Cambridge, Mass.: Harvard University Press.

Cockerill, A. (1974). *The Steel Industry: International Comparisons of Industrial Structure and Performance.* Cambridge: Cambridge University Press.

Cohen, Jerome B. (1958). *Japan's Postwar Economy.* Bloomington: Indiana University Press.

Cotter, Arundel. (1921). *United States Steel Corporation: A Corporation with a Soul.* New York: Doubleday, Page & Company.

Council on Wage and Price Stability (CWPS). (1977). *Prices and Costs in the American Steel Industry.* Washington, D.C.: Government Printing Office.

Crandall, Robert W. (1981). *The U.S. Steel Industry in Recurrent Crisis.* Washington, D.C.: Brookings Institution.

Dore, Ronald. (1986). *Flexible Rigidities: Industrial Policy and Structural Adjustment in the Japanese Economy 1970–1980.* Stanford, Calif.: Stanford University Press.

Fortune. (1960, December). "Steel: It's a Brand New Industry," pp. 123–27.

Fortune. (1966, October). "Steel Is Rebuilding for a New Era," pp. 130–37.

FTC (Federal Trade Commission). (1977). *Staff Report on the United States Steel Industry and Its International Rivals: Trends and Factors Determining International Competitiveness.* Washington, D.C.: Government Printing Office.

Henderson, Gerard C. (1924). *The Federal Trade Commission: A Study in Administrative Law and Procedure.* New Haven, Conn.: Yale University Press.

Hoopes, Roy. (1963). *The Steel Crisis.* New York: The John Day Co.

IISS (Institute for Iron and Steel Studies). (1977). *Steel Industry in Brief: Japan, 1977.* Green Brook, N.J.: IISS.

IISS (Institute for Iron and Steel Studies) Commentary. (1981). *Steel Plants USA, 1960–1980.* Green Brook, N.J.: IISS.

IISS (Institute for Iron and Steel Studies). (1977–1983). *Steel Industry in Brief: Databook, U.S.A.* Green Brook, N.J.: IISS.

Iron Age. (1949, April 7). "West Coast Export Men See European Competition," p. 120.

Iron Age. (1928, November 8). "Steel Code Is Prime Need," p. 1181.

Japan's Iron and Steel Industry, 1953–1954. (1954). Tokyo: Ministry of International Trade and Industry.

Johnson, Chalmers. (1982). *MITI and the Japanese Miracle: The Growth of Industrial Policy, 1925–1975.* Stanford, Calif. Stanford University Press.

Kawahito, Kiyoshi. (1972). *The Japanese Steel Industry: With an Analysis of the U.S. Steel Import Problem.* New York: Praeger.

Kodo, R. (1967). "A Proposal from the Industry, The Reorganization of Industrial Structure." In Kozo Yamamura (ed.), *Economic Policy in Postwar Japan*, p. 99. Berkeley: University of California Press.

Kolko, Gabriel. (1963). *The Triumph of Conservation: A Reinterpretation of American History, 1900–1916.* Chicago: Quadrangle Books.

Lamoreaux, Naomi R. (1985). *The Great Merger Movement in American Business, 1895–1904.* New York: Cambridge University Press.

Livesay, Harold C. (1975). *Andrew Carnegie and the Rise of Big Business.* Boston: Little, Brown.

Lynn, Leonard H. (1982). *How Japan Innovates: A Comparison with the U.S. in the Case of Oxygen Steelmaking.* Boulder, Colo.: Westview Press.

Marcus, Maeva. (1977). *Truman and the Steel Seizure Case.* New York: Columbia University Press.

McCraw, Thomas K. and Forest Reinhart. (1989). "Losing to Win: U.S. Steel's Pricing, Investment Decisions and Market Share, 1901–1938" *The Journal of Economic History*, 49, 593–619.

McCraw, Thomas K., and Patricia A. O'Brien. (1986). "Production and Distribution: Competition Policy and Industry Structure." In Thomas K. McCraw (ed.), *America versus Japan* (pp. 77–116). Boston: Harvard Business School Press.

McDiarmid, Orville J. (1966, June). "Japan and Israel." In *Finance and Development* (pp. 136–43). Washington, D.C.: The International Monetary Fund.

Miller, Jack Robert. (1984, May). "Steel Minimills." *Scientific American*, pp. 32–39.

Miyazaki, Yoshikazu. (1976, December). "Big Corporations and Business Groups in Postwar Japan." *Developing Economics*, 14.

Mueller, Hans, and Kiyoshi Kawahito. (1978). "Steel Industry Economics: A Comparative Analysis of Structure, Conduct and Performance." New York: Japan Steel Information Center.

Okumura, Hiroshi. (1982, Summer). "Interfirm Relations in an Enterprise Group: The Case of Mitsubishi." *Japanese Economic Studies*. 10.

Robinson, Maurice H. (1926, September). "The Gary Dinner System: An Experiment in Co-operative Price Stabilization." *Southwest Political and Social Science Quarterly*, 7, 137–61.

Sengo Sangyushi eno Shogen. Kyodaika no Jidai. (1977). In *Mainichi Shinbunsha* (pp. 57–76). Tokyo. (Published interview with Mr. Hosai Hyuga, president of Sumitomo Metals.)

Shinohara, Miyohei. (1982). *Industrial Growth, Trade, and Dynamic Patterns in the Japanese Economy.* Tokyo: University of Tokyo Press.

Stevens, William S. (1922). *Industrial Combinations and Trusts.* New York: Macmillan.

Stocking, George W. (1954). *Basing Point Pricing and Regional Development.* Chapel Hill: University of North Carolina Press.

Stocking, George W., and Myron W. Watkins. (1947). *Cartels in Action: Case Studies in International Business Diplomacy.* New York: The Twentieth Century Fund.

Sumitomo *Annual Report.* (1966).

Tarbell, Ida M. (1925). *The Life of Elbert H. Gary: The Story of Steel.* New York: D. Appleton and Company.

Temin, Peter. (1964). *Iron and Steel in Nineteenth Century America.* Cambridge, Mass.: MIT Press.

Thorelli, Hans B. (1955). *The Federal Antitrust Policy: Origination of an American Tradition.* Baltimore: The Johns Hopkins University Press.

Tiffany, Paul A. (1988). *The Decline of American Steel: How Management, Labor and Government Went Wrong.* New York: Oxford University Press.

TNEC (Temporary National Economic Committee). (1940, January). *The Iron and Steel Industry: United States Steel Corporation Studies, Prices, and Costs, Investigation of Concentration of Economic Power.* Part 26 (pp. 13914–979). Washington D.C.: Government Printing Office.

Tower, Walter S. (1947). "Address of the President." In *The American Iron and Steel Industry Yearbook* (pp. 628–38). New York: AISI.

U.S. Bureau of the Census, Department of Commerce. (1914). *Abstract of the Census of Manufactures.*

United States v. United States Steel Corporation et al. (1915). District Court, New Jersey, 223 *Federal Reporter.*

Urofsky, Melvin I. (1969). *Big Steel and the Wilson Administration: A Study in Business-Government Relations.* Columbus: Ohio State University Press.

Wall, Joseph Frazier. (1970). *Andrew Carnegie.* New York: Oxford University Press.

Webb, Steven B. (1980). "Tariffs, Cartels, Technology, and Growth in the German Steel Industry, 1879–1914." *The Journal of Economic History*, 40 (2), 309–29.

Westin, Alan F. (1958). *The Anatomy of a Constitutional Law Case.* New York: Macmillan.

Yamamura, Kozo. (1967). *Economic Policy in Postwar Japan.* Berkeley: University of California Press.

Yamamura, Kozo. (1982). "Success That Soured: Administrative Guidance and Cartels in Japan." In Kozo Yamamura (ed.), *Policy and Trade Issues of the Japanese Economy.* (pp. 77–112). Seattle: University of Washington Press.

Yonekura, Seiichiro. (1984). "Entrepreneurship and Innovative Behavior of Kawasaki Steel: The Post–World War II Period." Tokyo: Institute of Business Research, Hitotsubashi University. Discussion Paper No. 120.

Zimmerman, Erich W. (1951). *World Resources and Industries.* New York: Harper and Brothers.

Modes of Governance in the Shipbuilding Sector in Germany, Sweden, and Japan

Bo Stråth

The Market and the Sectoral Mode of Governance

The driving force behind the growth of the shipbuilding industry after World War II was the development of seaborne trade. Ever-increasing amounts of petroleum transported over longer and longer distances were an especially important commodity. The impressive growth in trade was also, of course, a logical consequence of the general economic boom after the war. The twenty-five to thirty years after 1945 were, despite minor recessions, a long period of expansion.

Shipbuilding output increased tenfold between 1950 and 1975. The need for new types of ships, rapid economic development, and political factors such as the temporary closure of the Suez Canal created a breeding ground for technical innovations in shipbuilding. Tankers and bulk carriers were built in ever-increasing sizes, and the technology of construction meant large-scale operations not only for the transport industry but also for the shipbuilding industry itself.

This technological development and the subsequent rapidly increasing capacity for building super tonnage also spread to newly industrialized countries like South Korea, Taiwan, and Singapore. Thus, there was no technological gap, which meant a potentially very vulnerable position for the old shipbuilding nations, including Japan, if the market declined. This is an *ex post facto* observation, hardly possible to realize at the time.

The 1960s brought the first signs of structural problems in the economy of growth. By the end of the decade it was obvious that the Bretton Woods agreement was a very weak basis for the international economy. Moreover, the 1960s and early 1970s brought the opening of new oil fields closer to the industrial centers of Europe and Japan, and therefore decreased the need for sea transportation. The reopening of the Suez Canal in 1974 had the same effect.

Hence the beginnings of a downswing in the demand for shipping were already clear when, in 1973, the October War between Israel and Egypt and the Arab reaction to it produced a dramatic drop in the international oil trade and, consequently, in international trade in general. Orders from shipowners decreased dramatically in the industry, which, during the bonanza years, had built up a capacity far exceededing demand under normal conditions. World production of ships decreased from 35.9 million gross tons in the peak years of 1975 to 17.7 million gross tons in 1984. German production fell by 80 percent, Swedish by 92 percent, and Japanese output by 48 percent during this collapse.

Government subsidies in shipbuilding were the subject of heated debate from as early as 1960. Structural problems in a rapidly changing industry had led to government intervention even in the 1950s, but a more consistent cash flow from governments began in the 1960s as a West European response to the Japanese challenge.

During the interwar period in Western Europe, the shipowner usually paid a part of the price during the construction period and the rest on delivery of the vessel. In the 1950s and 1960s the granting of credit by shipbuilders became a weapon of competition. The usual credit terms in Europe were 50 percent of the order sum over five years, but the Japanese shipbuilders escalated credits to improve their competitiveness, and by 1961 credits covering 70 percent of the order sum over a period of seven years had become quite general, often with an additional period of no installments during the first two years after delivery.

As shipbuilders became more and more concerned with being able to offer better terms of credit than their competitors, governments became increasingly involved in the problem of securing funds. Credits were generally supplied by government-backed financial institutions, and the outcome was a period of prosperity for shipbuilders and shipowners alike, coupled with a sharp increase in the size of the world fleet and shipbuilding capacity beyond the level of shipping requirements. Credit competition intensified, and in the period of expansion after 1964 and, above all, from 1970 to 1975, credit schemes were institutionalized. After the collapse of the shipbuilding market, credit schemes, which had been devised by governments to cope with a situation of high demand, came to be seen by these same governments as a solution to the problem of low demand (Stråth, 1987a: 15–20).

Although it is difficult to make a precise estimate, it was commonly held in the shipbuilding industry at the beginning of the 1980s that 40 percent of the price of a new ship in Western Europe was paid by government subsidies in one form or another. Shipbuilding brought governments into a situation where they were making interventions at the microlevel, where not only the prospects of individual enterprises but even individual orders were items on governments' agendas. The question of economic governability is clearly a very relevant one for the shipbuilding sector.

It is not completely clear why shipbuilding, when the market collapsed in the 1970s, was given such massive support in comparison with other industries; in most countries shipbuilding's contribution to the GNP and to industrial employment has never been more than a few percent. One crucial factor has been that shipbuilding has derived its national importance from its role in particular regions. The shipbuilding industry totally dominated many regions of Western Europe and Japan, and this in turn gave employers and employees, in cooperation with local and regional authorities and politicians, considerable strength as a pressure group. Moreover, unlike in another hard-hit industry—textiles—the vast majority of shipbuilding employees are men. This, too, may serve to explain the strength of the shipbuilding lobby. A more decisive factor has probably been that, for national security and commercial reasons, a large shipbuilding business was good on both political and economic grounds.

The oil shock in the mid-1970s occasioned and legitimized political action of a more immediate and spectacularly interventionist nature than earlier. Actions were governed by hopes for a cyclical change for the better in a few years. After 1982, the structural perspective gradually reasserted itself. Governments in Western Europe in the wake of the social rivalry between groups in stagnating economies began to cope with the inevitable retreat as flexibly as possible (Stråth, 1987a:20).

Two elements are particularly conspicuous in this rough draft of a development framework: the severe market fluctuations and the role of the public authorities in sectoral governance. Government credits for the shipbuilding industry amounted to a political question both during the bonanza years before 1975 and during the subsequent market collapse. One of the main purposes of this chapter is to discern the scope of strategic choices available to the shipbuilding companies during different phases of this market development, and how this scope has influenced and been influenced by social bargaining, provoked by the (internationally and technologically derived) market development and by national norms and traditions and institutional factors, to form a governance regime for the shipbuilding sector. What is similar in the three countries (Germany, Sweden, and Japan) in the mode of governance in the shipbuilding sector? What differences attributable to national norms, traditions, and institutions exist?

Clearly, shipbuilding has been a highly politicized sector that early on become a subject of subsidizing, particularly for reasons of credit. It then suffered from overcapacity, to which credit competition from government subsidies contributed a great deal. In all three countries, pressures from "below" for artificial conservation of employment in shipbuilding emerged when the shipbuilding market collapsed. The pressures were finally defeated in the mid-1980s owing to the high price of keeping the industry alive.

Thus far this story is nothing but a typical government versus market one. The next step of the analysis is to describe the government structures and institutional differences (firms, trade associations, unions, industrial relations). The main question addressed is whether differences in these respects are reflected in (1) the time when it was realized that the crisis in shipbuilding was structural and not cyclical and (2) the speed and efficiency of the divestment of the sector. Efficiency is analyzed in terms of the extent of the resource loss and waste.

The question structuring the analysis is the institutional infrastructure available to the three countries to manage the divestment process in their shipbuilding sectors, especially with respect to the outflow of labor. A sectoral governance mode, it is argued, is more efficient if it accomplishes a transfer of labor without long delays and high costs in terms of jobs that are more productive.

It goes without saying that the governance of a specific sector like shipbuilding is not merely a sectoral question. The institutions for sectoral governance are closely related to national patterns of political culture in general and even to more general power relationships among politicians, government administration, organized capital, and organized labor in the structure of society. Occasionally such links to the broader framework are touched upon.

More specifically, this chapter focuses on the following key questions:

What similarities were there with regard to sectoral performance in shipbuilding in West Germany, Sweden, and Japan?

What national differences reflecting a different organization of production and of society were there?

What were the key institutional arrangements involved in coordinating relationships among major actors involved in the shipbuilding industry?

What were the capacities of these institutional arrangements to adjust to problems of crises in their environment?

What were the linkages between these institutional arrangements and sectoral performance?

Germany

Between 1972 and 1977 the five biggest shipyards in what was then West Germany had a 70 percent share of the turnover in German shipbuilding. They were regionally concentrated in a few areas (Bremen, Hamburg, Emden, Kiel). All the big shipyards belonged to steel groups: AG Weser (owned by the Krupp Group) and Bremer Vulkan (the German-Dutch Thyssen-Bornemisza Group) in Bremen; Nordseewerk (the German Thyssen Group) in Emden; Blohm & Voss (the German Thyssen Group) in Hamburg; and Howaldtwerke Deutsche Werft (HDW) (state-owned via the Salzgitter Group) with yards in Kiel and Hamburg. This was mainly the result of a deliberate strategy within the German steel industry in the 1920s that aimed at vertical integration. One consequence of belonging to a vertically integrated organization was that it made possible a relatively rapid shift to production areas other than new construction of ships. By 1979 only 52.4 percent of the turnover of the five largest shipyards came from new construction (Wulf, 1980; Flieshardt and Sablotny, 1980; Kappel and Rother, 1982).

The combination of being a part of large conglomerates and of the federal political structure of West Germany (the name used throughout this chapter) together has often made the shipyards pawns in a game among the industrial giants, the federal government (*Bundesregierung*), and the *Länderregierungen* in the four coastal states (*Länder*) of Schleswig-Holstein, Hamburg, Bremen, and Lower Saxony. This first became clear in the early 1960s with the introduction of the first structural rationalization and federal government aid program. More than 10,000 employees were made redundant (lost their jobs), but in a generally expanding economy it was relatively easy for them to find new employment. All the big shipyards were members of the Federation of German Shipbuilders (VDS), which formed a business association that was to become influential during the contraction of the industry provoked by the market collapse in 1975. Before that time the association had less influence, and the mode of governance is best described in terms of "hierarchies" of vertically integrated firms, although these were not only private but also publicly owned firms, because of the state ownership of a substantial part of the industry.

The high financing costs constituted a problem for the privately owned industry, which did not *immediately* provoke government intervention with cheap credit. This kind of government intervention was introduced gradually and was particularly initiated for reasons of competitiveness on the world market when the use of the credit weapon escalated rapidly in the 1960s. The government's credit involvement, for competitive reasons, produced a converging interest among the sectoral actors in increased productivity through rationalization of the production process and large-scale operation. Gradually an institutional framework was developed, the more or less intrinsic logic of which implied a mode of governance where the government, with vested ownership interests in the sector, promoted capital investment and concentration, while the private firms were more hesitant because of the uncertainty of the market prospects and the yield on investments. Labor unions supported the government's approach even at the price of layoffs, in a situation where redundant labor could be transferred to other sectors in what was then the economy of growth.

The shipbuilding collapse of 1975 brought about union pressures. The unions were involved in tripartite bargaining where the *Länder* governments of the coastal region, VDS, and the metalworkers' union, IG Metall, formed a coalition on shipbuilding policy in Germany. This coalition was in close contact with the sponsoring government departments. In this interaction between private and public interests, the unions and the industry pressured the *Länder* governments, and all three participants in the sectoral coalition put pressure on the German federal government.

Although all three parties in the coastal coalition after 1975 were in agreement as to principles, the unions laid most stress on employment. This did not mean maintaining worker capacity at any price. Necessary reductions were accepted, but it was argued that such reductions must be made in a socially responsible way, under government and union supervision, and linked to plans for investment in new production areas. Subsidies should not be given "blindly" but be made conditional on restructuring. Reorganization, in turn, was to be governed by private interests and market economic principles, and there should be a development plan that took employment into consideration. The inevitable disappearance of jobs in shipbuilding should be offset by diversification in production (Der Gewerkschaftler, No. 9, 1976).[1]

At the beginning of the crisis in 1977, union officials in IG Metall went as far as to argue that, in the framework of such a national plan, the shipyards with the best chances of survival should be publicly named and differentiated from those where capacity reduction would have to be introduced (Der Gewerkschaftler, No. 1, 1977).[2] This was a far more radical proposal than the "slice-of-pie principle" by which equal number of workers would be laid off from every shipyard and, which, when the crisis deepened, became the only possible way to balance competing local interests. The proposal was rapidly withdrawn from the union scheme for handling the crisis. No doubt the proposal was also too radical for the Federation of German Shipbuilders (VDS): Although its professed commitment to a market solution pointed in that direction, in practice the VDS would have had difficulties in listing the condemned member enterprises.[3] Therefore, both the union and the shipbuilding industry not only agreed in theory on a market solution, but also found each other, in practice, ready to diverge from that principle.[4]

The more immediate importance of social and political factors in the sectoral mode of governance after the market collapse was visible in the increasing influence of the unions. This influence, in turn, was provoked for reasons of political legitimacy.

At the seventh national shipbuilding conference of IG Metall in the spring of 1978, the need for restructuring and reducing capacity receded into the background. Instead, it was argued that capacity should not be adapted in the short term to reduced demand, which was seen as a cyclical phenomenon. The proper strategy would be to increase the demand for ships by government measures within the framework of the EEC. The federal government was asked to prepare an "intermediate plan" guaranteeing full employment at the shipyards and in the regions in which they were situated. The more radical ideas of restructuring were put aside (IG Metall, 1978).

This new emphasis must be related to the deteriorating situation in shipbuilding. More immediate measures were demanded than a long-term restructuring plan. The new emphasis meant, of course, demands for more temporary government subsidies in the hope of weathering the crisis. This was not incompatible with the views of the VDS, which, nevertheless, had a clearer understanding than did IG Metall of the structural features of the shipbuilding crisis. The unions and employers were therefore united in demanding government funds, although for the former the money was intended to see them through the crisis, and for the latter to adjust the structure of the industry to a new situation (VDS, 1978).

Thus the ever-deepening conflict in shipbuilding did not result in the traditional conflict between management and labor but in a common campaign for more money. The object of the campaign was the German federal government, and this common object unified IG Metall and VDS, supported by the *Länder* governments in the sectoral tripartite coalition.

The first real strains in this tripartite coalition became apparent in the spring of 1981. Wide differences opened between IG Metall and VDS on the one hand and the *Länder* governments on the other. The latter were not prepared to continue the subsidies on the same scale as previously, an attitude that had immediate consequences. The *Länder* governments and the other interested parties in the coastal region had to agree in order to get federal funds. The disagreement in 1981, triggered by the *Länder* governments' refusal to contribute as much as before, meant that the federal government refused to allow a subsidy of 180 million marks (90 million US dollars) for 1982.

The continuing crisis and the pronounced reluctance of the new federal Conservative–Liberal government (which succeeded the Social Democratic–Liberal administration in October 1982) to proceed with subsidies to industries with poor future prospects brought new tensions into the coalition.

The federal government demanded a plan for the creation of a competitive industry in return for considering any more subsidies. This demand was not new: It had been made by the Social Democratic–Liberal government in 1979. What was new was that the demand was now made more vigorously. In order to consider new subsidies at all, the Conservative–Liberal government demanded a common forward-looking concentration scheme for the entire shipbuilding industry. The four coastal *Länder* governments were put under pressure in the spring of 1983, when they met with the shipbuilding industry and the unions to try to agree on such a scheme.

The meeting was held in April in Hamburg. VDS proposed a plan according to which 9,000 workers would have to be made redundant (laid off). The closure of entire shipyards would be considered. The per capita cost of the "social plans" (i.e., bi- or tripartite agreements on early retirement, voluntary redundancy instead of compulsory, retraining, and so on, for a "soft landing" for workers) had to be reduced. Shop-floor pressure and internal tensions between local unions made it impossible for IG Metall to agree to this. Thus, the coalition broke down (IG Metall, 1983).

The more limited supply of government money may be seen as a decline in the political propensity to spend funds on shipbuilding, which rested on the growing awareness that the crisis was structural and lasting and could not be countered by cyclical measures. This realization was further prompted by gigantic government deficits. This growing awareness set new limits for what political legitimacy required, with consequences for the sectoral mode of governance.

IG Metall's problems increased with the deepening of the crisis and as the industry became more and more dependent on state intervention. The union had only two weapons: the mobilization of its members and its influence on public opinion, which became increasingly problematic as a structural perspective gradually replaced the cyclical one.

By 1982/1983 it was obvious that any hope of a cyclic recovery in the shipbuilding industry had more or less vanished. Moreover, a point was reached from which management's economic perspective of further gradual reductions yard by yard became impossible. The political will or capacity to spend public money decreased. This was above all true of the federal government, for the sensitivity of local opinion and to the local effects of continued contraction was greater in the *Länder* governments. There, as in Bremen, continued financial support became a matter more of economic resources than of political will.

Officially, IG Metall always agreed to necessary reductions in shipbuilding, but the union argued that for every job lost a new job in another production field had to be created. However, in reality union officials had to accept a local "social plan" for gradual reduction of workers, which took no consideration of overall regional or national strategies for developing alternative production. Diversification is a rational claim of a union that is strong at the local company level through co-determination legislation but weak at the national level of the organization of society. Individual enterprises managed to diversify production to a certain extent. This was especially true of Blohm & Voss where military production (Leopard tanks) became increasingly important. But beyond the enterprise level, overall strategies involving other sectors all failed. Diversification was a matter of entrepreneurship in a Schumpeterian sense much more than a corporatist strategy from above (Stråth, 1987a:42–44).

The insight that capacity in shipbuilding had to be reduced and the hope that the crisis could be bridged by government support was the basis of the sectoral tripartite coalition. A prerequisite was that the reduction could be carried through by "social plans," which marginalized possible grassroots protest. When the federal government demanded much more severe cuts, and when for economic reasons management found the gradual contraction yard by yard more difficult, the maneuvring room of the members of the tripartite coalition decreased. To win federal support at all, the four *Länder* governments and VDS agreed on a scheme that IG Metall, exposed to local protests, could not accept.

By then IG Metall had already fulfilled a role of giving legitimacy to the shrinking process. The tripartite coalition should not be mistaken for a body where all interests were consensual. It was, rather, a group characterized by bargaining and traditional lobbying by pressure groups with conflicting interests, but which nevertheless developed a sphere where their interests in the future of shipbuilding converged and prevailed over other conflicting interests. Internal tensions were always visible, although much more so by the end of the period. Much more than being a matter of social engineering, the process became one of muddling through in social bargaining where the direction of the pressure was from the organized interests toward the political power at different levels. The organized interests influenced events more by virtue of the backing of local opinion, and by virtue of pressure on the political order, than by their consensual integration into that order.

Politicians, rather than the bureaucracy, reacted in a flexible way to the pressures by using the bureaucracy as instruments for the implementation of political responses. High political elasticity made it constantly possible to maintain legitimacy and overall stability. This high elasticity was not achieved in a static equilibrium system but in a dialectic process of responses to workers' pressure for their jobs and to the international market prospects and government problems with budget deficits.

Such a perspective of social bargaining in a power context provides important insights into the role of the welfare state. It is a perspective that focuses on the link between action and structure. The structure of the state is not impersonal. It is malleable as a result of political actions made by representatives of different social interests in a process of social bargaining. However, political leaders do not only represent group interests; they have a wider constituency. This process of social bargaining could be described as a political market. It is here that votes conveying political power are bought from the public for welfare and other social measures. The notion of political market is expressly *not* a functionalist concept presuming an analogy between political parties and politicians on one side and entrepreneurs in a profit-seeking economy on the other. Political parties do not generally formulate which policies they believe will gain the most votes, as do entrepreneurs who produce whatever products they believe will gain the most profits. Maximization of votes can never be an unconditional goal. For reasons of credibility among other things, a political party has to consider the interests of its core supporters, its traditions, ideology, and the need for a degree of continuity in political performance. The concept is expressly *not* used in the sense of a rational calculation of how to maximize votes, but in the sense of responsiveness to pressures and to changing public opinion in a process of social bargaining. Thus the political market is a place for political strife and social bargaining as much as it is a place where policy concessions are traded for votes (Stråth, 1987a:236).

In the 1970s there was massive support for subsidizing shipbuilding to maintain operations and save jobs. However, by the early 1980s the subsidies, in the wake of the budget deficits and the apparently never-recovering shipbuilding market, were rapidly called into question by a changing public opinion. Thus, the political trade-off costs in the early 1980s had become too expensive and therefore the subsidies had to be abandoned.

A special feature of West Germany has been its federal structure, which means that shipbuilding has been a matter of relatively small concern in Bonn but of much more importance in the coastal *Länder*. Hence, the intensity of the conflict has been more acute depending on the political level, between tiers of government (*Bund* versus *Länder*), than among political parties (Stråth, 1987a:51). Apart from this question of relative influence at different political levels, the decisive governance question during the decade of restructuring and contraction has been: Who has had the money to buy political and social stability and how much money has been considered necessary? In the early 1980s the question was transformed into "how much money was available?"

Sweden

Historically, the Swedish shipbuilding industry has been concentrated in Göteborg on the west coast, and in Malmö-Landskrona in the southwest. In Göteborg during the mid-nineteenth century, the three shipyards of Götaverken, Lindholmen, and Eriksberg were established as engineering workshops in the Göta Älv estuary. During the early 1900s they expanded to become more streamlined shipyards. Kockums in Malmö developed along similar lines. Öresundsvarvet in Landskrona some 40 kilometers north of Malmö and Uddevallavarvet in Uddevalla some 70 kilometers north of Göteborg were younger and more streamlined shipyards from the starts.

Before the period of government intervention in the 1960s all the shipyards were centers of strong local cultures. They did not, as in Germany, belong to a vertically integrated industrial conglomerate. Each shipbuilder had its own market segment within which business was influenced by personal contact between management and ship owners. In particular, the alliances established in the 1930s between the Swedish shipbuilders and Norwegian ship owners concentrating on oil freights resulted in "stable contracting arrangements" in the words of Schmitter. The symbiosis of Swedish shipyards and Norwegian ship owners, and the strength of local corporate cultures, prosperous by profitable niche production, provided mighty barriers preventing sectoral concentration and vertical integration. The strong local cultures were also resistant to mergers with the steel industry. The nationalization of the debt-ridden industry during the late 1970s was the culmination of a lengthy process of concentration starting in the 1960s, which had as one consequence the steady decline of the once-strong local cultures.

During the 1960s, with a market share of approximately 10 percent, the Swedish shipbuilding industry was the second largest in the world. This position had been reached thanks to investment in gantry cranes, welding equipment, computerized systems, and large docks. With regard to total employment, shipbuilding was never big: At most there were 30,000 shipyard workers (at the end of the 1950s). For the regional labor markets in Göteborg and in the Malmö-Landskrona region, its importance was, however, great.

Problems caused by the credit competition brought the Swedish government more immediately into sectoral governance. By the end of the 1960s the shipbuilding industry requested a government inquiry to investigate the problems of credit. The shipbuilding employers were organized into a federation that, owing to the strength of the owners of the member enterprises, was relatively weak, lacked organizational tightness, and could by no means be compared with the German VDS. The conflicting interests of the local cultures were too strong to allow for the development of real organizational strength. In dealings with the government it was the managing directors of the individual shipyards rather than the federation who spoke for the industry.

The government was also concerned, by the end of the 1960s, about the threat of overcapacity, and the inquiry committee on credits was given the additional task of presenting a scheme to coordinate shipbuilding. The industry was completely opposed to any such plan, and the outcome was an improvement in export credit guarantees (which had been in use since 1963) and a very loose agreement for cooperation among the major shipyards. Any attempt by the Swedish government to impose a tighter coordination of the sector was refuted by means of threats of redundancies. The industry wanted independence, along with the support of government credit subsidies, and the government could not do much to change this strategy.[5]

In the autumn of 1974 the first signs of a financial crisis at the Eriksberg shipyard hinted at the total collapse of the entire shipbuilding industry. From then on the question of employment and the union demands for co-determination in these matters assumed great importance.

In 1975 a formalized tripartite organization was established. The new organization could be seen as a part of the general transformation of industrial relations in Sweden at that time, but also as an indication of increased insight into the desirability of greater union participation in decision making in an industry facing difficulties. The crisis brought government influence to bear on the industry, and the government wanted a tripartite forum for the contraction talks (Government Bill No. 121, 1975/1976).[6]

The government's interest in getting the unions to agree to a reduction scheme was clear. In 1975/1976, there was unanimous agreement in the tripartite shipbuilding council not only to close Eriksberg but also to a 30 percent reduction in employment in shipbuilding. Some 8,000 people, including a few thousand subcontractors, were to leave the industry. But the redundancies were to be carried out within the framework of a "social plan."

By the mid-1970s a transition of the sectoral mode of governance had occurred. The closure of the Eriksberg yard was a catalyst in this development. In 1975 a government commission under the direction of Kockums' managing director, Nils-Hugo Hallenborg, began work on a rescue plan. Hallenborg was the leader of a competing yard but one that had a more progressive personnel policy than Eriksberg and therefore Hallenborg could command the confidence of the unions and the Social Democratic government that ruled Sweden.

For Hallenborg it was an Eriksberg crisis, not a general crisis in shipbuilding. His criticisms of the Eriksberg management and of the Boström shipping company, which owned the shipyard, were severe and formed part of the report of the commission. The yard had no competitive capability because the owners had failed to invest in new and modern equipment. The Boström family, who owned the yard, became a symbol of that form of decadent private capitalism that is totally governed by ideas of high profits, gained at any price, being spent on luxurious consumption rather than reinvested.

The other picture that was presented was that of the progressive Kockums boss Nils-Hugo Hallenborg, who was in charge of the most successful Swedish shipyard and who was a union man with few serious objections to Social Democratic government policies. Hallenborg, backed by the progressive management of the other big yard, Götaverken, succeeded completely in making the Eriksberg crisis look like one of bad management. This black and white picture of Eriksberg as a symbol of decadent private capitalism and of mismanagement, in sharp contrast to the well-run Kockums and Götaverken yards with a modern personnel policy, was arguably what the competitors and the government needed to effect the closure of Eriksberg and reduce capacity. A year later both Kockums and Götaverken were also close to bankruptcy.

Once Eriksberg was closed, the remainder of the shipbuilding industry formed a group with close relations to sponsoring government departments. However, this was only a step on the way to nationalization of the entire bankrupt industry, which occurred in 1977/1978.

Between 1975 and the early 1980s the sectoral mode of governance in Sweden was very similar to the tripartite coalition in Germany in the sense that the government, industry, and the trade unions formed a bargaining body. The decisive difference between the two countries was that the shipbuilding industry in Sweden was nationalized, the government in Germany was split between federal and regional levels, and local decision-makers from the shipyards were more directly involved at the central-level talks in Sweden. The focus of tripartite bargaining in Germany was more on the regional/sectoral level, whereas in Sweden it was at the national level where the shipbuilding talks were considered in a suprasectoral institutional framework.

When the Center-Right government, about 1980, discussed the closure of Öresundsvarvet in Landskrona, there were considerable strains between the metalworkers' union, Metall, and the government, and the union temporarily froze its participation in the tripartite talks. The closure of Öresundsvarvet meant that the "slice-of-the-pie principle" was abandoned. This principle of even distribution of the capacity reduction among the shipyards had been the cornerstone of the tripartite bargaining ever since the closure of the Eriksberg facility.

Since 1976 the shipyards had received 20 billion kronor (3 billion dollars) in direct support from the taxpayers with additional guarantees of some 22 billion kronor by the end of 1982. This amounted to considerably higher state support for shipbuilding than had been given to other ailing industries. For instance, the subsidy per employee in shipbuilding totaled about 320,000 kronor, whereas the figure for textile employees was 21,000 kronor (Hamilton, 1981). Increasing doubts also emerged among large and rapidly growing groups of Social Democrats about a continued policy of subsidies. This development can be understood in terms of the operation of the political market as defined in the discussion of the German case.

In 1983, under its new chairman, Leif Blomberg, the leadership of Metall began a new strategy that was built on the premise that subsidies had gone as far as they could and that the potential for employment in the shipbuilding industry had decreased. It was also a strategy based on the awareness that solidarity between shipbuilding workers and those in other industries was breaking down. According to Blomberg, not recognizing these realities would limit the union's influence on the outcome. Instead of a defensive rearguard action aimed at the hopeless task of saving all jobs, it was vital to develop an active policy, the emphasis of which was not opposition to the cutbacks themselves but the pace and the methods used in making the reductions and the possibility of transferring workers to other sectors.[7] The union's goal was to develop a competitive industry; research and technology developments, the diffusion of new technologies to small and medium-sized enterprises, and greater flexibility to adjust capacity to new market conditions would be the instruments to achieve this aim. Implicit in such a strategy, although this was definitely not said out loud, was the long-term abandonment of traditional shipbuilding.[8]

This new strategy coming from the union meant that it would be politically possible to continue the contraction of operations in shipbuilding. A reduction in the readiness of unions to support nonprofitable industries decreased the potential for protest and prepared the terrain for more radical change.

At the end of 1984 it was obvious that profitability would not return to Swedish shipbuilding. When the government consequently decided to halt the production of merchant ships in the two remaining large yards there were protests only from those shipyard workers immediately affected. The government had no problem in getting legislation through parliament, and it had at least the passive support of the union.

The Swedish government negotiated an agreement with two auto factories owned by Volvo and Saab to have the automakers take over the shipbuilding plants and transform them for vehicle production so as to keep expected laid-off shipyard workers employed. This meant that the diversification strategy "from above," which failed in Germany, was successful in Sweden, at least in the short-term perspective. After a few years, Saab decided to close its factory in Malmö and in 1992 Volvo decided to close the Uddevalla factory.

The strategy adopted by Metall in 1983 was not a completely new orientation, but it was based on old union traditions. This union culture emerged after decades of struggle with the employers over the content of the concept of rationalization, and a compromise formula was finally agreed on. An institutional framework to implement that formula was developed. In the 1950s the active labor market policy and the wage policy with solidarity emerged, according to which an important union goal was the structural development of Swedish industry. The unions even pushed for layoffs and contraction in less competitive industries, such as textiles, and encouraged the interregional transfer of labor. Union wage policy was a powerful instrument for structural change and for the transfer of workers from low- to high-productivity industries (Stråth, 1987b).

This traditional Swedish model of compromise based on the production and identification of mutually coincidental (rather than common) interests, which were stronger than the conflictual interests—which also existed—was, of course, a model for structural change based on a growing economy. However, many of these ideas survived in the new economic situation. The model continued to work in the context of slow growth and stagnation of the mid-1970s, although less well and not without tensions in regions dominated by one or two industries, as was the case with shipbuilding. The unions never wanted to defend obsolete structures at any cost: Their policies have been concerned with how best to achieve reductions rather than how to avoid them.

An important prerequisite of the Swedish model for restructuring was the active labor market policy under governmental auspices. This meant that unemployment in Sweden after World War II and before 1992 never exceeded 3.5 percent, which is far below the West European average figures from about 1975. The active labor market policy together with the introduction of the sector-specific massive but temporary subsidy policy to mitigate the consequences of the collapse of shipbuilding seems to explain the more far-reaching and less contested contraction process in Sweden.

Two general union roles stand out. One is the problem-solving role where the unions have faced problems jointly with management and have often cooperated in finding solutions. The other is that of defining and articulating union members' interests, which are often in conflict with the interests of employers. During the reduction process in shipbuilding in Sweden, union politics balanced these two roles, but during severe phases of contraction, there was an emphasis on the first role. Correspondingly, there has been far less conflict than in other West European countries where the unions have, to a greater extent, exerted influence by mobilizing their memberships. Swedish trade unions have tried to justify their existence by influencing the shape of the compromise.

In this general framework the focus of the sectoral governance after nationalization of the shipbuilding industry in 1977 definitely moved from the local cultures of the industry to the political axis of the government—the unions. The change of strategy and the closure of the remaining shipyards by the mid-1980s were carried out with the same governing focus and in the framework of the political market as defined in the discussion of the German case.

The decisive difference as compared to Germany was that in Sweden a compromise was made between organized labor and organized capital based on the content of the concept of rationalization and a cultural framework with specific institutions existing for the implementation of this compromise.

Japan

Japanese shipbuilding recorded remarkable gains in the rapid economic growth following World War II. In 1956 it occupied the top position in the world, exceeding that of Britain. The output in 1960 of 1.7 million gross tons was 20 percent of world shipbuilding production, in 1970 (of 10.5 million gross tons) 22 percent, in 1980 (of 7.2 million gross tons) 52 percent, and in 1984 (of 9.4 million gross tons) 53 percent. Despite the dramatic decline in production after 1975 and the stagnation in the 1980s, Japan's share of world production increased (Lloyds Register, 1960–1984).

Shipbuilding became one of the "big three" industries, along with iron and steel and motor vehicles, in the economic reconstruction after the war. The Japanese were pioneers in technical innovation in the postwar revolution of shipbuilding technology. The assembly-line system was established by 1954 and spread to shipyards throughout the country. Electrical welding became universal, and numerical control plate cutting was adopted. Introduction of these new techniques made shipbuilding with short delivery times and low costs possible by economizing on the consumption of steel, lightening the body of the vessel, and increasing loading capacity (Yamamoto, 1975).

In the 1960s, amalgamation of enterprises and selections of new locations were begun. Ishikawajima Heavy Industry Company and Harima Shipbuilding Company were amalgamated to become Ishikawajima-Harima Industry (IHI) in 1960. Three companies of the old Mitsubishi group were amalgamated to form Mitsubishi Heavy Industry in 1963. In 1964, IHI absorbed Nagoya Shipbuilding and in 1968 Kure Shipbuilding, thereby becoming the largest shipbuilding and heavy machinery trust in Japan. As for new locations, Mitsui set up operations in Chiba in addition to its large yard in Tamano (Okayama Prefecture), Hitachi located in Sakai (Osaka Prefecture), and IHI located in Yokohama in addition to its yard in Aioi (Hyogo Prefecture) (Yamamoto, 1975:168).

By the end of the 1960s most of the existing medium and small shipbuilding companies came under the control of the seven major shipbuilding enterprises. Among this group of major shipbuilders, new shipyards were developed by Kawasaki Heavy Industry at Sakaide on the Seto Inland Sea, by Nippon Kokan at Tsu on Ise Bay, and by Mitsubishi Heavy Industry and Hitachi Shipbuilding at Koyagi and Ariake, respectively, in northwest Kyushu. Sumitomo and IHI constructed new yards adjacent to the sites of their old works, which they abandoned.

In 1970, the new yard of IHI in Chita west of Yokohama was ready with a capacity of 800,000 dead weight tons (dwt). Mitsui had already built its yard in Chiba at the beginning of the decade. Except for Sumitomo and IHI, the new larger yards were often located in remote areas because physical conditions for yards large enough to permit construction of the enormous vessels being demanded had to be satisfied even at the expense of the agglomeration advantage, especially closeness to related industries (Yamamoto, 1975:169). In the 1970s, almost every enterprise undertaken by the major group of seven shipbuilders consisted of plans for large shipyards in Kyushu. However, many of these plans were suspended when the market finally collapsed.

In 1975, there were 184,000 regular employees in shipbuilding. There were forty-six yards with more than 1000 employees each. However, the small and medium-sized yards and the many frequent subcontracting firms were also important for the Japanese economy, although less so for the export market. There were also a total of about 1500 shipbuilding companies, 1600 related industrial companies, and 4000 subcontractors. If the employees in all these companies, both permanent and temporary, are included, total employment reached 361,000 (Yamamoto, 1975:163–64, 167).

The seven major companies involved in shipbuilding all belong to an enterprise group (kigyo shudan), which is an alliance built around a bank in a financial lineage, or network (kinyu keiretsu). These alliances have fundamentally transformed the operations of business. This organization of firms into coherent groupings operates through extended networks of relationships among companies (rather than hierarchically). The alliance consists of a central bank, other financial institutions, a trading company, and a highly diversified group of large manufacturing firms. The shipyards as a rule belong to the heavy engineering subgroup of the kigyo shudan. The network being constructed around the bank represents an organizational structure different from the hierarchical vertical integration of the German shipbuilding industry. Mitsubishi, Mitsui, and Sumitomo are direct descendants of the prewar zaibatsu. The other three groups were founded during the postwar period around the large commercial banks of Fuji (to which Nippon Kokkan belongs), Dai-Ichi Kangyo (Kawasaki and IHI), and Sanwa (Hitachi) (Gerlach, 1987:126–28; Aoki, 1988:119–21, 205–6, 223–34).

Business alliances have been important in Japanese shipbuilding because of their effects on structuring of the markets for capital and labor. Redundant workers have been transferred, if necessary after retraining, to other firms within the group. The existence in shipbuilding of a hierarchically ordered labor market—stratified rather than dual—with the frequent use of subcontractors at different hierarchical levels has worked supplementarily to this internal labor market structure, which has meant segmentation and marginalization of workers at the bottom of the subcontracting order during the contraction of the ship-building industry following the market collapse.

As to the structuring of the market for capital, this meant that cash deliveries to the central bank of the group during the bonanza years gave the shipbuilding companies balances in their favor when their accounts, after the market collapse, went into the red.[9]

Taken together with the subcontracting order and its stratified labor market, the *kigyo shudan* financing mechanism brought a considerable number of stabilizing elements to the shipbuilding industry when the market collapsed, although the possibilities of, and the interest in, trading the problems downward in the subcontracting hierarchy should not be exaggerated. A functioning subcontracting structure is hardly a matter of unilateral exploitation, but requires mutual confidence for long-term credibility (Aoki, 1988:204–22; cf. Lorenz, 1988).

The Japanese government and its administration constitute the third govern-ing element, or "governor," in the shipbuilding sector, in addition to the *kigyo shudan* structure and the subcontracting order (defined by Aoki as financial and capital *keiretsu*, respectively), both during the growth years up to the 1970s and during the years of "crisis" thereafter.

Using direct controls such as licensing, or indirect controls such as financial and tax incentives, the Japanese government could intervene in the shipbuilding industry. It could give direct subsidies to the shipbuilding companies or provide assistance to domestic or foreign shipping firms in order to raise demand. The Japanese shipbuilding industry is under the supervision of the Ministry of Transport. The Shipbuilding Bureau of the Ministry of Transport enacted thirty-two pieces of legislation between 1950 and 1982, and under the Shipbuilding Law of 1950 all construction, transfer, or leasing of building berths, docks, or equipment for manufacturing or repairing of ships over 500 gross tons had to be licensed by the Ministry of Transport (Yonezawa, 1988). Financial assistance through government financial institutions such as the Japan Development Bank and the Export-Import Bank of Japan formed the core of the Japanese shipping and shipbuilding policies from the early 1950s. Some 70 percent of the total domestic demand for ships in the early 1960s arose out of the planned shipbuild-ing scheme. Interest rates on loans were less than half the market rate of interest. This was the basis of the harsh credit competition on the world market for ships in the 1960s.

The index of demand for ships in terms of orders received fell from 100 in 1973 to 20 in 1975 and to 10 in 1978. The profit position in the shipbuilding industry deteriorated sharply in 1978/1979. In November 1976, the Ministry of Transport recommended curtailment of shipbuilding operations. Operation time was used as the basis for curtailments in the initial recommendations of the ministry. However, as the firms increased the intensity of work, the prescribed curtailment did not correspond to the fall in demand. Therefore, in December 1978 the Ministry of Transport shifted the basis of curtailment to production of tonnage, thereby taking recourse in direct production control while increasing the intensity of curtailments. The Antimonopoly Law was circumvented and a crisis cartel was formed. A Basic Stabilization Plan was passed, and the ministry asked the shipbuilding companies to submit capacity-scrapping programs by October 1979. The funds necessary for meeting costs of capacity reductions came from within the industry through the remaining companies (Yonezawa, 1988).

Guidelines adopted for the shipbuilding industry in 1978 were part of a stabilization package of fourteen specific depressed industries administered by MITI. The 35 percent reduction target set for shipbuilding was more than for the other thirteen industries except aluminium and urea. The target was exceeded by the beginning of the 1980s. It is debatable what role the contraction plan really played. The fact that the reduction went further than was proposed by the plan suggests that the outcome was more the consequence of the market than the plan itself (cf. Peck, 1987).

The massive intervention of the government demonstrates that the collapse of the shipbuilding industry was as spectacular as its rise in the 1960s. After 1974, thirty-seven medium and small shipbuilders went into bankruptcy (twenty-two alone in 1977). In 1978 the eighth largest shipbuilder, Sasebo, was almost ruined. Political pressure increased on the government and on local and regional authorities. In the summer of 1975, at a very early phase in the crisis, nineteen prefectures and thirty-six city authorities established a common lobby organization to persuade the government to intervene with support measures. The authorities acted especially on behalf of the small and medium-sized shipbuilders who could not, to the same extent as the big firms, trade off redundancy by means of interenterprise mobility (Nihon Zosen Shinkozaidan, 1983; Nakajima, 1987; cf. Kikkawa, 1983).

The internal labor market of the big shipbuilding firms was not a total guarantee against having laid-off workers. Several big shipbuilders announced voluntary lay offs and retirement for their regular employees. In 1979, thousands of workers were retired in the second largest firm, IHI (Kikkawa, 1983:241). The implication was that *the* pillar of strength of the industrial relations, the myth of lifelong employment for permanent employees, was threatened. Thus, the massive government intervention must be seen in this context.

During the elaboration of the program of the Ministry of Transport, the Council for the Rationalization of the Shipping and Shipbuilding Industries played a key role. The council, which was established in the early 1950s, is an expert committee for the shipping and shipbuilding sectors and exists to give the government advice on shipping and shipbuilding affairs. Members of the council are university professors and representatives of the industry and its trade associations, especially The Federation of Japan Shipbuilders, the banks, and, unique outside Japan, the mass media. Labor unions have one representative.

There is a Japanese expression that has been frequently used to describe the political operations, particularly the role of the Rationalization Council, during the restructuring of shipbuilding and other industries. *Nemawashi* means to dig around the roots of a tree (in order to lay the root system bare and make it easy to pull the tree up by the roots).

The expression indicates that the political implications of the economic and technological restructuring in Japan as well as in Western Europe have been a process of bargaining and muddling through with a considerable degree of dispute. The difference between Western Europe and Japan is that the political pressure in Western Europe has been more openly expressed in a public discourse.

In the shipbuilding sector, the Rationalization Council makes proposals, with the help of expert advice, to the government. In reality, during the process of *nemawashi*, the Ministry of Transport and its bureaucracy have the initiative in frequent unofficial and informal contacts with members of the council and with industry (with labor only at a late stage) where the product (i.e., the council's proposal) is elaborated in detail and adapted to the intentions of the ministry. The role of the experts is more to legitimize and give authority to political action than to provide the government with advice. After the hard informal work the ministry gets the proposal it desires. In this way the oligarchal interests of the industry, the government, and the politicians are expressed. It is then a bureaucratic task to sew up these interests—which are often interwoven in a network structure and difficult to distinguish between—into a single cloth.

This has been possible by means of setting a framework for the contraction of the shipbuilding industry. In the implementation of cutting capacity by 35 percent (or 20 percent as decided upon in 1986), the individual shipbuilding companies were given freedom of action. Typically, as in 1986, when the Ministry of Transport proposed a cartel for some of the companies, the proposal was much more difficult to carry through. The ministry wanted to organize the forty-three shipyards with a capacity of over 5000 gross tons into eleven groups. The seven largest shipbuilding firms were to be organized into four or five groups. Very soon the talks came to deal with a more "plastic" organization, leaving the seven large shipyards intact. Three of the big seven (IHI, Kawasaki, and Nippon Kokkan) had lengthy talks about a reduction plan and a common sales organization, but to involve all seven companies in the talks was impossible. The main obstacle was the role of the banks. Each of the seven enterprises was tied to its own bank in the *kinyu keiretsu* system, and that network was very hard to untie. Typically, two of the three firms (IHI and Kawasaki), which negotiated about closer cooperation, belonged to the same group. The network structure, comprised of the government agency and industry and institutionalized in the Rationalization Council, worked for only as long as the financial lineages in the networks constituting the enterprise groups remained intact. These networks had to be combined, not broken up.

As to the curtailment of production proposed by the Ministry of Transport, the possibilities of getting the firms to carry out what the ministry proposed was much easier, owing to the preceding talks with the Rationalization Council.

A manager of Mitsubishi expressed the view of management:

> If problems as to implementation arose the Ministry of Transport had talks with the board. They had no legal means to enforce the proposal but it was mandatory nevertheless. Otherwise the firm risked some kind of inconvenience.[10]

What role, then, did the trade unions play in the governance of the shipbuilding sector in Japan?

Obviously, their influence in the Rationalization Council was limited. However, this may be due to the Japanese union structure where the focus is at the enterprise level. The many company unions in shipbuilding are, as a rule, members of the Right-wing union confederation for the shipbuilding industry *Zosenjukiroren*. About 50 percent of the regular employees (blue-collar as well as white-collar) are unionized in *Zosenjukiroren*. The Left-wing *Zenzosen* was strong in shipbuilding in the 1950s when it was the biggest of the two unions. From the beginning of the 1960s its membership declined rapidly, however, when a management strategy, ongoing since the late 1940s, of busting progressive unions operating beyond the company level, was at last successful in shipbuilding as well. In all other industries the introduction of enterprise unions occurred as early as the 1950s. (This establishment could be linked to a line of continuity to a corresponding organization of industrial relations in both the prewar and World War II period.) *Zenzosen* only has a few thousand members. One distinctive mark is that only the permanent employees are unionized. Temporary workers, who constitute a cyclical buffer on the stratified labor market, are not allowed to join.

The unions have not been able to influence the market prospects any more than has management. They have not been able to prevent reduction of capacity. Appeals to the government have been of no use, not least because of the unions' weak organization at the national level. However, unions have been able to exert an influence on the shape of the reduction plans. Retraining and transfer to other jobs in the enterprise group have been accepted, provided wages, working time, and other working conditions have not been worsened. Unions seem to accept transfers as a "lesser evil" policy and to negotiate the features of their implementation within the framework of labor agreements and the formal and informal structures of consultation (Brunello, 1988:135).

This attitude of the unions has helped to keep up the relative value of worker transfers, as compared with outright dismissals. The employers, too, have preferred transfers. The cost of discharging an employee is high because of the long spells of unemployment and because of reverse seniority in involuntary separations. The numerous transfers of workers from steel and shipbuilding to automotive plants during the late 1970s and early 1980s were considered by car makers as substitutes for seasonal workers. The advantage, in the eyes of management, was that transferees were less likely to be "troublemakers" and were more "reliable" than seasonal workers. Seasonal workers are perceived by some employers as an indicator of low quality. The interest of both employers and unions in transfers had made the market for transfers function as an intermediate structure between market and organizations (Brunello, 1988:123–27). However, owing to the severity of the decline of the shipbuilding industry, the capacity of the market for transfers has occasionally been insufficient.

The sectoral mode of governance in Japanese shipbuilding has oscillated between business association networks and sponsoring departments, where the private business networks of the seven enterprise groups with the major ship-builders—loosely coordinated by the Federation of Japanese Shipbuilders—have been knit together with the government in the institutional form of the Rationalization Council and the Ministry of Transport. Occasionally, the ministry has intervened like a regulatory agency.

This conclusion confirms Aoki's opinion (1988:263–64) that the Japanese bureaucracy is "neither a monolithic, rational social engineer nor a passive black-box processer of pluralist interests." It is a multitude of entities that formulate and implement policy by drafting and enforcing laws, providing informal administration guidance, allocating cash flow resources, and so on, in a way that is not only a bureaucratic delineation of "public interests" but is closely intertwined with its status as a representative of sectoral interests providing constituents with access to policy-making and responding to political pressures.

In contrast to the hierarchical coordination and regulation in Sweden, this structural pattern "features relatively autonomous operating units connected horizontally without hierarchical control" (Aoki, 1988:298). The role of leadership has been to facilitate horizontal communication among the firms and *kinyu keiretsu* and to make strategic decisions in a constituent-based manner. This sectoral governance mode has allowed the adaption of operations to the changing market environment. In a regulative order like this, radical organizational innovation and strategic reorientation requiring some constituent groups to make a sacrifice are not likely to occur from within unless they are brought on by a significant external shock. There is a tendency toward "progressive conservatism" (Aoki, 1988:298). Whether the collapse of the shipbuilding market constituted such a shock is debatable. In any case, the response to the crisis, measured in terms of capacity liquidation, was smaller in Japan than in Sweden and Germany.

The fact that the bargaining model has been bipartite rather than tripartite as in Germany and Sweden does not mean that the role of the unions can be ignored. Their interests in improved wages and better working conditions (for the core of the work force constituting their membership) have made them important for the achievement of increased productivity (Muramatsu, 1984:121, 127; Freeman, 1984).

Integration of the unions at the company level has constituted a stabilizing feature of the contraction process. The fact that only permanent employees are members of the unions and derive the benefit of the company welfare arrangements means that the temporary workers, especially those in the subcontracting firms, have been used as cyclical regulators. The company-based welfare and industrial relations structure has worked well both for the companies and for the Japanese economy and also for those permanent employees who have been invited to participate in it in the form of an offer of permanent employment. Therefore, the defense of the system has also been strong during the period of decline.[11]

Concluding Remarks

In the sectoral framework for development from the 1960s onward, which has been drawn here, the market for ships and the political propensity of governments to intervene, either to underpin the growth of the market and organize the industry accordingly, or to mitigate the effects of the workings of the market, have been the organizing principle, or the common denominator, of the sector in all three countries studied. In this sense the development has had obvious common features in all countries, justifying the label "sectoral governance." There has been a convergence at the performance level, irrespective of the particular country.

However, as to the precise forms and causes for government intervention there have been clear national differences owing to different national political cultures and their institutional arrangements.

One crucial question has been to what extent it has been possible to go beyond the limits set by the sector to find solutions when the market broke down. Here, obviously, the Swedish and Japanese regulative orders have worked rather similarly and diverged from the German sectoral hierarchies. Sweden abandoned shipbuilding totally and established automobile production at the sites of the last two shipyards following a cooperative agreement between the Swedish government and the private automotive industry. In Japan the *kigyo shudan* system facilitated the transfer of labor to other sectors. The claims of the unions in Germany for alternative production and creation of new jobs in other sectors was problematic as a general strategy. Some but not all firms in the hierarchy managed to diversify, and success in this field was more a matter of individual entrepreneurship than a general counter-crisis strategy. This institutional difference as to capacity to find solutions beyond the sectoral bounds must be referred to the general union interest demonstrated in productivity gains in Japan and Sweden. The much lower unemployment figures in Japan and Sweden than in West Germany for the entire period since the early 1970s must be understood in this context.

It was realized that the crisis in shipbuilding was structural and not cyclical by the end of the 1970s in all three countries. The international nature of the market collapse and the penetration power of the crisis in the public discourse contributed to a simultaneous awareness of the magnitude and the structural dimension of the crisis beyond the cultural frameworks of national discourses.. While there was no real difference among the three countries in this respect, the responses to this insight differed among nations and within the bipartite or tripartite arrangements in each nation.

In Germany the unions first argued for a closure of unprofitable shipyards, but grassroots pressure caused them to abandon this approach in 1978. In Sweden the unions agreed to capacity reductions and contraction by the mid-1970s, provided that the principle of equal distribution of the reduction of workers among all the shipyards was maintained, with no closure with the exception of Eriksberg. As in Germany, unions demanded government funds to mitigate the contraction process and prevent compulsory redundancy (worker layoffs). Industry representatives early on were as aware as were the unions of the structural dimension of the problem.

In the Swedish political culture with its institutional arrangements, local decision-makers from the shipyards representing the unions in the central-level bargaining, and the nationalized shipbuilding industry (1977), especially made the bargaining less complicated with less friction than in Germany. There, the works council (*Betriebsräte*) system produced gravitation toward the local level, which was not counterbalanced by strong unions at the national level, although the union structure was hierarchical. Shipbuilding was mainly handled at the regional *Bezirk* level in Hamburg and pressures from the shipbuilding regions were "diluted" when they arrived at the national *Vorstand* level in Frankfurt where several other interests had to be considered. Moreover, in general terms, the German unions had a weaker position in the organization of society than did the Swedish ones.

The greater tensions within organized labor in Germany and the more fragmented contraction process were underscored by the competing interests on the owner side and between the regional and federal political levels.

This greater tension in the German divestment process as compared with Sweden was obvious from the early 1980s when the subsidy policy was abandoned. The rapidly increasing tensions between VDS and the shipbuilding firms and the unions when no money was available released latent tensions in IG Metall. However, the rapidly changing opinion against spending more taxpayers' money on a bankrupt industry was an important factor in stabilizing the contraction process and keeping the tensions under control and in establishing sectoral boundaries in both Germany and Sweden.

Although there were similar pressures "from below" in Japan, the retreat there was more planned and more of a bipartite affair. One important institutional factor was the internal labor market within the business networks. Also, the stratified labor market, with considerable marginalization of parts of the labor force and considerable division, worked in the same direction. The tradition of strategies with fast shifts to expansive and high productivity sectors prevailing in the *kinyu keiretsu* was important for the early start of a planned contraction process under government guidance. However, the planned contraction process not only brought an early start but also a less far-reaching capacity curtailment than in Sweden and Germany.

The Swedish case demonstrates speedy worker redeployment, as in Japan. However, the Swedish process went much further (all the yards closed down) than in either Japan or Germany, and under much less open friction and conflict than in Germany. As in Japan and Germany, the Swedish process was managed by nonmarket institutions, although these institutions were basically labor-dominated in networks that are universalist in the sense that they are nonsectoral and not firm-specific. The core of this institutional arrangement has been central bargaining in the labor market, with an active labor market policy, guaranteed by the government, and the unions' wage policy with solidarity, providing for wage maintenance, as the most important ingredients. This institutionalization of a universalist political culture is the decisive difference between Sweden and the informal and particularistic bipartite trading relationships in the Japanese networks. Sweden even more than Japan had a hierarchical corporatist structure transcending particular sectors.

The German case reveals particularistic traits of a different kind than in Japan. These traits are reflected in the sectoral trade union treatment of ship-building, the local gravitation force of the works council, internal labor markets within the vertical hierarchies of the shipbuilding companies, and the regionally fragmented state. However, there are also universalist traits, such as the absence of the stratified labor market and trading groups, as in Japan. The outcome of this German mix seems to be local management–union cooperation at the company level trying to exploit other such constellations, sectoral coalitions trying to exploit other sectors, and/or regional coalitions trying to exploit other regions.

In all these respects there have been similar tendencies in Sweden, but they have in the case of the contraction of the shipbuilding industry been absorbed by the dominating universalist tendency. (In other Swedish sectors and in the economy in general in the early 1990s fragmentation and breakdown of hierarchy and centralization are palpable.) In Germany there was neither a state nor a union capacity for an effective suprasectoral intervention as in Sweden, nor intersectoral networks for trade-offs as was the case in Japan.

Notes

1. The article was written by Karl H. Pitz, who was on the board of IG Metall and oversaw shipbuilding.
2. Written by Karl H. Pitz.
3. Interview with Volkhard Meier, Verband der Deutschen Schiffbauindustrie, VDS, March 1983.
4. IG Metall was certainly not exclusively market oriented: The union demanded extensive planning and public financial support for the creation of new jobs in other fields. The key concept of IG Metall was a *planned* reduction of the work force.
5. "De svenska storvarvens problem." Verkstadsföreningen, Stockholm archives F 727-1970: memorandum by Metall's economist Allan Larsson, 6 October 1971, and minutes from shipbuilding meetings 14 February and 10 April 1972 and 5 April 1973. Metall, Stockholm archives; Interviews with Per Nyström, chairman of the government committee on shipbuilding, October 1982, and with Gunnar Sträng, Minister of Finance, 1956–1976, January 1985.
6. Cf "Om Varvssamrådet." Memorandum 6 March 1975, Metall, Stockholm archives.
7. Interview with Leif Blomberg, October 1984.
8. Ibid.
9. Interview with Shigeya Takayama, Mitsubishi Heavy Industry, February 1988.
10. Ibid.
11. Interviews with Sukesada Ito, Zosenjukiroren's General Secretary; Yoshihiro Kawai, Ministry of Labor, and Naotake Kaibara, Rengo, March 1988.

References

Aoki, Masahiko. (1988). *Information, Incentives, and Bargaining in the Japanese Economy.* Cambridge: Cambridge University Press.

Brunello, Giorgio. "Transfers of Employees between Japanese Manufacturing Enterprises: Some Results from an Enquiry on a Small Sample of Large Firms." *British Journal of Industrial Relations*, 1988, March.

Flieshardt, Peter, and Reinhardt Sablotny. (1980). *Schliessung order Fusion—gibt es bald nur noch einige einzige Grosswerfte?* Bremen: University of Bremen.

Freeman, Richard B. (1984). "De-mystifying the Japanese Labor Markets." In Masahiko Aoki (ed.), *The Economic Analysis of the Japanese Firm.* New York: North-Holland.

Gerlach, Michael. (1987, Fall). "Business Alliances and the Strategy of the Japanese Firm." *California Management Review.*

Der Gewerkschaftler. (1976). Vol. 9.

Der Gewerkschaftler. (1977). Vol. 1.

Hamilton, Carl. (1981). *Public Subsidies to Industry: The Case of Sweden and Its Shipbuilding Industry.* Stockholm: Institute for International Economic Studies. (Stockholm University Seminar Paper No. 174.)

IG Metall. (1978). *7. Nationale Schiffbaukonferenz der IG Metall am 3. März 1978 in Hamburg. Protokoll.* Hamburg: IG Metall. *Bezirksleitung* archives.

IG Metall. (1983). *Entschliessung der Konferenz Norddeutschland am 21. April 1983.* Hamburg: IG Metall. *Bezirksleitung* archives.

Kappel, Robert, and Detlef Rother. (1982). *Wandlungsprozesse in der Schiffahrt und im Schiffbau Westeuropas.* Bremen: Bremen University.

Kikkawa, Mototada. (1983). "Shipbuilding, Motor Cars and Semiconductors: The Diminishing Role of Industrial Policy in Japan." In Stepherd Geoffrey et al. (eds.), *Europe's Industries: Public and Private Strategies for Change.* London: Frances Pinter.

Lloyds Register. (1960–1984). *Shipbuilding. Lloyds Annual Summaries.* London: Lloyds.

Lorenz, Edward. (1988). "Neither Friends nor Strangers: Informal Networks of Subcontracting in French Industry." In Diego Gambetta (ed.), *Trust: Making and Breaking Cooperative Relations.* London: Basil Blackwell.

Muramatsu, Kuramitsu. (1984). "The Effect of Trade Unions on Productivity in Japanese Manufacturing Industries." In Masahiko Aoki (ed.), *The Economic Analysis of the Japanese Firm.* New York: North-Holland.

Nakajima, Tomovoshi (1987). "Nihon ni okeru zosengyo 1970–1985. Sangyochosei seisaku taisho sangyo no jirei" *Senshu Daigaku Shakai Kagaku Ronshu*, 9.

Nihon Zosen Shinkozaidan. (1983). *Zosen fukyo no kiroku.* Tokyo: Japan Shipbuilding Association.

Peck, Merton I et al. (1987). "Picking Losers: Public Policy toward Declining Industries in Japan." *The Journal of Japanese Studies*, 13(1).

Stråth, Bo. (1987a). *The Politics of De-industrialisation.* London: Croom Helm.

Stråth. Bo. (1987b). "Social Change and Active Labour Market Policy: The Case of Sweden." Paper presented for the Conference of the International Working Party on Labour Market Segmentation in Torino, 16–21 July 1987. Göeborg: University of Göteborg.

Swedish Government. (1976). Bill 1975/1976, No. 121. Stockholm: Government Offices.

VDS. (1978). *Bericht über Struktur und Entwicklung des deutschen Seeschiffbaus. 1978.* Hamburg: VDS Archives.

Wulf, Peter. (1980). "Schwerindustrie und Seeschiffahrt nach dem 1. Weltkrieg: Hugo Stinnes und die HAPAG." *Vierteljahrschrift für Sozial- und Wirtschaftsgeschichte*, 1.

Yamamoto, S. (1975). "Shipbuilding." In Kivoji Kurata (ed.), *An Industrial Geography of Japan*. London: Bell & Hyman.

Yonezawa, Yoshie. (1988). "The Shipbuilding Industry." In Komiya, Sutsumura, and Okuno (eds.), *Industrial Policy of Japan*. Tokyo: Academic Press.

CHAPTER 5

Industry as a Form of Order

A Comparison of the Historical Development
of the Machine Tool Industries in the
United States and Germany

Gary Herrigel

THIS chapter compares the historical development of the machine tool industries in the United States and Germany. Its focus is on the self-regulatory arrangements that these industries constructed and how these arrangements influenced their strategies of adjustment, repeatedly, over time. The machine tool industries in Germany and the United States make an interesting case because, with the exception of the current period, both industries performed extremely well throughout the twentieth century, yet both have been organized in radically different ways and have followed different developmental trajectories. In the U.S. industry, all aspects of production are incorporated within the institutional framework of independent firms in and among whom the mechanisms of authority and price are chiefly used to govern. In Germany, production is governed by a complex network of public and private institutions (including firms) in which mechanisms of price, authority, and trust interact in complex, yet highly flexible, ways.

The chapter will argue that these various governance mechanisms in production are the consequence of the existence of different forms of industrial order in these countries. An industrial order is the peculiar social, political, and legal framework constructed over the course of the industrialization process that shapes the way that producers serving given product markets collectively define the legitimate boundaries of industrial practice. Such frameworks exclude certain types of behavior, make others possible, and establish procedures for dispute resolution within a community of transacting parties. An industrial order is thus not a governance mechanism, such as a market or a hierarchy; it is the politically and socially constructed framework that creates the conditions under which particular repertoires of governance mechanisms emerge and are employed. In this respect, industrial orders have more in common with modern political constitutions than with particular governance mechanisms (see Holmes, 1988; Ackerman, 1988; Hardin, 1989).

The argument begins with a brief theoretical discussion of the notion of industrial order. The two following sections then develop the notion of industrial order through a comparison of the two machine tool industries: The U.S. case will be presented first, the German second. Finally, a conclusion will discuss the implications that the notion of industrial order has for our understanding of the current predicament of the U.S. machine tool industry.

Industrial Order

The argument about industrial order made in the comparative cases below attempts to address a dimension of the boundary between the economy and society that has been exposed by, yet left unexamined in, current sociological critiques of neoclassical theories of governance mechanisms and the firm. The basic divide in the current debate between neoclassical economists and economic sociologists on the theory of the firm is that the latter view individual economic transactions as contingent upon and defined within larger social contexts, whereas the former do not. Neoclassical economists (e.g., Williamson, 1985; Jensen and Meckling, 1976; Grossman and Hart, 1986) focus on individual transactions among self-interested maximizers and view various governance mechanisms as mutually exclusive (uniquely efficient) alternative solutions to the problems of uncertainty and risk posed by discrete choice situations. Inefficient solutions are inevitably revealed to be so, at least in the long run. Contingency and structuralist sociologists (e.g., Stinchcombe, 1985; Bradach and Eccles, 1989) maintain with considerable legitimacy that this orientation assumes away precisely what is most significant in shaping economic exchanges, that is, the way in which noneconomic relations and transactions shape economic ones.

Eccles and White (1988), for example, show that, owing to the power and role calculations of individual managers, multidivisional corporations often use the market as a mechanism of control when neoclassical theory would predict they would use hierarchy, and vice versa. The economists go wrong, Eccles and White argue, because they take the boundary between the economy and society completely for granted. For Eccles and White, the contours of this boundary are crucial: Individual agents in industry, as well as their interests and evaluations of risk and uncertainty, are literally defined by the social contexts of power and value in which they are embedded.

Sociological theories of the firm have gone some way in applying these insights to a theory of governance mechanisms. Rather than as mutually exclusive, most efficient options, ranging on a continuum between market and hierarchy, the sociologists view the governance mechanisms employed by "embedded" agents as institutional techniques for achieving control or avoiding risk. Such techniques, moreover, can be deployed in diverse, often overlapping ways. Indeed, according to Stinchcombe (1985) and Bradach and Eccles (1989) governance mechanisms are deployed both in ways that complement one another (e.g., combining franchising and vertical integration) and in ways that can make one a substitute for another (e.g., hierarchical contracts in large-scale, deep-sea oil drilling projects). Which mechanisms are deployed in a particular situation and in what ways, they argue, depend upon the context and strategies of the transacting parties within it—what Bradach and Eccles refer to as the "broader architecture of control mechanisms" (1989:115).

Given the explanatory importance attributed to it, it is ironic that the sociologists have not yet addressed systematically the problem of how context or "architecture" is structured or how such structures may vary. Bradach and Eccles recognize the problem, but have no solution for it. They end their illuminating essay by pointing out that explanations for "when and why different mixtures of control mechanisms occur" still need to be developed (1989:116). The notion of industrial order as developed here is an attempt to get at the relationship between particular repertoires of control or governance mechanisms and the background architecture of social and political relations that make them possible.

The argument is that industries exist within specific frameworks of order that emerge historically and are partially created by the members of the industry themselves and partially established for them by historical currents at other levels of society. These frameworks are not identical to the boundaries of a firm or group of firms. Rather, they are ground rules for acceptable practice, created in the turbulent organizational and strategic ambiguity of the formation of an industry, which give rise to particular kinds of firms with a specific array of available governance mechanisms. In this view, industrial orders have a relationship to the agents within them that is analogous in some generic respects to the relation between a modern liberal constitution and its citizens. In particular, I believe there are three characteristics that constitutions and frameworks of industrial order share in common: exclusionary rules, dispute adjudication procedures, and identity creation.

First, like modern constitutions, industrial orders involve rules that prevent or bind members of the industry from engaging in specific practices. These exclusionary rules, however, encourage and in many ways even enable participants to act in other ways considered to be more desirable by the collectivity.[1] Thus as we shall see, in the U.S. machine tool industry, rules against collusion inhibited cooperation and encouraged the stabilization of competition through merger. In Germany, rules against broad technological diversification blocked merger as a strategy and encouraged cooperation as a stabilization measure.

Second, frameworks of order in industry, very much in the manner of constitutions (Hardin, 1989:113–15), establish general procedural guidelines (and institutions) for the adjudication of disputes among members. The norm councils in the German machine tool association in which members coordinate their specialization strategies is an example of institutionalized dispute adjudication. In the United States, dispute adjudication followed the rules of the market: It occurred through merger and was guided by the principles of survival of the fittest.

Finally, I want to suggest further, as some constitutional theorists do about constitutions (e.g., Ackerman, 1988), that the emergence of a framework of order in industry not only crystallizes the strategies of actors but it also either constitutes or validates general kinds of shared beliefs about the character and boundaries of the industrial community.[2] Industrial orders are generally the outcome of political and social conflicts among competing conceptions of industry and its relationship to society. Once established, industrial orders represent the institutionalization of such a view: People think about firms and their relationship to society differently within different forms of industrial order. This is important because crisis in an industry can provoke actors to engage in difficult reexamination of the boundaries between their own community and the rest of society.

Thinking of an industrial order as analogous to a modern constitution is helpful in characterizing the kind of role that I claim an industrial order plays in an industry. In the manner of a constitution it establishes a framework of order within which, among other things, particular repertoires of governance mechanisms emerge. Yet there are, to be sure, several limitations on the usefulness of the constitutional analogy that should be mentioned to avoid confusion.

First, unlike constitutions, the principles of industrial order are not typically written down, at least not in one place. They exist more as ways of collectively conceptualizing an industry and of institutionalizing acceptable practice within one. They must be discovered, therefore, through careful historical and ethnographic reconstruction. Second, such frameworks do not come into existence in one grand deliberative act, such as a constitutional convention. They are constructed piecemeal over time through an evolving dialogue and struggle over the way that acceptable practice in the industry should be defined. Finally, the boundaries of an industrial order are less sovereign than those of a polity framed by a constitution. Industrial order is often interpenetrated with principles of order outlined within actual constitutions as well as the rules that define and govern practice within the broader social communities in which industries are embedded.

All of these things make frameworks of industrial order more difficult than constitutions to identify and circumscribe precisely. The existence of an industrial order can nevertheless always be verified, I suggest, in two ways. One is to view the way in which two groups of producers making the same types of products in different places react to the same technological and international market pressures. If both successfully respond to the challenge, yet their reactions substantially differ, as did, we shall see, the mid-twentieth-century U.S. and German machine tool industries to the rise of large-scale mass production, then it strengthens the claim that the frameworks of order in each industry were different. Particular strategies of adjustment appeared obvious to those in one context of order that were made virtually unthinkable in the other—and vice versa.

The second way to identify the existence of industrial order is to identify rules that exclude certain governance mechanisms from the repertoire available to a community. The continued salience of those rules in situations where their absence could reasonably be considered to enhance the performance of the industry is a good indication of the existence of an industrial order. The current experience of the U.S. machine tool industry, which eschews both cooperation and participation in trust relations in a competitive environment that has shown these practices to be highly successful elsewhere, provides a test for the existence of industrial order. The current experience of the U.S. industry, as the conclusion to this chapter makes plain, also points to the kinds of issues involved in redefining industrial order. For the U.S. industry to adjust successfully in the current environment, it must recast the principles of industrial order that define it in a way that makes currently unavailable forms of governance possible to deploy. To do this, however, following the argument above, it will be necessary for industry members to reflect on their shared assumptions about what firms are and on the boundaries of their own community.

The U.S. and German Machine Tool Industries in the Twentieth Century

In the presentation of the machine tool case, the experience of the U.S. industry will be followed by the German. Each of the historical accounts of industrial development will have parallel structures. The industries will pass through three periods of change: an initial period of industry and industrial order creation in the late nineteenth and early twentieth centuries, and then two periods of adjustment within the twentieth century.

Industrial Order in the U.S. Machine Tool Industry

The production of machine tools in the United States has a very long and proud tradition. During the early nineteenth century, there was no independent machine tool industry, as such. Machine tools were constructed by firms engaged in industries that used them, such as weapons producers, textile mills, and locomotive works. Nevertheless, it was during this time that the most distinctively American innovation in machine tool technology took place. With government support, machinists working in armories developed the technological capacity to machine parts that resembled one another so exactly that they could be used interchangeably (Smith, 1977; Hounshell, 1984). The capacity to machine interchangeable parts was an essential technological precondition for the development of high-volume or "mass" production. Such machines were highly productive when used in the manufacture of standardized parts and were also labor-saving.

Although there is some disagreement concerning the precise time, the emergence of companies devoted exclusively to the production of machine tools occurred in the last two decades of the nineteenth century (Robertson, 1966; McDougall, 1966). The emergence of the industry in its modern form is completely bound up with the rise of the modern corporation and the related development of mass-producing industries: sewing machinery manufacturers, bicycle makers, office machinery producers, farm equipment and construction machinery makers, and, especially after the turn of the century, automobile producers (Chandler, 1977). Regional clusters of machine tool producers grew up in and around clusters of these industries in northern Illinois and southern

Wisconsin, Detroit, Cincinnati, Cleveland, while the former nineteenth-century centers of general machine tool production in the Connecticut River valley, Providence, Rhode Island, and Philadelphia fell into relative decline (Wagoner, 1968, chapter 3).

There is much debate about this transformation of the U.S. political economy, but recent evidence clearly indicates that the triumph of the corporation and mass production was in no way economically or technologically inevitable. On the contrary, the mass-producing corporation was the victor in a broadly political contest with an alternative, more regionalist, small producer, and republican vision for the emergent industrial society of late nineteenth-century America (e.g., Berk, 1987; Hattam, 1990; Livingston, 1986; Sklar, 1988). Only when a legal and institutional framework conducive to its development was established was the victory of modern corporate capitalism assured. Formation of the modern machine tool industry was at once shaped by the construction of this framework and was a microcosm of the types of conflicts that constructed it. Three significant aspects of this framework were expressed in the industrial order of the machine tool industry: exclusionary rules favorable to volume producers, procedures for dispute resolution based on market power, and a shared understanding that industry was a term of art for a grouping of sovereign hierarchically centralized firms.

Imposition of Exclusionary Rules

In the context of this general transformation of the American political economy, two different strategies for organizing production competed with one another to define order in the machine tool industry. On the one side were those machine tool producers who attempted to follow the strategy of their mass-producing customers, that is, to focus on the production of a narrow range of standard products that could be produced in volume (Buxbaum, 1920; Wagoner, 1968; Brown, 1957). Such standardized American machine tools were generally semi-dedicated: Although they were not single-purpose machines, they had a limited range of flexibility. Rather than build broad machining capacity into a single machine, these producers tended to make separate machines. The simple machines made up for what they lost in complexity and flexibility with labor savings, precision, and high-volume efficiency (Rosenberg, 1972; Woodbury, 1972). On the other side were craft production-based producers following a strategy of broadly diversified production with an emphasis on customization (Wagoner, 1968, chapters 2, 4). Such producers attempted to cover demand both from the old craft/industrial sectors and from the newer volume producers by emphasizing production flexibility and quality in meeting the precise production needs of the customer.

During much of the latter half of the nineteenth century, market characteristics were still sufficiently plastic to allow producers pursuing both of the above strategies to compete successfully in the market. Most recent research seems to show that neither strategy was technically superior to the other (e.g., Robinson and Briggs, 1991). The level of demand for most types of special machines was sufficiently large so that individual standardized volume producers could justify specializing production on a narrow range of machinery. Their earnings during boom times were usually enough to tide them over the rather dramatic cyclical swings that plagued the industry. Similarly, demand was robust enough to allow diversified customizers to spread resources across a broad product palette, offering an array of machines that they could deliver with modifications according to user wishes. Reliance on productive flexibility and skill enabled producers to find orders for some type of machinery even during downturns in the business cycle.

Although successful enough in a growing environment, the two strategies did not coexist harmoniously with one another. Each had particular vulnerabilities, and their differences ultimately gave rise to conceptions of acceptable practice and competition that destabilized those of the other.

The specialized volume production strategy was vulnerable in two ways. On the one hand, because by and large at the end of the nineteenth century direct control over the production process and the division of labor was in the hands of skilled workers, would-be volume producers found that their ability to achieve efficient economies of scale in production was blocked by worker control (Montgomery, 1979). On the other hand, in those cases where they succeeded in shifting their resources behind the specialized volume production strategy, such producers became extremely vulnerable to competition and the threat of market fragmentation. In a competitive market, it was always possible for diversified customizer competitors to offer a machine with precisely those capabilities that a standardized machine lacked. Volume producers could only respond to such challenges by offering to customize as well, but this then undermined their efforts to standardize and achieve economies of scale in production. Thus, among volume producers the desire gradually grew to establish a framework of order, or rules for acceptable conduct both in production and in competition, that protected them from such challenges. In its most radical guise, their strategy aimed at redefining the boundaries of industry in ways that completely eliminated the challenges posed by worker control and what they and their allies in other industries called "excessive" competition (Livingston, 1986; Sklar, 1988; Montgomery, 1979; and Wagoner, 1968, chapter 4).

Diversified customizers had an alternative strategy, different vulnerabilities, and, hence, wanted to construct an alternative type of order. Unlike the volume producers, the customizer's strategy was not blocked by the presence of powerful skilled workers in production. On the contrary, because the diversified and customizing strategy that they pursued depended upon a great deal of flexibility in production, these producers relied heavily upon strong, autonomous, and cooperative skilled workers. Indeed, republican "producerist" social and political traditions tended to draw class boundaries in ways that created affinity between the skilled and the small-scale manufacturer (Hattam, 1990). Also unlike the volume producers, the customizers were not threatened by market fragmentation—they thrived on it. A market of many desires, in their view, was a market of many possible contracts.

The vulnerability of the diversified customizer strategy lay not in market fragmentation but in market chaos. Downturns in the business cycle within a community of highly flexible producers always sent producer chasing after producer, nervously underbidding one another and seeking to win a dwindling pool of machine tool orders. This problem of underbidding among the generalists was compounded by the fact that the volume producers could win orders by dumping machines from their inventory on the market at cut-rate prices. The result in either case was the collapse of market prices. The classic solution to market breakdown of this kind is for participating producers to cooperate on the bidding process and collectively agree to put a floor on prices to preserve market order (i.e., construct a kind of dispute-adjudicating cartel). As we shall see below, this is precisely what the German producers did. Yet, in the United States the diversified customizers proved unable to implement successfully this kind of cooperation or establish it as a legitimate form of market order.

There are two central reasons for this. First, the customizers needed the cooperation of the specialist volume producers in the construction of those kinds of cartels. But volume producers had little incentive to cooperate with the customizers. They desired a *different* form of industrial order that excluded customization as a practice. Second, as time went on and the balance of power in American politics shifted toward an accommodation of large-scale corporate organization, the political and legal terrain in which the industrial economy was embedded became increasingly hostile to the vision of order shared by customizing industrial producers (Sklar, 1988). This was most crucially true in the way that court interpretations of legitimate competition and market order changed. Traditionally, the types of arrangements that the diversified customizers needed to organize cooperation had been permissible under common law (Hovenkamp, 1991, chapter 21). But, in the new corporate and progressive political order, older and classically liberal, or republican producerist, readings of restraint of trade and freedom of contract gave way to interpretations that viewed cooperation among producers almost exclusively as harmful collusion (Hovenkamp, 1991, chapters 20, 22).

Dispute Adjudication

Blocked by rules that excluded the practices needed to construct a framework for stable cooperation, diversified customizing production had to play by rules congenial to the volume producers. Essentially this meant that all disputes on the market concerning price or the character of technology were resolved through a contest of strength. Customizing firms, as a result, were either competed out of business by the financially more robust volume producers, or they were bought out by the same producers. In any case, the customization strategy followed a path of gradual decay in the early twentieth-century machine tool industry. Bludgeoned and decimated from brutal competition during downturns, surviving producers emerged weakened in the next upturn. Slowly, over many iterations of the business cycle, their ability to offer tools of sufficient quality to compete against the standardized tools of volume producers began to disappear. Healthy firms were frequently bought out by richer volume producers because that was the only way the former could protect their assets from the ravages of the business cycle. Weaker generalist firms either collapsed, or, as we shall see, turned to subcontracting.

Ultimately, the decline of diversified customization redefined the community of machine tool producers. The industry gradually developed an increasingly concentrated industrial structure dominated by specialized companies producing standardized machine tools in relatively large volume. Individual machine tool companies came to be associated with particular types of machines—such as the Gleason company and bevel gear machinery, or the Landis Tool Company and cylindrical grinders—because they dominated the U.S. market for that particular machine. This process had advanced far enough by the mid-1920s that Wagoner claims there were no more than four firms producing the same product in the entire industry and frequently far fewer (Wagoner, 1968:272–73).

Even though this dynamic of concentration shaped relations among individual producers in an important way, there are two reasons why it could not progress as far in the machine tool industry as it had in other branches of capital goods manufacture in the United States, such as textile and shoe machinery (Herrigel and Kazis, 1989; Kaysen, 1956). First, tremendous increases in the level of demand in the first quarter of the twentieth century, owing to the emergence of new industries, in particular the automobile industry, and large military orders during World War I far outstripped the ability of any single producer to cover all of demand completely, even for special types of machinery. In this context, smaller companies, which were either blessed with talented owners, such as the Lodge & Shipley Company in Cincinnati, or could find a profitable niche with an excellent product, such as the Bryant Chucking Grinder Company in Springfield, Vermont, could maintain their position among the leading firms in the industry (Geier, 1949; Broehl, 1959).

Second, because business cycles were far more dramatic in the machine tool industry than they were in other industries, firms were reluctant to increase their production capacity a great deal during periods of peak demand. Instead, they ceded a portion of demand to smaller, often less competitive companies. The structure of the industry in this way grew to be increasingly dualist, divided between a core of leading manufacturers and a secondary sector of smaller and more fragile producers. In many cases the smaller firms that absorbed surplus demand at the peak of the cycle produced their own tools; many other small firms specialized in producing tools for larger producers under contract. Many firms survived by doing both. In all cases, these producers rarely made enough money in boom periods to tide them over business cycle troughs, much less to commit resources to training, research, or product development to pursue systematically a strategy of fragmenting the larger firm's market (Brown, 1957: 413–14).

Consolidation of the Volume Producer Conception of the
Firm and Its Relationship to Society

These exclusionary rules and procedures for dispute adjudication basically validated the standardized volume producer conception of the firm and of the appropriate boundaries between industry and society. For them, the relative rigidity of high volume standardized production meant that profitability could only be achieved when as much uncertainty as possible could be weeded out of production and the market. Volume producers, therefore, placed great value on control (Noble, 1977). The hierarchical firm and the prerogative of its management were not only the practical organizational vehicles they used to achieve their ends of control; they also became the prestigious symbols of a new social order and of legitimate private authority (on this, see, classically, Veblen, 1906/1978, passim, and 1923, especially chapters 5–8).

Correspondingly, extra-firm influences on production, such as from suppliers, customers, or public bodies, were devalued in the developing understanding of good industrial practice. Such intrusions from the outside were viewed as disorderly, or collusive, or threatening, and in all cases obstacles to efficient production. As development within the new framework of order progressed, and producers with alternative conceptions of order slowly went into extinction, the machine tool industry lost all the vestiges of whatever republican, producerist community self-image it may have once had. Its members now understood themselves, not as a community, but as a collection of independent, nearly autonomous firms, each of which, like fathers in a bourgeois family, possessed absolutely sovereign authority over production.

Governance Mechanisms

As the framework of order in the industry increasingly affected producers in this way, it also became clear that it led them to rely on a narrow repertoire of governance mechanisms: primarily authority and price. Other governance mechanisms, such as cooperation, as we saw, had been self-consciously excluded, legally and practically, from the realm of acceptable practice. Still others, such as trust, could not emerge in an industry of producers that drew such rigid and strict boundaries between themselves and the rest of society.

The role of market mechanisms in governing the industry has already been discussed with reference to dispute adjudication. But the importance of hierarchy in the industry is very clear from its organizational development. By the mid-1920s, nearly all aspects of production, the organization of work, vocational training, product development, and market coordination had been taken off the market or ripped out of cooperative relations with others and incorporated exclusively inside the hierarchical and centralized structures of the firm. Large producers abandoned the traditional practice of purchasing parts from artisinal suppliers because they feared that the suppliers would gain access to proprietary information and use it to compete against them.

This kind of mistrust ultimately led to the decline of the artisinate in many manufacturing industrial districts, such as Cincinnati (Ross, 1985). Volume-producing firms wrested control over the labor process from skilled workers so as to be able to implement products and production processes that utilized simpler, more standardized machinery and less skilled, less expensive workers (Montgomery, 1979). These two developments, in turn, led to the total transformation of vocational education in the industry. Traditionally training had been organized by the artisanate (Ross, 1985; Montgomery, 1979). With its decline, companies made halting efforts to pick up the system themselves, but their production plans changed the type of workers that they needed (Elbaum, 1989; Jacoby, 1991). Ultimately, in those cases where the firm could not completely design away the need for skill, they wound up either stealing skilled workers from other companies or instituting informal on-the-job training regimes (Wagoner, 1968:346–47; BMMTPT, 1953).

The desire to standardize products, increase the scale of production, and vertically integrate ultimately brought product development almost completely in-house. Because producers wanted to avoid customization, innovation in the machine tool business rarely took place in direct response to communication with customers. Firms innovated during business cycle downturns: In an effort to create demand for their products, companies brought out new variations of their special machines, which made the old models obsolete (Brown, 1957: 411–12).

Finally, as production, training, and product development were brought increasingly under the control of individual companies, all vestiges of extra-firm forms of cooperation among machine tool producers disappeared. One can see this in the evolution of the activities of the trade association, the National Machine Tool Builders Association (NMTBA). The association was formed in 1902 in an effort by customizers to establish an institution that would foster cooperation on pricing in the industry to guard against harmful market behavior. But, with the general defeat of such efforts to create an alternative industrial order, the role and purpose of the trade association completely changed. Instead of attempting to foster cooperation among companies, the association was transformed into a public relations and lobbying organization (Wagoner, 1968). Within the framework of order in the machine tool industry, individual firms exclusively governed production.

First Adjustment Period: Mechanical Automation and the Military

By the middle of the 1920s, the framework of industrial order was firmly in place, and the industry whose development it shaped was extremely successful. Technologically, the kinds of special machines produced in high volume by the U.S. industry were unrivaled anywhere else in the world for their quality and sophistication. British, French, and German volume producers all looked to the United States for their specialized machine tools because their own industries did not produce machines capable of doing efficient high-volume work (Soltau, 1930). But at the very time that the American machines were being revered and (partially) imitated abroad, the industry that produced them began to undergo important changes at home. Two developments in the middle decades of the twentieth century—from roughly the mid-1930s to the mid-1970s—set processes of adjustment into motion. These were the implementation of mechanical automation in mass-production industries, and government–military interest in machine tools. As we shall see, the character of adjustment was importantly shaped by the framework of order that the period just described had put in place.

Mechanical automation completely transformed demand for machine tools in the United States. In the place of the independent, stand-alone, standardized, labor-saving machinery that the machine tool industry offered, nearly all mass producers, from automobiles to consumer electrical products, began to implement completely customized systems of linked machine tools in their production processes (Brown, 1957; Noble, 1984; Burawoy, 1979). Although these increased the productivity of the mass-producing user industries immeasurably, the various forms of mechanical automation these users demanded could not themselves be produced in volume, or even in small batches. In most cases they were contraptions completely customized for the particular needs of the user.

These changes in the character of demand were compounded by demand from the military, particularly after World War II with the development of the aerospace industry. Although they did not mass-produce in the same manner as the industries demanding mechanical automation, the military, and the prime defense contractors who did their manufacturing for them, consistently demanded production equipment from the machine tool industry with extremely special characteristics; for example, that used special metals and other (cutting) materials, or possessed particular dimensions and precision required for the manufacture of a military product (Melman, 1985).

RESPONSE. Both of these changes forced machine tool builders to move away from standard products to more customized ones and to relate to their customers in a different way. Because machine tool manufacture was governed primarily by hierarchically organized firms, the capacity to change in the industry was determined by the relative resources at the disposal of individual companies, rather than, for example, the collective resources at the disposal of the industry or of particular regions. This ultimately led to even greater concentration in the industry and the decimation of the secondary sector of small and medium-sized firms.

Greater concentration in the industry resulted from the high costs involved in the bidding process and subsequent construction of large-scale mechanical automation systems (LSMAS). To win an order—say, for a transfer line at an automobile company—machine tool producers had to invest considerable time and money in research, tooling, and machinery simply to be able to make a competitive bid. If they did not win the bid—which always went to the lowest bidder—then they were stuck with the investment. Moreover, the production of such systems had to be done in a fundamentally different and more costly manner than the standard tools that the firms in the industry had made their stock and trade. The LSMAS could not be produced in volume, nor could they be standardized. Customers wanted very particular constructions that would automate their particular production processes. However, to customize a system in this way, the machinery producers needed skilled workers, which they did not readily have—nor, as a result of previous developments, did they have access to a public system that could provide them. Hence, movement into the market for LSMAS involved extremely costly investments in training that firms had to bear entirely on their own.

Within the framework of order in the industry, large companies simply had a greater capacity to deal with these increased costs than did the smaller number of smaller producers within the core of the machine tool industry (Marx, n.d.). Generally, they had the capital needed to absorb the additional costs of entry and then still had enough left over to spread their risks by diversifying their businesses. Large firms such as Cincinnati Milacron, Giddings and Lewis, or the Ingersoll Milling Machine Company diversified in a number of ways: They broadened their product palettes so that they were not dependent upon a single line of machinery, and they offered both customized and standard products.

In contrast to the large firms, smaller companies within the core sector of the industry became increasingly trapped in a scissors situation. They could not afford to carry the bidding and training costs required to compete in custom markets, nor were they, owing to the exclusionary rules that framed the industry, able to cooperate by pooling together their resources. Yet at the same time, the larger the bigger competitors became, the more efficiently they could produce the standard items that remained in their product palette. Hopelessly outmatched, many smaller and medium-sized firms sold out to larger companies such as Milacron to get access to capital, or they merged their operations with one another to improve their capital base and gain economies of scale.

Either way, given the upheaval in the definition of markets and thus the possibility of disputes among firms, mergers and acquisitions were a constant feature of industrial practice in the machine tool industry throughout the postwar period: From 1944 to 1958 there were an average of eight mergers or acquisitions per year. The Bryant Chucking Grinder Company, for example, was purchased by the Ex-Cell-O Corporation in 1958. Between 1958 and 1968, the average number of mergers rose to 13.5 per year (Research Management Corporation, 1969:60). During the late 1960s and early 1970s, as growth in the main user industries began to slow down, this same dynamic began to affect even many of the large firms. Major mergers occurred between two Cleveland companies—National Acme and Cleveland Twist Drill—to form Acme Cleveland in 1968 and between the Cross Company of Fraser, Michigan, and the Kearny and Trecker Company of Milwaukee to form Cross and Trecker in 1978. Other firms sold out to larger manufacturing conglomerates such as Textron, Litton Industries, Colt, White Consolidated, and AMCA International of Canada. Indeed, by 1982, of the top fifteen companies in the industry, all were large, diversified machine tool producers, and at least nine were either themselves conglomerates or were owned by larger conglomerates (Holland, 1989).

This process of concentration among core firms in the industry was paralleled by the gradual decimation of the secondary sector of small and medium-sized firms. This followed from the way in which the increased costs involved in LSMAS production changed core firms' evaluations of risk. In the business of large-scale customization, cumulative knowledge became a competitive advantage. The more business that firms did with particular automobile producers, for example, the more they came to know about the auto manufacturer's purchasing and production strategies in general. This made it easier for companies to anticipate customers' needs and the possible paths of technological evolution in machine tool demand. Large firms jealously guarded these informational advantages. Old conjunctural subcontracting practices were abandoned because they were viewed as unsafe: Proprietary information could possibly "leak out" to the subcontractor this way and create the possibility that large LSMAS customers could use this to their advantage by playing smaller producers off larger ones to lower bidding prices. Over time, large machine tool producer efforts to keep this from happening killed the small secondary-sector sub-contractor. The increasing irrelevance of these producers in the industry comes through clearly in the statistics. Wagoner (1968:272) reported that, in 1947, the largest sixteen companies in the industry accounted for 43.2 percent of the industry's shipments, measured by value. In 1957, Brown (1957) claimed that the top forty companies in the machine tool industry accounted for 70 percent of the output in the industry. By 1981, however, the largest fifteen companies accounted for 73 percent of total shipments (CMTI, 1983).

All of these changes followed from the firm-dominated strategic calculus that the framework of order in the industry created. Significantly, the calculus made for an extremely successful industry. Large American producers pioneered many of the pathbreaking technologies employed worldwide in LSMAS. Their close work with the military in the development of special machinery produced many advanced forms of automation technology, including numerical control (Noble, 1984; Holland, 1989, chapter 3). Throughout the postwar period the industry was consistently among the largest and most technologically sophisticated in the world.

Second Adjustment Period: The End of Mass Production

The U.S. machine tool industry was singularly incapable of adjusting to the new forms of market competition that emerged in the 1980s. Two factors combined in this decade to transform completely the U.S. machine tool markets. First, firms engaged in the mass production of standardized goods found that their markets had become saturated. Partly as a cause and partly as an effect of this, markets that had once been stable began to fragment and break up. Competition from producers in Japan, Europe, and many newly industrializing countries caused the pace of technological change (particularly in micro-electronics) to accelerate in all industries, including machine tools. Product life cycles shortened dramatically at the same time that the costs of developing the new technologies began to increase (Piore and Sabel, 1984). Second, as an immediate response to increases in the level of risk that firms confronted on their markets, producers sought to reduce their fixed costs in manufacturing by subcontracting work to outside suppliers. On the one hand, this allowed them to be less vulnerable to a dramatic loss of market share at any point; on the other hand, the use of specialist subcontractors enabled them to spread the costs of development in specialized technologies (see Sabel, Kern, and Herrigel, 1990).

These changes qualitatively transformed the demand for machine tools in both of the areas of U.S. strength. Instability and rapid technological change in previously stable markets caused demand for rigid forms of LSMAS to evaporate completely. In its place, user firms demanded more flexible machine tools that, with the aid of computer numerical control, could be repeatedly reprogrammed to operate on a variety of production tasks. Moreover, in most cases user firms continued to demand customization, insisting upon special adjustments and features on the machinery itself or in its operating software. At the same time, with the decentralization of manufacturing operations, the demand for standard machine tools with computer numerical control (CNC) increased dramatically. Small and medium-sized specialist supplier firms and job shops found that computer numerical control standard machines were more precise and flexible than conventional machines. Moreover, as the price of CNC technology declined and as the level of work done by small and medium-sized companies in decentralized manufacturing networks increased, the market for all varieties of standardized CNC lathes, milling machines, and machining centers grew to be astronomical.

RESPONSE. American machine tool companies have not been successful in entering these new markets. They have ceded the high end to Japanese, German, Italian, and Swiss manufacturers and the low end to Japanese, Taiwanese, and, to a smaller extent, German and Italian producers. The share taken by imports in the total U.S. market for machine tools has been over 50 percent since 1984 (Holland, 1989; Friedman, 1988). American producers have had difficulty adjusting because the principles of order that shape the industry—no cooperation, dispute resolution through merger, and companies defining themselves as firms radically independent of one another and of society—led producers initially to overlook changes in the character of demand and then subsequently prevented them from responding competitively.

In standard machine markets, as we have seen, U.S. companies traditionally organized production on the assumption that there would be little competition in their product area. Production processes were rigid and vertically integrated, and companies eschewed customization. The larger and more diversified that firms became in the postwar period, the more entrenched these practices in standard machinery production became. American companies made a great deal of money off their military and mechanical automation operations and tended to let their standard machine operations evolve at a very slow rate. As a result, they lost touch with the market.

Japanese producers recognized the potential demand in the small metal-working sector in the mid-1970s, but it took U.S. producers until the early 1980s to respond with a downsized CNC unit of their own—White Sundstrand produced one of the first American CNC machining centers in 1980—and when they did, the response followed the logic of the old production practices exactly. Rather than produce a range of machining centers with different electric motors and gearboxes to fulfill different needs (perhaps saving on costs by purchasing the different motors from subcontractors), White Sundstrand chose to make one highly flexible machine that could be easily produced with traditional volume methods entirely in-house. The company soon discovered that this could not compete with Japanese firms that were producing a broad variety of different types of well-engineered, general-purpose tools that they could easily and quickly tailor to the needs of a particular customer (Ong, 1983).

The story of blindness and rigidity in the custom machinery market is more subtle but just as devastating. American firms developed production and product development strategies in both commercial and military markets that were bureaucratic and risk-avoiding just as competition and technological change in the industry began to reward risk-takers. The picture of the U.S. commercial machine tool markets during the 1960s and 1970s is one of increasingly large, bureaucratically organized machine tool sellers, in concentrated markets, courting even larger, more bureaucratically organized buyers. Successful machine tool companies knew that purchasers were reluctant to take risks on promising new technologies with no track record because the internal reward system in the largest corporations punished failed innovations. Machine tool salespeople, who needed to sell because of their own internal reward structures, learned to offer what they knew would sell: usually older and well-tested technologies. With little competition or trust within or among sellers or buyers, there was no pressure to act otherwise (*American Machinist*, 1986).

Military work compounded this propensity to avoid risk, only here the result was the development of incredibly advanced machining technologies. Government procurement in machine tools, as well as tremendous amounts of government-funded R&D in the industry, went overwhelmingly to the largest firms in the machine tool industry. Military contractors demanded extremely advanced machining techniques and consistently encouraged machine tool firms to push the frontiers of automation technologies. Contracts were always long term and extremely lucrative. The government paid for performance and was willing to overlook costs. Thus, whereas in commercial markets firms actively sought to minimize risks on the market, in military markets there was virtually no risk involved (Melman, 1985).

The problem, of course, was one that has turned out to be common among many large hierarchically structured American corporations (e.g., Boynton and Victor, 1991). When commercial purchasers of customized machine tools fell into crisis and began to demand advanced forms of production technologies, American machine tool producers were in no position to respond because their divisions producing advanced technology had little connection to those producing for civilian markets. Making linkages between them took time—precisely what the tumultuous and rapidly changing market environment did not allow—and the possibility of turning to cooperation with outsiders was mistrusted and in any case not considered to be in line with the principles of order that governed the industry. Years of bureaucratic conservatism, concentration, and vertical insulation left U.S. machine tool companies, despite their many resources, frozen in their tracks. European and Japanese producers, who organized their business in a different way, turned out to be far better at innovating and delivering advanced commercial technologies at acceptable prices.

Before asking the question of whether or not the firm-based form of industrial order in the United States will be able to recover from its present crisis, it will be interesting to look more closely at the evolution of industrial order in the

German case. German machine tool producers followed a different path of development in the twentieth century, which has made it possible for them to take advantage of current machine tool market opportunities.

Industrial Order in the German Machine Tool Industry

The Germans have a tradition of machine tool production equally as long and distinguished as that in the United States. An independent industry producing machine tools probably emerged slightly earlier in Germany than in America. The first company to specialize entirely on the production of machine tools was founded in the 1850s, and there was a wave of new companies in the 1870s following the unification of the German Reich. Most early nineteenth-century German machine tools were imitations of British and American designs, but by the early years of the twentieth century German companies were producing machines that the rest of the world imitated (Buxbaum, 1919). The actual tools that German firms produced tended on the whole to be heavier and far more flexible and general purpose than their American counterparts. Where U.S. producers continually sought to restrict the amount of machining operations that a single machine could accomplish, Germans tended to build more and more operations into their machines (e.g., Mommertz, 1981:140).

The Germans made more flexible machine tools because they sold in very different markets than existed in the United States. The quality of demand in Germany differed because the political, legal, social, and economic background conditions in Germany were far less favorable to the emergence of large-scale mass production than they were in America. German markets were fragmented by different regional, political, and economic boundaries and traditions not only within the Imperial Reich itself, but throughout Europe. This kind of fragmentation made it difficult to sell standardized products, and most producers, large and small, did not.

Indeed, in a way that is ironic only when compared to the United States, high-volume manufacturing was a niche phenomenon in Germany. Among machine-tool-using industries it was found primarily in weapons production and in the relatively small industries involved with the production of sewing machines, bicycles, office equipment, and, beginning in the 1920s, automobiles. But even in the case of these volume-production industries, the contrast with mass production practiced in the United States was dramatic. In 1929, for example, Germany was fifth in world motor vehicle production with a total output of 149,000 units. That same year, the U.S. industry produced 5,358,000 units (Overy, 1975). No auto manufacturer in Germany produced more than ten vehicles per day in the 1920s; no American firm produced less than forty vehicles per day (Soltau, 1930).

This peculiarity of German growth is significant because it means that the kind of struggle between incompatible visions of industrial production that plagued late nineteenth-century America and split the machine tool industry into two warring camps never emerged in Germany—at least not in the late nineteenth and early twentieth century when the industrial order in the machine tool industry came into being. The absence of mass production as an option in most industries made low-volume, flexible, specialty-product-oriented production an uncontested strategic orientation among both users and producers of machine tools, large and small.

It is true that beyond a common orientation toward customization and craft-based production, real practical and organizational differences existed between large and small firms in Germany. But these differences were prevented from becoming a source of conflict through the regional political and economic structure of the Imperial Reich. Large firms were primarily a regional phenomenon in *fin de siecle* Germany, and they were located in the Ruhr Valley, central Prussia, old court and trading cities (such as Hanover, Kassel, Augsburg, and Munich), and the Saarland.[3] Firms were large in these regions because they could draw on very little preindustrial infrastructure of artisans or home producers as suppliers. They were forced to produce everything that went into their product themselves (Kocka, 1980). In regions where there was a rich preindustrial infrastructure—for example, Württemberg, the Kingdom of Saxony, southern Hesse, or Baden—industrialization occurred within that structure, and the size of firms continued to be quite small. Moreover, most of the regions of small firms, with the exception of the Rhineland, were located outside of Prussia in states that entered the German Reich beginning only after 1866. One of the conditions of entry was that these regions retain sovereignty over their tax, education, and industrial policies. This structure effectively blocked all important background framework changes that could have made large and small producers play by the same rules (Herrigel, 1990, chapter 2).

Thus, in effect, industrializing Germany was replete with regional economies, each dominated by different sectoral mixtures of highly specialized, low-volume producers. Producers of different types of specialty machine tools emerged because they serviced different kinds of local demand. For example, producers in Württemberg made small precision machine tools for the fine mechanical and special machine industries in that region; producers in the Kingdom of Saxony manufactured machines suited for use in the local general machine and woolen textile industries; those in Berlin specialized in producing machine tools for the electromechanical, heavy machine, and weapons industries. So it went. The major centers of machine tool production coincided with the major agglomerations of industrial production in Germany. The largest concentrations of machine tool producers were, moreover, located in the regions dominated by small and medium-sized producers (Buxbaum, 1919).

Given this varied political and economic background in Germany, the problem posed to producers during the period in which the modern German machine tool industry was created proved very different from that which U.S. producers confronted. The Germans needed to discover a way to establish a framework of order within and among communities of highly flexible craft producers.

The Framework of Order

IDENTITY. Producers constructing a framework of industrial order in Germany thought about the boundaries of both the company and of industry in an entirely different way from their volume-producing American counterparts. The problems inherent in following a craft production-based strategy of customization led machine tool producers to assume that reliance on other firms and on other institutions in society was a necessary part of industrial practice. These bonds of mutual dependence engendered the belief that machine tool producers were part of a community.

Reliance on other producers was an unavoidable part of the strategy of customization. As a practical matter in the densely populated industrial districts of small and medium-sized firms it was extremely difficult to centralize production completely and to customize continuously at the same time. Vertical integration of craft production meant that a firm had to hire enough skilled workers to produce all elements of their machines in-house. The business cycle made this a risky strategy because it was fatal to lay off workers during downturns. Once let go into the labor market of the industrial district, such workers invariably would be lost to other firms. The best way to avoid this kind of disruption was simply to limit levels of employment by procuring special parts from the outside. Producers could use such purchases either to supplement their own capacity in periods of peak demand, or simply to provide materials that the firm was unable to produce itself—such as foundry castings. Either way, subcontracting was preferable to investing in more productive capacity than the market could absorb (Soltau, 1930; Pastor, 1937).

Moreover, the same logic that made these firms subcontract made them become subcontractors as well. Because companies were not completely autarkic as producers, they often did work for other machinery producers on a subcontract basis because they had more appropriate machinery, or simply temporary excess capacity. The ability to complete a custom order often depended upon the knowledge that a company could get something done at another machinery manufacturer within the region.

All of this meant that producers tended to think of themselves not as a group of independent firms coincidentally lumped in a common category because they produced the same technology, as was the case in the United States. Rather, they understood themselves to be a community of producers. The mode of interaction that underlay this self-conception, not surprisingly, resulted in a different, more egalitarian, industrial structure than was the case in the United States. Instead of dualism between large and small firms, there was a great deal of interdependence among firms of comparable size. Seventy percent of those employed in the 332 establishments in the industry in 1926, for example, worked in firms with fewer than 500 employees. Sixty-three percent of all employees worked in establishments employing between 30 and 500 workers. Only 20 percent worked in companies employing more than 1000 workers.

Predictably enough, the large firms in the industry were those that produced "American style" machine tools—mostly turret lathes and milling machines. Five manufacturers dominated that segment—Ludwig Loewe and Fritz Werner of Berlin and Wanderer, Pittler, and Reinecker in Saxony. These companies prospered primarily on the basis of demand from state arsenals and other volume-producing industries. They had been able to gain market power in their segments by licensing the designs of particular American machines useful in the mass production of weapons (Buxbaum, 1919; Ludwig Loewe & Co., 1929; Dominik, 1938). Companies were even able to standardize their machines and produce in series. The interesting thing about these firms, apart from the special character of their demand, is that they remained relatively isolated from the other smaller specialty producers in the German industry. Because their machines were so closely modeled after American designs, the firms never fostered a secondary sector of second- and third-rate producers as had companies in the United States. The reason: The segment of the market at the peak of the business cycle that the large German producers could not serve was generally serviced by American imports (Soltau, 1930; Pastor, 1937; Mengel, 1931).

The mutual dependence and sense of community that bound producers in the German industry together was enhanced by the multiple ways that these producers were also linked to a variety of institutions in society. The same kinds of risks associated with craft-based customization that led producers to rely on one another also led them (often in cooperation with craft producers from other local industries) to attempt to socialize many of their costs by constructing a broad infrastructure of institutions providing services to all producers. Four institutions in particular were important.

The first important institution was an extensive public system for vocational education. Emergence of the German dual system of industrial training in 1897—which combined practical training in actual workshops with public vocational training—represented a victory of an alliance of industrial craft producers and artisans over the forces of liberalism in Germany. Artisan organizations were entrusted by the state with the authority to oversee and organize the education of skilled workers. In return for a material and functional basis for survival, along with political legitimacy for their organizations, artisans trained skilled workers and thereby ensured that the costs of training highly skilled workers would not have to be borne by individual companies in the industrial sector (Schriewer, 1986).

The second important institution consisted of regional and national research institutes dedicated to the technological concerns of industry. The various German states sponsored the development of technical universities dedicated to the dissemination of advanced technologies into the economy. The Technical University of Berlin and, later, technical schools in Aachen and Stuttgart developed very important laboratories dedicated to technical research on problems related to the machine tool industry. Services provided by the technical universities were further complemented by more locally based institutes for applied technology (now known as *Fachhochschulen*). The most important of these for the machine tool industry were located in Esslingen, Chemnitz, and Remscheid. Initially, these institutes were established by the producers themselves, often with other metalworking-machinery-user firms, to address in a cooperative way the applied technological problems of common concern and to educate technicians and engineers. Although financial support gradually was taken over by the state, these regional institutes became a crucial source of external know-how for small and specialized individual firms.

Third, small and medium-sized manufacturers also created a cooperative banking system to improve their access to capital. Much like small manufacturers in the United States at the time, German small producers were disadvantaged in the national capital markets because they provided smaller returns on investment than did the larger and rapidly growing Ruhr and Berlin combines. But unlike the Populists in the United States, the broadly based late nineteenth-century cooperative banking movement in Germany succeeded in establishing a system that pooled the resources of local small industrialists and artisans for collective investment needs. These "banks" actually were institutions that mediated between individual small industrialists and artisans and the money and credit markets controlled by the larger banks. In 1895, the Prussian state government helped create a Central Bank for Cooperative Societies (*Central-genossenschaftskasse*) in Berlin, which pooled capital from the local cooperative banks so as to provide even more clout in the credit markets to the economic and social interests served by those banks (Heiligenstadt, 1910; Gemming, 1911).

Finally, at the turn of the century, the machine tool industry formed its own trade association, the *Verein Deutscher Werkzeugmaschinenfabriken e.V.* (VDW) Aside from the many political and service tasks that this association performed for the industry, it grew to be intimately involved in the coordination of research. Most precompetitive research projects among firms that were members of the association were managed and coordinated by the association. Also important, the VDW ran the Leipzig (later Hanover) trade fair for machine tools, the largest in the world (Kappel, 1966).

Exclusionary Rules and Dispute Adjudication

By itself, the fact that producers understood themselves to be part of a community that included not only other producers but also important supporting institutions was not enough to provide stability in the industry. The major problem that producers faced was the tendency for competition among firms to degenerate into competitive pricing, underbidding, poaching, and so forth during cyclical downturns. The threat of market chaos, described earlier among the American customizers, needed to somehow be conquered before the German industry could stably reproduce itself.

This problem plagued German machine tool producers—along with the rest of the mechanical engineering trades—a great deal in the three decades preceding World War I. Beginning in the early 1900s, efforts were initiated by the general machinery industry trade association Verein Deutscher Maschianbau Anstalten (VDMA) to regulate competition through the construction of industry-wide guidelines for delivery and payment. These conditions did not attempt to set prices or limit production in the industry—both the range and the variation of products were too vast for that—but they did seek to remove the terms of sale, form of payment, and delivery from competition.

The problem of poaching was directly addressed through the creation of specialized confederations, or "finishing associations" (Liefmann, 1932). Here member firms agreed to specialize in one or several lines of machinery while ceding other lines to other members of the association. The consensus in these agreements was that all parties agreed not to poach on other members' technologies, even in bad periods of the business cycle. The Germans rarely codified these specialization arrangements into formal cartels because the evolution and change in technology was so completely fluid that the construction of a legal arrangement would only have substituted rigidity for instability. Even so, the kind of arrangements they established would have been illegal under U.S. antitrust law. Instead of binding one another legally, firms simply agreed to commit themselves to continual negotiations over the definition and demarcation of markets (RDI, 1929; Muellenseifen, 1926; Schultz-Mehrin, 1926).

This arrangement solidified a framework of order in the industry. First, poaching practices and technological diversification were by agreement excluded from the industry. This not only had the positive effect of preventing the breakdown of market competition but it also stimulated innovation in the industry. By forbidding diversification in economic downturns, the associations forced companies to remain innovative in their chosen specialty or leave the industry. Second, because the commitment to specialize and not poach was simultaneously a commitment to engage in continuous negotiation with other producers about the terms and boundaries of that commitment, a procedure for the adjudication of disputes in the industry was thereby established.

Ultimately, the process of adjudicating disputes was institutionalized in the Norm Council of the VDW trade association. All manufacturers in the industry sent representatives to this council where they engaged in negotiation that defined the relationship between their various specialties. Once agreement was reached, all received the right to attach the association's quality stamp to their machines—at once a symbol of technical quality and industrial order. This institutionalized practice of negotiation was a crucial condition for the reproduction of the community identity in the industry. Because it effectively eliminated merger as a mechanism of stabilization, the system of permanently negotiated specialization blocked the emergence of firms with disproportionate market power.

Governance Mechanisms

Within this framework of industrial order, normal interaction in the industry virtually conflated the boundaries between individual company and society. Correspondingly, the industry governed itself with overlapping mixtures of market and hierarchy: A firm making a customized machine for a customer—in which customer, client, and other suppliers collaborated on the design—were linked together exclusively by neither contract nor authority but by both of these together. In addition to these, the framework of order in the industry also created conditions under which certain types of governance could only occur through relations of trust and loyalty.

For example, the interpenetrated division of labor between the individual specialized craft firm and the infrastructure of the industry as a whole was self-reinforcing in a way that made trust crucial. The more specialized that each firm became, the more that the pursuit of its particular interests required loyalty to the common understandings of appropriate market behavior, which the framework of order had created, and defense of those superordinate institutions—

training institutes, banks, trade associations, and government agencies—that safeguarded the interests of the industry as a whole. If participants in the system did not believe or trust that others would embrace the same cooperative rules of the game that they did, the entire system simply would not work.

First Adjustment Period: Mass Production and Mechanical Automation

The system described above began to fall into place during the 1920s. By that time, German machine tools were already renowned for their high quality, flexibility, and durability. By 1913, Germany had become the second largest producer of machine tools in the world, behind the United States, and the world's biggest exporter. During the first third of the twentieth century, the United States, Britain, and Germany regularly accounted for over 80 percent of the world market in machine tools. American firms served the world with standardized, semi-dedicated, labor-saving machinery for volume producers, while the Germans provided general-purpose machines to low-volume and specialist producers (Froehlich, 1914; Mengel, 1931; Pastor, 1937; Levy, 1933).

Differences in technology and export orientation between the two countries reflect the fact that German producers concentrated on markets where there were highly skilled workers and little mass production, whereas the American producers did precisely the opposite. This division of labor, already unstable in the 1920s as a result of changes wrought by the war, changed over the course of the following four decades. The Nazi economic recovery program, preparation for war, and, finally, the reconstruction of Europe and the formation of the Common Market transformed both German and European markets. Various market conditions were created that made mass production on a Europe-wide basis possible with a pervasiveness and at a scale that had never before existed (Piore and Sabel, 1984). Market conditions in Europe and the United States began to converge in the post–World War II period. Demand for LSMAS and "American-style" labor-saving machinery dominated the order books of machine tool producers.

RESPONSE. The German industry proved surprisingly able to adapt to the new character of machine tool demand. Even though the ravages of war and the division of Germany caused the collapse of the five largest American-style machinery-producing firms mentioned above, the number of firms in the West German industry exceeded the number from 1926 by over 100 in 1970. Employment in the industry grew to 125,000 workers in 1970. Indeed, there is much evidence to suggest that the industry became even less concentrated during the postwar period—particularly after the formation of the European Common Market (Baumann, 1964; Daley and Jones, 1980). By 1970, the West German machine tool industry was not only the world's largest exporter of machine tools but also the largest absolute producer of machine tools in the world.

As in the U.S. case, the framework of order in the industry shaped the character of German adjustment. This was true in two ways. First, because they could spread costs across an array of firms and supporting institutions, the relatively smaller German producers were not overwhelmed by the large costs associated with the production of LSMAS. Second, the framework of order had created a dynamic of practice in the industry that simply prevented certain kinds of costs that had plagued their U.S. counterparts from emerging.

As an example, training costs in Germany were partially absorbed by the dual system of vocational training. Moreover, German tool makers, unlike their U.S. counterparts, were already richly supplied with skilled workers because their previous strategy had not been devoted to their elimination. Furthermore, many R&D costs were absorbed or shared through the continuous exchange of know-how with other firms in noncompeting lines, with faculty members and students at the regional research institutes, and through joint "precompetitive" research projects at technical universities organized and administered by the VDW.

Significantly, firms also continued to learn from their suppliers. Although most manufacturers preferred not to subcontract the pieces of the machinery which carried the "know-how" of the firm, many companies did maintain long-term trusting relations with suppliers. In contrast to producers in America, West German companies were not as aggressive about trying to eliminate the threat of competition from suppliers to protect their proprietary knowledge as customizers. They preferred to coordinate and control competition rather than eliminate it. New entrants did not survive long without entering into the complex process of negotiation within the industry over the definition of relationships among firms and technology. In this way they were included in the community of producers. This obligated them to abide by the principles of order that governed it. But, importantly, it also made adherence to some of the principles, such as the use of trust as a governance mechanism, possible as such: Newcomer identification with the community established a sense of common fate without which trust and cooperation would be impossible.

Second Adjustment Period: Crisis of Mass Production

As in the U.S. case, the machine tool industry in Germany suffered considerable turmoil when the long postwar boom in the international economy came to an end. Market saturation, new competitors—above all the Japanese—new technologies, high development costs, and rapidly changing markets all transformed the character of demand in the industry as well as the conditions under which competition took place. The difference between the German and American case is that the German industry was able to recoup its initial losses. Much of this, again, can be explained by the character of order in the industry.

Several developments combined to throw the industry into crisis. First, domestic investment in machine tools in West Germany stagnated throughout the 1970s. In 1975, domestic investment in capital goods, including machine tools, was 7 percent below the level of 1970 in the electromechanical industry, 22 percent below the level in the machinery and automobile industries, and more than 35 percent below 1970 levels in the metal products sector of the economy. Moreover, machine tools declined as a percentage of total capital goods investment throughout the 1970s in West Germany, from 41 percent to 35 percent (Horstmann, 1984).

Innovation in the industry slowed down as a result of this stagnation. Because the demand for machine tools was far lower than the potential supply, prices were driven downwards. Companies, especially small and medium-sized ones, found little incentive, and as the decade wore on, they had increasingly little capital for experimentation with design. This tendency to avoid the risks and costs involved with technological innovation in the 1970s was compounded by a shift in the direction of West German exports. To compensate for stagnation in the more advanced industrial markets, German producers found that they had to enter markets in Eastern European and in developing nations more extensively than they had ever before. The demand in these markets was not terribly sophisticated, and firms found that increasing portions of their output was in machinery that had been in their product palette for a considerable period of time (Borst, 1976; Horstmann, 1984).

When investment demand for machine tools began to pick up at the end of the decade in West Germany and in the broader EEC, the Germans were initially unable to compete with Japanese producers in markets for CNC equipment. In 1980, some 73 percent of the domestic demand for computer numerical control equipment was supplied by imports. Japanese producers grabbed 43 percent of the import market for CNC lathes that year. What was worse, the West Germans appeared to have completely missed the significance of CNC technology. Very few companies in the industry even manufactured the technology. In 1980, the Japanese produced 22,000 CNC machines while German producers made only 4800 (Handelsblatt, 1986; SHfdM, 1987, 1985). By 1984, however, the picture had completely changed. The percentage of domestic demand for CNC equipment supplied by imports fell from 73 percent to 30 percent. Moreover, in that year, West German machine tool builders produced 10,600 CNC machines. This was 34 percent of the total value of turnover in the industry and more than the combined total of American, British, and French machine tool producers measured in terms of units. By 1986, 53 percent of the value of output in metalcutting machines was accounted for by CNC. Machine tool producers in West Germany have exported more CNC machines than were imported every year since 1981.

This relatively rapid turnaround was possible because of the availability of technological know-how in the public space created by the framework of order in the industry. In the early 1980s when it appeared that the West Germans had been overtaken by technological change in the industry, all of the institutions and actors involved in the industrial order focused their attention on CNC technology and the problem of microelectronic applications on machine tools. The VDW and the machinery producers' association (VDMA) worked with the Federal Ministry of Research and Technology (BMFT), together with other associations, to develop a special subsidy program that allowed small and medium-sized firms to discount all research and application expenses related to CNC technology on their machines (Ziegler, 1989). Innumerable joint "precompetitive research" projects were conducted at the major technical universities. The regional government of Baden-Württemberg launched a significant program to extend the consulting services provided by regional research institutes to small and medium-sized companies without increasing the cost of those services.

The machinery producers association and the metalworkers union (IG Metall) each advocated the need for a qualification offensive in vocational education and advocated cooperation in the construction of a curriculum that would educate German skilled workers in computer programming. Interfirm cooperation was also a central aspect of the industry's adjustment strength. By reducing their fixed costs, and relying on the specialized know-how of outside suppliers, firms were able to integrate the new technology and bring products to market faster with less cost and greater flexibility. Typically, machine tool producers cultivated a core circle of suppliers with which they could work very intimately and provide them with know-how. Important suppliers to the machine tool industry, such as Siemens, which supplied the industry with the computer numerical controllers that they placed on their machines, worked individually with companies to help them adapt CNC technology to their special machine tool products. In most cases, the transfer of know-how goes in both directions: Machine tool firms provide their suppliers with mechanical engineering know-how, often by collaborating on production engineering of single parts and subassemblies, in exchange for the specialists' expertise in electronics, plastics, or hydraulics, among other areas.

This list of factors could be easily extended. No single factor alone can be isolated as "most significant" in facilitating the industry's successful adjustment. Rather, successful adaptation in the industry in many ways was produced by the logic of order in the industry itself.

Conclusion: Industrial Order and Industrial Adjustment

The comparative historical experience of machine tool producers in the United States and Germany over the course of the twentieth century is a good case for developing the notion of industrial order. Given different political and economic starting points, producers of machine tools created very different framework rules for the way they practiced their trade. In each case, producers shared common beliefs about what industry was and how it legitimately related to the rest of society. Moreover, the different frameworks of industrial order in the two countries created a repertoire of governance mechanisms that shaped the character of adjustment in the industry throughout the twentieth century. Thus, even though the German and American machine tool industries faced the same technological challenges in the middle of the twentieth century, because they were different forms of industrial order they responded (successfully) in radically different ways. The framework of order in the United States made strategies of adjustment, which resulted in concentration and vertical integration, appear obvious and inevitable to American firms. In Germany, under the same technological pressures in their product markets, not only were such strategies not inevitable, they were not pursued.

A similar logic was at work during the 1980s, only this time without mutual success. All comparative evidence, in Germany as well as Japan (e.g., Friedman, 1988), suggests that an industry that practices according to rules that exclude cooperation, that foment mistrust and hostility among producers by resorting to contests of strength on the market to resolve disputes, and that delegitimate the potential contributions to production that players in society outside the boundaries of the firm can make will not be able to survive in the current international environment. And, yet, it was precisely according to such rules of practice that the American machine tool industry attempted to cope with the transformation of world markets in the 1980s.

Many ironies abound in the case of the U.S. machine tool industry. It has for most of the twentieth century been conventional among students of industry in the United States to think of the machine tool industry as the great exception inside an industrial economy. Unlike other industries, machine tool producers were not mass producers; they relied disproportionately on skilled workers; they were flexible. A straight kind of market logic has always been employed to explain the distinctiveness of the industry: Because their market was for a single purpose—often unique machine that let their users efficiently mass-produce—machine tool producers were forever blocked from implementing mass-production techniques themselves. Following this logic, many at the beginning of the 1980s believed that if any U.S. sector were to have the inner resources to compete in a turbulent world market that seemed to favor flexibility, it would be the machine tool industry. This kind of thinking made the total collapse of the industry that much more shocking—and, perhaps, the success of others that much more suspicious.

But, if we put the folk understanding of the industry aside, the comparison with Germany makes it easier to see what kind of an industry the U.S. machine tool industry actually was. That is, only in an industrial economy in which the rules of industrial practice are defined as they have been in the United States is the machine tool industry reasonably considered a craft-production industry. In comparison to the radically decentralized craft production that exists within the framework of order in the German industry, U.S. toolmakers don't look like a craft-production-based industry at all. Indeed, the story of the development of the American industry has much more similarity with the organizational forms prevalent in other American industries than it does with the foreign competitors it confronts in its own sectoral markets.

This point casts the entire question of adjustment in the current U.S. industry into a very particular light. The challenge that the industry faces is not simply a technological one. Nor is it rightly characterized, as has been done, as a problem of unfair competition on the part of major competitors (see the excellent discussion of the Houdaille Industries case in Holland, 1989:171–222).

Rather, the challenge to the United States posed by German and Japanese competitors is to the way in which producers in America have traditionally defined the rules of the game in industry and to the way that they have under-stood the proper relationship between industry and society. The Germans and Japanese are not playing *unfairly* by engaging in cooperative research and production or by utilizing the resources of extra-firm institutions and governments—they are playing according to different rules. The relationship between industry and society exists within a different framework of order, and they view the relationship between industry and society differently. If the U.S. industry, or what is left of it, is going to compete in world markets as they are currently defined, manufacturers are going to have to rethink who they are and what the proper boundaries between industrial practice and the rest of society should or can legitimately be. Finally, for the achievement of this task, the Germans exist less as a model that can be directly transferred, than as an example of possibilities that the Americans, because of the way their indigenous understanding of industrial order shapes their capacity to recognize available strategies, are unable to see.

Notes

This research was supported by a grant from the German Marshall Fund of the United States. An earlier, longer, and subsequently much revised version of this chapter appeared in Eckardt Hildebrant, ed., *Betriebliche Sozialeverfassungen* (Berlin: Edition Sigma, 1991).

1. According to Stephen Holmes (1988:227): "Constitutions [are] binding in a possibility-engendering way." Russell Hardin (1989:115) similarly remarks: "The point of a constitution is to tie our hands in certain ways in order to discipline them to more productive use."

2. "Like it or not," writes Ackerman about the way that the Constitution has shaped the character and possibilities for political self-reflection in the United States, "it is these symbols and structures, not any of my own devising, that set the terms of my own efforts at political communication with my fellow citizens" (Ackerman, 1988:156).

3. Eighty-one percent of the top 100 firms were located in these regions in 1908 (see Herrigel, 1990:202, n. 112).

References

Ackerman, Bruce. (1988). "Neo-Federalism?" In Jon Elster and Rune Slagstad (eds.), *Constitutionalism and Democracy* (pp. 153–94). New York: Cambridge University Press.

American Machinist. (1986, January). "GM Studies US Machine Tool Firms. One Problem: The Way Automakers Buy."

Baumann, Hans. (1964). *Strukturwandlungen des deutschen Maschinenbaus*. Munich: IFO.

Berk, Gerald. (1987). *Corporations and Politics: American Railroads, 1870–1916* (Doctoral dissertation, MIT).

Borst, Manfred. (1976). "Nur nicht den Kopf haengen lassen!" In *Werkstatt und Betrieb: Zeitschrift fuer Maschinenbau, Konstruktion und Fertigung*, 109(4), 193–94.

Boynton, Andrew, and Bart Victor. (1991, Fall). "Beyond Flexibility: Building and Managing Dynamically Stable Organization." *California Management Review*, pp. 53–66.

Bradach, Jeffrey, and Robert Eccles. (1989). "Price, Authority, and Trust: From Ideal Types to Plural Forms." *Annual Review of Sociology*, 15, 97–118.

British Metalworking Machine Tool Productivity Team (BMMTPT). (1953). *Metalworking Machine Tools: Report of a Productivity Team Representing the British Machine Tool Industry, Which Visited the United States of America in 1951*. London: British Productivity Council, pp. 25ff.

Broehl, Wayne. (1959). *Precision Valley*. Englewood Cliffs, N.J.: Prentice-Hall.
Brown, William. (1957). "Innovation in the Machine Tool Industry." *Quarterly Journal of Economics*, 3(71), 406–24.
Burawoy, Michael. (1979). *Manufacturing Consent*. Chicago: University of Chicago Press.
Buxbaum, Berthold. (1919). "Der deutsche Werkzeugmaschinen- und Werkzeugbau im 19 Jahrhundert." *Beitraege zur Geschichte der Technik und Industrie*, 9, 97–129.
Buxbaum, Berthold. (1920). "Der Amerikanische Werkzeugmaschinen- und Werkzeugbau in 18 und 19. Jahrhundert." *Beitraege zur Geschichte der Technik und Industrie*, 10, 121–54.
Chandler, Alfred. (1977). *The Visible Hand*. Cambridge, Mass.: Harvard University Press.
Committee on the Machine Tool Industry (CMTI), Manufacturing Studies Board, Commission on Engineering and Technical Systems, National Research Council. (1983). *The US Machine Tool Industry and the Defense Industrial Base*. Washington, D.C.: National Academy Press.
Daley, Anne, and Daniel T. Jones. (1980). "The Machine Tool Industry in Britain, Germany and the United States." *National Institute Economic Review*, 92, 56.
Dominik, Hans. (1938). *Fritz Werner AG Berlin* (Serie: Deutsche Grossbetriebe Band 17: Der Werkzeugmaschinen- und Werkzeugbau). Leipzig: J. J. Arnd.
Elbaum, Bernard. (1989). "Why Apprenticeship Persisted in Britain But Not in the United States." *Journal of Economic History*, 49(2), 337–49.
Enquette Kommission. (1928). *Wanglungen in den Wirtschaftlichen Organisationsformen; Entwicklungslinien der industriellen und gewerblichen Kartellierung: Arbeitsplan, Maschinenbau*. Berlin: E. S. Mittler & Sohn.
Friedman, David. (1988). *The Misunderstood Miracle*. Ithaca, N.Y.: Cornell University Press.
Froehlich, Fr. (1914). *Stellung der deutsche Maschinenindustrie im deutschen Wirtschaft und auf dem Weltmarkt*. Charlottenberg: VDMA.
Geier, Frederick V. (1949). *The Coming of the Machine Tool Age—The Tool Builders of Cincinnati*. New York: Newcomen Society Publication.
Gemming, Alfred. (1911). *Das Handwerkgenossenschaftswesen in Wuerttemberg*. Stuttgart: Verlag von Ferdinand Enke.
Grossman, Sanford J., and Oliver D. Hart. (1986). "The Costs and Benefits of Ownership: A Theory of Vertical and Lateral Integration." *Journal of Political Economy*, 94(4), 691–719.
Handelsblatt. (1986, February 4).
Hardin, Russell. (1989). "Why a Constitution?" In Bernard Grofman and Donald Wittman (eds.), *The Federalist Papers and the New Institutionalism* (pp. 100–120). New York: Agathon Press.
Hattam, Victoria. (1990). "Economic Visions and Political Strategies: American Labor and the State, 1865–1896." *Studies in American Political Development*, Vol. 4.
Heiligenstadt, C. (1910). "Die Preussische Centralgenossenschaftskasse." In Conrad's *Handwoerterbuch* (3rd ed.). Reprinted in English in a volume published by the National Monetary Commission (U.S.): *Miscellaneous Articles on German Banking*.
Herrigel, Gary. (1990). *Industrial Organization and the Politics of Industry. Centralized and Decentralized Production in Germany* (Doctoral dissertation, MIT Department of Political Science).
Herrigel, Gary, and Richard Kazis. (1989). *The Politics of Industrial Adjustment: The Case of U.S. and West German Textile Machinery*. Unpublished manuscript.
Holland, Max. (1989). *When the Machine Stopped*. Cambridge, Mass.: Harvard Business School Press.

Holmes, Stephen. (1988). "Precommitment and the Paradox of Democracy." In Elster and Slagstad (eds.), *Constitutionalism and Democracy*. New York: Cambridge University Press, pp. 195–240.

Horstmann, Axel. (1984). "Branchentrends und Unternehmerstrategien im Werkzeugmaschinenbau," In Wolfram Elsner and Siegfried Katterle (eds.), *Wirtschaftsstrukturen, neue Technologies und Arbeitsmarkt* (pp. 166–213). Cologne: Bund-Verlag.

Hounshell, David Allen. (1984). *From the American System to Mass Production, 1800–1932*. Baltimore: Johns Hopkins University Press.

Hovenkamp, Herbert. (1991). *Enterprise and American Law, 1836–1937*. Cambridge, Mass.: Harvard University Press.

Jacoby, Daniel. (1991). "The Transformation of Industrial Apprenticeship in the United States." *Journal of Economic History*, 51(4).

Jensen, Michael, and William H. Meckling. (1976). "Theory of the Firm: Managerial Behavior, Agency Costs and Ownership Structure." *Journal of Financial Economics*, 3, 305–60.

Kappel, Fritz. (1966). *75 Jahre VDW, 1891–1966*. Frankfurt/Main:VDW.

Kaysen, Carl. (1956). *The US Versus the United Shoe Machinery Comapny*. Cambridge, Mass.: Harvard University Press.

Keller, Morton. (1980). "Regulation of Large Enterprise: The United States Experience in Comparative Perspective." In Alfred Chandler and Herman Daems (eds.), *Managerial Hierarchies* (pp. 161–81). Cambridge, Mass.: Harvard University Press.

Kocka, Jürgen. (1980) "The Rise of Modern Industrial Enterprise in Germany." In Alfred Chandler and Herman Daems (eds.), *Managerial Hierarchies* (pp. 77–117). Cambridge, Mass.: Harvard University Press.

Lévy, Hermann. (1933). "Die europaische Verflechtung des amerikansiche Aussenhandels." *Weltwirtschaftliches Archiv*, 1(37), 164.

Liefmann, Robert. (1932). *Cartels, Combines and Trusts*. New York: E. P. Dutton.

Livingston, James. (1986). *Origins of the Federal Reserve System: Money, Class and Corporate Capitalism, 1890–1913*. Ithaca, N.Y.: Cornell University Press.

Ludwig Loewe & Co. AG. (1929). *Die Geschichte der Ludwig Loewe & Co. A. G. Berlin: Sechsig Jahre Edelarbeit 1869–1929*. Berlin: VDI-Verlag.

McDougall, Duncan. (1966). "Machine Tool Output, 1861–1910." In National Bureau of Economic Research, Conference on Research in Income and Wealth, *Output, Employment and Productivity in the United States After 1800*, Studies in Income and Wealth, Vol. 30 (pp. 479–517). New York: Columbia University Press.

Marx, Thomas G. (nd). "Technological Change and the Structure of the Machine Tool Industry." *MSU Business Topics*, 41–47.

Melman, Seymour. (1985). *The Permanent War Economy: American Capitalism in Decline*. New York: Simon & Schuster.

Mengel, Heinrich Wilhelm. (1931). *Strukturwandlungen und Konjunkturbewegung in der Werkzeugmaschinen-Industrie*. (Doctoral dissertation, Technische Hochschule, Berlin.)

Mommertz, Karl-Heinz. (1981). *Bohren, Drehen und Fraesen: Geschichte der Werkzeugmaschinen*. Hamburg: Rowohlt.

Montgomery, David. (1979). *Worker's Control in America*. New York: Cambridge University Press.

Muellenseifen, Heinz. (1926). *Kartelle als Produktionsfoerderer unter besonderer Beruecksichtigung der modernen Zusammenschlusstendenzen in der deutschen Maschinenbauindustrie*. Berlin: Julius Springer.

Noble, David. (1977). *America by Design: Science, Technology and the Rise of Corporate Capitalism*. New York: Oxford University Press.

Noble, David. (1984). *Forces of Production.* New York: Knopf.

Ong, Paul. (1983). *NC Machine Tools.* Unpublished manuscript, University of California, Berkeley. Part of *BRIE Final Report to Office of Technology Assessment on Programmable Automation Industries: Structure, Conduct and Performance.*

Overy, Richard. (1975). "Cars, Roads and Economic Recovery in Germany, 1932–8." *Economic History Review,* 28, 166.

Pastor, J.J. (1937). *Die Ausfuhr des deutschen Maschinenbaus und ihre Wirtschaftliche Bedeutung.* (Dissertation, Universitaet Koeln.)

Piore, Michael, and Charles Sabel. (1984). *The Second Industrial Divide: Possibilities for Prosperity.* New York: Basic Books.

Reichsverbandes der Deutsche Industrie (RDI). (1929). *Produktionsfoerderung durch Kartelle.* Berlin: RDI.

Research Management Corporation (RMC). (1969, May). *The Defense Dependency of the Metalworking Machinery and Equipment Industry and Disarmament Implications.* ACDA/E-130, Prepared for the U.S. Arms Control and Disarmament Agency.

Robertson, Ross M. (1966). "Changing Production of Metalworking Machinery, 1860–1920." In National Bureau of Economic Research, Conference on Research in Income and Wealth, *Output, Employment and Productivity in the United States After 1800,* Studies in Income and Wealth, Vol. 30. New York: Columbia University Press.

Robinson, Robert V., and Carl M. Briggs. (1991). "The Rise of Factories in Nineteenth-Century Indianapolis." *American Journal of Sociology,* 97(3), 622–56.

Rosenberg, Nathan. (1972). *Technology and American Economic Growth.* New York: Harper Torchbooks.

Ross Steven J. (1985). *Workers on the Edge: Work, Leisure, and Politics in Industrializing Cincinnati.* New York: Columbia University Press.

Sabel, Charles, Horst Kern, and Gary Herrigel. (1990). "Kooperative Produktion. Neue Formen der Zusammenaibeit zwischen Endfertigern und Zulieferern in der Auto-mobilindustrie und der Neueordnung der Firma." In Hans Gerhard Mendius and Ulrike Wendling-Schroeder (eds.), *Zulieferer im Netz. Neustrukturierung der Logistik am Beispiel der Automobilzulieferung.* Cologne: Bund-Verlag.

Schriewer, Juergen. (1986). "Intermediare Instanzen, Selbstverwaltung und berufliche Ausbildungsstrukturen im historischen Vergleich." *Zeitschrift für Paedegogik,* 1(32).

Schultz-Mehrin, Otto. (1926). *Specializierungs- und Verkaufsgemeinschaften im Maschinenbau.* Berlin: VDMA.

Sklar, Martin. (1988). *The Corporate Reconstruction of American Capitalism, 1890–1916.* New York: Cambridge University Press.

Smith, Merritt Roe. (1977). *Harpers Ferry Armory and the New Technology.* Ithaca, N.Y.: Cornell University Press.

Soltau, Friedrich. (1930). *Der Absatz der deutschen Werkzeugmaschinenindustrie.* (Doctoral dissertation, Vereinigte Friedrichs-Universitaet Halle–Wittenberg.)

Statistisches Handbuch für den Maschinenbau, various years, Frankfurt: VDMA, abbreviated as SHfdM.

Stinchcombe, Arthur. (1985). "Contracts as Hierarchical Documents." In Carol A Heimer (ed.), *Organization Theory and Project Management* (pp. 121–71). Oslo: Norwegian University Press.

VDMA. (1985/1987). *Statistisches Handbuch fuer den Maschinenbau.* Frankfurt: VDMA.

Veblen, Thorstein. (1906/1978). *The Theory of Business Enterprise.* New Brunswick, N.J.: Transaction Books.

Veblen, Thorstein. (1923). *Absentee Ownership and Business Enterprise in Recent Times.* New York: B. W. Huebsch.

Wagoner, Harless D. (1968). *The US Machine Tool Industry from 1900 to 1950.* Cambridge, Mass.: MIT Press.

Williamson, Oliver. (1985). *The Economic Institutions of Capitalism.* New York: Free Press.

Woodbury, Robert S. (1972). *Studies in the History of Machine Tools.* Cambridge, Mass.: MIT Press.

Ziegler, J. Nicholas. (1989). *The State and Technological Advance: Political Efforts for Industrial Change in France and the Federal Republic of Germany.* (Doctoral dissertation, Harvard University, Department of Government.)

CHAPTER 6

The Chemical Industry:
A Study in Internationalization

Wyn Grant and
William Paterson

W E SHALL argue in this chapter that the chemical industry is a highly internationalized industry, one in which the integration of world markets has led to a considerable degree of convergence in regimes of governance. Even so, there are still important national differences that may bear on the competitive performance of the chemical industry in different countries. These differences do not always lead in an expected direction. For example, although Japan is a major player in the world chemical industry, it is not a dominant, or even a leading producer, as is the case with industries such as consumer electronics. We also caution against forging too many generalizations regarding the chemical industry, an industry with many distinctive features. The chemical industry should also not be seen as a model for future developments in other industries, but rather one whose particular pattern of development and distinctive characteristics have produced various interrelationships among firms, markets, interest associations, and governments that have a number of special features.

Before proceeding to a discussion of the extent of internatonalization in the chemical industry, some preliminary remarks have to be made about the definition of the industry, and the institutions with which it comes into contact. An important distinction may be made between how industrial sectors are defined in schemes of classification because of the need to find a location for every product group (an important consideration in categorization), and how sectors actually see themselves. It must be stressed that many subsectors classified as being part of the chemical industry either resent being so classified (notably cosmetics and toiletries) or regard themselves largely as *users* of basic chemical products with very different sets of interests from their suppliers of raw materials. Hence, our analysis focuses on ISIC 351 (basic industrial chemicals) rather than ISIC 352 (consumer products such as paints, pharmaceuticals, soaps and detergents, etc.). In terms of value-added, ISIC 351 and ISIC 352 are of similar size in the developed world. It should also be noted that the space available to us here does not pemit any discussion of the distinctive problems

129

of the fertilizers and pesticides subsector within ISIC 351. Agrochemicals are sometimes viewed with some suspicion by other parts of the industry as giving it a bad name: "the killers," as one of our German respondents labeled agrochemicals.

Because of its international character, the chemical industry is more directly influenced by a variety of international organizations than most other industries. Some of these bodies (e.g., the Organization for Economic Cooperation and Development [OECD] and certain specialized UN agencies) clearly qualify as intergovernmental organizations through which national governments are able to reach agreements on matters of common concern (e.g., rules for the international transportation of potentially hazardous chemicals). The European Community (EC), however, poses conceptual problems of a rather different order. One view would be to regard it as yet another intergovernmental organization, albeit one with a wider remit and greater resources at its disposal than most. Such a perspective would see its effectiveness as limited by the difficulty of reaching agreement on issues among member states, and the limitations of the enforcement mechanisms at its disposal once legislation has been agreed to. There is much truth in such a perspective, but we would wish to argue that, even if the European Community does not yet qualify as a state, it has certain statelike properties: It is able to make authoritative decisions that apply to a defined territory, and it does have mechanisms of enforcement, not least the European Court of Justice. The European Community is also displaying a growing interest in the way in which EC legislation is implemented.

Internationalization

Our discussion of the extent of internationalization in the chemical industry will be organized around four dimensions: internationalization of production; internationalization of trade; international cartelization; and internationalizaion of control. The first two dimensions could be observed in a number of industries, although they are developed to a greater extent in the chemical industry than elsewhere. The second two dimensions are, we would argue, more highly developed in the chemical industry than in any other industry.

Internationalization of Production

The multinational corporation operating in a number of countries is not a new phenomenon, and is certainly not confined to the chemical industry. Even so, chemical firms, particularly those originating in Britain and the United States, tend to have particularly widespread production locations. For example, only 44 percent of Imperial Chemical Industries (ICI) net operating assets in 1988 were located in Britain, with 24 percent in North and South America, 16 percent in the Asia-Pacific region, and 13 percent in continental Europe (with the remainder elsewhere, including the Indian subcontinent).

Of the top ten chemical firms in 1985 (ranked by sales), three were American, three were German, one was British, one was Swiss, one was Dutch, and one was Anglo-Dutch. There was, in fact, a gap of $3.5 billion between the fifth and sixth places, with only one American firm (Du Pont) in the top five. If one examines the top twenty-five chemical companies, only eight are American-based firms, and only two are Japanese. This is an industry in which Western Europe has a strong presence. In this connection, it is important to note the extent to which German firms have been internationalizing their production and research, gradually moving away from their former strategy of exporting from a German base.

As a generalization, it can be claimed that production is dominated by a relatively small number of companies, with an increasing tendency for companies to concentrate in areas where they perceive that they have technological and/or marketing strength; for example, ICI through its joint venture with ENI—European Vinyls Corporation—which is the leading producer of polyvinyl chloride (PVC) in Western Europe; or British Petroleum's concentration on the development of its gas-phase technology for the manufacture of polyethylene.

Polypropylene, a highly versatile plastic much in demand, provides a good illustration of the way in which global production is dominated by a relatively small number of companies. The leading world producer is Himont, which is 80 percent owned by Montedison; it has about 14 percent of world capacity, with plants in the United States, Italy, and Canada. It is also a partner with Petrofina in a joint venture in Belgium and has a minority share in businesses in Taiwan and Brazil.

The second major player in the world market is Shell with 10 percent of world capacity, and major plants in the United States, Britain, France, and the Netherlands (plus a joint venture with BASF in West Germany). Shell tends to produce a more limited range of polypropylene grades. The third largest producer is also an oil company subsidiary, Amoco, with an estimated 6.5 percent share of world capacity. Two majors chemical companies each have about 5 percent of the world market (Hoechst and ICI). Thus, some 40 percent of global capacity is accounted for by the five leading producers.

The cost of research and development (R&D), and the need to recoup this cost in an international market, is itself a cause of extensive internationalization in the chemical industry (see Mussati and Soru, 1991). This is done, of course, not just through international production, but also by licensing process technology. For example, in the case of polypropylene, about twenty companies license the Spheripol process originally developed by Montedison.

Some companies, such as Dow, Du Pont, and Solvay, prefer to keep their technological breakthroughs in-house. Licensing may, however, offer quicker returns, although, as Spitz observes (1988:546), "it is not inappropriate to suggest that companies in the past have too often taken the easy road and have licensed their new technology to competitors, rather than using it exclusively for their own benefit." It should also be noted that "The patent cross-licensing agreement has been an important device used by American and foreign firms to establish a degree of control over international markets much greater than would have been possible under a separate and independent exercise of their respective monopoly privileges based on patent grants." (Stocking and Watkins, 1950:10).

One factor affecting the licensing decision will be the level of available patent protection. Protection of intellectual property raises complex issues, but it is not possible to discuss these at sufficient length here. What is evident in the chemical industry is that new technology has not always been covered by strong patents. In the case of vinyl chloride, for example, "The patents involved were always easy to get around" (Spitz, 1988:550). Cooperation may be the most cost-effective way for two companies working in a similar area to move ahead. In the case of the Spheripol technology for polypropylene production, Himont (whose parent company is Montedison) concluded a joint research agreement with Mitsui. Mitsui has made a significant contribution to development in the catalysis area, enabling the reduction of energy and operating costs.

Internationalization of Trade

As the former chairman of ICI, Sir John Harvey-Jones, has commented, "The chemical industry is one of the most integrated industries in the free world as measured by the proportion of output which enters into world trade" (Harvey-Jones, 1985:451). Clearly, the proportion of output that is exported by any one country depends on the size of its home market and its export orientation. At one end of the spectrum, the United States exported a little over 10 pecent of its chemical output in 1985 compared with 85 percent for Switzerland; the figure for EC countries was just under 50 percent. Over time, new producers such as those in the Middle East will become an increasingly important factor in world markets. By 1995 it is estimated that developing nations will account for nearly a quarter of the world's chemical output. One consequence of growing internationalization of production may be that trading will become more opportunistic—that is, short term in character rather than based on long-term contracts to supply a particular market.

The future role of the Middle East in the global chemicals trade will be considerably affected by developments in the political relationship between the European Community and the six nations organized in the Gulf Cooperation Council. Up to now, the low-cost feedstock advantage of these countries has been offset by the application of standard GATT tariffs by the United States, the EC, and Japan. An agreement giving advantageous access to the EC market for Gulf states petrochemicals, particularly if it occurred against a background of rising oil prices, would have serious implications for EC producers. The United States and Japan would presumably continue to apply their tariffs, and the EC markets would absorb an even larger share of a growing Gulf states output. Following the adoption of a new negotiating mandate by the EC in September 1989, talks on a comprehensive free trade agreement between the EC and the Gulf Cooperation Council began in 1990, but made little progress.

Within Western Europe, trade among individual countries has grown steadily, helped by the elimination of tariffs, by easy transportation or pipeline connections, and by the practice of arranging "swaps" between producers of commodity chemicals to avoid or reduce transportation costs. The impact of the single European market 1992, which is in any case often exaggerated by observers from outside the EC, will be less marked in the chemical sector than in other industries, particularly in terms of the definition of the sector we have used here. (There are implications for reductions in registration costs in associated sectors such as pharmaceuticals.) Nevertheless, important developments should occur in areas such as transport deregulation, and CEFIC, the organization of the European chemical industry, has set up a special Steering Commitee 1992 to identify the key issues for the chemical sector.

International Cartelization

It is sometimes remarked that "C is for chemicals is for cartels," and certainly one of the distinctive characteristics of the chemical industry is its ability to create international cartels that share markets. There is a long history of such behavior in the industry, with a major network of cartels developing in the interwar period. By 1939, "ICI alone was a party to some *eight hundred* agreements covering its chemical business" (Mirow and Maurer, 1982:131). ICI took the British Empire as its domain; IG Farben (and, to a lesser extent, Solvay) took the European continent; Du Pont, North America and parts of South America. The single most important document setting up these arrangements was the 1929 Patents and Processes Agreement between Du Pont and ICI. It is often referred to as the "Grand Alliance," a not surprising title when one considers that it reads something like a diplomatic treaty. ICI's historian calls this agreement "the bedrock of ICI *foreign policy* [italics added] throughout the thirties" (Reader, 1975:34).

What were the underlying dynamics of cartel formation in the chemical industry, and were they replicated in other internationally organized industries? There is, of course, a general incentive, identified by Adam Smith, for rational economic actors to form cartels so as to avoid "ruinous" competition. The literature on economic governance has often downplayed the importance of cartels as a mechanism for sectoral collaboration as the national and international level. (For an interesting study of cartels, see Mirow and Maurer, 1982.) Cartel formation is a particularly attractive option in industries where there is overcapacity; where demand is relatively inelastic; and where the industry is relatively highly concentrated. The last two conditions have been generally present in chemicals, whereas fulfillment of the first condition triggers off new periods of cartel formation, as happened in Western Europe in the 1980s (see below).

Another internationalized, highly concentrated industry with a long history of cartel formation is the aluminium industry. As one observer has noted: "In 1901, a comprehensive cartel agreement was concluded by the important aluminium producers in Europe and the Northern Aluminium Company of Canada" (Graham, 1982:18). There were seven distinct cartels up to 1930, culminating in the highly cooperative "aluminium alliance" in the depressed economic conditions of the 1930s. Technological innovation, government intervention for strategic reasons, and changes in relative company size stimulated a new period of competition after World War II, just as in chemicals (Holloway, 1988:36–37). However, there was a resurgence of cooperation in the 1960s, further stimulated in the 1970s by the growing militancy of third-world bauxite producers. The formation of the International Primary Aluminium Institute in 1982 "represented a partial return to the monopoly capitalism of the old cartels as all the leading aluminium companies closed ranks to co-ordinate members' investments, control prices and avoid over-production" (Graham, 1982:257). Reviewing the experience of the aluminum industry, Mikdashi (1974:189) unconsciously highlights the similarities with the chemical industry: "The strategies adopted by the aluminium companies could only have appeared in a highly concentrated and international industry, in which the component parts were deeply aware of their interdependence."

Although concentration and overcapacity are important contributory factors in explaining the process of cartel formation in both the chemical and aluminium industries, "Development and control of technology was the basis for the original establishment of cartels among chemical manufacturers" (Spitz, 1988:202). In particular, the eagerness of firms in the interwar period to obtain access to superior German technology produced a complex web of bilateral and multilateral agreements. Once established, these technology exchange agreements "were used as a springboard for market sharing, price fixing, and other actions characteristic of cartels" (Spitz, 1988:199). Similarly, in the aluminium industry, the Heroult process, which (along with the discoveries of Hall in the United States) transformed aluminum from a precious metal to an industrial metal, led to a series of license agreements that parceled out the global market and provided the basis for the subsequent formation of cartels (Graham, 1982:15–18).

It has been noted how the years after World War II saw a collapse of cartel activity in the aluminium industry. Similarly, in the chemical industry in the postwar period the combined effect of antitrust activity in the United States, the increase in the number of participants in the industry as the result of the entry of the oil companies, and the dissolution of IG Farben meant that the prewar cartels could not be maintained. However, the habit of cartelization is not completely dead in the industry. On the night of October 13–14, 1983, EC officials simultaneously raided offices of ten major polypropylene producers and found "A mass of evidence [that] led to the exposure of an industry-wide cartel that had operated from 1977–1983, in contravention of Article 85 of the Treaty of Rome. It was the EEC competition department's biggest case ever." (*European Chemicals News*, 8 September 1986).

In its most developed form (by 1982), this was a highly structured cartel:

1. At the top level were the four largest producers accounting for 50 percent of the EC polypropylene market (Hoechst, ICI, Shell, and Montepolimer, part of Montedison). They constituted an unofficial directorate known as the "Big Four," which from 1982 onwards met the day before "the bosses."

2. There were monthly meetings of "the bosses," senior managers, or directors. ICI took over the presidency in 1982 on condition that "more determined efforts [be] made to increase prices" (*European Chemicals News*, 8 September 1986). Zürich appears to have been the favored location for international meetings (an anonymous information exchange had been set up there in 1976) with twenty-eight out of fifty-five meetings there between September 1979

and September 1983. London's Heathrow Airport also provided a suitably anonymous location.

3. Meetings of marketing managers twice a month decided on concerted efforts to raise prices and to implement and monitor a system of annual quotas. After the system of quotas settled down, they were worked out by ICI on its computer after negotiating with participants.

4. Local meetings discussed the detailed implementation of the agreed-on measures in national markets, often down to the price of individual truckloads to each consumer. In local meetings, pricing anomalies were discussed and explanations given for any transgressions. Forty-three such meetings are known to have taken place between February 1982 and October 1983.

In 1988, the European Commission fined twenty-three West European companies (many of them members of the polypropylene cartel) a record $67 million for illicit price-fixing and production sharing in low-density polyethylene and PVC. The price-fixing occurred during the early 1980s at the height of the overcapacity crisis. Directors of the companies met in Switzerland to work out a market-sharing strategy, which was then passed on to product managers for implementation. The aim was to establish a "posted price" that was generally accepted as the market rate from which only large customers might get a discount. In 1989, the EC began investigations into an alleged soda ash cartel.

It might seem that antitrust laws would inhibit any similar actions in the United States. Certainly, the managers of American chemical companies operating in Europe were anxious to stress the importance of antitrust laws as a major constraint on their behavior when interviewed. Even so, matters might not be quite as straightforward as they appear. It is interesting that the one American-based participant in the polypropylene cartel, Hercules, was at the forefront of suggesting methods of developing the arrangements that were made. According to an ICI document inspected by the EC, Hercules suggested in 1982 that the system should be elaborated by the introduction of account leadership. Major customers would be identified and allocated to a chosen "leader." Other companies ("contenders") would cooperate on price guidelines with the account leader. Any other producers ("noncontenders") approached by the customer were to quote prices above the target level. Despite the stringency of antitrust law, the occurrence of cartellike practices in the United States cannot be ruled out.

Internationalization of Control

ICI has probably pursued a conscious strategy of internationalization more vigorously than any other chemical company. The company refers with pride in its annual report to "the ever-increasing internationalism of ICI." The company has pursued a strategy of internationalizing its board with the appointment of American, Canadian, German, and Japanese directors. For example, members of the board in 1988 included Shoici Saba, adviser to the board of Toshiba and vice-chairman of Keidranren; and Walter Kiep, managing partner of a leading West German insurance group, a member of the supervisory board of Volkswagen, and a leading member of the Christlich Demokratische Union (CDU). The former chairman of ICI has expressed the hope that in the future the board of an international company like ICI would be constituted in proportion to its share of the market in different parts of the world (Harvey-Jones, 1988:165).

About 10 percent of ICI's equity is held in the form of American depositary receipts (ADRs). ICI ADRs have been traded in the United States since 1983, when ICI first became listed on the NYSE Big Board. In an important symbolic move, the company's board of directors met outside Britain for the first time in 1987. The meeting was held in New York at the invitation of the New York Stock Exchange. In 1988, the chairman of ICI, Denys Henderson, was the first representative of British industry invited to join the Listed Company Advisory Committee of the NYSE. In December 1988, ICI obtained a listing on the Tokyo stock exchange. Similarly, the leading German companies are quoted on all major stock exchanges including Tokyo.

Perhaps most significant of all, ICI has announced that the proportion of R&D it carries out in Britain will be cut; usually financial control and R&D are the two functions that multinationals keep in their home base. ICI's view is that "we have to get this last activity nearer the marketplace—which is increasingly outside the UK" (*Financial Times*, 7 September 1988). The German companies tend to have more centralized research policies, with BASF having three-quarters of its research workers in Ludwigshafen. However, by 1988, Bayer undertook only 65 percent of its research in West Germany, with 20 percent in the United States and 12 percent in the rest of Europe.

ICI has taken the process of internationalization further than the major German companies. Its chairman has justifiably claimed that "we are undoubtedly the most international of all the big chemical companies" (interview in Heller, 1987:68). Its major U.S. acquisitions have included Beatrice Chemicals in 1985 ($750 million), Glidden Paints in 1986 ($580 million), and Stauffer Chemicals in 1987 ($1.69 billion). ICI Americas has plants in thirty states. It should be noted, however, that the principal German have also been substantial purchasers of American chemical businesses (e.g., Hoechst's acquisition of Celanese, and BASF's purchase of Inmont).

The Chemical Industry in Japan

Japan is a major player in the world chemical industry, but it is not a world leader. Although there is a significant domestic industry, with a turnover in 1986 accounting for 20 percent of the comined turnover of the United States, Western Europe, and Japan, Japan's chemical exports are less than one-tenth of the value of West European exports, and less than half of those of the United States. Japan's export share of chemicals (expressed as a percentage of total OECD imports) declined from 10.1 percent in 1973 to 7.6 percent in 1986; Britain's share increased over the same period from 8.8 percent to 10.6 percent. Indeed, Japan ran a small deficit in its chemicals trade in the mid-1980s. Perhaps most significant, there has been no "Japanization" of the West European and American industries through significant levels of inward investment, as has happened in consumer electronics and the auto industry. Indeed, in 1988, ICI made its first major inward investment in Japan.

Given the general concern of this text with Japan, the position of the chemical industry there requires some explanation. Government production of chemicals followed the Meiji Restoration (1868), and the industry expanded rapidly between the two world wars, partly in response to the needs of the military. The Japanese chemical industry was more seriously damaged by bombing raids in World War II than occurred in Germany, and recovery only began after the Korean War. "By world standards, Japanese chemical companies in the mid-1950s were quite small" (Spitz, 1988:376). One constraining factor was that the American Occupation authorities had followed a policy of not allowing Japan to build large refineries whose off-gases could be used as a basis for a petrochemical industry (Spitz, 1988:378). Even today, Mitsubishi Chemical, the largest Japanese chemical company, is several times smaller than industry leaders such as ICI, Du Pont, and the major German producers, and is really no more than a medium-sized enterprise by global standards.

Production of ethylene and its derivatives began in the late 1950s following a study by a Petrochemical Technology Committee set up by the Japanese Ministry of International Trade and Industry (MITI). Imported crude oil was allocated in such a way as to encourage the construction of chemical plants next to refineries. The industry is totally dependent on imported raw materials, and it was severely impacted by the oil shocks of the 1970s, leading to a substantial reduction in its international competitiveness. MITI responded by initiating a substantial reduction in the industry's production capacity. Proposals put forward in December 1982 by the Industrial Structure Council, a MITI advisory body, recommended a reduction through closure and mothballing of 36 percent of the total ethylene capacity, and between 24 percent and 36 percent of capacity for the main derivatives. Temporary cartels were to be formed to eliminate excessive capacity and avoid overproduction.

These proposals were put into effect in May 1983 under the Temporary Measures Law for the Structural Adjustment of Specific Industries. By March 1985, Japanese ethylene capacity was cut from 6.3 million tons annually to just over 4 million tons. Against a background of low and stable world oil prices, demand recovered significantly in 1987. By September 1987, the petrochemical industry was removed by MITI from the list of designated industries under this law, and the government-sponsored cartels were abolished. Petrochemical companies have announced plans for the reopening of mothballed plants, and for the construction of new complexes. Sumitomo has plans to switch the emphasis of its production from commodity chemicals to more specialist products, a strategy already put into practice by firms such as ICI.

According to some observers, the Japanese chemical industry's "structural weakness stems from the fact that it relies heavily on imported naphtha" (*Japan Economic Almanac*, 1985:126). This has led to a price gap between Japan and countries that use natural gas as a primary feedstock. For example, the price differential for most basic polymers was of the order of $400 a ton in favour of the U.S. Gulf Coast in 1980, admittedly a period of high oil prices (see Fayad and Motamen, 1986:119). Western Europe also uses naphtha as its principal feedstock, but has access to North Sea oil, whereas Japan has no hydrocarbon resources. One Japanese response has been "to establish direct contacts and joint ventures with oil producers of South-East Asia and the Middle East" (Fayad and Motamen, 1986:56).

An alternative explanation centers on the weakness of the scientific infrastructure in Japan. In 1985, Du Pont spent 186.2 billion yen on R&D investment, and Hoechst spent 169.1 billion yen, compared with a 28 billion yen average for the two leading Japanese firms (*Japan Economic Almanac*, 1988:159). In 1982, the Japanese chemical industry spent 3.1 percent of its total sales on R&D, compared with 3.5 percent (1980) in the United States and 4.4 percent (1979) in West Germany (*Japan Economic Almanac*, 1985:129). Both countries had, of course, much higher levels of sales than did Japan, leading to an even higher level of total spending.

It should not be supposed that contacts between the industry and the scientific community are absent. In Tskuba, new research institutes are being built by nearly thirty chemical companies to develop the technology needed for effective competition in the twenty-first century. However, the earlier development of the industry was based on a conscious decision to follow a "catching up" strategy centered on importing the best available technology from abroad. There were close links with American contractors, with substantial discounts being obtained through skilled joint bargaining techniques executed with guidance from MITI (Spitz, 1988:378). Spitz also notes:

> Initially very much behind in chemical technology development, Japan was able to purchase modern processes from the West in order to be able to build plants employing the most modern technology available at the time. While the amount of indigenous technology development was initially modest, Japanese firms were often able to improve the technology licensed from the outside, thus making it suitable for reexport. As time went by, an increasing amount of technology was also developed in Japan. (1988:382)

Japan has built up a significant chemical industry, but it is always going to have difficulty competing with countries that have their own cheap feedstock supplies, or countries such as Germany with a specialized training and research base. Some companies have made substantial progress in the specialist chemicals field (e.g., Shin-Etsu, a leading world producer of semiconductor silicon). Although Japan is likely to continue to succeed on an international level with particular products, it is doubtful whether Japanese companies will supplant the existing world leaders from the United States and Western Europe. In light of OECD figures showing that there are 388 biotechnology plants in the United States, 105 in Japan, and only 17 in Germany, it may be that this area offers the greatest future prospects for the Japanese chemical industry.

The Internationalization of Governance

The highly internationalized character of the chemical industry requires no further emphasis. What, then, are the consequences for governance structures? To a large degree, coordination of markets is achieved by the firms themselves, or by interfirm coordination that does not involve either business associations or governments. It is important to bear in mind that in areas like northern Europe or the Texas-Louisiana region of the United States, companies are physically linked to one another through a network of pipelines through which they can swap products. Indeed, isolation from this pipeline network can be a potential competitive disadvantage. In an oligopolistic industry, a firm with a large market share can substantially influence the operation of the market, a possibility enhanced by the specialization of companies in particular product lines referred to earlier. Companies are also involved in an elaborate network of joint ventures and capacity swaps; as was noted earlier, they may also engage in illicit forms of joint action.

Several examples may help to illustrate the way in which companies cooperate with one another to improve their market position. In 1988, ICI and Du Pont formed a "business alliance" involving a joint investment of £50 million by the two companies to improve their position in the European car paint market. The new business is headquartered in Bonn in an Inmont factory that ICI bought from BASF in 1986, as a consequence of a decision by the Bundeskartellamt (BKA). The joint investment includes a £10 million technical application center where car factory conditions can be exactly reproduced while paints are being developed and tested. It should be noted that car paints are increasingly high-technology products, expensive to develop and needing global markets to give good returns. Globalization of car design and production is also creating a dmand for greater product consistency.

The PVC joint venture between ICI and ENI (named European Vinyls Corporation) provides a mechanism for rationalizing the European market, which has suffered from overcapacity (contributed to by ICI's decision to construct a new plant in West Germany in the 1970s). It should be noted that PVC producers throughout Europe are vertically integrated through chlorine, ethylene, and vinyl chlorine monomer production to the final product, making extrication from the market difficult. As part of the merger deal, ICI closed 100,000 tons of PVC capacity while ENI closed 200,000 tons. Subsequently, European Vinyls has built up its market share by purchasing three other European PVC producers (Interplastic Weis of Austria, Davinyl of Sweden, and Weston Hyde of Britain).

Many of the challenges facing the industry are therefore dealt with within vertically integrated firms, or by arrangements between firms. Government, however, plays an important role in setting the framework within which companies operate. It is important to remember that a number of aspects of national economic policy, which have a considerable impact on the chemical industry (e.g., taxation and energy policy), remain a matter for national governments. Competition policy also shows significant national variations.

The United States has a more stringent competition policy than does the EC, meaning that it has not been possible to deal with overcapacity problems through joint arrangements and capacity swaps to the extent that has happened in Western Europe.

Within Western Europe, competition law is more stringent in Germany than in Britain. Thus, ICI's attempt to acquire Norddeutsche Faserwerke in 1988 was blocked by the West German Federal Cartel Office, although it was supported by the European Community as a necessary contribution to the reduction of overcapacity in European fibers production. This was seen in some circles as an indication of a more protective attitude on the part of the German competition authorities in looking after German interests. The key question for the companies is the extent to which, in the future, cross-border mergers will be cleared at a European rather than a member-state level. This has been the subject of considerable political controversy, with Britain, France, and Germany concerned that Brussels is seeking to encroach too far on national controls. Compromise proposals put forward in April 1989 by the competition policy commissioner, Sir Leon Brittan, would limit advance vetting of cross-border mergers (as distinct from after the event as at present) to takeovers with a combined turnovers of over $5.6 billion dollars.

Of course, apparent differences in national regimes may not be so great as they appear to be. Bower (1985) presents a picture of the American chemical industry respoding promptly to market signals of overproduction through the exit of the weaker companies. In fact, the market process may not have worked in such a pure way. One observer of the American chemical industry commented in interview:

On paper the closures were unilateral, but down in the Houston spaghetti bowl all the plants are connected, a lot of product swaps, although they stay on the right side of the law. There's great discussion between producers; in my opinion they say "it's your turn to take the next plant." There is a need for companies to meet in order for the price structure not to go to hell. They tend to be able to work together so that the industry proceeds on an orderly basis. (Interview information)

In the area of environmental regulation, which is where government had its greatest impact in the late 1980s on the industry, the requirements of international trade (e.g., registration) and the exchange of information between scientists and environmentalists produced major pressures for regulatory convergence, particularly within the European Community. However, the regulatory regime in the United States continues to differ from that of the EC insofar as it appears to be more onerous and unpredictable in terms of process (although no necessarily more effective in terms of outcome). These points are discussed more fully in the section on environmental regulation later in the chapter.

Intergovernmental Authorities

The European Community has had an increasing impact on the chemical industry in a number of key areas of its operations. Reference has already been made to its competition policy activities, both in terms of exposing cartels and penalizing their members, and giving permission for agreements between companies. The EC plays an increasingly significant role in environmental regulation, a topic discussed more fully below. It also conducts trade policy, an area of considerable significance for the chemical industry, given the expansion of petrochemical production in the Middle East and the continuous pressure from countries such as Saudi Arabia to be given unrestrained access to the European market.

Since the early 1970s, the OECD chemicals program has served as a major forum for international discussion on specific chemicals and on issues relating to the general control of chemicals. In particular, it offers a forum where bargains between the United States and Western European countries can occur on chemical-control matters. International chemical companies do not want different requirements for bringing new products to the market in Europe and the United States. The OECD has taken the lead "in a strong and successful effort to harmonize testing guidelines, principles of good laboratory practices, a minimum premarketing set of data, and mutual acceptance of data" (Gusman, von Moltke, Irwin, and Whitehead, 1981:48). In particular, agreements on premarketing notification issues contributed toward countering "the most serious threat to international trade in chemicals in the postwar period" (Brickman, Jasanoff, and Ilgen, 1985:299).

Business Interest Organization

Increased globalization is likely to have an impact on the resources and policy attention the chemical giants give to their national trade associations. A major feature in the Federal Republic of Germany has been the amount of policy attention the giants pay to their national trade associations, particularly the *Verband der Chemischen Industrie* (VCI) and the *Bundesarbeitgeberverband Chemie* (BAVC). This is already beginning to change (note the emergence of European coordinators), but is likely to alter much more in the coming years as the proportion of production and research located outside the Federal Republic continues to climb.

Globalization has been accompanied by a restructuring of the boards of directors, especially at Bayer. Members of the management board are no longer responsible for operating units. Instead of product divisions, as before, dominating the main board, Bayer has grouped its global activities into six sectors, most of which contain several operating business areas (e.g., plastics/fibers/rubber and agrochemicals/veterinary products). Although board members no longer have individual responsibility for product divisions or for administrative or service areas, they do retain responsibility for several countries where the company operates.

The main board has been reduced in size to twelve members, and further reductions are planned. Immediately below the main board are seven committees dealing with broad areas such as finance, R&D, environment, and coordination. The heads of the product divisions now occupy the next level in the hierarchy rather than as was the case in the past, sitting on the main board as head of the product division.

We have discussed these changes in the internal organizational structure of Bayer in some detail because there is a linkage between them and the organization of associative activity. These changes at the company level have obvious if unintended consequences for the firm's representation on the executive committees of the specialist associations. While the managing directors were represented on the Präsidium of the VCI, main board directors with specific responsibilities were on the equivalent committees of the specialist associations. The rationalization of the main board has meant that some of these representatives are now no longer on the main board of Bayer, although they retain the same responsibilities. These changes, however unintended, reflect a situation in which the companies are increasingly concentrating on retaining and expanding global market share rather than fine-tuning the coordination of their domestic activities.

Despite this global market orientation, business interest organization in the chemical industry still occurs largely at a national level. This is particularly so if one counts the European Community as the "national level" in the case of Western Europe, for the major international business organizations in the chemical industry operate only at a regional—, that is, European—level. They include the European Chemical Industry Council (CEFIC), the organization of national chemical industry associations in Western Europe (including non-EC countries). By the standards of such "associations of associations" at the European level, CEFIC is relatively well resourced and, after recent reforms during the presidency of Sir John Harvey-Jones, has reasonably effective decision-making structures. In particular, the creation of a new category of corporate associate member (in effect for major multinationals) was not seen as a bureaucratic detail. Rather, this innovation was viewed as a means of building "new bridges between the Federations who are the legal members of CEFIC and the major trans-national companies operating in several member states whose practical and financial support and commitment is essential to the success of CEFIC in all its European and international lobbying activities" (Chemical Industries Association Activities Report, 1986:14).

Another important innovation was the formation within CEFIC in 1985 of the Association of Petrochemical Producers in Europe (APPE). This is a direct membership organization of the leading multinational petrochemical producers in Western Europe. Company representation in APPE is confined to senior executives dealing with petrochemicals operations. Formation of a Europe-wide direct membership association of leading multinationals is a significant development against the background of the difficulties that associations of associations have faced in winning agreement from their national members to anything more than "lowest common denominator" policies.

A considerable number of associations serve particular subsectors or product groups of the chemical industry at the European level, many of them functioning as sector groups or affiliated organizations of CEFIC. Apart from ten major sectoral or subsectoral associations, there are over sixty product-based or technical associations operating at the West European level. New organizations continue to be formed. For example, in 1988 the European Council of Vinyl

Manufacturers was founded within the Association of Plastic Manufacturers in Europe to defend PVC against what were described as "ill-informed and harmful public attitudes" and to "convince detractors to consider this material [PVC] as being one of the standard plastics" (APME Newsletter No. 27, May 1988).

One or two sectoral organizations function at a global level, such as GIFAP, the International Group of National Associations of Agrochemical Manufacturers (headquartered in Brussels), which has Latin American and Asian organizations as members as well as those from the United States and Western Europe. Chief executive officers of plastics industry associations worldwide convene once a year in the International Plastics Associations Director (IPAD) conference. Frequent bilateral or multilateral contacts occur among the various national associations, especially those of Western Europe, the United States, and Japan (e.g., there is a regular cycle of meetings between CEFIC and the Chemical Manufacturers' Association [CMA] in the United States). CEFIC noted in its 1987 annual report that, given the growing number of issues directly affecting the chemical industry, which are addressed in globally oriented international bodies, there was a need "for intensified cooperation with the sister associations of the United States, Japan, or of other parts of the world." In the late 1980s, there has been cooperation among CEFIC, CMA, and the Japan Chemical Industry Association (JCIA) on chemical weapons questions.

Given that the chemical companies are the key global actors, attention should perhaps focus on their own political capabilities. The chemical companies, particularly those of Britain and the United States, have been pioneers in the development of the government relations function, and they devote considerable resources to it. (One company's total public affairs and government relations budget is £7 million to £8 million a year, far in excess of the resources available to most business associations.) These government relations divisions operate in all significant locations: For example, ICI has government relations operations in London, Brussels, and Washington, D.C. German companies have been less interested in the development of a government relations capability, preferring to rely on their industry association. However, the leading German companies have recently appointed high-level coordinators to handle relations with the European Community.

We would suggest that internationalization of the chemial industry is likely to lead to further development of the political capabilities of individual companies, rather than the emergence of effictive global-level business associations. There are, after all, important national differences of perspective and interest in areas such as trade policy, whereas multinational companies should, in principle, be pursuing a agreed-upon corporate strategy (in practice, matters are more difficult given the sheer size of the companies and their complex organizational structures).

To analyze in greater depth the mechanisms that govern the economic transactions of large chemical firms, and the extent of cross-national convergence, we shall now present two case studies: one on the handling of the overcapacity problem in petrochemicals, and the other on environmental regulation.

Overcapacity Problems in the West European Petrochemical Industry

In 1981, capacity utilization for most of the bulk polymers in the West European petrochemical industry was in the low sixties in percentage terms (the main exception was polypropylene, which had a number of attractive qualities). By 1987, capacity utilization was in the 95 to 105 percent range (it is possible for chemical plants to produce above what is known as their "nameplate capacity"). Between 1980 and 1987, about one-fourth or low-density polyethylene capacity had been closed: 25 percent of ethylene capacity and 18 percent of PVC capacity. The petrochemical industry successfully sorted out its own overcapacity problem without very much government involvement. The APPE has claimed that "The result has been a textbook example of how to overhaul an industrial sector in line with the European Commission's precepts for creating a genuine Common Market by 1992." In short, this experience provides us with an opportunity to examine a successful example of industry self-governance that operated at a cross-national level.

The focus here is on Western Europe; the crisis was less acute in the United States. It has been argued that this was because the U.S. industry anticipated problems at an earlier stage and moved out of the less promising product lines. However, it should also be borne in mind that, while the chemical industries of the United States and Western Europe are roughly the same size, Europe exports 50 percent of its output, as against only 10 percent in the United States. Even allowing for the fact that the greater part of Europe's exports go elsewhere in Europe, the Europeans are far more vulnerable to the growth of capacity elsewhere. Admittedly, the new producers are, as yet, small players in the market; the Middle East producers, for example, have added only about 3 percent to global capacity.

Although there have been unilateral withdrawals by companies from the petrochemical business, or unilateral closures of particular plants, most of the rationalization has taken the form of product swaps or the formation of joint companies, often across national boundaries. Product swaps involve companies trading plants between them, concentrating on their technological strengths (thus, British Petroleum has built up its holdings in polyethylene; ICI has done the same in PVC). The classic example of a joint venture is the ICI–ENI operation in PVC, which gives them the leading share of European production and provides them with a basis for the further rationalization needed in the case of this particular bulk polymer.

Rather than provide a detailed account of the various phases of the process, the analysis presented here will focus on the five main mechanisms identified by the project organizers. It is our contention that the categories of "markets" and "corporate hierarchies" are not centrally important in this particular case. Of course, we recognize that the decision to close a particular plant, or engage in a product swap, ultimately has to made by the corporate hierarchy of a particular firm. However, there were relatively few examples of firms making a market judgment *on their own*. (Where they did, they often seem to have got it wrong, as in the case of the Esso plant in Cologne.) The clearest examples of autonomous commercial judgment are by American firms (always nervous of taking any actions that might violate antitrust laws).

"The state" in this context means the European Community (EC) rather than national governments: Remember that we are talking about companies that generally treat Western Europe as an integrated market. It was the European Community that decided that it did not want a "crisis cartel" in the industry on the lines of steel, and the European Community that had to reconcile the various interfirm arrangements that occurred with its competition laws. It was also, of course, the European Commission that staged dawn raids on the premises of chemical companies, which provided evidence of cartel activity.

National governments are significant actors in those countries where there are state holding companies in the chemical industry. However, in countries such as Italy and France, the tendency in the 1980s was for the state to stand back from using the industry as an instrument of national economic policy, and instead to create conditions in which chemical companies could find commercial solutions to their problems (such as the ICI–ENI joint venture; see Grant and Martinelli, 1991). In the Netherlands, the leading chemical company, DSM, has been privatized, although the government retains five golden shares. In countries such as Britain and Germany, national governments have been marginal actors in relation to overcapacity issues, although they have become increasingly interventionist (along with the EC) on environmental control questions, an arena of increasing importance for the chemical industry.

Associative action has been of some importance in terms of the formation of APPE to represent directly the major petrochemical producers at the important EC level. It must be stressed that APPE's role is not to suggest *solutions* to the overcapacity problem; that is a matter for the companies. What it can do is to increase understanding and awareness both within the industry and outside it of the nature and scope of the overcapacity problem. It can also represent the industry to the European Commission on such vital issues as the terms on which petrochemicals from the new producers enter the Western European market. It is interesting that the industry should consider that such a new association is necessary, but it forms part of the context within which the overcapacity problem has been resolved, rather than an authoritative mechanism for organizing and enforcing cooperative behavior (a role that would not be compatible with competition law).

We would argue that the crucial governance mechanism in the resolution of the overcapacity problem in the petrochemical industry has been community in the sense of "informal networks." Transactions have been conducted between individual or corporate actors on the basis of mutual trust and confidence vested in stable informal relationships of an obligatory character. The intercompany agreements contributing to the resolution of the overcapacity problem could only have been achieved on the basis of intensive contacts based on mutual trust.

In a formal sense, what one has seen is a non-zero-sum game in which cooperation has benefitted all the participant parties. However, as is well known, the fact that cooperation can produce greater benefits than conflict in particular circumstances does not always lead to cooperative outcomes. One has to examine particular features of the chemical industry that facilitate cooperation. First, it has to be remembered that one is talking about a relatively small number of players (thirty ethylene producers in Western Europe in 1980). That is still quite a large number, but it also has to be remembered that some of these producers are more significant in market-share terms than others. Many of the producers are also *physically* linked with one another by an ethylene grid. This is largely used to cope with temporary supply interruptions resulting from accidents or maintenance (see Molle and Wever, 1984:81–2), but the fact of such cooperation in the production process strengthens interfirm links. (It is interesting to note that some of the most commercially dubious plants left at the end of the rationalization process have been those isolated from the ethylene grid.) It should also be remembered that many of the managers in the industry have a shared professional background as chemists, or chemical engineers.

Above all, the industry has a long historical tradition of interfirm cooperation (discussed earlier). Although the days of substantial international cartelization are over, many opportunities exist for informal exchanges that can lead to entirely legitimate (EC approved) restructuring arrangements. Apart from informal contacts at general gatherings of business people (say, in Switzerland), there are the meetings of the European Chemicals Market Research Association, the annual conference of the European Petrochemical Association, and the Society of Chemical Industry European Conference. Managers also have an opportunity to speak informally before and after meetings of CEFIC and APPE. In-between these meetings, views can be exchanged through the specialist journals and newsletters of the chemical industry such as *European Chemicals News* and *Chemical Insight*. Our research suggests that these and other journals are used to "launch trial balloons." Indeed, there is evidence to suggest that *European Chemicals News* was used (without its knowledge) to communicate between members of the alleged polypropylene cartel. One of the seized documents contained the following somewhat cryptic message: "June volume—restrict. 122.5 [ton] = June market assumed 130 + [ton] likely. Shell to lead. *ECN* article two weeks. ICI informed." (Reproduced in *European Chemicals News*, 8 September 1986.)

The polypropylene cartel and other cartels represent a negative example of the industry's historic tendency to engage in collusive action. On the more positive side, the various "product swaps" and joint ventures that permitted a relatively orderly and generally successful reduction of capacity were made possible by the presence of a sense of "community" within the industry. This sense of community clearly transcends national boundaries. In terms of a typology developed by Philippe Schmitter, the solutions adopted combined elements of "alliances" ("the autonomous calculations of mutual advantage strictly among business enterprises") and "networks" ("elaborated on the basis of interpersonal or intergroup reciprocity"). Neither "economistic" nor "sociological" motives would be themselves have been sufficient to provide a satisfactory outcome (see Schmitter, 1988).

One note of caution: Cooperation to reduce overcapacity was easier and more effective against a background of crisis in the industry. Ethylene profitability improved substantially between 1987 and 1989 against the background of a tight market. This has led to a number of announcements of new plants, substantial expansions, or recommissioning of mothballed units. When account is also taken of "capacity creep" through "debottlenecking," production in Western Europe could increase from the 1989 level of around 15 million tons a year to 20 million tons annually by 1995. Even if there is not a recession, the best available forecasts suggest total demand of around 17 million tons by 1995, leaving a 3 million ton surplus. (See *European Chemicals News Northern Supplement*, July 1989.) The industry could thus face renewed problems of excess capacity and poor profits. A less severe crisis than that of the 1980s might be more difficult to deal with, as it would provide a weaker impetus for effective cooperation.

The Environmental Challenge: Problem Zone for the Chemical Industry

The chemical industry in Western Europe has been noticeably successful in managing its relationship with government to produce what it regards as successful "framework conditions." This success has been a product of its organizational skill, its notably good labor relations, and its technological achievements. This very favorable balance is now threatened by the steeply rising salience of the environmental challenge, a challenge that many of the chemical industry's established practices and assumptions make it ill equipped to deal with.

The Background

The reactive processes involved in chemical production carry with them some risk of environmental damage. In the large-scale expansion of the industry in the nineteenth century, a central process—the Leblanc process for the production of alkalais—produced very visible pollution through the large-scale emission of clouds of hydrogen chloride into the air. This led to the imposition of environmental controls on the industry, especially in Britain, where the Alkalai Inspectorate became the first pollution-control agency in the world.

The regulatory balance soon began to shift very strongly toward self-regulation by the industry. The technical achievements of the industry created a dependence on the part of government, particularly in wartime. Perhaps more important, however, was the replacement of the Leblanc process. This had the effect of rendering environmental damage by the chemical industry largely "socially invisible," as its effects were not noticeable to the general public. There was very little expert dissent within the chemicals policy community, and the VCI, through a network of prizes and foundations, invested a great deal of effort in maintaining consensus in relation to nonindustrial chemists. Issues of environmental protection were argued by experts in a dialogue between industry and the bureaucracy with the dominant role being played by the industry. Participation in this dialogue by political parties and environmental groups was almost completely excluded.

The Changing Agenda

Environmental concerns began to move up the political agenda beginning in the late 1960s in most Western democracies. There were pronounced national differences of pace and emphasis, with environmental concerns relatively high on the agenda in the Federal Republic, and very low in comparative terms in Britain. Despite the increased saliency of environmental concerns, this pattern largely persisted in West Germany through the SPD/FDP governments of 1969–82 (Paterson, 1989). Very little of the environmental legislation enacted was sector specific. The major exception was the Chemicals Law of 1980, which was concerned with regulating the entry of new chemicals into the market. The Chemicals Law was the German implementing legislation of an EC directive, and the break with the principle of self-regulation was minimal. It is essentially a notification procedure where the firms rather than the state regulatory agencies carry out the great bulk of the tests, and the agencies are largely concerned with monitoring the results of these tests for plausibility. In this sense, it is best characterized as an example of "controlled self-regulation" (Klöpfer, 1981:20).

In this period the chemical industry unlike the nuclear power industry (Campbell, 1988) was able to preserve a depoliticized model of decision making. The chemical industry was expanding in the 1970s, but almost exclusively on the basis of existing sites where people in the surrounding areas were already employed in the industry. Unlike the nuclear industry, there was almost no expert dissent within the scientific community. The result was that environmental groups devoted relatively little attention to the chemical industry. IG Chemie (the chemical workers' union in West Germany) played a very effective role within the SPD (German Social Democratic Party) and the wider labor movement in keeping the environmental effects of the chemical industry off the political agenda.

The Changing Political Climate

Paradoxically, the transition to an unequivocally "industry friendly" government in the Fedeal Republic in 1982 has almost exactly coincided with the onset of real difficulties for the chemical industry in maintaining its core principle of self-regulation. The entry of the Green party (an environmental party) into the Bundestag after the German federal electrons of March 1983 began to dissolve the previous consensus based on the primacy of industrial values. The effect of the Green party's electoral surge was felt first and principally by the SPD, which now saw the need to compete with the "Greens" on environmental issues. In a major departure from previous policies, the SPD introduced a "chemicals policy" in April 1986; the main feature of this policy was to suggest that the key criterion for the registration of a new chemical substance ought to be social net benefit.

The Greens

In their first Bundestag period, the Greens concentrated on nuclear issues and the peace movement, and their impact on the chemical industry occurred at the *Länd* level when a leading green, Joschka Fischer, became environmental minister of Hesse in December 1985. There was little possibility of introducing new environmental legislation, so Fischer concentrated on the implementation stage of existing legislation, where the prevailing pattern was one of cozy relationships between a tight circle of government bureaucrats and chemical industry experts. Fischer's decision to concentrate on the implementation stage, his disinclination to proceed in a "cooperative" manner, and his readiness to staff the new ministry with outsiders who were much less sympathetic to industrial imperatives than their predecessors, all seemed very ominous to the VCI, the German chemical industry's trade association.

Regulation of the chemical industry was now well and truly on the political agenda, and issues were being generated not by a bureaucratic/expert milieu at either the national or the EC level but for the first time by political parties and environmental groups. These changes moved the VCI to develop a set of industry guidelines (*Leitlinien*), which restated its commitment to self-regulation in what it argued was a more plausible manner. In particular, the guidelines stated:

If required in terms of health care and environmental protection, it will also restrict the marketing of products or stop their production, irrespective of economic interest.

The guidelines were to apply to all plants belonging to VCI members, whether the plants were located in the Federal Republic or not. The force of the guidelines was weakened by the absence of the mention of exclusion for firms that broke the guidelines.

The *Leitlinien* had been timed to influence the German federal elections of January 1987, but the campaign was overshadowed by a series of major chemical spillages, first from Swiss plants, and then from all three major German producers, into the Rhine and Main rivers. The coincidence of the spillages with the election campaign threw the industry on the defensive and significantly weakened the case for self-regulation. These events very seriously undermined the position of Walter Wallmann, the federal environmental minister, who had given a notably warm welcome to the industry guidelines.

Self-regulation took another hit in the Imhausen Chemicals scandal where it appeared that a small company had played a major role in the construction of a chemical weapons plant for Libya despite the existence of a voluntary agreement on the export of dangerous chemicals.

A Red-Green coalition at the federal level after the December 1990 election, or even the creation of a number of Red-Green coalitons at the *Länd* level, would have meant very significant constraints on the production and distribution of chemicals. Even at present, the existence of strict emission regulations and the possibility of further restrictions in a future law on gene technology have persuaded Bayer and BASF to develop gene techology in the United States rather than the Federal Republic. Hoechst, which elected to stay in Germany, has been unable to open its $70 million plant for genetically engineered insulin. The attempt to draft a new German law on the regulation of genetic research has been beset by difficulties. In particular, it appears as though public hearings will be necessary for a genetic engineering license to produce even the most harmless products with associated opportunities for delay.

The difficulties the chemical industry has had in meeting this challenge are in stark contrast to their previous success in dealing with governments. A number of explanations suggest themselves. First, the expert leadership of the chemical industry, which is still largely dominated by chemists, finds a politicized discussion difficult. Wolfgang Hilger, the managing director of Hoechst and a distinguished chemist, responded in a very clumsy manner to the appointment of Joschka Fischer as environmental minister of Hesse. A director of one of the big three chemical companies commented in an interview, "The chemical industry suffers from the difficulty that people rely on their specialization and often find it difficult to talk to anyone else." The public affairs director of a medium-sized company argued that, while the government–industry relationship "was formerly characterized by its *sachlich/fachlich* (technical/expert) nature oriented to practical problem solving, the intrusion of ideologies and ideologists, particularly now in the bureaucracy, and the effect of the media, makes this more difficult to sustain at present. This poses particular problems since the leadership of the industry are themselves also exclusively chemist, and are much better suited to a *sachlich/fachlich* atmosphere." (Interview information).

Second, as the chemical industry admits, difficulties are inherent in the production process itself. Neither in nature nor in laboratory or production conditions can the outcome of reactive processes be predicted with absolute certainty. Risk, albeit small as the industry would argue, is inherent, and this has always been the case. The difference now is quite different public susceptibilities, and a decreasing level of risk acceptability.

The response of the chemical industry has been to beef up the resources of the chemical association. One quarter of the employees of the VCI are now involved with the work of the Environment Department. Much of the work of the Press and Documentation Center is concerned with monitoring the media comment on the environment. Since 1979 the industry has had a special organization to finance advertisements stressing the environmental achievements of the chemical industry. As Wolfgang Munde of VCI observed, "All the Greens' news automatically gets into the newspapers. I have to pay for advertisements." The industry also continued to rely on the association in dealing with the changing political environment (that is, it continued to work through its Bonn lobbyist who had been so successful in the past).

Reliance on the VCI proved much less effective than had been hoped. Advertisements had no measurable impact on public opinion, in stark contrast to the negative impact of chemical accidents. The VCI's arrangements for handling the political interface proved totally unequal in dealing with the issue once it had been politicized. The *Leitlinien* were notably weak in order to take along the smaller firms. The response of the VCI to the series of chemical spillages into the Rhine was hesitant, confused, and totally counterproductive. Since then the industry has instituted a number of changes. There is now less reliance on the VCI, and large companies stress the positive things they are doing. Bayer has produced its own "environmental perspective." All the large companies now run very expensive advertising campaigns of their own.

Not all of the time and resources invested in the VCI have been wasted. The close alliance between the VCI/BAVC (Bundesarbeitgeverband Chemie) and IG Chemie (the chemical workers' union) has been used to advantage. IG Chemie's positions on environmental issues are closely coordinated with the VCI. The link with the unions gives the industry some leverage in the SPD to try to contain environmental proposals and to work against any proposals for accommodation between the Greens and the SPD. The industry and unions have now set up a joint foundation, GIBUCCI, which concerned with environmental protection at the plant level.

The chemical industry has also continued to derive considerable benefits from associative activity at the European level. If self-regulation is becoming unsustainable in the context of the domestic politics of the Federal Republic, then the industry has a considerable interest in fostering European-wide environmental standards (e.g, in the area of gene technology). The increasing involvement of the EC in the implementation stage of environmental decisions has been a strong element in the decision of the chemical companies no longer to rely totally on the association for representation at the European level:

> Behind this change lies a realization that more and more matters have become important which simply have to be dealt with between companies and authorities at the international level. For example, in relation to all practical measures to deal with pollution, the *Verband* can issue guidelines, but the actual work must be done by the companies. (Personal communication from a Hoechst director to William Paterson.)

The difficulties experienced by the German chemical industry in this area, already more acute than in other Western European nations, would have become more grave had the Red-Green coalition emerged after the 1990 federal electrons. German pressure, the commitment of the European Commission, especially DG XI (the environment directorate general), the Single European Act, which modified the Treaty of Rome, and changing public perceptions now mean that many of the same pressures are also beginning to impinge on the chemical industry in Britain and other Western European states. The commitment of the European Commission is demonstrated by its increasing readiness to use Article 100A on environmental questions rather than Article 130, which specifically deals with environmental matters. Article 100A envisages majority voting in the Commission, which Article 130 R, S, and T practically excludes. The political leverage of the British chemical industry within the British government may have been weakened by the abolition of the chemicals sponsorship division (along with other sponsorship divisions in the Department of Trade and Industry) by Lord Young of Graffham as part of his effort to convert the department into a "department for enterprise," although Michael Heseltine reintroduced sector divisions in 1992.

This increased intervention and regulation will vary across the field of chemical production. There are very definite limits in relation to the products themselves since the regulatory authorities are necessarily almost totally dependent on the producers for information. In broad outline, there are three separate models for regulation: self-regulation, state regulation, and the model currently used—notification. This involves most of the testing being done by the firm according to rules laid down by the regulatory authorities. The regulatory authorities could not undertake this task themselves without an unimaginable increase in scientifically trained staff. Even so, regulation of the industry is likely to become much more intense on issues like emissions.

Indeed, it was on the issue of a tightening of the emissions law that BASF announced its decision to transfer the building up of a gene technology capacity to the United States. The chemical industry is likely therefore to be confronted with increasing re-regulation at a time when the rest of European industry is benefitting from deregulation.

Perhaps even more worrisome for the industry than the host of new regulations and directives are indications of changing attitudes among the regulators themselves, a change of attitudes that would significantly erode the existing advantages of the industry at the implementation stage. The net effect of environmental pressures has been to increase the process of globalization and to render Western Europe a less attractive area for the manufacture of chemical products.

Conclusions

A central theme of many of the other chapters in this volume is the process of transformation from Fordist to post-Fordist methods of production, and the implications for work organization and forms of governance of the development of flexible specialization. This theme has not been pursued in this chapter because, as Allen notes (1989:163), "the sector never fully adopted the Fordist mass production model—completely standardized products with simple and repetitive work processes—of such other leading sectors as automobiles." In a statement that would also apply to countries other than Germany, Allen notes (1989:164):

> In short, from its inception the chemical industry in Germany has been characterized by a mix of capital-intensive mass production, and only in the postwar period did flexible specialization among skilled workers become important. This mix of production processes dependent on product line has enabled the chemical industry to avoid some of the upheavals characteristic of other industries that had to make the transition to flexible specialization from a much heavier reliance on mass production.

In this chapter we focused on the pressures that are leading to further globalization in an already highly internationalized industry. The recovery of R&D costs for new speciality chemicals requires a global market. Acquisition opportunities in the United States have been, and continue to be, vigorously pursued by European companies. The resolution of the overcapacity problem in Western Europe has required cross-border cooperation among chemical companies. The industry has a history of international cartelization, and cartelization has continued as a business practice in Western Europe in the 1980s. ICI, which is in the vanguard of the internationalization process, has moved toward an internationalization of control. State-owned chemical companies in Italy have been obliged to develop a more commercial orientation in response to the internationalization of the Italian economy. (Ses Grant and Martinelli, 1991) Environmental pressures have developed in all Western democracies, and, in the case of Western Europe, these have led to the relocation of some research and production activities elsewhere in the world.

Even so, one must be aware of the limits of internationalization. Business association activity still takes place largely at a national or European level. Contacts between, for example, European and American business associations take the form of negotiation among different centers of power. Differences in national policy still have an impact on the chemical industry. Development and implementation of competition policy in Western Europe is shared between the European Community and the member states, a situation that will continue beyond 1992. Within Western Europe, EC environmental policy is implemented at national level, and there are clear divergences in the attention given to the task of implementation by national authorities, and the effectiveness of their actions. (See Grant, Paterson, and Whitston, 1988.) Although we have not had space to discuss U.S. environmental policy in any detail here, it is clearly more dependent on interpretations made by the courts than is the case in Western Europe.

One must also be careful about using the situation of the chemical industry to make more general statements about the process of internationalization and cross-national convergence. In the consumer electronics sector, for example, one has seen a very different process at work from that in chemicals. In the chemical industry, apart from the arrival of the major oil producers after World War II, the principal actors in the industry are essentially the same as those that were present in the interwar period. They have consolidated their position and extended the geographical range of their operations. The consumer electronics industry has been transformed by the emergence of Japanese (and subsequently South Korean firms), first through import penetration into American and West European markets, and later through foreign direct investment.

Although a process of growing transnationalism can be observed in the chemical industry, it does have some limits. Some of these are related to the physical characteristics of particular products (e.g., the transportation problems that limit trade in ethylene), but others are political in character. Spitz (1988:539) goes as far as to specify "government policies and actions, including social forces acting on these agencies" as an area that has had a negative impact on the financial performance of the industry, but over which the industry had no control. Clearly, the chemical industry does have a considerable capacity to exert political influence. The development of the European Community and passage of the U.S.–Canada free trade agreement open up new commercial possibilities. The emergence of the new producers, and growing political pressures in relation to the environment, present the industry with a new set of commercial and political problems. These concerns will have to be confronted at a variety of levels both within the company and in terms of the company's relations with external actors.

The overall picture is thus a very complex one that has not been possible to explore comprehensively within the confines of this chapter. We have been able to refer only briefly to intellectual property issues; we have not been able to discuss the implications of the future decline in the availability of oil as a feedstock, or financial relationships within the chemical industry at a national and international level. Even so, the general picture that emerges is of a cosmopolitan industry with stable actors, clearly demarcated boundaries, and distinctive technologies constituting a highly internationalized sector.

References

Allen, Christopher. (1989). "Political Consequences of Change: The Chemical Industry." In Peter Katzenstein (ed.), *Industry and Politics in West Germany* (pp. 157–84). Ithaca, N.Y.: Cornell University Press.

Bower, Joseph. (1985). "Restructuring Petrochemicals." In Bruce Scott and George Lodge (eds.), *U.S. Competitiveness in the World Economy* (pp. 263–300). Boston: Harvard Business School Press.

Brickman, R., S. Jasanoff, and T. Ilgen. (1985). *Controlling Chemicals: The Politics of Regulation in Europe and the United States*. Ithaca, N.Y.: Cornell University Press.

Campbell., John. (1988). *Collapse of an Industry: Nuclear Power and the Contradictions of U.S. Policy*. Ithaca, N.Y.: Cornell University Press.

Fayad, Marwan, and Homa Motamen. (1986). *Economics of the Petrochemical Industry*. London: Frances Pinter.

Graham, Ronald. (1982). *The Aluminium Industry and the Third World* London: Zed Press.

Grant, Wyn, and Alberto Martinelli. (1991). "Political Turbulence, Enterprise Crisis and Industrial Recovery: A Comparison of ICI and Montedison." (pp. 61–90). In Alberto Martinelli (ed.), *International Markets, State Policies and Business Interests: The Case of the Chemical Industry*. London: Sage.

Grant, Wyn, William Paterson, and Colin Whitston (1988). *Government and the Chemical Industry: A Comparative Study of Britain and West Germany*. Oxford: Clarendon Press.

Gusman, S., K von Moltke, F. Irwin, and C. Whitehead. (1981). *Public Policy for Chemicals: National and International Issues*. Washington, D.C.: Conservation Foundation.

Harvey-Jones, John. (1988). *Making It Happen: Reflections on Leadership*. London: Fontana/Collins.

Heller, Robert. (1987). *The State of Industry* London: Sphere.

Holloway, Stephen. (1988). *The Aluminium Multinationals and the Bauxite Cartel*. London: Macmillan.

Klöpfer, M. (1981). "Das Gesetz zum Schutz vor gefahrlichen Stoffen." *Neue Juristische Wochenschrift*, 1/2 17–22.

Mikdashi, Zuhayr. (1974). "Aluminium." In Raymond Vernon (ed.), *Big Business and the State: Changing Relations in Western Europe* (pp. 170–94). London: Macmillan.

Mirow, K., and H. Maurer. (1982). *Webs of Power: International Cartels and the World Economy* Boston: Houghton Mifflin.

Molle, Willem, and Egbert Wever. (1984). *Oil Refineries and Petrochemical Industries in Western Europe*. Aldershot: Gower.

Mussati, G., and A. Soru. (in 1991). "International Markets and Competitive Systems in the Chemical Industry." In Alberto Martinelli (ed.), *International Markets, State Policies and Business Interests: The Case of the Chemical Industry* (pp. 18–46). London: Sage.

Paterson, William. (1989). "Environmental Protection, the German Chemical Industry and Government: Self-regulation under Pressure." In Simon Bulmer (ed.), *The Changing Agenda of West German Public Policy* (pp. 73–89). Aldershot: Dartmouth.

Reader, W.J. (1975). *Imperial Chemical Industries: A History, Vol. 2: The First Quarter Century, 1926–52*. Oxford: Oxford University Press.

Schmitter, Phillipe. (1988). "Sectors in Modern Capitalism: Modes of Governance and Variations in Performance." Unpublished manuscript.

Spitz, Peter. (1988). *Petrochemicals: The Rise of an Industry* Chichester, U.K.: John Wiley.

Stocking, George, and Myron Watkins. (1950). *Cartels in Action*. New York: Twentieth Century Fund.

CHAPTER 7

Sectoral Governance in the Automobile Industries of Germany, Great Britain, and France

Ben Dankbaar

FOR OVER fifteen years, auto manufacturers in traditional car-producing countries in North America and Western Europe have been under pressure to adapt to a series of challenges and changes in their environment. This chapter is concerned with the competitive strategies of the auto manufacturers in three European countries in reaction to these challenges and more specifically with the relation among these strategies, their relative success or failure, and the systems of governance and modes of coordination of economic activity of the automotive industries in these countries.[1] The central question of our investigation is whether cross-national differences in institutional arrangements (in "industrial order" or "mechanisms of industrial governance") have made a difference in the competitive performance of the auto manufacturers in France, Germany,[2] and Great Britain.

Challenges

Ever since the oil crisis of 1973–74 the market for passenger cars has become much more of a real-world market than before. Of course, the market was already dominated by a few American and European multinational corporations long before the oil crisis, but the demand profiles of the various regional and national markets were quite different. Also, the corporations tended to follow an unwritten rule—that vehicles were to be produced where the market was. The oil crisis had an important impact on demand patterns in the United States: there was a sharp increase in the demand for small, fuel-efficient cars, which had several consequences. The American manufacturers now envisaged possibilities to produce the same size car for both the North American and the European market, to explore further the path of mass production that they had been

156

following since the days of Henry Ford. Thus, the "world car" concept was born: a vehicle that would not just be *sold* all over the world but that would also be *produced* all over the world. More important, however, was the opportunity offered to the Japanese automakers. For years they had specialized in precisely the type of cars the American consumer was now asking for. They did not hesitate to seize this golden opportunity to enter the world's largest single market. In Europe, too, the market share of Japanese manufacturers began to increase slowly but steadily. Market share was conquered first in European countries that did not have an indigenous auto industry. Investment in production activities was undertaken later in Great Britain, where the indigenous car industry was already extremely weak.

Quite apart from possible competitive advantages in price and/or quality, the mere appearance of a number of additional independent manufacturers will lead to losses in market share for the existing producers. In this case, the new competition had important price and quality dimensions as well. The new suppliers were often able to provide cars with the same or even higher quality at a lower price. Japanese manufacturers set new standards for "fits and finishes" of standard cars. Interestingly, they didn't achieve this quality advantage by expanding their quality-control apparatus (and thereby increasing costs), but by more quality-conscious production work. By doing so, they could avoid the trade-off between quality and cost that was considered normal in Western ("Fordist") production systems.

Traditionally, American automakers were leading the world in productivity, being the inventors of the mass-produced automobile and of mass production in general. The European producers, on the other hand, had gained ascendance in innovativeness, especially in product innovation, and increasingly also in product quality. The European car market never was a homogeneous market like the North American market and consequently offered fewer opportunities for refining the techniques of mass production. For the Americans, the "Japanese challenge" was first of all that Japanese manufacturers had achieved higher levels of productivity together with higher levels of quality than what had seemed possible in the U.S. As it turned out, the Japanese could do this not just with small cars but also with the larger models that are at the core of the American market.

Finally, car manufacturers were confronted by the challenges and chances flowing from new technologies, especially microelectronics, but also new materials (plastics, ceramics), that can be used both in product and in process innovation. Again, the new competitors on the world market turned out to be quite capable in dealing with the new technologies. This was especially worrisome to the European producers, whose competitive strength was based to a large extent on innovative product technology. The Japanese have shown a respectable capability in applying new technologies, microelectronics, sensors, new materials, both in product and process innovation. Moreover, the Japanese manufacturers have organized product design and renewal in a way that allows them to shorten lead times and product life cycles, thereby increasing their capacity to incorporate the newest technologies and to react quickly to changes in consumer demand.

Sectoral Governance and Performance

Naturally, if a group of companies is doing as well as the Japanese car manufacturers, all their competitors want to know why this is so. Explanations of the Japanese performance have by now flooded the industry. The business press is replete with references to "just-in-time" production, partnership relations with suppliers, quality circles, total quality concepts, the search for continuous improvement, and so forth. In the more serious studies, of course, the question is raised how all these elements of the Japanese system of manufacturing hang together and how they are related to the social context (i.e., to Japanese society). It is now widely accepted that the Japanese production system, as it has developed—for instance, at Toyota—consists of several interdependent elements (Cusumano, 1985; Schonberger, 1982). The adoption of just one or two elements is unlikely to be very productive. The question then arises whether the entire system can be adopted in a different social context. Will it be necessary to allow for changes and adaptations of the system to local circumstances, or will such imitation efforts lead to changes in the system of governance in the industry, to accommodate the Japanese system?

There is an obvious analogy to be made here with the development and diffusion of the Fordist production system. Rooted firmly in the "American system" of manufacturing, the Fordist system underwent considerable modifications when it was adopted in Europe and indeed in Japan following World War II. At the same time, the adoption of the Fordist system was also at the basis of important institutional changes in these countries. In the three nations under investigation here, the automakers performed quite well and survived for several decades under the conditions of three national variants of the Fordist system (Tolliday and Zeitlin, 1986). Confronted with the new challenges mentioned above and beset with new performance standards and new recipes for success, automakers had to develop new competitive strategies. Did the prevailing system of governance in the automotive industries determine in any way the choices made by the car manufacturers in these countries?

On several occasions Wolfgang Streeck (1988a, b) has made the point that the sectoral system of governance of the automobile industry in Germany, especially in the field of industrial relations, has contributed to the relative success of the industry over the past decade by forcing the industry's strategic choices in the direction of upmarket product policies and product innovation. Streeck argues that this was probably the only viable strategy to choose in the long run, but companies would not have chosen it had not the often criticized institutional rigidities of the German political economy forced them to.

For many years the upmarket, high-quality strategy presented itself as the appropriate "German" way to deal with the Japanese challenge. Going upmarket, however, also meant avoiding a direct confrontation with the new standards for productivity set by the Japanese manufacturers in the lower market segments. Now that the Japanese manufacturers are rapidly moving upmarket, their standards of performance in productivity and quality will be enforced by competition in the higher market segments. The question arises whether the German manufacturers will find ways of meeting these standards.

This is not impossible, according to John Krafcik (1988), who has made a comparative analysis of the performance of auto assembly plants in Europe, Japan, and North America. He argues against the "country explanation for high performance":

> Intra-regional variation in operating performance was found to be significant in North America, Europe, and Japan. Substantial overlap among these regions and relatively consistent international intra-corporation performance supports the notion that corporate parentage is at least as important as location in determining the performance of an assembly plant. (Krafcik, 1988:115)

Krafcik and others, who base their arguments on the same research (Jones and Womack, 1988), basically argue that "world class" performance levels can be achieved by adopting the Japanese system of production management. They point to evidence from the United States that such performance can indeed be transferred to other countries quite easily.[3] In a not too distant future, the Japanese-owned North American auto plants will have reached output and performance levels that will allow for volume exports to Western Europe, adding to the Japanese challenge and certainly making it more difficult to keep out by protectionist measures.

American-owned plants in the U.S., moreover, confronted with competition from across the road instead of form a foreign country, are now also improving their performance rapidly, which turns out to be "stressful" but "easier than expected." Krafcik's findings suggest that the system of sectoral governance has little impact on performance:

> [A]n effective production management policy can be shaped in any location. (Krafcik, 1988:115)

Streeck's argument about the German auto industry suggests differently. If the existing system of governance has forced the industry into an upmarket and into a confrontation-avoiding strategy, will not that same governance system prevent the industry from following a cost-cutting, confrontational strategy?[4] What about the British car industry? Can its demise be explained in terms of sectoral institutions that do not allow the introduction of new management methods, even if it means the destruction of the industry? Or was it just a failure of British management that was unable to adopt "an effective production management policy"?

Some of these questions have been dealt with by another plant-level, international-comparative research project, which has paid explicit attention to the social ramifications of plant performance (Jürgens, Malsch, and Dohse, 1989). It should be noted that, in each of these studies, performance has a somewhat different meaning. Streeck is referring to such things as size and growth of production, exports, domestic employment, and technical prowess of an industry. Krafcik is looking at product quality and productivity at the individual assembly-plant level. An industry can perform very well according to Streeck's measures and still be scoring low on Krafcik's scales. Jürgens and colleagues investigated performance in terms of work organization and quality of work (team concepts, lengths of work cycle, integration of tasks, supervisory structure, automation levels) in plants of three different car manufacturers in three countries (Germany, Great Britain, and the United States). They come to a more differentiated conclusion regarding the "country explanation." They distinguish between corporate strategies and plant strategies, where the latter are the local implementations of the former. The plant strategies, they find, are clearly influenced by the national and sectoral institutions of industrial relations, vocational training, labor market organization, occupational health and safety regulations, and other labor-related policies. In fact, differences in work organization among plants of different firms in one country were often smaller than differences between countries. That doesn't mean, however, that different corporate strategies are not clearly recognizable in plant practices. Corporate strategies are much less clearly related to the institutional context.

Jürgens and co-workers find that the basic thrust of a corporate strategy—for instance, whether it emphasizes technical innovation or worker rationalization— shows up in plant practice of every country. However,

> the influence of location of the plant is modifying and overruling many aspects of the influence of corporate decision making. . . . The national system of industrial relations and other labor-related policies and institutions in the three countries each have a particular selective effect on aims and priorities of restructuring activities in the plants. . . . These country-specific patterns of selection interact with the corporate strategic profiles, which leads to characteristic blends and mixtures. (Jürgens et al., 1989:361–63; translated by Ben Dankbaar)

Note that these country-specific patterns of plant-level work organization do not necessarily exclude the possibility of large differences in productivity and product quality between plants in the same country, as they have been found by Krafcik. On the contrary, Jürgens and colleagues find similar differences in plant productivity, not only between countries but also within the same country and even within the same corporation.[5] Where Krafcik and Jürgens et al. differ is where Krafcik underlines that a "Japanese" model of production management can be introduced everywhere. Jürgens and co-workers are inclined to emphasize the modifications this model would undergo in different institutional settings. To some extent this is just a difference in perspective. Jürgens et al. are interested in risks and chances for the workers, arising from the restructuring of work organizations in the auto industry. They would like to know if and where industrial relations and government labor policies made for a difference in the quality of labor. Krafcik is working from a management perspective, which basically is not interested in country-specific modifications of work organization or in the quality of work as long as they do not affect plant performance.

Krafcik's findings ("an effective production management policy can be shaped in any location") can be interpreted in two ways: that the system of sectoral governance has no impact on performance, or, that managements will really have to "shape" the production system to allow for the peculiarities of sectoral governance, while still achieving "Japanese" performance standards. The interesting question is: What happens if sectoral governance is indeed affecting the implementation ("shaping") of corporate strategy to the extent that productivity and quality goals cannot be realized? Jürgens et al. suggest that the system of governance will then come under pressure. Efforts will be undertaken to develop new institutions and rules that will allow the corporations to achieve world market standards (cf. also Dankbaar, 1989).

For corporate performance, what counts is only that world-class standards *are* achieved, not *how* they are achieved. Even if Krafcik is right in saying that Japanese plant performance can be achieved everywhere, the "how" can and will be governed by the prevailing sectoral institutions and/or by such changes in the institutions that the various sectoral actors can agree with or impose on each other. In the remaining part of this chapter, several aspects of sectoral governance of the auto industries in Germany, Great Britain, and France will be investigated and related to the performance of the automobile manufacturers in these countries. Special attention will be paid to signs of national or European adaptations of the high-performance model presented by the Japanese car manufacturers as well as to changes in the sectoral governance system arising from the efforts to achieve the new standards.

Performance

The automobile industries of Great Britain, Germany, and France have performed quite differently over the past twenty years. According to practically all criteria, the British industry has performed worst, whereas German industry has done best, and the French assumes a position somewhere in-between these two.

Before the first oil crisis, British production of passenger cars was already below the previous peak year 1964. Since then, it declined even further and has stabilized since the early 1980s (see Table 7.1). French and German production in 1971 was much larger than in 1964, and after the big downturn of the early 1970s, production grew to new record levels. Similarly, the contribution of automotive activities to the balance of payments of Great Britain turned negative in the course of the 1970s and deteriorated further in the following decade. The automotive balance of France remained positive, although imports have been slowly rising as a share of exports. The German industry, however, managed to improve its contribution to the balance of payments, so that in 1985 the value of exports was four times the value of imports (see Table 7.2).

Naturally, the automotive balance is also visible in the market shares that the car manufacturers are able to glean in the country where they are located. The British industry is supplying less than half of the cars being sold in the country, whereas two French manufacturers, Peugeot (PSA) and Renault, had a market share in France of almost 64 percent in 1987. The German producers topped this performance by supplying almost 71 percent of the new car registration in West Germany in 1987.

In all three countries, the economic importance of the automobile industry

Table 7.1. Passenger Car Production in Western Europe, 1957–1987

	Passenger Cars (1000s)				
	Year				
Country	1957	1964	1971	1978	1987
Germany	1040	2650	3697	3890	4374
France	738	1384	2466	3112	3052
Italy	319	1007	1685	1509	1713
Great Britain	861	1868	1685	1223	1143
Spain	–	119	453	986	1403
Sweden	56	162	287	254	432
Belgium	–	61	272	282	294
Netherlands	–	30	78	65	125
Austria	10	3	1	–	7
Total	3024	7284	10,624	11,321	12,543[a]

SOURCES: Hild (1986), Table 3; VDA, *Das Auto international in Zahlen*, 1988.
[a] Double-counts included.

Table 7.2. World Imports as a Percentage of World Exports (Cars, Trucks, Parts), 1970–1985

	1970	1975	1980	1985
France	41	37	51	68
Germany	27	30	30	25
Italy	59	51	128	125
Great Britain	21	48	103	169
Spain	131	67	44	40

SOURCE: OECD, *Statistics of Foreign Trade*, several years; author's own calculations.

is beyond doubt. Even in Britain, after many years of decline, employment in the motor vehicle industry as a share of total employment in manufacturing was almost 5 percent in 1986. It was 9.6 percent in France, and over 11 percent in Germany. In the same year, investment in the motor vehicle industry as a share of total investment in manufacturing was 15.8 percent in Germany, 8.1 percent in France, and 9.2 percent in Great Britain (the last figure is for 1985; all data from the Association of the German auto industry (VDA)).

If we go from the industry level to the firm level of analysis, some interesting patterns emerge, which enlighten but also complicate the discussion about successful versus unsuccessful industries. Table 7.3 shows profits over sales for all major car manufacturers in the three countries for the past ten years. Inter-country comparisons are somewhat hazardous in this regard because of differences in accounting rules, tax policies, and banking institutions; but the data clearly show the various ups and downs of the corporations during this difficult decade, which was characterized by a significant and long-lasting period of depression between 1980 and 1985.

Table 7.3. Percentage of Profits/Sales of German, British, and French Automakers, 1978–1987

Year	1978	1979	1980	1981	1982	1983	1984	1985	1986	1987
West Germany										
VW	2.07	2.22	0.93	0.59	-0.62	-0.33	0.54	1.27	1.18	0.80
Daimler	2.44	2.33	3.54	2.24	2.43	2.58	2.63	3.31	2.76	2.58
Adam Opel	4.62	–	4.45	-5.87	0.71	1.99	-5.40	-0.91	-0.95	2.79
BMW	2.46	2.87	2.25	1.79	1.94	2.44	2.41	2.04	2.23	2.06
Ford AG	5.24	4.43	-5.32	1.36	2.77	1.13	-2.33	-1.74	3.52	4.76
Great Britain										
British Leyland	-1.23	-4.83	-18.61	-17.32	-9.53	-4.43	2.37	-4.04		
Ford UK	4.37	12.36	9.98	7.14	6.96	-2.99	1.10	3.04	1.51	3.76
Vauxhall	0.25	-3.82	-10.87	-7.53	-3.65	-0.10	-0.72	-3.03	-4.12	1.86
France										
PSA	2.83	1.47	-2.07	-2.75	-2.83	-3.02	-0.37	5.41	3.42	5.68
Renault	0.02	1.50	0.84	-0.77	-1.23	-1.43	-11.74	-8.94	-4.78	2.50

Daimler (Mercedes-Benz) and BMW are the only two automakers in these three countries to remain profitable throughout the decade. Both are different from the other car manufacturers presented in Table 7.3, in that they are "specialist" producers supplying only the higher segments of the market. Table 7.4 demonstrates changes in employment of these car manufacturers, which gives a first indication of the competitive strategies that the firms have followed in this turbulent decade. It is obvious that Ford AG and Opel have followed a completely different approach from the three German-owned manufacturers. Ford AG and Opel have trimmed personnel by 15 percent to 20 percent since 1978 and followed a clear policy of rationalization. Employment at Daimler, BMW, and VW, on the other hand, has grown more or less steadily. It would seem here that the "German model" presented by Streeck fits the German-owned firms far better than the American-owned firms. Apparently, the German system of governance can accommodate a broad variety of company policies. Interestingly, the notion that Opel is a more "German" company, whereas Ford is more "British" but closely held by Ford US and therefore more inclined to use layoffs as a means of policy, also seems to show in these figures.

In France, Peugeot (which includes Citroen) became profitable again in 1985 after five years of losses and is now showing the highest profits/sales ratio in the industry. Renault, after a period of very heavy losses, also seems to be recovering. Both companies have been shedding labor, Peugeot more than Renault and both more than even Ford in Germany. Clearly, it took Renault much longer than PSA to rationalize its production, reflecting the status of Renault as a government-owned company with special social obligations.

In Britain, British Leyland (Austin Rover) has recently become profitable again and has been taken over by British Aerospace, in 1988, with employment and production down dramatically. Vauxhall has also been doing very poorly, with losses in eight out of the past ten years and a very poor employment record. Ford UK, has an almost perfect record of profitability over the decade, with constantly diminishing employment levels since 1980. Even though its performance in terms of employment is better than that of the other two "British" firms, it is still worse than that of any of the German or French companies.

Let us now turn to the various institutional ramifications that conditioned, guided, or hindered these automakers in their efforts to stay or become competitive in this difficult decade.

The Industrial Relations Systems

In their efforts to design competitive strategies, car manufacturers naturally have to deal with organized labor, their organizations, and all the other institutions that make up the industrial relations systems of the respective countries. In all three countries, the car industry is prototypical of mass production, and workers in the huge auto assembly plants have been a central element of industrial unionism, taking the lead in national movements on key issues of economic and social policy. The state, of course, is also present in this context as a regulator and mediator. In the field of industrial relations the three countries

Table 7.4. Employment Index of Automakers

Year	1978[a]	1979	1980	1981	1982	1983	1984	1985	1986	1987	1987 Total Employment
West Germany											
VM	100	113	114	115	114	112	115	122	122	122	170,000
Daimler	100	105	108	110	110	112	117	120	127	124	166,144
Adam Opel	100	102	92	93	92	92	92	88	85	85	55,282
BMW	100	106	106	106	108	115	119	127	135	148	55,769
Ford AG	100	99	85	85	84	82	80	79	80	81	47,104
Great Britain											
British Leyland	100	88	75	61	55	53	42	40	38	36	70,000
Ford UK	100	103	103	96	89	82	75	66	63	60	47,000
Vauxhall	100	98	92	71	62	35	38	37	38	34	11,492
France											
PSA	100	98	91	82	78	95	86	81	76	74	118,477
Renault	100	99	98	95	95	93	89	79	73	81	111,846

SOURCE: WZB Datenbank; author's own calculations.

[a] 1978 = 100.

show remarkable differences, both in union organization and in industrial relations legislation.

In Germany, we find large industrial unions that speak for all workers in the industry. For the German car industry, the metalworkers' union, IG Metall, is the only relevant organization of the workers. Especially in the car plants, membership is very high. In France, there are several major competing trade union confederations, each with their own ideological affiliation, that bind together all kinds of trade- or company-related unions. These confederations are stronger at the national level than at the branch or firm level. Union membership is weak and has been declining, although there is a much larger group of workers that is inclined to follow the unions' directives during strikes and other forms of industrial action. In Great Britain, there is only one trade union confederation (the TUC), but it is rather weak compared to the different unions representing the various trades. In the auto industry, this means that firms have to deal with a considerable number of unions representing all the different trades found in an assembly plant.

Turning to statutory rights of the workers, apart from laws protecting workers against arbitrary dismissals and regulations on health and safety, there is strong legislation on codetermination in Germany. The law on codetermination provides for elected (by the workforce) works councils, which in the auto industry consist mostly of IG Metall members, and grants these councils specific rights and influence regarding the management of plants and firms. The works councils cannot negotiate over the level of wages, which remains the exclusive domain of the union and are mostly dealt with at the branch level. In France, there is more negotiating on wages at the company level, albeit within the framework of branch-level agreements. This may explain why the unions have been less interested in participating as actively as their German counterparts in the so-called enterprise committees, the equivalent of the German works councils. These committees have some rights regarding information and bargaining. In Great Britain, such legislation is not only almost completely lacking, but seems to be rejected by management and union alike. There is no legislation creating representative bodies with statutory rights comparable to the works councils in Germany or the enterprise committees in France. Representation at the plant or enterprise level is by shop steward committees, with each member representing different trades and groups.

How do these differences translate in the behavior, functioning, and performance of the car manufacturers? Bamber and Lansbury (1987), for instance, have studied the works councils in the German automobile industry and conclude:

> One consequence of co-determination has been to lengthen the planning horizons for technological change and to heighten the priority given by managers to "the human resource implications." This has increased the role and status of personnel managers in German industry.... In recent years, compared with their German rivals, the car manufacturers in ... other countries have been less successful in the marketplace, have placed

less emphasis on personnel planning, training and consultation, but have experienced more industrial disputes. (Bamber and Lansbury, 1987: 169–70)

Much more than in the other countries, IG Metall and the works councils in the car industry have engaged in debate about work organization and job design in relation to new technologies (Mueller-Jentsch, 1988; Muster, 1988; Roth, 1988). Their strategies in this respect aim to protect the skilled worker. The semiskilled are protected by agreements to prevent involuntary dismissals on the one hand and by various training measures and job redesign on the other. These strategies are a quite natural complement to high-tech, high-skill strategies of management.

In France, conditions for the development of these types of strategies were less favorable. The importance of company-level bargaining on wages, the necessity to show strength by the mobilization of the (partly unorganized) mass of unskilled workers, and the limited importance of formally certified qualifications in the French vocational structure (see below) made for a strong emphasis on wages and the grading of jobs (Eyraud, 1983). Only in the last few years has there been growing interest on the part of the unions to participate in bargaining on training and new technologies on the basis of the so-called Auroux laws. These laws, introduced during the first years of Mitterand's presidency, provide for some forms of formal representation of the work force inside plants and companies. Thus, in what can be considered a typical French approach, the central government has intervened to improve the position of the unions and of the workers, at least partly motivated by the "German lesson" that says involvement of workers can contribute to the competitive performance of the industry. It is probably too early to say that this move has been successful and that industrial relations in France are conducted on a new footing (see Pene, 1985, for an early, skeptical judgment, complaining of stifling, tripartite management), but there seems to be widespread agreement that things are changing.

The literature concerning British industrial relations, and their presumably negative impact on industry, is voluminous. A lot of it relates to the auto industry, with emphasis on British Leyland (Rover). Just as in France, but somewhat earlier in time and under a different political constellation, the British auto industry went through a period of confrontation in industrial relations. Opinions differ over whether this has resulted in a fundamental change in the industrial relations system, but the immediate results were spectacular. When Michael Edwardes was appointed head of British Leyland (BL) in 1977, the company recorded 500 strikes per year and productivity and quality were way below continental European levels. By the end of 1982, strikes had become rare and quality had improved; productivity was up by more than 100 percent. Lewchuk (1986) has argued that the problems of the industry should be blamed not on particularly aggressive unionism, but on the production strategies chosen by British management in the early days of the auto industry. These were characterized by weak managerial control over labor, low wages, low capital-labor ratios, low levels of machine integration along flow principles, and piecework payment systems. The role of unions naturally evolved from that strategy.

At the end of the confrontation period under Edwardes, new streamlined corporate collective bargaining arrangements were agreed upon. The joint committee of shop stewards was reconstituted and a new procedure for the avoidance of disputes adopted, which no longer adhered to the principle that no change could be effectuated by management as long as the dispute over it had not been settled. Both the number of shop stewards at BL and the facilities they had access to had been reduced.

Throughout this period, the Conservative government put pressure on the unions by various pieces of legislation (concerning closed shops, strike ballots, picketing), some of which greatly divided the TUC. Changes in the industrial relations system have been quite fundamental and seem to be irreversible. This is also underlined by Marsden and co-workers (1985), who discern considerable continuity in industrial relations over the past decade and note that some of the reforms were a continuation of the processes set in motion by the Donovan Commission in the late 1960s.

If we compare the impact of unions and the industrial relations systems of these countries on corporate performance, it is only in Germany that the unions and works councils get some credit for the performance of "their" industry, even from management. Apparently, the system in Germany has a built-in flexibility that makes it relatively easy for management and unions to reach agreements on productive changes in work organization, job descriptions, and even work force reductions. In Great Britain, this has been most difficult for various reasons, especially the fact that the traditional strength of the British unions was located exactly at the shop-floor level, where most changes were considered necessary to improve competitiveness. In France, the unions were much less well organized on the shop floor, nor did they dispose of substantial strike chests. Despite some massive actions, plant occupations, and demonstrations, unions could not prevent dismissals enforced by the fierce competition on the international car market, while changes at the plant and shop-floor level could be introduced comparatively easily.

Conversely, changes in the industrial relations system seem to have been most pronounced in Britain and least important in Germany. In all three countries, however, continuity as well as change is to be noted. There are some signs of convergence of the systems, because workers and unions everywhere show a growing interest in issues of further training, upskilling, and job (re)-design. The possibilities to express and act upon this interest, however, are circumscribed by the traditional organizational patterns of unionism, the skill composition of the work force, and the statutory rights of the workers. There is clearly no convergence of government policies concerning statutory rights. In France there is a movement in the direction of German legislation, whereas the British government is not interested in strengthening the statutory rights of workers. The actual practice in both countries is far removed from the reality of the works councils in the German auto industry. An important reason for this continuing divergence is to be found in the differences in skill levels of the work forces and in the educational systems, to which we now turn.

Educational Systems

Ever since the early days of mass production the automobile industry has been employing masses of unskilled and semiskilled workers in some of the largest plants and industrial complexes of the world. Not only the work organization developed by Ford, but also the concurrent development of workplace industrial relations and industrial unionism in the industry became in many countries a general model for the social organization of production. It was only fitting that the name "Fordism" was given to this system and to this era. Recently, however, it is often argued that the days of Fordism are over and that the character of mass production is changing. Long gone already are the days when the auto industry produced large numbers of identical vehicles. The wide variety now offered to customers has made production more complicated. Besides that, cars themselves have become more complicated, especially during the last decade. New automotive technologies, many of them based on microelectronics, have rejuvenated the product. Also, in the production process, new technologies, most visibly robotics, have changed the face of the industry. Quality and quality standards have improved greatly (the average lifetime of a motor vehicle has been lengthened by several years over the past decade by better protection against corrosion, by automatic welding techniques, improved materials, and so forth). The end effect of all these changes has been that the auto plant is much less a domain of the semiskilled than it was a quarter century ago.

Although there are still large numbers of semiskilled workers employed in assembly plants, there is a general feeling in the industry that more skills are needed now and certainly in the future. Automation of assembly operations will not happen as swift and radically as in the body shop, but it is progressing steadily, and already the preparations are changing the organization of assembly (the use of automated guided vehicles, and off-line assembly of large components like the cockpit and the doors).

The supply of skilled workers is therefore an increasingly important element in the environment of the auto manufacturers. The educational systems of the three countries have to supply these workers. We will concentrate here on the systems of vocational training, as these are most relevant for the mass of the workers in the immediate future. Intercountry differences probably are also largest here. In all three countries, the government, employers, and unions are the major actors involved in defining the vocational training system.

The German system is widely seen as one of the best-functioning vocational training systems in the world. Regular school attendance is compulsary up to the age of fifteen (or sixteen in some *Länder*). After completion of any one of three types of high school, students can enter the vocational training system. In this so-called dual system, apprentices attend public vocational schools for one or two days a week where they are taught some general subjects as well as more theoretical aspects of their occupation. The rest of the week they work at a regular workplace where practical skills are acquired. As a rule, vocational training programs have a duration of three years. Workplace training is based on training regulations that, under the federal Vocational Training Act, are negotiated among the organized social partners, decreed by the Federal Republic, and supervised by the chambers of commerce and industry.

Two points about the German system need to be emphasized. The first one is its size: Training in the dual system is the classic way of entering the employment system in Germany, with about 60 percent of young people in an age cohort completing a training program in the dual system. The second point is the close and highly structured cooperation among state agencies, employers' associations, and trade unions in the development of regulations for workplace training and their coordination with the curricula for vocational schools.

In France, we find a very defferent situation indeed. One of the great problems of the French educational system—which is now generally recognized and slowly being amended—is an elitist and selective emphasis, with the result that (in 1987) almost 50 percent of the national work force had no certified skill or general education beyond the primary level (nine years) (Gambier and Vernières, 1988:68). Legislation and organization concerning vocational training, apprenticeships, and further learning have been developing together (which is different from Germany, where further learning is a more separate entity). The role of the state is much more dominant in France. For the initial training and apprenticeship system, rule-making is a responsibility of the state alone. The central government and regional authorities decide on the content of the teaching programs and the teaching and testing methods, albeit after consultations with unions and management. Only in further training is this responsibility shared with employers and unions—as far as it is paid for by the companies involved. (Further training refers both to the training programs that firms provide for their employees and to the retraining of employees threatened with layoffs; it also includes training of individuals who exercise their right to training leave.) Employers decide about their own training programs but are obliged to consult with the enterprise committee. The role of the unions in vocational training has ramained limited, but it is increasing in those places where the state is delegating some of its responsibilities to the employers and to joint bodies of unions and management.

Altogether, the system of vocational training in France seems to be adapting to the requirements of new technologies and new production methods in industry, even though there is more friction with the unions than in Germany. All these changes take time, and a large shortage of skilled workers will continue to exist in the foreseeable future.[6] Comparing the French system with the German system, the French had moved further down the Fordist trail, both in production organization (with a larger gap between skilled and unskilled labor) and in the educational system (where this gap was produced and reproduced). Now that the signals point in the opposite direction, the French have a longer road ahead of them and find it quite difficult to reintroduce skills into manufacturing practice at the shop-floor level (Maurice and Sorge, 1989).

There seems to be general agreement that in most British industries the training situation is worse even than in France and is improving less rapidly. Although the British government has recognized the problems and undertaken various actions to improve vocational training since the early 1970s, it has so far not been very effective. The traditionally decentralized organization of the training system, the relative independence of the local education authorities

(LEAs), and the lack of mechanisms for conveying the needs of industry apart from demand on the labor market were factors that were slowing down all attempts to improve the system. Also, the Conservative government's own ideology prevented a stronger, direct intervention and instead called for stimulating changes through the (labor) market mechanism, which is not very effective on this account. There is no legal basis for putting training into the collective bargaining agenda. Collective bargaining during the past decade was very much concerned with the problems created by the dividing lines existing between the skills of an earlier era. Union strength and workers' rights had been based on these demarcations, and they were therefore difficult to remove, even though they were causing high costs of inflexibility. Now that these inflexibilities have been removed after long and intense struggles, skills are clearly lacking to exploit the new opportunities to the full (Mason and Russell, 1987).

The situation in the auto industry does not differ much from that in other industries. Although the British auto industry shows similar developments as in other countries regarding the growth of new functions in a new technology environment, there is curiously little debate in the copious literature on the crisis of the British automobile industry about skill shortages and changing skill requirements. New skills have not led to the definition of new occupational profiles. They have been added onto existing skills (sometimes involving intense competition between different trades). This pattern is only slowly changing because of the many vested interests involved. As one study notes:

> Whereas the key to the West German apprenticeships and skilled work lies in access to technical competence, the pattern of regulation in Britain relies more on access to "job territories," that is, sets of tasks and the use of certain tools which are the exclusive right of certain groups of workers. (Marsden and others, 1985:79)

Thus, new tools and new tasks immediately call for a decision (and bargaining) on the occupational group (and therefore the union) that needs to be involved. Apart from the lack of a training tradition and the difficulties involved in defining new occupational profiles, the relative lack of interest in training also seems to be rooted in a lingering doubt about the significance of training for competitiveness, both among employers and unions.

Clearly, then, to the extent that competitiveness, flexibility, and optimal use of new technologies in the auto industry depend on the supply of skilled workers, the German training system is more supportive for the industry than its French or British counterparts. Moreover, British institutions seem to be more resistant to change than the French ones. It is also clear that the positive effects of the German industrial relations system are closely tied to the opportunities offered by the vocational training system.

Industry Structure: Assembler–Supplier Relations

Vertical integration and control by ownership over the full length of the production process was a long-standing strategy of the major car manufacturers.

Not too long ago, it was considered one of the strong points of firms like General Motors and Volkswagen that they produced a high percentage of the value of a car in-house. Opinions have changed, however. All major automakers are now reconsidering the production of parts in their companies, selling off some of these activities and entering into contractual relations with independent suppliers. There are at least three reasons for this development, all of which are expressions of the intensity of competition within the automobile market.

The first is financial. By concentrating on their core activities, the auto manufacturers hope to free the immense resources necessary for the development of new models and the construction of new production lines. The second reason is technological change. Many components of a modern car contain technologies (microelectronics, plastics, ceramics, and other new materials) that do not belong to the traditional knowledge terrain of the auto industry. The third reason for vertical disintegration is the example of the Japanese vehicle industry, where manufacturers are much less integrated, or rather, where vertical integration is organized differently. Japanese automakers have built hierarchical networks of subsystem suppliers (seats, braking systems, lighting systems, cooling systems) and their subcontractors around them. These suppliers may be partly or wholly owned by the car manufacturer, but the important point is that these suppliers have been given a large responsibility for product design and optimization of production of the subsystem, which often has to be delivered just-in-time to the assembler. Suppliers are associated with the design process of a new model at an early stage and contribute to it with their own specific know-how. Thus, a larger potential for innovation as well as productivity improvements is being tapped than in the traditional Western strategy of vertical integration in one enterprise with centralized R&D. Obviously, such "partnership" relations between assembler and supplier are often characterized by large differences in leverage. Japanese suppliers are subjected to extreme pressure to be competitive, but that doesn't make partnership an empty phrase. It is based on long-term relations of trust, exchange of information, and support. The creation of such relations of partnership in other countries will not happen overnight. It will depend, among other things, on the structure of the supplier industries in the different countries. In this respect Germany, France, and Britain again show some differences.

All German automakers have a strong engineering capability, but they can also rely on the considerable engineering strengths of the German components manufacturers and the machine tool industry. Volkswagen has produced its own robotic systems and has reached a relatively high level of vertical integration. Obviously the transactions between carmakers and the independent engineering firms are governed by the market mechanism, but some elements of "community" are also present, but only in the sense of being part of the same high-quality engineering tradition. These elements of mutual understanding and trust become increasingly important by the rapid growth of just-in-time delivery systems.

Relations between car manufacturers and suppliers of components in Britain have been rather complex. The British engineering industry has been historically strong, and automakers have been inclined to buy a relatively high share of the value of their products from independent parts manufacturers. Components manufacturers have suffered from the decline of vehicle production in Great Britain. Still, the overall balance of trade in motor vehicle components remains positive, although declining. The balance with the rest of the European Community (EC), however, has turned negative (House of Commons, 1987). There are probably too many components manufacturers that are too small to remain technically competent in the present period of rapid technological change. There are, on the other hand, a couple of large, technologically well-versed components manufacturers (like Lucas, ICI, GKN). These, however, have been moving an increasing part of their business overseas and in the case of Lucas seem to consider selling (parts of) their automotive business. A "community" of car manufacturers and components producers does not appear to exist.

In France, the vehicle manufacturers have long kept technological, financial, and even managerial control over their suppliers and subcontractors who did not get a chance to develop into independent entities. As a consequence,

a major part of the French component industry is under the control of foreign multinational corporations such as Bosch, Fiat Componenti, General Motors, Associated Engineering, GKN, Rockwell International, Dana, Automotive Products, etc. In terms of employees, the part under foreign control is nearly 60%. The French component industry is now integrated in a "world parts" system dominated by a number of multi-national companies whose objective is to win control of complete functions: motorisation, transmission, suspension, ignition, etc. (Chanaron, 1988:294)

Whether this will become a real disadvantage for the French manufacturers, if they try to develop "partnership" with their suppliers, remains to be seen. The big multinational components suppliers should be able and willing to supply the required components as "world class" conditions everywhere. There is no reason to assume that a French subsidiary of Bosch would be less interested in having a relation of trust with Renault than a French-owned components manufacturer. More problems can be expected in relations with the smaller suppliers, where technological knowledge is lacking and distrust of the big car assemblers is great, based on bad experiences with unprofitable contracts and lack of support. It is here that relations of trust between unequal partners will have to be built from scratch. That will take some time and it could very well be that circumstances in Germany are more favorable for such a development than in France or Britain. The latter country is suffering here too from the poor quality of its vocational training system; the former is struggling with a clash of cultures between the craft orientation of many small supplier firms and the "industrial" orientation of the big car manufacturers (Maurice and Sorge, 1989).

It should be noted that there is not just vertical disintegration but also some significant integration going on. Several automakers have taken an interest in high-technology firms, with the aim of acquiring technological know-how in the new areas that count in the international auto market.

The Role of Government

In every industry and certainly in the auto industry, many different "interventions" by government can be discerned. In his study of the effects of government policy on the British motor industry, for instance, Dunnett (1980) deals with government policies regarding exports and imports, (re)armament, distribution, taxation, roads and transport, labor relations, competition, consumer credit, economically backward regions, and safety and the environment. Dunnett concludes that "government policy did have a considerable influence on the UK motor industry [but] much of that influence was unintended and undesirable" (Dunnett, 1980:181). In the following section, no effort will be made to give a comprehensive description and assessment of government policies affecting the auto industries of Britain, France, and Germany. We will concentrate mainly on direct (financial) support by national governments for "their" car manufacturers or for the industry as a whole (i.e., on "intentional" industrial policy in the narrower meaning of the word). However, the point made by Dunnett must be kept in mind: Financial aid to an industry may be useless if other policies at the same time have (unintended) contrary effects.

Table 7.5 provides a no doubt incomplete but still illuminating overview of government assistance to the motor vehicle industries of France, Germany, and Great Britain. Looking at Table 7.5 and knowing the performance of the auto

Table 7.5. Selected Government Assistance to the Motor Vehicle Industry

Country	Period	Company	Aid (millions)	
			Reported currency	Dollar equivalent[a]
France				
3 liters research project	1981–85	Peugeot-Renault	FF500	55
FIM modernization loans	1984–85	Peugeot-Renault	FF1200	86
	1984–85		FF1250	102
Capital injections	1975–80	Renault	FF1520	169
	1982–85	Renault	FF7200	800
	1986	Renault	FF5000	557
Germany				
Auto 2000 research project	1980–84	VW/DBenz/Berlin Univ.	DM148	50
United Kingdom				
Capital injection	1978–83	BL	£2009	2612
Regional & other grants	1976–83	Ford	£158	205
	1979–82	Peugeot	£59	77
	1979–83	GM Vauxhall	£25	33
	1988–91 (projection)	Nissan	£112	146

SOURCE: Jones, 1988:51.
[a] Dollar equivalent is calculated at 1985 exchange rates.

industries in these countries, opponents of government aid to industry will certainly find their case made out for them. Although some hidden support may not show up in Table 7.5, it is clear that the industry that performed best received the least assistance from government, whereas the worst-performing industry received the most.[7] As noted above, in the case of state support through protectionist measures against Japanese imports, a similar relationship seems to exist. Even though Volkswagen is partly state-owned, it is generally agreed that government support for the car industry in Germany has been small. Explanations for the relatively successful performance of the (West) German economy and of the German car industry in particular vary, but do not normally include active government intervention, let alone financial support for individual companies (there is more of it than meets the eye and more than most Germans would like to think, but it is limited compared to other West European countries (Dankbaar, 1987). About British government assistance to the auto industry and particularly about its failure to have much of a visible impact, a voluminous literature has by now come into existence, which we will briefly review below. Probably just as interesting, but not as much a subject of academic discussion and scrutiny, is the case of France. State support for Renault may not have been cheap, and it may not have been efficient, but at least it seems to have had some positive effect. The question arises: What factors of positive influence were present in France that were apparently absent in Britain?

Production of motor vehicles in Great Britain grew steadily throughout the postwar period, reaching an all-time peak in 1972. However, productivity growth was lower than in neighboring countries, and poor labor relations in the automotive industry had become a cause of concern and subject of special public inquiry on several occasions in the 1950s and 1960s. Moreover, the industry seemed to be unable or unwilling to consider the consequences of the opening up of the British market to foreign competitors (entrance into the common market in 1973), and far too long its export strategies remained focused on slow-growing Commonwealth countries.

By the mid-1970s Britain was facing a trade deficit in passenger cars, which to no small extent was due to "captive imports" by Vauxhall and Ford, which found it easier and cheaper to produce in Spain, Belgium, or Germany than in their British plants. The British Leyland Motor Company (BLMC), the only British-owned manufacturer, was doing so poorly that it had to close its assembly operations in Belgium, Italy, and France. BLMC had been created in 1968 by the last of a long series of mergers in which all British producers participated. As such, BLMC contained the remains of Austin, Morris, Daimler, Standard Triumph, Leyland, Rover, and Jaguar. By 1974 this complex enterprise had not managed to streamline its various operations, was practically bankrupt, and was subsequently purchased by the British government. Its name was changed to BL and more recently into Austin Rover Group and then simply Rover Group. Jaguar regained its independent status in 1983 to become quite successful again (subsequently, Ford gained control in 1989).

Furthermore, in 1987 the commercial vehicle activities (Leyland Trucks) were taken over by DAF (Netherlands). Other businesses that belonged to the

Austin Rover Group were also sold off over a period of two to three years, so that the work force had been reduced from about 70,000 in 1986 to about 40,000 by mid-1988, when the Group was taken over from the British government by British Aerospace. Thus, in retrospective, the fourteen years of government ownership proved to be a period of prolonged rationalization, cutting out some of the healthier parts of the corporation and ending with the disappearance of the Rover Group as an independent entity.

All students of the role of government in the British auto industry over the postwar period emphasize that government has been insensitive to the needs of the industry (cf. Wilks, 1984). Williams, Williams, and Haslam (1987) suggest that even if management had been perfect at Austin Rover (and it was not), it would not have been successful because government policies created a wrong economic environment. They argue that the main aim of government should have been to safeguard a larger share of the British car market for the British manufacturers, presumably by protectionist measures. Thatcherism, so they say, misrepresented the problems of manufacturing and exaggerated what management could do. As long as imports were not slowed down, any management of Austin Rover would have been forced to retreat into mere assembly operations. Thus, even before the expensive program of product renewal had run its course, BL found out that it could not recoup its market share without further and other types of support that the government was not willing to provide.

To speed up the new product program, cooperation was initiated with Honda, a first important step away from the goal of an independent British-owned, full-line car manufacturer. A few years later, the government actively encouraged (with a grant of over £100 million) the establishment of a new assembly plant by another Japanese manufacturer, Nissan. Starting up in September 1986, this plant has reached a local content (EEC content) of over 60 percent in 1988, which means that its products will no longer fall under the limits set on Japanese vehicle imports. This government-supported pressure on Rover's market share no doubt contributed to the latter's continuing decline. Since then, Honda has expanded its activities in Britain, and Toyota has announced that it will start assembly operations as well. Because of this, production and employment will increase again in the British automobile industry. Whether direct implantation of the Japanese model is sufficient to drag the rest of the auto industry and British industry at large out of the vicious circle of bad management, insufficient vocational training, conflictive industrial relations, and "incoherent" government action remains to be seen.

The situation in France is in many respects quite different. Renault has been state-owned since World War II, and although privatization is no longer a forbidden theme, the French government has long been reluctant even to change the status of the firm from a *Regie Nationale* (whose losses are automatically absorbed by the state) to a normal corporation (that would have access to the private capital market).[8] France has a long-standing tradition in industrial policy and conscious state intervention in the economy, which is not tied to one specific political current (Groenewegen, 1989). That does not mean that the French government has in any sense managed Renault (although, as in

Britain, it did not hesitate to appoint a new chairman when it considered that necessary). It did show more awareness of the complex interrelations in an industrial economy and seems to have been better equipped and more willing to deal with them. Up till now, it has also enforced protectionist measures that have kept the market share of the Japanese automakers down to a mere 3 percent.

In 1962, when Renault received financial support for the first time to invest in a large program of model diversification, the company presented a five-year plan to the government that was to be revised annually. The plan remained secret and was discussed only with the Ministry of Industry and responsible representatives of the Finance Ministry. In the 1960s, the financial backing of the government enabled Renault to grow significantly. Production was doubled and exports increased along with a growing number of assembly plants all over the world.

The 1970s were more difficult, but Renault followed the same expansionist line and took control of the U.S. auto manufacturer American Motors (AMC) in 1979. At the same time, without comparable state backing, Peugeot grew by merger, first buying Citroen in 1975 and then Chrysler-Europe (Simca) in 1978. Thus, the difficulties and costs of rationalizing the industry and integrating diverging company cultures, which made British Leyland stumble in the mid-1970s, were borne by Peugeot (PSA) and not by state-owned Renault. Now, of course, Renault did have a price to pay for the support from the government. It was expected to set an example in the field of social policy and industrial relations. It therefore came to pay higher wages than the other French car manufacturers and until 1985 never made any compulsory layoffs. In the early 1980s, when both French firms ran into considerable problems, Renault's social policy became a handicap. By the end of 1986, Renault's debt amounted to 62 billion francs and PSA's to 30 billion francs. Both firms now received financial support from the government and both were allowed to cut down on employment considerably. Various measures of rationalization, such as lowering the break-even point and the sale of loss-bringing assets (selling AMC to Chrysler in 1987) seem to have been quite effective so far.

The French have not found an infallible method of government intervention, but rather a willingness to accept government as a strategic actor in the industry, an actor who can make costly mistakes and design policies with unintended detrimental effects, but who is strongly—some might say excessively—supportive of the survival of a French-owned motor vehicle industry.

A similar point can be made for Germany. Even though there is a much greater reluctance to engage in direct (financial) government support for industry, all major actors accept the fact that government has a role to play in the economy. Government seeks to play that role within a framework of more or less corporatist institutions, which provide for participation of major social groupings. We have encountered such institutions in the field of industrial relations as well as in the area of vocational training. It can be argued that this has resulted in interventions that were less costly than in France and more coherent than in Britain, and apparently also more effective.

Conclusions

The increasingly international character of the passenger car market and the intensity of competition have forced all auto manufacturers to adopt new technologies quickly and to review their operations with an eye on best practice and best performance on a world scale. At the level of strategic decision making, the location of enterprise headquarters does not seem to matter very much. Even at the plant level, internationalization seems to lead to similar developments in all countries, independent of the specific institutional settings (Krafcik). Of course, this is nothing new, and the assembly line ("Fordism") is an older example of this phenomenon.

However, if one takes a closer look, it is possible to see that the governance structures in the various countries offer different opportunities for strategic choice to the car manufacturers. It would seem that the governance structure in Germany offered the choice of a relatively early start along a high-tech, upmarket trajectory. It remains to be seen whether the industry can adjust to intensified competition in the higher market segments, but there are signs that it will be able to do so. The crucial point is that in many fields of action the German environment seems to dispose of institutions and procedural rules, to accommodate differences of interests and also—if necessary—to provide for changes of the rules. In Germany, as opposed to Great Britain, the regime of governance consists not only of old solutions to old problems of achieving acceptable performance but also of rules to find new solutions to new problems arising in the marketplace.

The governance structure o France and Great Britain apparently did not provide the options that the German industry had, especially in the areas of industrial relations and vocational training. Strategies subsequently followed by the French and British manufacturers were far from successful and raised the question of the necessity for institutional change. Here, the role of government turns out to be of crucial importance. The British government was prepared to provide huge sums to the auto industry (Chrysler/Talbot, British Leyland, Nissan); it also applauded institutional change (both in industrial relations and vocational training), but mostly by supporting selected actors (mainly employers) and not by initiating a national dialogue and a broadly based process of institutional transformation. The French government has been more inclined to insist on its own responsibilities in this respect. The result is, as most observers agree, that things are moving much slower in Great Britain than in France.

If institutions are changing under the pressures of a new competitive environment, they do not necessarily change in the same direction. What counts is the outcome (a larger supply of skilled workers, more involvement of workers in the production process, more flexible arrangements for the division of labor in the plant). Naturally, the example of successful countries provides some direction. In French legislation on industrial relations, the "German model" is clearly present. In British debate about vocational training, the German system is also regarded as a model to be followed. As a result, the institutional systems of the three countries will show a tendency to converge. This is also happening for other reasons, most prominently because of the integration of Europe itself.

Convergence, however, is not to be confused with being identical. There will in all likelihood remain substantial differences, just as there always have been differences among these countries that did not prevent their manufacturers from being competitive. Competitiveness is the final and indeed often the only criterium. As long as competitiveness seems to be ensured, no one is interested in engaging in the difficult political process of changing institutions. The globalization of markets has put more institutions to the "competitiveness test" than ever before. The process of change, however, is still to a large extent a process of national actors and traditions.

Is there a shift visible in the mixture of governance mechanisms prevailing in the different countries? Not in the sense that in any specific area one mechanism is replaced by another. What we see is an increasingly complex constellation of different mechanisms regulating an activity or relation. The relations between assemblers and suppliers can no longer be characterized by the simple dichotomy of markets and hierarchies ("buy or make"). Strong elements of cooperation and partnership have been introduced. The same can be said for industrial relations, where associations of employers and employees are discovering common ground. Where the state is withdrawing as a supplier of finance, change seems to be greatest and unidirectional, but our discussion has clearly shown that the function of government as a mediator and organizational framework for institutional change is more important and not decreasing. Perhaps we can draw the conclusion that a new emphasis on "community," on shared values, shared history, and common interests has been superimposed on the existing regulatory mechanisms that continue to function. This is no doubt a result of the discovery of the importance of community for the "Japanese model," but was already present in the German/Scandinavian model as well.

Finally, community does not replace the market or the firm (hierarchy) or the state or the associations and interest groups, but it does point to the limits of these various governance mechanisms when they are employed to the exclusion of each other. It underscores the need for a more complex and more subtle mixture of regulatory mechanisms to deal with the problems of change and stability in a highly internationalized and highly politicized industry.

Notes

Apart from the indispensable support and encouragement provided by the editors and other participants in the project, the author gratefully acknowledges critical questions and comments by Stephen Wood (London) and George Eads (Detroit), who nevertheless can in no way be held responsible for the final product.

1. This chapter is mainly concerned with the manufacturers of passenger cars, that is, with those assemblers who are usually responsible for the production of such basic components as the engine and power train, and for the activities going on in an automobile assembly plant: pressing, welding, painting, and final assembly. Independent component manufacturers (suppliers) and manufacturers of commercial vehicles will not be considered in any detail.

2. Throughout this chapter, "Germany" refers to the Federal Republic of Germany (West Germany) before unification with East Germany.

3. Krafcik (1988) finds that production management policy has a great effect on

plant operating performance. Production management policy is found to have greater explanatory effect on productivity than Japanese partentage. Data used to construct an indicator of production management policy refer to elements of the Japanese production system, but they are quite crude and would seem to allow for considerable variation in actual practice.

4. In this analysis, Krafcik (1988) has made corrections for differences in product, so that his findings express "real" differences in productivity, as if all plants were producing more or less the same car.

5. Jürgens, Malsch, and Dohse (1989) have not corrected for product differences as Krafcik has done, but they have selected plants that are producing comparable models (sometimes the same) for the same market segment. Their data show that, especially in the United States, plant performance is showing strong cyclical movements through the years. Plant comparisons should therefore preferably be based on data over a period of several years.

6. On the other hand, because of the same elitist characteristics of the educational and social system, French industry is very strong in such technologies as computer-aided design (CAD).

7. Table 7.5 does not mention a five-year plan that was agreed to in June 1985 between the British government and the management of the Austin Rover Group (ARG), providing additional state guarantees on the company's private borrowings with the understanding that this would be the last time that government would provide public funding for the ARG. Williams, Williams, and Haslam (1987:110) come to a total cost of £2,100 million in equity capital and £1,500 million of state guarantees on borrowings since 1977. *The Financial Times* (18 June, 1988) mentions an even higher total of £3.8 billion since 1976.

8. The Right-wing government under Jacques Chirac has proposed to write off 12 billion francs' worth of debt at Renault, and in its request for approval from the European Community linked this to a change in the legal status of Renault. The new Socialist government decided to go on with the debt write-off without changing the status of Renault. The chairman of Peugeot, Jacques Calvet, was strongly opposed to further state aid for Renault, saying that it had already received 12.7 billion francs in capital grants from the state since 1982 (*Financial Times*, 6 January 1989).

References

Amadieu J. F. (1987). "Employment Flexibility, Unions and Companies in France." *Industrial Relations Journal*, 18(2), pp. 117–123.

Bamber G., and Lansbury R. (1987). "Codetermination and Technological Change in the German Automobile Industry." *New Technology, Work and Employment*, 2(2), pp. 160–71.

Boyer, Robert. (1989). "New Directions in Management Practices and Work Organisation." Paper presented at the OECD Conference on Technological Change as a Social Process, Helsinki, December 11–13, 1989.

Brody M. (1985). "British Unions go Japanese." *Fortune*, December 9, pp. 62–65.

Chanaron J. J. (1988). "Productivity, Vertical Integration and Competitiveness: Some Methodological Reflections and Empirical Evidences." In B. Dankbaar et al (eds.), *Die Zukunft der arbeit in der automobilindustrie*. Berlin: Edition Sigma.

Cusumano, Michael A. (1985). *The Japanese Automobile Industry. Technology and Management at Nissan and Toyota*. Cambridge, Mass: Harvard University Press.

Dankbaar, Ben. (1987). "Industriebeleid in West-Duitsland." In Hans Schenk (ed.),

Industrie- en Technologiebeleid: Analyse en Perspektief (pp. 141–72). Groningen: Wolters-Noordhoff.

Dankbaar B. (1989). "Technical Change and Industrial Relations: Theoretical Reflections on Changes in the Automobile Industry." *Economic and Industrial Democracy*, 10, 99–121.

Dankbaar Ben; Ulrich Jürgens; and Thomas Malsch (eds.). (1988). *Die Zukunft der Arbeit in der Automobilindustrie*. Berlin: Edition Sigma.

Dunnett P. J. S. (1980). *The Decline of the British Motor Industry. The Effects of Government Policy, 1945–1979*. London: Croom Helm.

Eyraud F. (1983). "The Principles of Union Action in the Engineering Industries in Great Britain and France. Towards a Neo-institutional Analysis of Industrial Relations." *British Journal of Industrial Relations*, 21(3), 358–76.

Gambier D., Vernières, M. (1988). *L'emploi en France*. Paris: La Découverte.

Groenewegen J. P. M. (1989). *Planning in een Markteconomie, Indicatieve Planning, Industriebeleid en de rol van de Publieke Onderneming in Frankrijk in de Periode 1981–1086*. Limburg: Proefschrift, Rijksuniversiteit.

Hild, Reinhard. (1986). "Japans Druck auf den Pkw-Weltmärkte. Zunehmendes Engagement in Nordamerika und Westeuropa." *Ifo-Schnelldienst*, 33/86, pp. 7–21.

House of Commons. (1987). *Third Report from the Trade and Industry Committee, Session 1986–87: The UK Motor Component Industry, Report, Proceedings of the Committee, Minutes of Evidence and Appendices*. London: Her Majesty's Stationery Office.

IG Metall. (1988, April). *Die Entwicklung der Fertigungstiefe in der Autoindustrie, Eine Information der IG Metall Vorstandsverwaltung (Wirtschaftsabteilung)*, Frankfurt.

IG Metall Vorstand Abteilung Wirtschaft. (1988). *Unternehmensvergleich, fur das Geschäftsjahr 1987*, Frankfurt.

IG Metall Vorstandverwaltung Wirtschaftsabteilung. (1988, Juli). *Fertigungstiefe der Automobilindustrie, Fortschreibung des Papiers vom April 1988*, Frankfurt.

d'Iribarne, Alain, and Annick Lemaitre. (1987). *The Rule of Unions and Management in Vocational Training in France*. Berlin: Cedefop.

Jones D. T. (1988, April). "Structural Adjustment in the Automobile Industry." *STI Review, Science Technology Industry, OECD*, No. 3.

Jones D., and J. Womack. (1988, October 28). "The Real Challenge Facing the European Motor Industry." *Financial Times*.

Jones, Daniel T. (1985). "Vehicles." In Christopher Freeman (ed.) *Technological Trends and Employment 4: Engineering and Vehicles* (pp. 128–87). Aldershot: Gower.

Jürgens U., T. Malsch, and K. Dohse. (1989). *Moderne Zeiten in der Automobilfabrik: Stragtegien der Produktionsmodernisierung im Länder- und Konzernvergleich*. Berlin: Springer-Verlag.

Krafcik J. F. (1988). *Comparative Analysis of Performance Indicators at World Auto Assembly Plants*. MA Thesis, Massachusetts Institute of Technology.

Lewchuk W. (1986). "The Motor Vehicle Industry." In B. Elbaum and W. Lazonick (eds.), *The Decline of the British Economy*. Oxford: Clarendon Press.

Marsden, David, Timothy Morris, Paul Willman, and Stephen Wood. (1985). *The Car Industry. Labour Relations and Industrial Adjustment*. London and New York: Tavistock.

Mason, Charlie, and Russ Russell. (1987). *The Role of the Social Partners in Vocational Education and Training in the United Kingdom*. Berlin: Cedefop.

Maurice, Marc, and Arndt Sorge. (1989, January). "Dynamique industrielle et capacité d'innovation de l'industrie de la machine-outil en France et en RFA, discussion paper, LEST-CNRS, Aix-in-Province.

Mueller-Jentsch, Walther. (1988). "Arbeitsorganisation und neue Techniken als Gegenstand betriebs- und tarifpolitischer Konzeptionen und Strategien der IG Metall." In B. Dankbaar et al (eds.), *Die Zukunft der Arbeit in der Automobilindustrie* (pp. 263–80). Berlin: Edition Sigma.

Muster M. (1988). "Neue Formen des Arbeitseinsatzes in hochautomatisierten Fertigungsbereichen der Automobilindustrie." In B. Dankbaar et al (eds.), *Die Zukunft der Arbeit in der Automobilindustrie* (pp. 95–113). Berlin: Edition Sigma.

Prais, S. J., and Karin Wagner. (1985, May). "Schooling Standards in England and Germany: Some Summary Comparisons Bearing on Economic Performance." In *National Institute Economic Review*, pp. 53–76.

Pene D. (1985). "L'industrie automobile française: Problèmes et solutions." *Revue d'economie industrielle*, 31, 51–56.

Roth S. (1988). "Gruppenarbeit in deutchen Automobilbetrieben: Perspektiven aus Gewerkschaftlicher Sicht." In B. Dankbaar et al (eds.), *Die Zukunft der Arbeit in der Automobilindustrie* (pp. 185–210). Berlin: Edition Sigma.

Schonberger, Richard J. (1982). *Japanese Manufacturing Techniques: Nine Hidden Lessons in Simplicity*. New York: Free Press.

Streeck W. (1988a, January). "Successful Adjustment to Turbulent Markets: The Automobile Industry." discussion paper, *Wissenschaftszentrum Berlin*.

Streeck W. (1988b, May). "Kollektive Arbeitsbeziehungen und industrieller Wandel: Das Beispiel der Automobilindustrie." discussion paper, *Wissenschaftszentrum Berlin*.

Streeck, Wolfgang et al. (1987). *The Role of the Social Partners in Vocational Training and Further Training in the FRG*. Berlin: Cedefop.

Tolliday, S., and J. Zeitlin. (1986). *The Automobile Industry and Its Workers: Between Fordism and Flexibility*. Cambridge: Polity Press.

l'Usine Nouvelle. (1987, April 2). "Renault ne sera plus une 'vitrine sociale': Une interview de Michel Paderie, directeur du personel et des affaires sociales," pp. 92–93.

Wilks S. (1984). *Industrial Policy and the Motor Industry*. Manchester: Manchester University Press.

Williams K., J. Williams, and C. Haslam. (1987). *The Breakdown of Austin Rover: A Case-Study in the Failure of Business Strategy and Industrial Policy*. Leamington Spa, Hamburg: Berg.

Wood S. (1988). "Some Observations on Industrial Relations in the British Car Industry." In B. Dankbaar et al (eds.), *Die Zukunft der Arbeit in der Automobilindustrie* (pp. 229–48). Berlin: Edition Sigma.

CHAPTER 8

Industry or Infrastructure?
A Cross-National Comparison of Governance: Its Determinants and Economic Consequences in the Dairy Sector

Franz Traxler and Brigitte Unger

THIS chapter analyzes the relationship between economic conditions and governance with regard to the dairy sector, specifying two main questions: How do economic conditions, especially efficiency pressures, influence sectoral governance, and to what extent does governance affect the sector's economic efficiency? To investigate these questions cross-nationally, one must select countries with variation in their governance arrangements. Thus it is for this reason that the United Kingdom, Germany, and Austria have been chosen. Even so, governance of the dairy industry has only modest variation in the governance arrangements in advanced Western *countries* but differs remarkably from other *sectors* within those countries. More specifically, national systems governing the dairy industry are higly corporatist institutions with unusual and complex governance priorities in which efficiency criteria typical of industries (like profitability) and other criteria typical of an infrastructure (including social benefits) are of nearly the same importance.[1]

To explain the impact of economic conditions on governance and the impact of governance on economic performance, this chapter directs attention not only to the factors accounting for national variations of the dairy sector, but also to those making dairy extremely different from most other sectors. Responding to the complexity of governance priorities, a multidimensional concept for measuring economic efficiency and linking it to governance is developed. The chapter outline is thus: a short description of the economic characteristics of the dairy sector in the U.K., Germany, and Austria; an overview of the national governance systems[2]; an analysis of the determinants of governance; and, finally, an inquiry into the consequences of national governance systems for economic efficiency.

Economic Characteristics of the Dairy Sector

The most striking difference between the three countries occurs when considering the size of farms. In 1985 the average number of cows per dairy farm was seven in Austria, fifteen in Germany and fifty-eight in the U.K. Large differences also exist in the average return of milk per cow. Austria has the lowest annual average return per cow and the U.K. the highest (see Table 8.1).

The main problem of the dairy sector in Austria and Germany concerns overcapacity in the European Community (EC) as a whole. Historically, the increase of milk production was aimed at assuring national independence in case of crisis. In Austria, for example, milk is considered to be of such importance as nutritive food that a certain level of excess supply (21 percent of production) is argued to be necessary for reasons of safeguarding capacity for political crises and independence (Bellak, 1988). The problem of overcapacity is managed partly by subsidized exports, partly by the inevitable increase in milk stocks.

Development of Domestic Demand

Demand for fresh milk products (cream, yogurt, etc.) is increasing only in Germany, while it is stagnant in Austria and even declining in the U.K. The demand for butter has been declining in all three countries since 1970, because health considerations have resulted in a substitution of margarine for butter.

Milk Processing

A remarkable difference of concentration of dairy enterprises exists in the three countries. In 1983 in the U.K., the five largest enterprises consisting of 157 firms absorbed 80 percent of cow's milk delivered, while on the other hand 43 percent of the smallest firms absorbed only 5 percent (Ifo, 1985). The British dairy industry is therefore highly concentrated. In Germany a higher percentage of firms is of medium size. Forty-six percent of firms processed between 20 million and 100 million tons of milk and absorbed 48 percent of the milk delivered. In Austria there exists a lot of small firms (especially for cheese production), but no large firm processes more than 100 million kg of milk. A German firm on average absorbs twice as much milk as in Britain and four times as much as in Austria (see Table 8.1). Raw milk is the most important input factor in all three countries, accounting for about 70 percent to 75 percent of dairy firms' turnover.

The dairy industry employed 5869 people in Austria (1986), 46,888 in Germany (1983), and 41,633 in the U.K. (1983). Six percent of those employed in the food processing industry (food, beverages, and tobacco industry) worked in the dairy industry in Austria in 1986, while in Germany it was ten percent and in the U.K. seven percent.

Distribution of Dairy Products

Distribution of milk and other dairy products in Germany is characterized by a highly complex system of distribution and many types of wholesale and retail trade (Ifo, 1985:63). Retail pressure is weakened by the fact that a big share of

Table 8.1. Economic Characteristics of the Dairy Industry

	Austria	Germany	U.K.
THE PROCUREMENT MARKET			
Contribution of milk to final agricultural production 1986	22%	27%	22%
Average dairy farm size	very small	medium	large
Average number of cows per farm 1985	7	15	58
Average return of milk per cow 1986	3,815 kg	4,843 kg	5,100 kg
Cow milk production 1986 in 1000 tons	3,790	26,349	16,230
Share of raw milk delivered to milk plants 1984	64%	93%	97%
THE SALES MARKET			
Foreign demand for dairy products	net exports	net exports	net imports
Domestic demand for dairy products			
demand for liquid milk	low and stable	very low and stable	very high and declining
demand for other fresh milk products	high and stable	high and increasing	low and declining
demand for cheese	moderate and increasing	high and increasing	low and increasing
demand for butter	low and declining	high since 1984 rising	low and declining
DAIRY PROCESSING			
Milk absorbed by a dairy plant on average (in millions of kg)	12.5	50	25
Concentration of firms	low	moderate	·very high
Most important input cost	raw milk	raw milk	raw milk
Number of employed persons	5,869	46,888	41,633
Excess supply:			
Butter stocks 1987	5,000 tone	416,000 tone	267,700 tone
skimmed milk stocks 1987	12,000 tone	474,000 tone	41,300 tone
cheese stocks 1987	9,000 tone	46,000 tone	123,400 tone
Retail pressure	zero	low	low

SOURCE: OECD, *Milk and Milk Products Balances in OECD countries 1976–1984*, Paris: 1986; EUROSTAT, *Yearbook of Agricultural Statistics 1985 and 1988*.

milk product distribution is under the control of processor-owned trading companies that have created efficient centrally located stocks, which supply retailers. In the U.K. wholesale trade of dairy products varies according to the kind of product being traded. In the domain of liquid milk distribution, processing firms dominate the market, especially in England and Wales. In Austria every processor is obliged to supply marketers within fixed areas, and marketers are obliged to buy only from the designated processor, giving perfect monopoly power to processors (see also below). The dairy industry does not suffer from high pressure from the demand side, unlike the food processing industry as a whole (see Farago, 1987).

Governance of the Dairy Sector

Exchange relations performing the transfer of resources within a sector and its environment comprise a multiplicity of economic issues such as the division of labor among sectoral companies, their interaction with suppliers and customers, and their procurement of capital, labor, and knowledge. Analyzing the governance of these and all the other transaction issues shaping the dairy sector would exceed the scope of this study. Moreover, such an all-encompassing approach is not necessary as economic restructuring serves as the main point of reference for this comparative analysis. Because the sector' main problem is excess supply, arising primarily from a glut of raw materials (especially of raw milk), the governance of processors' relations with the primary producers who supply raw milk is an economic transaction of special importance for this analysis. Another issue of importance is the governance of the processors' relations with wholesalers and retailers. This is an important issue because of the glut of raw milk resulting in excess production within the dairy industry. This creates a problem of equating the industry's supply with the demand for processed products.

The following are the parameters of economic transactions to which governance mechanisms are being related:

   the selection of transaction partners by sectoral firms; this parameter also refers to the conditions of market entry;
   the determination of quality of the subject of transaction;
   the determination of quantity of the transaction subject; and
   the setting of prices.

Combining these parameters of economic transactions with transaction issues most relevant for restructuring the dairy industry provides a two-dimensional framework for empirical investigations (Table 8.2). According to this, the comparative analysis of the governance of the dairy sector in the United Kingdom, Germany, and Austria outlined below will focus on mechanisms governing the following:

   the selection of transaction partners/market entry, and the determination of the quality, quantity, and price of the subject of transaction as far as the dimension of *parameters* is concerned, and

Table 8.2. A Framework for Empirical Investigations

	Transaction issues	
Transaction parameters	Relations with primary producer	Relations with customers
Selection of partners/market entry		
Quality of transaction subject		
Quantity of transaction subject		
Price of transaction subject		

the sector's exchange relations with suppliers (of raw milk) and customers in the dimension of *transaction issues.*

United Kingdom

Beginning with the dairy sector's relations with suppliers, no choice between possible transaction partners is left to processors owing to the operation of farmers' coalitions, the so-called Milk Marketing Boards (MMBs), which effectively control the supply of raw milk in the U.K. The boards purchase almost all the milk produced by farmers and organize selling it to the dairy companies; they negotiate with the dairy industry's representatives on a wide range of marketing matters including the boards' selling price.

The MMBs perform this marketing function with legally constituted governance powers and they have certain obligations as well. All farmers intending to produce cow's milk for sale must first obtain government authority to do so.[3] They must then apply to their area MMB to be registered as a producer and take up board membership. The central obligation of the boards to their members is to buy and find a market for all milk offered for sale, provided it complies with certain standards of quality.

Given this legal framework, the MMBs have a "dual personality" (Giddings, 1974), being a quasi-governmental organization and a representative of primary producers (Grant, 1983a). For processors, this milk marketing system means that they are confronted with a state-empowered monopoly that controls the supply of raw milk. Furthermore, setting the buying price for raw milk is beyond the direct influence of processing firms because price negotiations must be conducted centrally with the MMB.

The MMB of England and Wales "undertakes to market all the milk the farmer wishes to sell; to arrange for its collection and transport; to maximize return by giving priority, in the allocation of supplies, to the most remunerative markets" (Grant, 1983:8). For this purpose, it is characteristic of this MMB that it has moved forward into the processing sector. Owning and controlling processing plants can contribute to realizing the milk board's marketing goals since this provides additional opportunities of promoting the sale of processed dairy products in general and of launching new products in particular, all of which results in absorbing greater quantities of milk (Grant, 1983a:13). In managing these various activities, the board's commercial goals resulting from its processing activities have been subsidiary to producers' objectives.[4]

Among all its marketing activities, the board's key function is negotiating with the dairy industry's representatives on selling prices for raw milk. This takes place institutionally in a Joint Committee, the composition and competence of which are defined by law. According to the Milk Marketing Scheme of 1979, the Joint Committee consists of members appointed by the MMB and members appointed by the Dairy Trade Federation (DTF). The DTF is a peak association with four constituent member associations through which it organizes manufacturers, wholesales, and retailers. As a consequence of this encompassing domain and its specific relation to the MMB in the Joint Committee, all other business associations outside the DTF are irrelevant.

Within this procedural framework the selling price for raw milk is negotiated product by product by the MMB and by the DTF. This means that separate prices are set for different uses to which the milk is put. In this respect, pricing is split for processing milk differentiated according to twelve categories of different milk products and for liquid milk. An important condition for price negotiations is the EC target and intervention system for butter and skimmed milk powder, which sets the floor price for milk for manufacture and also, indirectly, the price for liquid milk. Ultimately, the prices achieved in the Joint Committee depend on market forces and the skill of the negotiators (Grant, 1983a:14).

This pricing system has been in operation since 1985. While setting prices for manufacturing milk has been under control of the Joint Committee since 1954, fixing prices for liquid milk before 1985 was the responsibility of the Minister of Agriculture, who set the maximum wholesale price (at which the MMB sold to the processors) as well as the maximum retail price.

Among the different statutory powers that have devolved to the Joint Committee, overseeing quality is another parameter of transaction central to our study. Quality standards for raw milk are laid down in a Code of Practice agreed upon by the Joint Committee. Quality control is implemented by the MMB, which pays the farmers a price depending on the milk's quality according to a quality payment differential.

Relations between producers and processors are additionally governed by EC regulations. Since 1977 a levy designed to contribute to financing excess production is charged on the price of raw milk, which is subject to EC quality directives beginning in 1989. EC regulation is most important for governing the quantity of milk production. In 1984, a quota system was introduced by the EC for a five-year period in order to cut back surplus production of milk. It constituted a "super" levy to be charged on all milk produced above a specified national quota set for all members states according to their 1981 milk deliveries.[5] The quota system applies, with very few exceptions, to all production of milk and milk products, not just deliveries to dairies.

Although this quota system is directly related to reducing excess production of the agricultural sector, it has important implications for the dairy industry. To the extent to which excess production of raw milk can be reduced by establishing quotas, dairies capacities suited to process this part of agricultural production grow obsolete. Since the U.K. (as well as the EC as a whole) has succeded in cutting back milk production, this has resulted in a corresponding cutback on the part of processors, especially where those products yielding comparatively narrow profits have been affected. For instance, about 25 percent of the U.K.'s butter-making capacity has been shut down because butter is one of the least profitable operations.

Turning now from the dairy industry's exchange relations with suppliers to those with customers, there are also nonmarket mechanisms of governance at work. In the case of product quality, the dairy industry is subject to national and EC state regulation. At the national level, the industry, like other groups involved, can exert influence on this matter based on consultation rights (De Vroom, 1987), while there is no proper consultation with the industry at the EC level (Pestoff, 1987).

Aside from this, the dairy industry's relations with customers are also governed by (supranationally) established regulations in terms of price, quantity, and even market entry. According to the EC regime for milk, a target price is set for raw milk at 3.7 percent fat content delivered to the dairy companies. Intervention prices are then fixed for butter and skimmed milk powder at a level to ensure that the producers receive a price close to the target price for milk. The obligation to purchase has been limited to maximal amounts (butter and milk powder) and to certain seasons in the year (milk powder) accompanied with the possibility of reducing the buying price (butter). This system is flanked by EC foreign trade practices. Threshold prices set a minimum entry price for imports. Export subsidies are paid and grants are given to processors for improving their storage capacity.

With regard to product quantity, this system provides processors who manufacture intervention products with a large guaranteed outlet. Concerning pricing, the system not only determines the price of products subject to intervention but also has an indirect influence on setting prices for the remaining processed dairy products. This impact upon quantity and price results from the opportunity of manufacturing "for intervention": Processors can, in principle, take advantage of the intervention price.

In all, nonmarket mechanisms are central to the governance of all transaction parameters significant for this study. This nonmarket governance is based on activities initiated and implemented by the state and/or associations. While state activities basically can be distinguished as to whether they are conducted by national or supranational authorities, in the case of associations one can differentiate between those primarily advancing commercial goals (cooperatives) and those performing political tasks (interest associations). State and/or associative activities clearly prevail in governing all parameters shaping the industry's relations with suppliers as well as in governing intervention products and product quality in relation to customers. Table 8.3 presents a brief summary of the governance of the U.K.'s dairy industry (as well as those of Germany and Austria) according to the two-dimensional scheme introduced above. Prevailing governance mechanisms are arranged within of each of the cells.

Table 8.3. Governance Mechanisms Prevailing in the Dairy Sector of the U.K. (England and Wales), Germany, and Austria

	Transaction issues					
Transaction	U.K.		Germany		Austria	
	Processors' relations with:		Processors' relations with:		Processors' relations with:	
Parameters	Producers	Customers	Producers	Customers	Producers	Customers
Selection of partners/ market entry	State-licensed associations[a]	State and market	Market	State and market	State-licensed associations	State-licensed associations
Quality	State-licensed associatons	State and market	State	State	State-licensed associations	State
Quantity	State	State	State	State and market	State and state-licensed associations	State-licensed associations
Price	State and state-licensed associations	State and market	State	State and market	State-licensed associations	State and state-licensed associations

[a] "State" refers to national as well as to supranational authorities.

Germany

Looking at nonmarket mechanisms of governance first, exchange relations of the dairy industry with suppliers are considerably mediated by state regulation. Additionally, associations are not fully absent in governing these relations, although associations of importance compared to that of the British MMBs do not exist. Among the different transaction parameters studied here, the influence of associative action is most significant for governing the quantity of supply. Similar to the British case, governing functions are performed by the cooperative type of association. However, an important difference between the U.K. and Germany is that German producers' cooperatives have been remarkably more successful in moving forward into the processing sector. At the beginning of the 1980s approximately 80 percent of all raw milk produced was bought by cooperatives or processing firms owned by them (Hilbert, 1983:24). This associative link between the processing and the producing sector has given rise to guaranteed outlets for farmers, which may be considered a functional equivalent to the farmer-controlled MMBs in the U.K. Since cooperative manufacturers have formally committed themselves to buying all the raw milk produced by their members, proprietary (noncooperative) dairy companies have been forced to do so de facto. Otherwise, they would have lost their suppliers to their cooperative competitors (Hilbert, 1983:19).

This commitment of processors is backed up by the EC system of target and intervention prices for butter and skimmed milk powder since this also gives processors an opportunity of entering into a market with (moderately) guaranteed outlets, which facilitates carrying out their obligations to buy all the milk delivered. However, farmers are not able simply to maximize their output regardless of the processors' commitment to buy. This follows from the EC quota system already pointed out in the example of the U.K. As in the case of the U.K., the introduction of the quota system has led to increasingly scarce supplies of milk and to a reduction of processing capacities (primarily for manufacturing intervention products) (Stöckl, 1988).

By analogy with the quantity of supplies, the selling price of producers is determined more by the state than by associations. Again, the governing function of the state resides in the EC system of target and intervention prices while a specifically national system of pricing by government is not established. Complementarily, quasi-governmental organizations play a minor role with regard to selling prices of producers. The *Landesvereinigungen der Milchwirtschaft* (regional associations of the dairy sector) contribute to reconciling conflicts between producers and processors resulting when a producer supposes he is paid a lower price by his dairy company than other companies pay. The company involved can take this case to the *Landesvereinigung*, which then provides a neutral evaluation (Hilbert, 1983:118). Functions, composition, and even the procurement of the resources of the *Landesvereinigung* are laid down by law. Primarily, their functions are advising the authorities (in regulating dairy issues) and processors (e.g., on matters of improving product quality) and balancing the interests of all groups in the dairy sector.

While they have little influence on price and quantity, interest associations are of major importance for governing product quality, although state intervention at national and EC level is the dominant mechanism with regard to these transaction parameters. Concerning the national formulation and implementation of quality standards, interest associations representing interests beyond the dairy sector have a legal right to be consulted by the state. This arrangement basically applies to quality matters pertaining to raw milk as well as to processed dairy products. Considering processed dairy products brings us to the subject of the industry's relationship to customers. In this respect, product quality is most extensively regulated by state intervention, leaving little room for determining the products' composition autonomously by manufacturers. The state is also engaged in governing price and quantity according to the EC milk regime. In contrast to the U.K., there is a statutory instrument aimed at improving the dairy industry's performance by promoting its concentration process.

Apart from the state, associations are also involved in governing product quantity to a limited extent. This especially applies to the farmer-controlled cooperatives, which are organized under the umbrella of *Raiffeisen*. Organizationally, the *Raiffeisen* system is functionally and vertically differentiated. The aim of the system is to coordinate all the activities of its members. At the top level, this task is performed by the *Deutscher Raiffeisenverband*, which additionally audits the second- and third-order cooperatives and represents the *Raiffeisen* system in interest-political matters. At the lower levels, coordinating functions concerning the cooperatives' commercial activities are fulfilled by the sector-specific, higher-order cooperatives. With regard to the dairy sector, this means that higher-order cooperatives, aside from conducting business in their own right (e.g., launching name-brand goods and import and export trades), also attempt to centralize the sales of all the decentralized first-order processors as effectively as possible (Bellak, 1988). However, this type of associational governance does not result in completely supplanting market competition. This is manifested by the fact that higher-order cooperatives are not able to suppress price competition even among their members (Hilbert, 1983:108).

Together with the state, market competition dominates the governance of the industry's transactions with customers while the state largely prevails over all other governing mechanisms with regard to the industry's relations with suppliers. This is reflected by the fact that the prices paid to farmers display only little regional differences, which would not be the case without deliberate state intervention given the different conditions of production in Germany (Hilbert, 1983:19). Associational governance is not completely absent, albeit of less importance, than in the U.K. (see Table 8.3.).

Austria

Governance of the Austrian dairy sector rests mainly on a close cooperation between associations and the state. The concrete mode of this cooperation varies according to different parameters and issues of economic transactions (Traxler, 1985). Basically, three modes of cooperation can be distinguished:

1. By law, regulatory functions are delegated to a sector-specific board (*Milchwirtschaftsfonds*/MWF) to which the "big four" interest associations are each empowered to send the same number of delegates: These big four consist of: The Conference of the Presidents of Chambers of Agriculture (*Präsidentenkonferenz der Landwirtschaftskammern*/PKLWK), which is the federal association of farmers; the Federal Chamber of Trade and Industry (*Bundeswirtschaftskammer*/BWK), which represents all the business firms outside agriculture; the Austrian Trade Union Federation (*Österreichischer Gewerkschaftsbund*/ÖGB), and the Austrian Association of Chambers of Labor (*Österreichischer Arbeiterkammertag*/ÖAKT), both representing the interests of employees and, additionally, of consumers in the MWF. The four associations decide on employing the regulatory powers attributed to the MWF, and they are under very strong pressure to reach consensus. Since the MWF is part of the state administration from a juridical point of view, its activities are subordinated to state control. Among the different institutions dealing with governing the dairy sector, the MWF is most important.

2. Regulatory functions have not formally devolved to the big four by the state but are performed by associations on a voluntary and autonomous basis. This is characteristic of the Parity Commission for Wage and Price Matters (*Paritätische Kommission für Lohn- und Preisfragen*), which participates not only in governing the dairy sector, but is a sector-nonspecific institution central to corporatist policy formation and implementation in Austria. Its main function is income policy.

3. Regulatory functions are fulfilled by the state while interest associations participate on the basis of consultation. Again, the big four enjoy a privileged

position insofar as authorities prefer dealing with them rather than with other associations.

The main property of these arrangements is that all those associations and, partly, the boards involved in governance are sector-nonspecific in their domain, although the dairy sector and its problems are highly specific. More precisely, the interest organizations are national peak associations of farmers, business, and labor that prevail in Austria's system of interest intermediation and are characterized by a highly encompassing domain and a centralized decision-making process. However, this does not mean that sectoral actors are excluded from participation in governing the sector since each of the big four usually sends delegates representing the dairy sector within their domain to the MWF.

A fifth interest association exerts considerable influence on governing the sector although it is not formally integrated into one of the arrangements desribed above. This is the peak association of the *Raiffeisen* cooperatives (*Österreichischer Raiffeisenverband/ÖRV*). The Austrian *Raiffeisen* system is organized quite similarly to its German counterpart. In the dairy industry, it is even more influential than in Germany. About 90 percent of all the raw milk delivered is bought by processing companies owned by *Raiffeisen* (ÖRV, 1981:68). Analogous to the German case, second- and third-order cooperatives perform an allocative function by handling storage and marketing of the local cooperatives' excess production. Not least, *Raiffeisen*'s economic predominance in the dairy sector results from its privileged position in export, which comes close to a monopoly. Export is implemented almost exclusively by two firms owned by *Raiffeisen*, which are also entitled to administer the state subsidies designed for companies exporting dairy products (Bellak, 1988:52ff). In interest-political respect, *Raiffeisen's* influence in the dairy sector rests on the fact that its cooperatives are organized in the BWK as well as in the territorial subunits of the PKLWK, to which the ÖRV itself is affiliated. As in the German case, Austrian cooperatives are legally subject to a special form of auditing that is periodically implemented by their associations. Because of this, the ÖRV is much better informed about the course of business of dairy companies than any other interest association dealing with the sector. All this places the ÖRV in a key role in governing the dairy sector.

Investigating the powers of the different governance arrangements shows that they constitute a coherent system of nonmarket mechanisms covering nearly all transaction parameters and issues of the dairy industry. Dealing with the industry's relations with suppliers first, the price that farmers receive regardless of the use of their milk delivered is fixed by the Minister of Economic Affairs, and the big four interest associations play a central role in price determination. Concerning the other transaction parameters, procurement markets are fixed by the MWF for each processing company, with companies obliged to buy all the milk from farmers designated, provided that quality standards defined and controlled by the MWF have been maintained. Conversely, farmers are required to deliver their milk to those processing firms to whose procurement area they belong. To cope with excess production of raw milk, a quota system was established by law in 1978. Each farmer who exceeds his individual quota is liable for a special levy designated to subsidize the sale of excess products at home and abroad.

The dairy industry's interactions with customers are governed in an analogous way. Corresponding to the allocation of procurement markets, sales markets are also allotted to processors by the MWF. Within their fixed sales areas, processors are obliged to deliver to the trade and the trade to buy only from the designated processor. The production program of dairy companies is also under control of the MWF. The MWF regulates which firm may produce which products and also determines the quantity to be manufactured. The retail price for liquid milk is formally fixed by the Minister of Economic Affairs while the big four interest associations prevail in setting the price de facto. Prices for processed dairy products are fixed directly by the big four within the framework of the Parity Commission.

For processors this implies that their profitability is politically preestablished and guaranteed. The realization of profit or loss is directly tied to the MWF's decision on the production program and markets allotted to individual firms. Hence, the actual profits or losses realized by the individual companies are corrected by standard costs and standard returns. They are calculated and set by the MWF with reference to the principle of economic efficiency. Standard costs and returns are designed to serve as an incentive to increase productivity.

According to the encompassing domain of all the actors involved, all prices to be fixed (including those of labor power) and costs to be calculated in this system are brought together into a corporate package deal. The big four interest associations govern collective agreements on wages and also fix the price for milk products autonomously in the Parity Commission. This governance arrangement is completed by regulations on foreign trade and on quality standards of dairy products. To protect the dairy sector against imports coming in below the price of domestic products, countervailing duties are fixed by the MWF. Quality standards for dairy products are largely formulated and implemented by the state. Certain interest associations advise the responsible government minister on questions relating to quality standards.

Governance by state and associations in Austria is remarkably more developed than in the U.K. and Germany. In a coordinated mode, state agencies and associations employ an encompassing system of nonmarket mechanisms governing not only the industry's selection of partners, quality, quantity, and price in relation to suppliers as well as to customers, but also investment and profits. Opacity is the side-effect for the actors who have to manage this highly complicated system (Traxler, 1985:163–67). Especially the MWF, which plays the key role in implementing the system, is burdened by these grave information problems. The MWF needs information about the companies' course of business in order to bring its allocative decision in line with the principles of economic efficiency. Above all, exact data on each single company's costs are required for calculating the standard costs upon which the entire system is based. Unfortunately, the MWF has no access to this information since costs are insufficiently accounted for and documented by the firms. Although the MWF is entitled by law to impose upon firms a system of cost accounting according to its requirements, it does not enforce such a system but accepts information on costs provided by the firms without auditing them (Bellak, 1988). Owing to this information problem, the MWF is governed by (*Raiffeisen*) companies rather than governing them concerning costs, prices, and profits. Some evidence from economic studies indicates that the Austrian dairy industry enjoys higher margins than the dairy industries of other Western countries (see section entitled The Consequence for Economic Performance later in the chapter).

In 1988, this system was revised by government in concert with the big four interest associations. Essentially, this amendment somewhat enlarges the autonomy of processors with regard to production programs, investments, and sales, and empowers the big four to determine the price of raw milk in place of the formerly responsible minister and makes a certain percentage of a quota forfeit if bought from one farmer by another one. This amendment is designed to serve as a first step toward simplifying the system and harmonizing it with the EC regime since Austria at present seeks a closer association with the EC so as to participate in the EC's liberalized Common Market to be established in 1993.

The Determinants of Governance Arrangements

The aim of this section is to investigate the conditions that may have led to the formation of governance arrangements discussed above. In this context, two questions should be distinguished:

1. What are the factors accounting for the differences among the arrangements established in the U.K., Germany, and Austria?

2. What are the determinants underlying the common feature of these arrangements?

While the former question assumes a nationally comparative perspective in order to investigate the differences among countries, the latter contributes to a sectorally comparative analysis by elaborating the common properties of the dairy sector that distinguish it from other sectors of the economy.

National Differences in Governance

Discussing national differences first requires, however, reference to the countries' most significant sectoral commonality. This is the predominant role of the state and associations in the sector's governance, which has resulted in a mode of institutional arrangements that have been categorized as (neo)corporatist in social science literature (e.g., Lehmbruch and Schmitter, 1982). This means that, for reasons to be analyzed in detail below, sectoral interests are advanced primarily in a *collective* way while the market as the classical institution for pursuing interests *individually* is a governance mechanism of rather subordinate relevance. Given this predominance of pursuing interests collectively, the main factor accounting for national differences in sectoral governance arrangements is the mode of how collective interests are *organized* in the sector.

Generally, associations, whether they be cooperatives or interest organizations, are more important for governing the sector the higher the organizational development of associative interest representation is. Associational structures are more developed the more encompassing they are in scope and purpose, the more coordinated they are internally, and the more they are capable of imposing binding decisions on their members (Schmitter and Streeck, 1981: 124ff.)[6]

Austria's interest associations dealing with dairy problems clearly surpass the other countries' associations in terms of organizational development. Corresponding to this organizational differential, of the three nations considered here, Austria's associations are most involved in performing governance functions. Those of Germany are least involved. Apparently, highly developed associative structures are better functions than are other associations. Owing to their encompassing domain they can internalize collective/public goals underlying these functions rather than other associations. They also have at their disposal more effective means of making their members comply with governance goals. However, encompassing associations that claim to perform governance functions are also burdened with more collective action problems than are other associations. As a consequence, the governance capacities of highly developed associations are ultimately dependent on state sponsorship in all three countries. This sponsorship enables the state to place a lot of the burden of governance upon associations (Streeck and Schmitter, 1985). In Austria and the U.K., these "private governments" have proved to be so successful from the state's perspective that additional functions of price determination were devolved to them in the 1980s. Conversely, it is a common feature of all three countries that the state is engaged most directly in quality regulations of dairy products, which is primarily in the interest of consumers. Because consumers face particular collective action problems and, thus, are the group least developed organizationally, governing on their behalf is left to the state.

Sectoral Properties and the Mode of Governance

Turning now to the question of what distinguishes the sector's governance from that of other sectors, it is important that the dairy industry's relations with suppliers are more extensively governed by the state and/or associations than those with customers. Additionally, as far as relations with customers are governed by the state and associations, they are largely the consequence of regulations on producer–processor transactions. This indicates that the industry's exchange relation with primary producers is the key to understanding the formation of a highly corporatist governance system in the dairy sector.

Among the factors making the dairy industry prone to corporatist governance, the asymmetry of power between suppliers and buyers of raw milk in the industry's procurement market is most decisive. In any market, the distribution of powers between suppliers and buyers essentially depends on their scope of choice in terms of defining the parameters of transaction (Offe and Hinrichs, 1985:14). The central parameters involved are determining the price, quality, and quanity of the commodity, and the location and timing of the selection of partners. The more that suppliers are capable of varying and specifying their offers within these dimensions, the more they can improve their market position in relation to buyers.

Conversely, buyers will gain an advantage over suppliers to the extent to which they become independent of a specified kind of supply and, thus, can extend their options for procurement. Both strategies affect the power relations between suppliers and buyers by influencing competition on each side of the market. For instance, product specialization is a strategy that contributes to moderating competition among suppliers since this shifts competition from price to quality. Buyers can extend their market options by finding possibilities of substituting other sources for one particular source of supply.

Considering the scope of strategies available to dairy producers and processors shows that the producers' scope of choice is remarkably more restricted in every transaction dimension. This issues from differences between producers and processors in their conditions of production and in their type of product. In the case of farmers, one main characteristic of production is that the number of cows and the amount of milk produced are strongly associated. There is only a limited possibility to slow dow or expand production given a certain number of cows. This decisively restricts the adaptability of supply according to market conditions in terms of quantity. Restraints in varying and specifying the other parameters are set by the property of raw milk. Its homogeneity leaves little room for specifying product quality, and its perishability makes it difficult for farmers to vary supply in terms of timing and location. For these reasons, farmers cannot withhold their product until prices change in a way favorable to them (Grant, 1985:187).

In comparison with farmers, potential buyers of raw milk are much better equipped with options for rational market strategies. The industrial mode of manufacturing renders processors more able to adjust their products' content and thus of substituting for milk other raw materials (e.g. nondairy fats) to some extent. Ultimately, all these differences resulting in an asymmetrical distribution of power between farmers and processors in the market stem from the fact that the development of productive forces in the primary sector lags behind that of the industry structurally. In conjunction with this, the market position of each single producer is weakened in relation to processors insofar as the number of farms is greater, and their economic potential is smaller, compared to dairy companies.

However fundamental these differences in production and product between producers and processors may be, they constitute an asymmetry of options only for *individual market* strategies. This implies that they affect just one dimension of the overall power configuration since farmers can attempt to overcome their individual inferiority through a market- and/or nonmarket-oriented strategy of *collective* action. Basically, two market strategies and one nonmarket strategy can be distinguished of which producers can make use collectively. They can try to form a coalition in order to

1. merge forward into the processing sector (processing cooperatives),

2. centralize and coordinate selling milk to processors (bargaining cooperatives), and

3. lobby for favorable state regulaton (interest associations).

According to Olson (1965), it can be argued that dairy farmers are burdened with difficulties in forming a coalition because of their great number, the homogeneity of product (and correspondingly of interest), and their regional dispersion. In this respect, it is common to the U.K., Germany, and Austria that farmers have succeeded in forming strong lobbies but largely have failed to organize effective market coalitions autonomously. Before the state began providing a legal framework supporting collective action of farmers in the market, farmers found themselves caught in a ruinous price competition accompanied by strong fluctuations of production and income. State assistance was indispensable for the rise of cooperatives, which are presently the farmers' main instrument for influencing the dairy market. In the U.K., a legal basis for the establishment of marketing organizations was the necessary precondition for setting up the MMBs (Grant, 1985:183). In Austria and Germany, co-operatives would not have been able to attain such a dominant position in the processing sector without being equipped with privileges by tax- and cartel-legislation in relation to their proprietary competitors.

Why was there a discrepancy between the farmers' capability of forming nonmarket associations and their difficulties in forming market coalitions? There are differences in the kind of conformity required for advancing different collective goals. If these differences are linked to different opportunity costs with which the cooperating actors are burdened for the sake of the collective interest, then the possibilities of forming collective action will vary even within one and the same group (Traxler, 1990). For organizing an interest-political lobby, a rather simple kind of conformity, essentially consisting of paying dues, is sufficient.

In contrast, forming a market coalition presupposes that each single actor subordinates his individual market strategy to the collective goal. This type of conformity creates opportunity costs that are more of a burden than just paying membership dues since defection (e.g., undercutting a collectively fixed price) makes it possible to improve the individual's own market position at the costs of those complying with the collective goal. This collective action problem, which farmers had to face in the market, could not be solved without governing capacities provided by state intervention for which, in turn, the farmers' lobbies paved the way.

However, it would be misleading to reduce the formation of corporatist governance arrangements in the dairy industry to a matter of farmers' lobbying for this, for (1) these arrangements also contain regulations corresponding to interests other than those of farmers (e.g., quality standards in which, for instance, consumers are interested), and (2) it must be taken into consideration that state policies are susceptible to interest politics but are not simply determined by them. From a theoretical perspective, the point of reference of state activities is not only maintaining social integration (reconciling conflicting interests mainly advanced by lobbies) but also maintaining system integration (satifying the imperatives of societal reproduction).[7] For mediating these conflict-provoking functions, the state's "interest in itself" can be seen as serving as the guiding principle (Offe, 1975). According to this perspective the state itself has a strong interest in regulating the dairy sector. Historically, the emergence of this interest has been strongly linked with sustaining national security. Two main objectives that, together, affect all transaction parameters studied here can be distinguished with regard to this interest. First, it is related to protecting domestic production so as to make the country as autarkic as possible. Given the instabilities inherent in the dairy market, this implies guaranteeing an assured income for farmers based on a legal framework for determining prices, quantities, and even the selection of transaction partners. The second objective is ensuring the provision of goods of faultless quality so as to secure public health. This gives rise to state-directed systems of quality regulation.

While all these public goals are affiliated with the imperatives of system integration, their implementation in detail is influenced by the requirements of social integration. As already discussed above, sectoral governance arrangements of the countries studied differ primarily owing to the organizability of the interests involved and their specific organizational form as far as forming a coalition has been successful. The state has to consider the demands of the interest groups involved, not the least for reasons of legitimacy. In this respect, governance arrangements of the U.K., Germany, and Austria have in common that there is a remarkable consent to them, especially of farmers and processors. Farmers are generally in strongest accordance with this form of governance since it has been introduced primarily to strengthen the market position of farmers in relation to processors by depriving them of a lot of discretionary power usually held by firms. Seen from this perspective, the fact that processors also largely consent to these arrangements may seem surprising, at least at first glance.

Among the system's different effects in which processors may be substantially interested, the most important one is that they moderate or even exclude competition among them and, thus, reduce uncertainty. Corporatist arrangements on the procurement of raw milk offer the dairy industry an opportunity to regulate competiton, given its high degree of fragmentation and the relative importance of the costs of raw milk compared to other production costs.

What makes it easier to regulate competition through corporatist arrangements than through autonomous coalition-building by the particular groups involved is that corporatist arrangements can rely on a mutual transfer of governance capacity among several actors, which increases each actor's capacity to overcome collective action problems in a way that also strengthens the governance capacity of the arrangement as a whole. In Austria, the membership dues that processors are obliged to pay to their associations are recognized as a cost factor by the MWF (Traxler, 1985:162). In the U.K., the DTF's funds are raised largely from a levy, which is charged obligatorily to the buyers of milk by their supply contract with the MMB, and this levy is also collected by the milk board on behalf of the DTF (Grant, 1985:190).

Apart from these organizational interests of their associations, the essential interest of dairy processors, which is realized by corporatist arrangements, is that their extensive regulations on the industry's interactions with suppliers result in strengthening the processors' market position in relation to customers even when downstream relations are not governed in an analogously extensive way. While the food processing industry as a whole suffers remarkably from retail pressure (Farago, 1987), this does not apply to dairy processors in the same way since they benefit from the fact that the determination of their buying price directly or indirectly "spills over" to their outlets (Bellak, 1988; Grant, 1983a; Hilbert, 1983). Furthermore, from the perspective of processors, demand for dairy products does not allow expansion but requires reduction of capacities. This enhances the processors' interest in stabilizing prices and sales by corporatist arrangements. The inelastic demand for milk at the retail level makes it easier for farmers, processors, and retailers to externalize the costs of their collusion to consumers.

Simply put, farmers and processors benefit from this form of governance to the disadvantage of consumers, as will be outlined in more detail below. Whatever kind of mental reservations on the side of consumers this may provoke they are hardly transformed into political protest and therefore do not endanger the governance system's stability. This is because consumers are the group least developed organizationally, as already stated. Their low degree of organizability makes any attempt to change the system very expensive for consumers, with the consequence that organizing costs are likely to exceed the benefits of change to be expected. By contrast, maintaining the system creates relatively low costs for farmers and processors, owing to their high organizational development, while this provides them with comparatively high payoffs. It is this distribution of costs and benefits that decisively contributes to the maintenance of the corporatist accord in the dairy sector.

What remains to be explained with regard to the formation of corporatism in the dairy sector is the question of why in the three countries considered (as well as in other countries) this sector is much more governed by corporatism than are other parts of agriculture and the food processing industry, which comparative studies show (Grant, 1987). The determinants of the dairy sector's "corporativization" as outlined above apply, in principle, to the food processing sector as a whole or at least to some segments of it. There is a general asymmetry of power between agricultural producers and industrial processors due to the unequal development of productive forces in these two sectors. According to national security interests, autarky may be the economic objective of state policy not only with regard to dairy products but also to other "security-sensitive" food.

It is primarily a matter of political priorities when products all belonging to this type of food are governed in different ways. Basically, governance tends to become more corporatist the higher a product's political relevance is. What renders a certain food more politically relevant than others depends on a complex interplay of economic, cultural, and natural conditions. In the three countries in question here, dairy is of special political relevance mainly for two reasons. First, milk is a very important staple food. Second, it is an especially relevant source of income for farmers because milk production is less sensitive to weather and climate than other agricultural products. Hence, it can be carried out by farmers whose land is not suited for alternative uses as far as location is concerned and, with regard to timing, it can be done during all seasons, thus providing for a continuous flow of income.

This special political relevance makes dairy the focal arena for state policy protecting domestic agriculture and results in a special need for a nonmarket type of governance that concerns itself primarily with the provision of collective goods like avoiding fluctuations in supplies and prices.[8] Correspondingly, the way in which the actors involved tend to perceive the sector and to deal with its problems is to consider it an infrastructure of society rather than a "conventional" industry. Yet it has become increasingly difficult to maintain this perception. This especially holds true for the state that in the last resort, has to sponsor the sector's peculiar status of being some kind of infrastructure. Intensified global competition imposing growing resource constraints on domestic economies has created severe fiscal problems for the state, which thus has come under pressure to cut subsidies and to economize the dairy sector. Interestingly, this led not to a "remarketization" in any country studied, but to a reinforced reliance on direct state regulation, concentrating on the quantity dimension of sectoral transactions: Introducing quota systems was the main element of economizing efforts. In Austria and the U.K., where elaborated corporatist systems governing prices already existed, these efforts were accompanied by devolving additional functions of price determination to them; obviously, this complementary corporativization was initiated by the state to relieve itself of increased distributional conflicts resulting from its economizing measures.

In an era of worldwide deregulation, this convergence of extended state regulation and corporatist governance is a very striking pattern of restructuring. Above all, it indicates that distributional issues are still central for the governance of the sector, for introducing quotas is a strategy of reducing overcapacity, which is inspired primarily not by *performance criteria* but by the *principle of equality* since it also gives less competitive producers an opportunity to survive. It is most characteristic of the sector that it becomes increasingly subject to a dialectic of "infrastructural" and "industrial" goals. The economic consequences of governance arrangements for the realization of both categories of goals will be studied in the final section.

The Consequences for Economic Performance

Performance and Its Indicators

The economic performance of a sector can be evaluated by taking the attainment of economic objectives as a yardstick. In principle, four types of economic objectives should be distinguished: allocative efficiency, dynamic efficiency, "fair" distribution, and stabilization. Whereas economic performance evaluation very often only takes into account allocative efficiency criteria, dynamic efficiency and distributionary aspects are also included here. Stabilization (i.e., the dampening of business cycles by safeguarding employment, demand, etc.) is of no importance for the dairy sector and will not be discussed here.

1. *Allocative efficiency*, in a strict neoclassical sense, is defined by Pareto-optimality, implying technical efficiency of production as well as the production of those goods that maximize the utility of consumers. One can show that under certain limited conditions, perfect competition leads to Pareto-optimality. However, on the empirical grounds that market imperfections and externalities are significant real phenomena, one might doubt the optimality of a real market economy. Other governance mechanisms of a sector can perform better, even if we accept the ideal market as a point of reference. In the case of externalities, the Pareto-conditions do not hold. Furthermore, the formal conditions that have to be fulfilled for a Pareto-optimum have to be replaced by a set of loose but observable indicators in order to operationalize the concept of allocative efficiency. Such loose criteria are, for example, low prices and low costs; high productivity; profitability; market clearing, and independence of subsidies (except in the case of externalities, where subsidies can increase efficiency).

2. *Dynamic efficiency* concerns the sector's capacity for structural change and development. This means the ability of a sector to respond to such changes in environmental conditons as changes in demand, technology, or market conditions. The concept of dynamic efficiency—in the narrow sense of innovative efficiency—dates back to Joseph Schumpeter (1942). While there are (at least theoretically) exact criteria for allocative efficiency, dynamic efficiency has to be defined in a less precise way, as, for example, a satisfying rate of innovation, high flexibility, and so forth. Criteria for dynamic efficiency are, for example, the diffusion of technological progress, product innovation, a sector's growth rate, and an increase in productivity.

3. *"Fair" distribution (distributional performance)*, besides efficiency, which takes the market as a point of reference, the "fair" distribution of goods and income for transactors within the sector is a further economic objective. What a "fair" distribution is largely depends on the values of a society. While the neoclassical ideal market is the most efficient governance mechanism, its distributional outcome may be unacceptable from an ethical, social, or political viewpoint. Criteria for distributional aspects are sufficient regional provision of goods, improved income of producers or consumers, and so forth. In any case, the question that arises is how to operationalize this performance indicator. Distribution—however it is defined as being fair—always means that some individuals or groups are better off to the disadvantage of others. For this reason, any operationalization of distributional performance implies the identification of the group that should be favored. This study deals with this normative question in a pragmatic way: Since in addition to the state the associations of farmers and processors play the key role in governing the dairy sector and thus decisively influence the formulation of governance goals, development of the farmers' and processors' income will serve as the

point of reference. More specifically, distributional performance is understood as the governance system's capability of supporting the income goals of farmers and processors. In other words, the more that farmers and processors are able to externalize the costs of realizing their income demands, the higher the governance system's distributional performance. From a methodological point of view, this operationalization is only a formal device for ranking the distributional outcome of governance systems but does not mean a value judgment concerning the question of how desirable a certain distribution of income is. What is measured is nothing but the extent to which the interests of special groups are satisfied. By no means does this procedure imply neglecting either interests of other groups or governance goals other than distributional ones.

Table 8.4 presents an overview of the scope of performance indicators and of governance goals that are selected by reference to the interests of *all* the groups involved. As outlined, governance goals can either claim to improve

Table 8.4. Performance Indicators and Governance Goals of the Dairy Sector

Performance Indicators	Sectoral Governance Goals
Allocative Efficiency	
	Provision of a sufficient supply
	Provision of adequate production capacities
market clearing	
overcapacity	Adjustment of production to demand
subsidies	Sales promotion
producer and consumer prices	
profitability	
productivity	
processing costs	
Dynamic Efficiency	
change in productivity	Increase in productivity
change in the number and size of farms	Rationalization of production
and firms	
change in the structure of delivery	Rationalization of marketing
diffusion of technical progress	
flexibility of restructuring	
product innovation	
"Fair" Distribution (Distributional Performance)	
	Protection of producer's income
improved income of producers	Protection of domestic production
	Avoidance of price and quantity
	Fluctuations
improved welfare of consumers	
quality	Provision of high-quality milk for health
	reasons
regional provision	
consumer price	
improved income of processors	

efficiency in the case of market failures or to improve the distribution of goods and income. Performance indicators are related to sectoral governance goals, declared relevant by the governing actors involved. For instance, distributional performance as indicated by improved welfare of consumers can be transformed into the governance goals of the provision of high-quality milk for health considerations. This makes it possible to analyze the sector's economic performance by proceeding from theoretically based indicators that are linked to politically relevant governance goals.

The Sector's Allocative Efficiency

MARKET CLEARING. Overcapacity is the main problem of the dairy sector. A comparison of the degree of self-supply (domestic production of milk/total indigenous utilization of milk) shows a systematic increase from 1970 to 1984 in all three countries (see Table 8.5).

Among the three countries Austria consistently has the highest excess supply of raw milk. In Austria excess of milk has been produced since the 1950s and has increased continuously until 1984. Although a lot of milk is used for feed, 27 percent of domestic milk production was not absorbed within the country in 1985. In Germany, overcapacity of milk emerged later than in Austria. In 1970, German domestic production entirely met domestic demand (100 percent). Since then the degree of self-supply has increased. The U.K. presents quite a different picture. It does not produce enough milk to meet domestic demand for milk and milk products. The U.K. still has no homemade overcapacity, but suffers from the excess supply in the EC as a whole, which has led to tougher competition, an increase of the supply of diversified foreign dairy products, and consequently to more imports. Only since 1987 has there been a clear tendency to reduce milk production in all three nations studied. Among the three countries, the U.K. manages the problem of overcapacity best, followed by Germany, while Austria's performance is the worst.

PRODUCER AND CONSUMER PRICES. Comparison of prices in the three countries is complicated by product differentiation, the impact of subsidies, taxes, differences of price definitions, and exchange-rate effects. A comparison of producer prices (value added tax and producers' levies deducted) in the three countries reveals that the dairy industry in the U.K. is supplied at the lowest

Table 8.5. Degree of Self-Supply of Milk (in percent)[a]

	1970	1976	1980	1984	1985	1986	1987	1988
Austria	116	120	123	132	127	127	123	120
Germany	100	116	122	123	115	116	104	100[b]
U.K.	—	76	87	88	88	90	86	83[b]

SOURCE: Vas (1988); Agrarbericht der Bundesregierung Bonn 1988; OECD (1986); MWF (1970–1988).
[a] Basis of calculation: dairy fat.
[b] Estimates.

price (in 1986 an average of $21.40 per 100 kg of milk); Germany's price lies in the middle (in 1986, $27.90 per 100 kg of milk), and Austria's producer price is the highest (in 1986, $28.70 per 100 kg of milk). These figures correspond to the difference between farm size and average return per cow in the three countries, economies of scale being much more favorable for the U.K. than for Germany and least favorable for Austria. British consumers have traditionally paid more for milk than have consumers in Germany and other EC countries, partly as a result of expensive doorstep delivery. Nevertheless, the Austrian consumer price for liquid milk is still higher.

While German farmers get 48.8 percent of the price the consumer pays for milk, British farmers receive 41.5 percent and Austrian farmers only get 39.5 percent. In Austria, high costs and profit margins of processing and the high cost of milk collection (owing to a very inefficient way of collecting milk in cans) are responsible for high consumer prices. Consumers are also obliged to subsidize export dairy products (cheese and milk powder) through higher prices for milk, butter, and other dairy products. In the U.K., transport costs for milk collection are very low. The MMB has succeeded in installing a very efficient low-cost transport system. Milk is collected in tanks, and farms have corresponding refrigeration systems (Ifo, 1985:15). The U.K. also has the lowest liquid milk processing costs. This can be blamed on the high concentration of dairies. A very small number of firms specializing in liquid milk production produce on a large scale. The top 8 of Britain's 464 dairies had a market share of 75 percent in 1982 (Ifo, 1985:20). Trade margins are the highest in the U.K. because of doorstep delivery. Germany's liquid milk costs are lower in all components compared to Austria's. Its processing costs and milk collection costs are higher than in the U.K.; thus it ranks in the middle with regard to the efficiency of liquid milk production. Butter prices were also the highest in Austria in 1986 and the lowest in Britain. The same holds true for cheese and skimmed milk powder prices.

A comparison of prices and costs of dairy processing among the three countries comes out definitively in favor of the U.K. followed by Germany and Austria.

PRODUCTIVITY, PROCESSING COSTS, AND PROFITABILITY (DAIRY MARGINS). Margins on all dairy products except liquid milk are higher in the U.K. than in Germany. This can either be due to higher profits of the highly concentrated sector and/or higher processing costs. In Britain both higher processing costs and higher profits seem to be responsible for higher dairy margins. The very low labor productivity in dairy processing as compared to Germany indicates higher processing costs. Experts also assess higher profits in the British dairy industry than in that of Germany. However, profits are only realized by a very few large firms, whereas small firms are closing (see section titled Determinants of Governance Arrangements). A rough indirect estimate of profits can be arrived at by adding investment, labor, and intermediate consumption costs and dividing this figure by the turnover. According to these calculations, the U.K. had higher profits (costs are 85 percent of turnover in the U.K. but 90 percent in Germany) in 1983, which confirms the experts' assertion. The highest dairy margins are realized in Austria. In 1984–85, Austria's dairy margins for butter were five times the German margins, three times higher than German cottage cheese margins, and nearly double German skimmed milk powder margins (Steger and Moser, 1987). Austria's processing costs are extremely high (see OECD, 1987a), partly due to the small size of dairy firms. Nevertheless, profits are the highest in Austria. The fact that all overcapacity of production goes into subsidized export and the fact that these exports are, to an increasing extent, handled by the dairy sector itself, gives rise to higher profit margins in Austria. Also, high labor productivity and low labor costs in the dairy industry contribute to higher profit margins. Because there is no cost-price competition among dairy firms at all due to the specific governance of the sector in Austria, it has the highest profits and processing costs of the three countries compared.

In terms of profitability and productivity, Germany is the most efficient country, having the highest competition and therefore lowest profits and processing costs of the three countries. The U.K. rank in the middle. Austria has the most profitable and least productive dairy industry among the three countries.

All together in what concerns allocative efficiency, the U.K. is leading followed by Germany and Austria. Only with regard to profitability and productivity does Germany perform better than the U.K.

The Sector's Dynamic Efficiency

CHANGE IN THE NUMBER AND SIZE OF FARMS AND FIRMS. A significant structural change has taken place in the production of milk in all three countries. The number of dairy farms declined drastically between 1975 and 1985. Germany had the sharpest decline of farms (36 percent), closely followed by the U.K. (35 percent) and by Austria (27 percent); the average number of cows per dairy farm increased in Germany and Austria, and declined slightly in the U.K.

Since 1965 the number of dairy plants has dropped by half in all three nations. The structure of dairy plants changed in favor of larger plants in all countries, but there are significant differences in the speed of adjustment. Germany shows the highest dynamic for medium and large plants. Between 1976 and 1982 the share of small firms processing between 1 million and 10 million kg of milk declined by 13 percent, while the share of medium and large firms increased respectively. The U.K. ranks second. There is especially a tendency for the share of medium plants to decline in favor of large firms. Austria has the lowest dynamic among the three countries.

PRODUCT INNOVATION. Product innovation can be roughly expressed by the increase in the number of dairy products. Product innovation is the highest in Germany, where there is an especially large and increasing number of fresh milk products. The U.K. ranks second, although there has been much effort undertaken in the few past years to increase product diversification. Austria has the lowest rate of product innovation (Hager, 1986).

DIFFUSION OF TECHNICAL PROGRESS. The diffusion of technical progress in production is highest in the U.K., where there are highly specialized dairy farms. Nearly all of them have milking machines. The high specialization of dairy farms in the U.K. is nevertheless also responsible for low flexibility in changing from dairy to meat production (Ifo, 1985:9). Germany ranks second. In Austria, the diffusion of technical progress in farming is extremely low because of the small farm size. Farms are often too small even to use milking machines.

As far as technological progress of processing is concerned, Germany again leads, although it is far behind other EC countries (especially the Netherlands and Denmark) and is therefore judged to be only moderately progressive (Ifo, 1985). Germany's average firm size is far bigger than in Britain (see opening section of this chapter), and investments are also much higher (in 1983 23.6 percent of gross value added at factor costs; in the U.K., 18 percent). The high specialization of British companies seems to be a hindrance to further technological progress. Highly specialized firms are less flexible and less able to accommodate to change in environmental conditions. In Austria, because firms are extremely small, technological standard is the lowest.

In terms of dynamic efficiency, Germany is leading among the three countries followed by the U.K., while Austria is far behind.

The Sector's Distributional Performance

The high degree of regulation of the dairy sector has often been justified as protecting the income of farmers, who would otherwise be threatened by downward pressure of prices in times of excess supply. Also, the protection of consumers with regard to better quality and the assurance of good regional provision of milk products are cited.

In terms of *quality*, British raw milk ranks above Germany, while Austria is far below both. Determining the quality of milk products is very subjective. However, one quantifiable criterion is the number of artificial additives. Austrian and German products rank above British products in terms of this index owing to stringent laws restricting the use of additives.

Doorstep delivery guarantees a high degree of *regional distribution* in the U.K. (England and Wales). About 92 percent of households in England and Wales are supplied. This does not hold true for scattered rural communities in Scotland (Grant, 1983a). In Austria, regional provision of milk and milk products is also very good. About 95 percent of Austria is regularly supplied with milk, which is a far better distribution than in Germany (only 50 percent: Bellak, 1988:128).

Real income data for the dairy sector are not compiled separately from the rest of the agricultural sector as a whole. Therefore, real income in agriculture (measured as real net value added at factor costs per person working in agriculture) will be evaluated. Farmers' real income declined in EC countries from 1973 to 1975 and has been stagnant since (though there are some slight fluctuations in different years). German farmers lost the most income. Between 1975 and 1986 their real income fell by 15 percent. British farmers had income losses of 10 percent in the same period (Eurostat, 1987). While there were income losses in Germany and the U.K., Austria had a real income increase of 5 percent in the same period (Kovarik, 1987:58). Although in Austria income distribution among farmers is still a big problem, Austria clearly performs best among the three countries, followed by the U.K. and then Germany.

The most interesting question is whether consumers, processors, or producers profit most from sectoral governance. In Austria the high degree of nonmarket governance, which has induced extremely large surpluses, is to the disadvantage of producers and consumers. The cost of every liter of excess production of milk is about 10 percent higher than the price the producer gets. This means that it would be much cheaper to pay some of the Austrian milk producers to stop production and do nothing (Steger, 1988:153). The Austrian consumer pays about 36 percent of its consumption expenditures for dairy products in order to subsidize the dairy system. This is extremely high, the EC average being 23.7 percent (OECD, 1987b). The Austrian dairy system clearly favors processing firms, having higher processing costs but also higher profits than the Austrian manufacturing industry on average.

The U.K., when it joined the EC in 1973, had lower prices for dairy products than other EC countries. To prevent high price increases, which would undermine the British exchange rate, larger consumer subsidies were accorded to Britain than to other EC countries (e.g., for butter until 1985). It has therefore been argued that the U.K. system favors consumers. Nevertheless, the increase in prices for British dairy products attributable to EC entry, although they are still lower than in Germany, could also be considered a disadvantage to consumers. Compared to Austria, consumers are charged less. Producers are protected by entry barriers (MMB admission). The comparatively low producer price in the U.K. does not necessarily mean a disadvantage of British farmers, since they can produce much more cheaply through large-scale operations. The setting of entry barriers and low transport costs for delivery favor producers. Although British processing firms profit less from the system than those in Austria, they take higher profit margins than in Germany. Nevertheless, profits in the U.K. dairy industry are below those of manufacturing as a whole.

In Germany, processing firms profit the least among the three countries. Producers profit from the possibility of producing excess supply at supported producer prices. As is typical in the EC, the system favors producers to the disadvantage of consumers (OECD, 1987b).

Impact of Governance on Performance

How are these differences in country-specific performance profiles affected by governance arrangements? Dealing with this question poses the methodological problem that economic performance is not only contingent on governance. Additionally, a "subjectivistic" and an "objectivistic" cluster of performance determinants can be distinguished. Subjectivistic factors refer to the individual intentions, resources, and actions at the company level, especially to the strategies of management. Clearly, management's abilities influence a company's success, and the aggregated effects of management strategies have an impact on the performance of a sector. However, management strategies can be successful only to the extent to which they present an adequate response to the firm's environment. In this respect, the governance arrangement is an important element of the environment, which, by constituting opportunities and constraints, defines a feasible set of management options. Hence, management strategies can be seen as factors dependent on governance, at least for the purpose of an aggregated analysis of sectoral performance. Unlike subjectivistic factors, some elements of the firm's environment are determinants of economic performance but cannot be reduced to a matter of governance. These objectivistic factors comprise natural and economic conditions (e.g., climate and the volume of sales markets as a result of a country's size).

To assess the impact of governance arrangements on the sector's economic performance it is necessary to keep constant all the objectivistic factors that cannot be treated as dependent variables of the governance system. Since these factors are largely invariable over time, this can be achived through a combined synchronic and diachronic analysis of performance as presented above: Differences in the development of each country's performance over time, as found in this analysis, can, for reasons already outlined above, be interpreted as the result of the impact of country-specific governance systems. In Table 8.6 the three countries studied are ranked according to their economic performance as well as to their governance properties.

Although the national performance scores differ in the three performance dimensions, nevertheless, they reveal an instructive pattern when associated with the ranking of governance. Germany, where corporatism is least developed and the market has the most important role among the three countries, displays the worst score in the distributional dimension, but is most successful in modernizing the dairy industry as indicated by the findings on dynamic efficiency. Just the opposite applies to Austria, whose governance system is most corporatist and whose dynamic (and allocative) efficiency ranks last; it exhibits the best results in distribution. The U.K. ranks between the other two countries on the degree of corporatism and also obtains a middle position with regard

Table 8.6. Economic performance and governance

	Economic performance			Degree of established corporatist governance*
	Allocative efficiency	Dynamic efficiency	Distributional performance[†]	
U.K.	1	2	2	2
Germany	2	1	3	3
Austria	3	3	1	1

1 = high, 2 = middle, 3 = low.

[†] Criterion for ranking: the extent to which the producers' and processors' income demands are realized.

* According to Table 8.3.

to dynamic and distributional performance. It has the best allocative efficiency, although this good performance is qualified by the fact that it has deteriorated remarkably since the U.K. dairy sector became integrated into the EC regime, being more interventionist than the original U.K. system. Additionally, Germany performs better in terms of allocative efficiency as far as profitability and productivity are concerned. In sum, the U.K. lies in an intermediate position between Germany and Austria if all three performance dimensions are taken into account.

Above all, two main conclusions can be drawn from these findings: First, allocative and dynamic efficiency and distributional performance are apparently conflicting goals. The more that distributional demands of producers and processors tend to be satisfied the worse becomes the sector's ability to adapt to restructuring requirements and to attain a market clearing, and vice versa. Second, a high degree of corporatism is an appropriate means for solving the sector's distributional problems, while it obviously impedes progress pertaining to modernization and market clearing.

How does this fit with earlier cross-national studies of the interrelations of corporatism and economic development during the 1960s and 1970s (e.g., Schmitter, 1981), which consistently showed that highly corporatist countries proved better in terms of macroeconomic performance? In this respect one might put forward formal and substantial arguments. From a formal point of view it should be mentioned that the conclusions of sectoral and macroeconomic studies may diverge simply owing to their different focus. Substantially, it might be argued that the governance capacity of corporatism and other nonmarket institutions has decreased as a result of significant changes in the economic and political conditions. Although offering a way to harmonize distributional demands with other economic goals in the context of an interventionist policy made corporatism attractive in the 1960s and early 1970s, this function has become much more difficult to perform in the 1980s. Given a growing divergence of these two sets of goals, interest groups integrated into a corporatist system will presumably use their governance power for advancing their income goals at the expense of other economic goals and thus externalize the costs of resolving their distributional conflict.

However, increased governance problems do not necessarily imply that non-market institutions fail to master them. Even externalizing costs by nonmarket institutions does not always lead to economic failure. On the contrary, this can provide competitive advantages as recent studies on the machine tool industry (Herrigel, 1989) and the steel industry (O'Brien, 1989) demonstrate. For instance, nearly the same nonmarket governance measure (protectionism in foreign trade, regulation of prices, and quantities of production) that perform poorly in the case of the dairy industry have played a decisive role in making Japan's steel industry the strongest in the world.

Thus, it can be seen that stating a structural inferiority of nonmarket institutions in relation to the market, as often argued when calling for deregulation, is obviously an overgeneralization. The consequences that result from a certain kind of governance can therefore only be clarified by reference to the very specific circumstances under which it is applied. What makes the dairy sector differ from the machine tool and steel industries in this respect can be summarized as follows:

- *Policies at the global level.* Although it is true that many countries follow a protectionist policy because steel has been undergoing a severe crisis ever since the mid-1970s, Japan adopted such a policy early in the postwar period and has been consistent in strictly enforcing it. Setting the pace in this respect helped Japan to gain competitive advantages, yet protectionism when generalized among all relevant countries leads to a prisoner's dilemma. This is exactly the case of dairy where protectionism has a long and worldwide tradition, with the result that product costs are above the world market price and exports require subsidies in nearly all Western nations.

- *Sectoral properties.* In both the machine tool industry and steel industry, the significance of nonmarket institutions consists of socializing costs of solving key problems of increasing competitiveness. Because of the sector's high technological complexity, public support for vocational education and research and development can decisively improve competitiveness in the machine tool industry (Herrigel, 1989), while institutions enabling the adoption of long-term perspectives are strategically relevant for the steel industry owing to its capital-intensive production (O'Brien, 1989). Leaving aside natural differences in the preconditions for production, comparable key problems of competitiveness do not exist in the dairy industry, given the relatively little capital required and the low degree of technological complexity and product differentiation. Since competition is comparatively less sophisticated, nonmarket institutions offer a smaller potential for achieving competitive advantages and can be established nationally with less difficulty in the dairy sector.

- *Governance priority.* As already mentioned, governance arrangements are primarily suited to solve distributional problems in the dairy sector. This unusual priority thwarts the realization of other performance goals because they conflict with distributional demands. For instance, progress in productivity just tends to increase the sector's overcapacity under the condition of a predominance of distributional goals and generalized protectionism.

Conclusions

In conclusion, governance mechanisms aimed not at *socializing* costs, as in the case of machine tool and steel, but at making the actors *internalize* their costs of production and transaction as much as possible would be required under the special circumstances of the dairy sector so as to improve allocative and dynamic efficiency. Redesigning governance in this way can only be done by the state, which sets the basic elements of the sector's institutional framework. Generally, the state is confronted with more problems in realizing this institutional redesign the more that relevance accrues to distributional issues as a result of a former attribution of governance powers to interest groups. Therefore, highly corporatist governance arrangements, however successful they may be in income policy, are particularly burdened with difficulties in economic restructuring of sheltered sectors like dairy.

Notes

1. On this, see several national case studies (Farago, 1985; Grant, 1985; Traxler, 1985; Van Waarden, 1985; Young, Lindberg, and Hollingsworth, 1989), and a cross-national inquiry into the public role of business associations (Jacek, 1985).

2. This overview includes only developments up to the end of 1988.

3. Granting government authority entails compliance with regulations concerning clean milk production.

4. One important reason for this priority may reside in the fact that the MMB's revenue as a market institution considerably dwarfs its revenue as a processor (Grant, 1983a:13).

5. In the case of the Irish Republic and Italy, national quotas have been allotted to them based on their 1983 milk deliveries.

6. By "associational structures" we mean interest organizations as well as associational systems in this context.

7. For this differentiation, see in detail Lockwood (1964).

8. Owing to variations in economic, cultural, and natural circumstances, this special political relevance does not accrue to dairy in all countries. For instance, rice is the food that has political top priority in Japan. Correspondingly, the Japanese mode of governing rice shows interesting similarities with the governance of dairy in the three countries considered.

References

Annual Review of Agriculture. (1988). *Agricultural Act 1947*. London: Her Majesty's Stationary Office.

Bellak, Christian. (1988). *Regulierungsproblematik und wettbewerbliche Wirkungen von De- und Re-Regulierungsmaßnahmen am Beispiel der österreichischen Milchwirtschaft.* Typescript. Vienna: Wirtschaftsuniversität.

Bericht über die Lage der österreichischen Landwirtschaft. (1986). Vienna: Bundesministerium für Land- und Forstwirtschaft, 1987.

De Vroom, Bert. (1987). "The Food Industry and Quality Regulation." In Wyn Grant (ed.), *Business Interests, Organizational Development and Private Interest Government: An International Comparative Study of the Food Processing Industry* (pp. 180–207). Berlin and New York: de Gruyter.

Eurostat. (1987). *Theme 5, Series D, Landwirtschftliches Einkommen.*

Farago, Peter. (1985). "Regulating Milk Markets: Corporatist Arrangements in the Swiss Dairy Industry." In Wolfgang Streeck and Phillippe C. Schmitter (eds.), *Private Interest Government: Beyond Market and State* (pp. 168–81). Beverly Hills and London: Sage Publications.

Farago, Peter. (1987). "Retail Pressure and the Collective Reactions of the Food Processing Industry." In Wyn Grant (ed.), *Business Interests, Organizational Development and Private Interest Government: An International Comparative Study of the Food Processing Industry* (pp. 166–79). Berlin and New York: de Gruyter.

Grant, Wyn. (1983a). *Gotta Lotta Bottle: Corporatism, the Public and the Private and* the *Milk Marketing System in Britain*, Paper prepared for the ECPR Joint Sessions, March 1983, Freiburg.

Grant, Wyn. (1983b). *The Organization of Business Interests in the U.K. Food Processing Industry*, International Institute of Management Discussions Paper IIM/LMP 83–11, Berlin.

Grant, Wyn. (1985). "Private Organizations as Agents of Public Policy: The Case of Milk Marketing in Britain." In Wolfgang Streeck and Philippe C. Schmitter (eds.), *Private Interest Government. Beyond Market and State* (pp. 182–96). Beverly Hills and London: Sage Publications.

Grant, Wyn. (ed.). (1987). *Business Interests, Organizational Development and Private Interest Government: An International Comparative Study of the Food Processing Industry*. Berlin and New York: de Gruyter.

Giddings, Philip J. (1974). *Marketing Boards and Ministers*. Farnborough, UK: Saxon House.

Hager, Robert. (1986). *Die österreichische Milchmarktordnung*. Typescript der Wirtschaftsuniversität, Vienna.

Herrigel, Gary. (1989). *Industrial Order in the Machine Tool Industry: A Comparison of the United States and Germany*. Paper prepared for a Conference on the Governance of Capitalist Economies, May/June, Bellagio, Italy.

Hilbert, Josef. (1983). *Verbände im produzierenden Ernährungsgewerbe der Bundesrepublik Deutschland — Eine Studie zu Strukturen, Problemen and Wirkungen der Organisation von Wirtschaftsinteressen*. Typescript, University of Bielefeld.

Ifo. (1985). *Studien zur Agrawirtschaft, Milcherzeugung, Milchverarbeitung und Handel mit Milch und Milcherzeugnissen in den Ländern der EG*, Vol. 3. München: Ifo.

Jacek, Henry J. (1985). "Business Interest Associations as Private Interest Governments." In Wyn Grant (ed.), *Business Interests, Organizational Development and Private Interest Government: An International Comparative Study of the Food Processing Industry* (pp. 34–62). Berlin and New York: de Gruyter.

Kovarik, Georg. (1987). *Darstellung der direkten und indirekten Agrarförderung in Österreich*. Typescript. Wirtschaftsuniversität, Vienna.

Lehmbruch, Gerhard, and Philippe C. Schmitter (eds.). (1982). *Patterns of Corporatist Policy Making*. Beverly Hills and London: Sage Publications.

Lockwood, David. (1964). "Social Integration and System Integration." In George K. Zollschan and Walter Hirsch (eds.), *Explorations in Social Change*. London: Routledge and Kegan Paul.

MWF annual. *Tätigkeitsbericht des Milchwirtschaftsfonds*, 1970–1988, Vienna.

O'Brien, Patricia A. (1989). *Steel: The United States and Japan since World War II*. Paper prepared for a Conference on the Governance of Capitalist Economies, May/June, Bellagio, Italy.

OECD. (1986). *Milk and Milk Product Balances in OECD Countries 1976–1984*. Paris: OECD.

OECD. (1987a). *National Policies and Agricultural Trade*. Paris: OECD.

OECD. (1987b). *Working Party No. 1 of the Economic Policy Committee: Effects of Agricultural Policies in OECD Countries Main Issues for Discussion*. Paris: OECD.

Offe, Claus. (1975). *Berufsbildungsreform. Eine Fallstudie über Reformpolitik*. Frankfurt: Suhrkamp.

Offe, Claus, and Karl Hinrichs. (1985). "The Political Economy of the Labour Market." In Claus Offe (ed.), *Disorganized Capitalism* (pp. 10–51). Cambridge: Polity Press.

Olson, Mancur. (1965). *The Logic of Collective Action: Public Goods and the Theory of Groups*. Cambridge, Mass.: Harvard University Press.

ÖRV. (1981) *Raiffeisen in Österreich,* Vienna: Oesterreichischer Raiffeisenverband.

Pestoff, Victor. (1987). "The Effect of State Institutions on Associative Action in the Food Processing Industry." In Wyn Grant (ed.), *Business Interests, Organizational Development and Private Interest Government: An International Comparative Study of the Food Processing Industry* (pp. 93–116). Berlin and New York: de Gruyter.

Schmidt, Erich (ed.). 1987. "Der Agrarsektor in Österreich." *Beiträge zur Wirtschafts- und Gesellschaftspolitik.* Band 3, Verein für Gesellschafts- und Wirtschaftswissenschaften, Vienna.

Schmitter, Philippe C. (1981). "Interest Intermediation and Regime Governability in Contemporary Western Europe and North America." In Suzanne D. Berger (ed.), *Organizing Interests in Western Europe* (pp. 285–330). Cambridge: Cambridge University Press.

Schmitter, Philippe C., and Wolfgang Streeck. (1981). *The Organization of Business Interests: A Research Design to Study the Associative Action of Business in the Advanced Industrial Societies of Western Europe.* International Institute of Management Disscusion Paper IIM/LMP 81–13, Berlin.

Schumpeter, Joseph. (1942). *Capitalism, Socialism and Democracy.* New York: Harper and Brothers.

Steger, Gerhard (ed.). (1988). *Grünbuch, Krise und Perspektiven der österreichischen Landwirtschaft.* Vienna: Erwin Schwaiger-Verlag.

Steger, Gerhard, and Erhard Moser. (1987). *Wer profitiert von den Überschüssen in der Landwirtschaft?* Vienna: Schriftenreihe der Gemeinwirtschaft.

Stöckl, Jakob P. (1988). *Die Milch-Garantiemengenregelung in ihren Konsequenzen für die Milchverarbeitung—Eine Bestandsaufnahme.* Unpublishd manuscript.

Streeck, Wolfgang, and Philippe C. Schmitter (eds). (1985). *Private Interest Government Beyond Market and State.* Beverly Hills and London: Sage Publications.

Traxler Franz. (1985). "Prerequisites, Problem-Solving Capacity and Limits of Neo-Corporatist Regulation: A Case Study of Private Interest Governance and Economic Performance in Austria." In Wolfgang Streek and Philippe C. Schmitter (eds.), *Private Interest Government: Beyond Market and State* (pp. 150–67). Beverly Hills and London: Sage Publications.

Traxler, Franz. (1990). "Political Exchange, Collective Action and Interest Governance." In Bernd Marin (ed.), *Governance and Generalized Exchange: Self-Organizing Policy Networks in Action* (pp. 37–67). Frankfurt-Boulder: Campus-Westview.

Van Waarden, Frans. (1985). "Varieties of Collective Self-Regulation of Business: The Example of the Dutch Dairy Industry." In Wolfgang Streeck and Philippe C. Schmitter (eds.), *Private Interest Government: Beyond Market and State* (pp. 197–220). Beverly Hills and London: Sage Publications.

Vas, Janos. (1988). *Bericht über die internationale Milchwirtschaft,* Unterlage zur Sitzung der Verwaltungskommission am 16.3.1988. Vienna Milchwirtschaftsfonds.

Young, Brigitta, Leon N. Lindberg, and J. Rogers Hollingsworth. (1989). "The Governance of the American Dairy Industry: From Regional Dominance to regional Cleavage." In William D. Coleman and Henry J. Jacek (eds), *Regionalism. Business Interests and Public Policy* (pp. 127–52). Beverly Hills and London: Sage Publications.

CHAPTER 9

Sectoral Governance in Consumer Electronics in Britain and France

Alan Cawson

THIS chapter examines the dynamics of sectoral governance in the British and French consumer electronics industries during a period of rapid change from the mid-1970s to the present. At the beginning of this period the industries were relatively self-contained: Both national industries comprised firms producing mainly for the national market; both were dependent on a single product—color television (CTV)—for the major part of their output; and both industries were afforded a measure of protection from international competition by patents on their respective CTV technologies.

By the end of the 1980s the situation had been transformed to the extent that it was no longer possible to analyze the industries in terms of distinctive national sectors. Today, every major consumer electronics producer in Britain and France is now part of a multinational corporation competing at a global level. Distinctive institutions of sectoral governance in each country have decreased in importance at the same time that mechanisms of governance have begun to be developed at a European level, principally through an extension of the role of the European Commission. The European consumer electronics industry is now dominated by three major multinational groupings: Philips, Thomson, and Nokia.

This transformation has taken place in response to the competitive pressure exerted by Japanese firms from the mid-1970s. As Table 9.1 shows, by 1986 seven of the world's ten largest consumer electronics firms were Japanese. The chapter traces the source of Japanese success to the particular "production system" characteristic of Japanese firms, both in terms of their internal mechanisms, which give them a wholly different character to European firms, and in terms of their location within a highly effective mode of sectoral governance.

The nature of the response of firms in the British and French industries to Japanese competition has been radically different. Over a period of ten years from 1977 to 1987 every major British consumer electronics manufacturer left the industry, and the bulk of British production is now accounted for by Japanese

Table 9.1. The World's Top Ten Consumer Electronics Firms, 1986

	Sales (in millions of dollars)
Matsushita Electric–JVC (Japan)	11,019
Philips (Netherlands)	6,898
Sony-Aiwa (Japan)	6,432
Toshiba (Japan)	5,885
Hitachi (Japan)	4,880
Sharp (Japan)	3,840
Mitsubishi (Japan)	3,721
Sanyo (Japan)	3,175
Thomson (France)	3,169
RCA (United States)[a]	2,506

SOURCE: Observatoire des Strategies Industrielles, *Cent acteurs dans la competition mondiale.* Paris: Economica, 1990, p. 374

[a] Acquired by Thomson in 1987.

companies. By contrast, the leading French firm, Thomson, has become the second largest European producer, and French government policy has restricted the role of Japanese competition in France. This chapter examines the extent to which these different outcomes can be explained by differences in the institutions of sectoral governance in the two countries, and especially in the willingness of the French government to promote its leading firm first as a "national champion" and then as an "international champion." The chapter concludes by showing how the process of adjustment of Japanese competition has led to the emergence of embryonic mechanisms of sectoral governance at a European level, especially as a consequence of the changing nature of competition.

The European Consumer Electronics Industry

The consumer electronics industry produces a range of audiovisual equipment (often referred to as "brown goods" to distinguish them from household electrical appliances—"white goods"). The principal products manufactured by the European consumer electronics industry are color televisions (CTVs), car radios and tape players, hi-fi equipment, video cassette recorders (VCRs), and, recently, compact disc players (CDs). Less significant products are radios, tape recorders, electronic watches, and TV computer games.

The growth of the consumer electronics industry in the Far East, initially in Japan but later in Korea, Taiwan, Hong Kong, and elsewhere, initiated a period of fierce competition that led European manufacturers to retreat from the production of low-cost items such as transistor radios, tape recorders, and monochrome (black-and-white) TVs.

It can be seen from Table 9.2—which compares the major consumer electronics items produced in Britain, France, and (West) Germany—that CTV represents by far the most important single product, although VCR production has grown rapidly in the period between 1979 and 1985, and the application

Table 9.2. Consumer Electronics Production in Britain, France, and (West) Germany, 1985 (in millions of dollars)

	Britain	France	(West) Germany
Color television	629	500	986
Monochrome television	13	23	—
Videotape recorders	187	19	538
TV games	—	11	—
Audio products	70	137	450
Other*a*	26	126	204
Total	925	816	2178

SOURCE: *Mackintosh Yearbook of West European Electronics Data 1987.* London: Benn Publications, 1986.

a Including electronic watches, but excluding home computers.

Table 9.3. The EEC Consumer Electronics Market, 1981–86, (millions of dollars at 1986 prices)

	1981	1986
Color television	5458	8044
Video cassette recorders	1627	4229
Audio systems	4340	3329
Compact disc players	—	599
Portable/personal audio equipment	2585	2456
Video camcorders	—	708
Other	116	718
Total value ($M)	14,126	20,083

SOURCE: BIS-Mackintosh.

of digital technologies to sound reproduction in the form of compact disc and digital sound recording is leading to a renaissance in the audio market. Table 9.3 shows the development of the market for a range of consumer electronics products between 1981 and 1986; the market shows continued growth in CTVs and VCRs, as well as new products such as CD players and camcorders.

The consumer electronics industry is highly concentrated, and various rationalizations and mergers in the last few years have led to a European industry dominated by the two leading European firms, Philips and Thomson, facing the Japanese majors such as Matsushita, Hitachi, and Toshiba, all of whom have now established manufacturing facilities in the EC (European Community). European firms have managed to hold their own in CTV production and have retained a major slice of VCR production, albeit using technology licensed from Japan. In newer products such as digital audio and camcorders, the Japanese have an important technological lead, with only Philips among the Europeans able to maintain a stake through its development of the compact disc and now the digital compact cassette (DCC). The strength of the European firms in CTV production is likely to be challenged by the Japanese firms with developments in digital TV technology and flat-screen alternatives to the cathode ray tube.

Table 9.4 shows the major CTV producers in Western Europe and illustrates the leading position of Philips–Grundig and Thomson. Philips is now the world's largest CTV producer, and it controls almost one-third of European production with plants in seven countries, although it is now in the process of reducing these to three. Thomson now accounts for almost a fifth of production, with plants in four countries, and together the two companies control over half of European production. Japanese firms are steadily increasing their output of CTVs in their European plants, and have now been joined by the Korean firms Samsung and Goldstar, with plants in Britain and Germany, respectively, so that it is unlikely that the process of rationalization among existing production has run its course.

The European VCR industry shows a much stronger presence of Japanese producers: As Table 9.5 shows, in 1986 Japanese companies accounted for nearly 40 percent of production, compared to about 14 percent in CTVs. Here too Korean firms are entering the industry in Europe. Unlike in CTV, joint ventures between European and Japanese producers have been an important factor: The JVC-Thomson company (JT, previously J2T) is the largest, producing 750,000 units annually in Britain and Germany, and it has been joined by Matsushita-Bosch and Amstrad-Funai.

Table 9.4. Western European Color Television Production, 1986

Company	Production (000s)	(%)
Philips	3100	20.4
Thomson	2000	13.2
Grundig	1950	12.8
ITT	1305	8.6
Thorn-EMI-Ferguson	800	5.3
Salora/Luxor	680	4.5
Blaupunkt	600	4.0
Sony	535	3.5
Sanyo	410	2.7
Hitachi	370	2.4
Toshiba	310	2.0
Matsushita	310	2.0
Other Japanese	130	0.9
Other Far East	410	2.7
Other European	2295	15.1
Total Japanese	2055	13.5
Total Far East	2465	16.2
Total	15,195	

SOURCE: BIS-Mackintosh based on industry estimates.

NOTE: Philips assumed managerial control of Grundig in 1985 and Thomson acquired Thorn-EMI-Ferguson in 1987. These two major firms thus control 33.6 percent and 18.5 percent, respectively, of total European production.

Table 9.5. Western European Video Cassette Recorder Production, 1986

Firm	Production (000s)	(%)
Philips	800	19.0
Grundig	750	17.9
J2T	750	17.9
Hitachi	450	10.7
Matsushita/Bosch	335	8.0
Sanyo/Fisher	240	5.7
Mitsubishi	165	3.9
Sharp	160	3.8
Toshiba	160	3.8
ITT	150	3.6
Others	240	5.7
Total European	2605	62.0
Total Japanese	1595	38.0
Total	4200	

SOURCE: BIS-Mackintosh based on industry estimates.

Color Television

Color television (CTV) was developed during the 1950s in the United States, and a transmission standard (NTSC) was adopted by the National Television System Committee which included a picture resolution of 525 horizontal lines. The Japanese government also adopted this standard, and Japanese manufacturers built up very high levels of production by developing the home market and exporting sets to the United States. The Europeans declined to adopt the NTSC system, and a struggle ensued between two rival systems, both of which were technically superior to the NTSC system, in part because the pictures comprised 625 horizontal lines (Crane, 1979). The PAL (Phase Alternate Line) standard was developed by Telefunken and cross-licensed to Thorn, and was adopted by most of Western Europe in the late 1960s and early 1970s. The rival French SECAM (Séquence à Memoire) system was adopted by France and later Greece alone in Western Europe, but given away to the Soviet Union and Eastern European countries.

The consequence of the failure to agree on a single technical standard in Europe was to segment the CTV market, and in effect if not in intention to insulate the French market from international competition, at least until dual PAL/SECAM sets were produced at little extra cost in the 1980s. The importance of transmission licensing in general was to offer a substantial degree of protection to the European industry against Japanese competition, which was not present in other consumer electronics products such as radios, tape recorders, and hi-fi systems.

The PAL licences were initially refused to Japanese producers by Telefunken and Thorn, but when the Japanese threatened to disrupt the market by exporting inferior but very low cost 300-line sets, Telefunken gave way and allowed licences for smaller-screen sets, subject to restrictions on the volume of exports to Europe. The European felt secure that there was relatively little demand for small-screen sets, but they failed to predict the substantial growth of a market for second sets, and for use in conjunction with home computers and video games. Japanese producers who located in Europe were permitted to make large-screen sets, but were prevented from exporting more than 50 percent of their production, thus restricting their ability to serve the entire European market from a single base.

Success of Japanese firms in the 1970s in exporting to Europe despite the PAL/SECAM barrier was not built on superior product technology, but rather on more efficient manufacturing processes based on the widespread use of automatic insertion of parts, and on higher standards of quality and reliability, which in part derived from the use of far fewer components. The social system of production, which lies behind the success of the Japanese firms, is examined in the following section. The European industry was fragmented into a large number of plants with relatively small production volumes serving segmented markets; Japanese firms had the advantage of the large combined NTSC markets in Japan and the United States in which to exploit scale economies (OTA, 1983). European firms that stayed in the industry after the upheavals of the 1970s and early 1980s were forced to modernize their production processes to remain competitive. In the medium to long term, however, competition in the TV industry will increasingly develop around product innovations, as has happened with VCRs. In this new phase the European firms may not be so well placed as in the last phase, unless they can once more reap the benefits of incompatible transmission standards.

In the late 1970s, PAL patents began to expire and are now no longer a significant barrier to trade. The race is now on to develop the next generation of high-definition television (HDTV) technologies (over 1000 lines to the picture compared to today's 625 or 525 lines). A consortium of European firms led by Philips is collaborating to produce a standard in competition with the Japanese industry. A proprosal to adopt the prototype Japanese system at the 1986 conference of the international standards body CCIR was defeated, and the Europeans had the chance to come up with their own working system by 1990. They were able to do this, and the result has been that CCIR has not agreed on a single world standard for HDTV. The European Community has, however, declined to offer the substantial package of subsidies to broadcasters demanded by consortium members in order to launch a service. and the future of the European HDTV program is now in doubt. Success would have resurrected a set of technical barriers such as those that had protected the industry in the 1970s (Watson Brown, 1987).

Video Cassette Recorders

Despite Philips having developed the first VCR suitable for domestic use in 1972, all VCRs now produced in Europe use proprietary Japanese technology, and innovation in video technology is dominated by the Japanese industry.

Unlike the case of television systems discussed above, where governments were involved in the adoption of broadcasting standards, a single VCR technology emerged out of a competitive struggle in the marketplace in which there have been Japanese as well as European losers.

The dominant format worldwide is the VHS system, developed by the Japan Victor Company (JVC), a subsidiary of the world's largest consumer electronics company, Matsushita. A rival format, Beta, was independently developed at the same time by the Sony Corporation, and both formats were in competition on the European market with a succession of formats introduced by Philips (the N-1500 and N-1700) and Philips-Grundig (the V-2000). At present the VHS system is being challenged by Sony's 8 mm format, and a new Super VHS format has been developed. The Europeans have opted out of the struggle.

In comparison with VHS and Beta models, the early Philips VCRs were bulky, expensive, unreliable, and restricted to short recording times. When the Japanese firms began to ship large numbers of VCRs to Europe in 1978 and 1979 they quickly achieved significant levels of market penetration. Earlier, JVC had signed agreements with the major competitor to Philips and Grundig in the three largest European markets: with Thorn-EMI in Britain, Telefunken in Germany, and Thomson in France, so that their machines would appear under European brand names and be marketed through existing channels. The 1977 agreements also included the provision for the eventual development of a joint manufacturing operation. By the time that Philips and Grundig were seeking cooperation from other manufacturers for their new V-2000 system, introduced in 1981, their European competitors were firmly ensconced in the VHS camp.

In 1981 the only manufacturers of VCRs with a base inside the EEC were Grundig, accounting for under 10 percent of total EC sales of 2 million VCRs, although the following year Philips opened a second VCR factory in West Germany, in addition to its existing plant in Austria. The failure of the attempt by these manufacturers to establish wider support for the V-2000 system was signaled in 1982 with the agreement between JVC and its European partners to manufacture VCRs in a joint venture, initially J3T, but in the end J2T (JVC-Thorn-Telefunken) when the French government vetoed Thomson's participation in the venture. In response to their failure to secure backing for the V-2000, and facing a cost difference of some 40 percent between V-2000 machines and VCRs imported from Japan, Philips and Grundig initiated an antidumping suit that led to the voluntary export restraint agreement negotiated between the EC and Japan. By the time the agreement was signed the V-2000 format was effectively finished, and Philips-Grundig moved into the VHS camp.

The most significant recent development in VCR technology has been the combined camera-recorder (camcorder), where another format war is being fought between JVC's VHS and Sony's 8 mm systems. This product began to grow rapidly just as VCR markets were reaching saturation point, and sales increased annually by 20 percent up to 1991. At present, no camcorders are manufactured in Europe, but it is likely that Philips and some of the Japanese firms in Europe will begin to do so in the near future.

The Nature of the Japanese Competitive Challenge

As was suggested in the previous section, Japanese success in penetrating European markets for CTV was based initially on incremental improvements in existing technologies, and it was the European industry through the introduction of teletext that introduced the most significant product innovation. Among the most important factors accounting for the early success of Japanese firms in European markets in the 1970s are the following:

labor costs were one-third to one-half that of European levels;

set designs required up to 30 percent fewer components because of the greater use of integrated circuits;

greater use of automation in the production of sets, with 65 to 80 percent of components inserted automatically (compared to 0 to 15 percent in the case of European firms);

larger scale of plants, with output per plant about 500,000 CTV sets per year, compared to a European average of half that;

superior-quality components delivered promptly to factories, which held fewer inventory stocks;

fast design cycles allowing for constantly improving product models.
(Franko, 1982:79–80; Shepherd, 1982:145; Negishi, 1985:25).

These factors enabled Japanese firms to produce CTVs at price/quality combinations that European producers were unable to match. To discover *how* the Japanese were able to achieve these advantages, we must explore the nature of Japanese firms as "social production systems" and locate the sources of their competitiveness in the distinctive social relations of production in Japan. This goes well beyond seeing companies as autonomous agents of production; the social relations underpinning efficient manufacturing technology must be understood in the context of an institutional framework that has encouraged companies to develop corporate strategies rooted in the long term. Both of these dimensions will be explored by contrasting the specific features of the Japanese industry with those that obtain in Europe.

Dore (1987:53–4) has argued that Western firms can be distinguished from Japanese ones in terms of a dimension of "community," which gives as polar types the "company law model" firm and the "community model" firm. In the Company law model, the firm is defined as the property of the shareholders, who exercise paramount rights, including the unconstrained right to sell their stake to others. Management act as trusted agents of shareholders, but relations of trust do not extend to the contract between managers and workers. This is ultimately based within an adversarial relationship, despite what may be scrupulous conformity to market contract rules.

In the Community model, by contrast:

1. The firm is primarily defined as a social unit made up of all the people who work full-time in it ("in" rather than "for").

2. The shareholders are, like customers and suppliers and local

authorities, one group of outsiders who have to be satisfied if the firm is to prosper. Members of the firm would feel entitled to vociferous protest if they had no say in the transfer of a controlling interest.

3. Every member of the firm can act on the assumption that other members share a desire to make the firm prosper, and this gives enough fellow feeling for those who have less than a full understanding of the accounts to trust managers not to conceal things from them for manipulative purposes. They are likely to believe that the distribution of rewards is what it appears to be, and is fair. (Dore, 1987:54)

The communitarian nature of Japanese business finds expression in many of its features, but perhaps the most far-reaching is in the system of lifetime employment practiced by all major Japanese companies. Workers are pushed back into the labor market only *in extremis*, and managers would expect to stay with a single company for the duration of their careers. This system is at the heart of the social relations of the firm, and it enables working practices that amount to a formidable competitive weapon. The relations of trust that it engenders permit a considerable degree of flexibility in the deployment of labor. Workers who are confident of continued employment are more ready to accept new technologies or retraining. Managers whose career expectations are confined to a single company identify their interests with those of the company, with beneficial effects on company performance (Kono, 1984:60; Dore, 1987:109). Reduction of employment mobility in the Community model firm might be expected to prevent a flexible response to changing market conditions, but in practice it promotes a strong impulse toward innovation. Faced with deteriorating markets for its existing products, the Japanese firm responds by making efforts "to find new products and markets to occupy the people they are more or less committed to employing anyway" (Dore, 1987:33). Response of the Japanese consumer electronics producers to emergent competition from the newly industrialized Southeast Asian countries in "mature" products such as CTVs and more recently VCRs has been to shift their production to plants in those countries while at the same time intensifying innovative activity by manufacturing higher value-added products at home.

The ability of Japanese firms to combine lifetime employment with adaptive managerial practices is considerably enhanced by the extensive practice of subcontracting, which has developed into a tightly regulated set of relationships between major firms and a large number of small enterprises in which the social relations of production extend beyond the boundaries of the company. "Obligational contracting" has developed as an alternative to vertical integration and component procurement via market relationships (Sako, 1989). It involves the development of long-term and relatively stable ties between manufacturers and suppliers, in which priority is given to the quality and stability of supply so that substantial economies can be achieved in the final assembly stage of production. Once a satisfactory relationship has been forged, counting and preassembly testing of components can be dispensed with (Trevor, 1988:146). The Japanese manufacturing philosophy, in which quality is built into each stage of the production process, rather than achieved by testing and repair at the end, depends crucially on these relationships with suppliers.

For the larger firms the latter are organized into associations of suppliers of a particular company (Trevor, 1988:141), with regular monthly meetings that are of particular importance when new products are being introduced. Japanese firms that have set up manufacturing bases in Europe cite component procurement as their most important problem, well ahead of labor quality (Negishi, 1985:22). They have not yet set up their own supplier associations, but have organized conferences of suppliers and subcontractors so as to begin to foster mutual obligations.

Obligational contracting offers other important advantages to Japanese firms. Lifetime employment in the parent company can be protected in adverse market conditions by squeezing suppliers so that they rather than the major firms bear the brunt of employment contraction. Tight discipline can be exercised over suppliers by using past performance as the criterion by which firms receive different treatment. Accommodation to the demands made by the big firms leads to preferential treatment in any future phase of expansion. Another advantage arises from the practice of redeploying managers in mid-career to supplier firms; they carry with them both technical expertise and the corporate philosophy of the major firm. This allows companies to reduce the immobility of the lifetime employment system and accelerate the career progress of the most promising managerial talent.

It must be stressed, however, that the specific social system of production in the Japanese corporation developed in the context of a unique institutional framework. One crucial aspect of this concerns the relationship between businesses and financial institutions, and the particular role of shareholding. Explanations of the greater capacity of Japanese firms to operate on a longtime horizon have frequently emphasized the close relationships between businesses and banks, low interest rates on industrial borrowings, and the absence of immediate pressures arising from fluctuations in the price of a company's stock (Aoki, 1984:7–15; Abegglen and Stalk, 1985:161–67; Kono, 1984:60–62; Dore, 1986:45ff.; Dore, 1987, chapter 6).

Aggressive pricing and strategies geared toward building market share over the long term were an important part of the first phase of competition between European and Japanese firms in consumer electronics. But "patient money" also helps to sustain the investments in research, training, and product development that lie behind the later phase of competition through innovation. What characteristics of the Japanese financial system sustained this crucial competitive advantage?

Constraints arising from company shareholdings differ greatly from the British or American pattern. In these countries there is a direct relationship between short-term profitability and share price, with pressure on the latter likely to lead to intervention by institutional shareholders or a takeover bid. In 1985 an attempt by the British firm STC to develop a long-term information technology strategy by diversifying from telecommunications equipment into computers led to intense pressure on the company's stock price and the eventual removal of Sir Kenneth Corfield. In Japan, shareholdings must be seen within the larger pattern of obligated long-term trading relationships. Shareholdings held by banks, insurance companies, or other firms are often an expression of commitment to customer or supplier relationships. "A high proportion of the holders of Japanese equity have more to gain from the other business they do with the companies whose shares they hold than from profits or capital gains on the shares themselves" (Dore, 1987:113).

Besides overt pressure, Japanese firms are less dependent on equity financing through the capital market than are their Western competitors. Some companies (such as Matsushita and Toyota) are able to finance investment out of reserves, but most have long-term debt relationships with a number of banks, and in turn borrowings by these banks from the Bank of Japan affords a chain of influence through which the long-term perspectives of the Japanese bureaucracy can be transmitted to individual companies. The banking relationship is not a simple debtor-creditor one: Banks acquire extensive knowledge about the firms, advise on long-term strategies, and often nominate directors to the company board (Dore, 1987:110). Abegglen and Stalk (1985:157) argue that the willingness of Japanese banks to permit high debt-to-equity ratios was a major factor behind the ability of Japanese firms to sustain very high growth rates in the 1970s and early 1980s. Besides technical factors (such as the undervaluation of the asset base through the omission of land holdings) the willingness of banks to permit high gearing reflects the priority they accord to growth rather than short-term profitability.

Finally, this brief overview of the source of the competitive advantages of Japanese versus Western businesses would not be complete without stressing the role of trade associations. In the electronics industry all of the major firms are members of the Electronic Industries Association of Japan (EIAJ), which has 600 members drawn from consumer and industrial electronics firms, as well as components producers. It maintains more than 200 standing committees covering all aspects of the industry, but its major priorities lie in the fields of technical standards, trade policy issues, and technology forecasting (EIAJ, 1988). The EIAJ established a European office in Dusseldorf in 1962, before any of its member firms had established its own European organization. This office provided detailed analyses of the European electronics industry, as well as specific assistance to firms on such issues as complying with different national standards legislation. It acted as an intermediary between companies and national governments, and it disseminated valuable information on subsidy regimes and inward investment policies.

Following the establishment of European manufacturing operations in the 1970s, and the admission of Japanese companies to some European trade associations such as BREMA, the EIAJ continued to operate a structure of "parallel representation." In the British case Japanese subsidiaries would send their senior British managers to BREMA to act as good corporate citizens, maintaining a low profile on trade policy issues. At the same time, the EIAJ maintained extensive contacts with Japanese management and met independently with government officials to try to head off protectionist pressures.

This section has emphasized the formidable competitive advantages the Japanese firms possessed in comparison to their European counterparts. These advantages arise from fundamental differences in the nature of Japanese businesses, their relationship to suppliers as well as to financial institutions, and their greater capacity for collective organization. The next section examines the differences in the patterns of sectoral governance in the British and French industries, which helps explain why the effect of Japanese competition was so dissimilar in the two countries.

Divergent Governance Mechanisms

The response to Japanese competition on the part of industries and governments in Britain and France was markedly different, reflecting differences both in industry structure and the role of government. In Zysman's (1983) terminology, government in France was a player; in Britain it was a regulator. French industry expected government to champion the interests of French capital abroad and expected discretionary intervention at home. By contrast, British companies jealously guarded their autonomy and sought from government a stable macroeconomic climate that would reduce market uncertainty. Only when Japanese firms began to locate in Britain in the context of a depressed market did the industry move toward a defensive coalition involving a more active role for government.

In France, the consumer electronics industry is heavily concentrated, both in terms of its domination by Thomson and the French subsidiary of Philips, and its reliance on color television (62 percent of production in 1985, of which Philips and Thomson contributed 73 percent). Until 1982 the French government was strongly opposed to inward investment in this sector, and Philips-France trod a delicate path with a French name (La Radiotechnique), French top management, and support for idiosyncratic French standards (e.g., SECAM).

Thomson had emerged as the dominant French manufacturer in the consumer electronics industry through a series of mergers in the 1960s, facilitated by the fiscal and subsidy policies of the French government. It was chosen with CGE as a "national champion" of the electronics industry, and a state-supported "Yalta" agreement in 1969 divided the industry into spheres of influence, with Thomson the flagship for consumer products, military electronics, and semiconductors.

Consumer electronics had been chosen in the fourth national plan (1961–65) as one of six growth sectors, and under the Barre administration a more selective industrial policy was developed that sought to identify areas of comparative advantage and focus state aid on specific firms and products. Selected companies were offered financial assistance, export subsidies, and preferential public purchasing contracts, such as the Minitel program for interactive videotext, which created a large public market for television tubes and components. The focus of government–industry relations was thus a bilateral relationship between ministries and the national champion, formalized in the *contrat de plan*. The trade association was relatively insignificant as an instrument of sectoral governance, certainly compared to its role in Germany or even Britain.

The strategic priority accorded to consumer electronics, and the goal of French technological independence, was emphasised once more in the early 1980s by the Mitterrand government, which developed the concept of the *filière électronique*. According to this, French firms should be active at all stages in the production chain, from raw materials to finished products. Inward (direct foreign) investment was to be discouraged, because foreign corporations tended to import their technology and components, which would lead to important gaps in the *filière*. For such a concept to work, the government could not be indifferent to the fate of any link in the chain; thus, it strengthened the hand of the national champions who could use it to bargain for extra resources or public contracts. Conversely, its success would depend on the capacity of the national champions to develop indigenous technology, and that of the government to harmonize the corporate strategies of the firms with its own ends.

For a while in the 1970s the economic conditions in the industry and Thomson's commercial success were combining to make such goals appear feasible. The market for color televisions was expanding strongly, and import penetration was kept to very low levels by the technical barrier of the SECAM system and import quotas that predated the Treaty of Rome. But, as we shall see in the next section, by the time the *filière* was made moot, two of its preconditions had disappeared. Thomson's attempts to retain independent technological capability in consumer electronics had ended in expensive failure, and despite nationalization in 1981 the government proved unable to control its corporate strategy.

In Britain, the consumer electronics industry was much less concentrated than in France, with some dozen companies manufacturing televisions in the late 1960s. They were linked through a trade association, BREMA, which began in 1973 to serve as the focus for trade negotiations with the Japanese associations (EIAJ) leading to bilateral voluntary restraint agreements. Governments have preferred not to be directly involved in these negotiations, offering tacit support rather than playing a leading role.

The severity of the impact of Japanese competition was moderated by technical barriers to trade. Britain had opted for the German PAL color television system in 1967, and under the conditions of that licence firms from non-PAL countries (such as Japan) were prevented from exporting sets with a screen size larger than 20 inches. Japanese manufacturers were thus faced with the option of setting up production facilities in Europe (where they could produce large sets, but not export more than 50 percent of production), or contain their exports to small sets for which there appeared to be only a very small market in Europe.

With official encouragement (and government regional aid amounting to 28 percent of costs) two leading Japanese firms, Sony and Matsushita, established plants in Wales in 1974 and 1976, respectively. The initial decisions to invest in plants in Britain were taken at a time when the Health government was pursuing an expansionist economic policy, and the television market was expanding rapidly. British manufacturers were unable to keep pace with demand, and thus had no reason to fear the Japanese arriving in their back yard. The level of import penetration rose sharply, and then most importantly, remained high as the market suddenly collapsed at the end of the "dash for growth" in 1974.

Successive British governments had until the mid-1970s tended to view the consumer electronics industry as a relatively successful sector that had a good record of innovation (the world's first solid-state color television had been introduced by Ferguson in 1972) and that could be left alone to adapt to changing market conditions. This abstentionist policy, so different from the French penchant toward the *grand project*, was reinforced by the attitudes of the firms lulled into a false sense of security by the rapid expansion of the market. During this period sectoral governance was characterized by absence of formal mechanisms of regulation and control, and by the convergence of interests between government and industry on the efficacy of the market.

Challenges to the Stability of Governance Mechanisms

Although sectoral governance in consumer electronics in Britain and France showed marked contrasts in the late 1960s and early 1970s, both systems performed relatively well under similar external conditions: (1) The sector was dominated by a color television market that was expanding rapidly, in both cases but to a different degree sheltered by the degree of protection afforded by the adoption of different technical standards from those prevailing in the United States and Japan; and (2) the technology was stable and protected, which had the twin effects of reducing the incentives for European companies to innovate while at the same time offering the prospect of long-term rewards to the Japanese industry to develop new products.

The stability of the sector was rapidly undermined in the late 1970s by a combination of factors that are explored in this section. In both countries government policies were sharply challenged within the industry and the practice of sectoral governance was called into question. In addition, both industries had to adjust to the arrival of the most significant innovation in consumer electronics since television: the domestic video cassette recorder (VCR).

Figure 9.1 shows graphically how the structure of the industry in Britain changed radically after a long period of stability. In the space of ten years a predominantly British-owned industry was transformed into one dominated by Japanese, Dutch, and French firms. This outcome has been the unintended consequence of the explicit policy of both Labour and Conservative governments to encourage the modernization of the industry by inducing and subsidising inward investment by Far Eastern, predominantly Japanese, producers. The intention of the policy was that British companies would reinvest and compete successfully with Japanese best practice; the effect was that, sooner or later, all the British producers chose to exit the industry.

The British Labour government of 1974–79 was the first to propose a specific strategy for the industry and an alternative form of sectoral governance to the

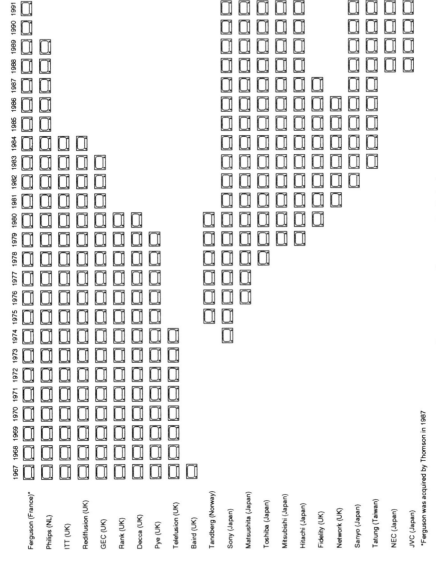

Figure 9.1. Television Manufacturers in Britain, 1967–91.

229

reliance on spontaneous adjustment through the market. As part of its overall industrial strategy, a network of tripartite Sector Working Parties (SWP) was created, including a Consumer Electronics SWP. The first eighteen months of the SWP's existence was dominated by a bitter struggle over the plans by Hitachi to establish a greenfield factory in the northeast, which would import TV tubes from Hitachi's plant in Finland and supply British and EC markets. This investment was fovored by the British government, but opposed by a coalition of employers and trade unions, led by the Philips subsidiary Mullard, which saw an immediate threat to its own tube-making interests. In the event Hitachi withdrew its plans, the government agreed to a set of new guidelines for inward investment, which it would seek to negotiate with incoming firms.

These guidelines included three key stipulations: that foreign firms would not invest in greenfield sites, but would acquire existing plants; that they would undertake to move quickly to 45 percent local content; and that they would seek EC markets for a substantial proportion of the output from their British plants.

The background to the concerns voiced by British firms was starkly drawn by the SWP's first report. Following the collapse of the short-lived boom of 1972–73 there was 50 percent excess capacity in the industry, and import penetration had risen from 18 percent in 1970 to 41 percent by 1976. The situation was particularly acute in the audio and monochrome TV subsectors, but there were also unmistakeable signs of disinvestment in CTV. To avoid a knee-jerk protectionist response, the SWP took the bold step of commissioning the Boston Consulting Group (BCG) to undertake a comparative study of the British electronics industry and its major competitors—Germany, Japan, and Korea.

The BCG report was received in the autumn of 1978 under conditions of great secrecy for fear that its contents, if leaked to the retail trade, would further damage the position of the British electronics industry. It found that, although British products were broadly competitive with those of the West German industry, there was a large gap between European and Far Eastern costs. In the case of Japan, the cost advantage was achieved not by lower labor costs but by much more efficient production technologies, superior set designs, and the insistence of manufacturers on reliable supplies of very high-quality components. Very large volumes per plant had allowed the Japanese firms to take full advantage of these benefits. The Koreans, by contrast, achieved their cost advantages largely through low wages and government subsidies.

The SWP advocated a strategy of increasing the competitiveness of the British industry by concentrating on four aspects:

1. rationalization of production units into a small number of plants, each with an annual volume of 500,000 TV sets instead of the then British average of 100,000;

2. increased involvement of existing Japanese technology in the CTV sector;

3. greater readiness to incorporate cost-saving innovations; and

4. improvements in the quality and supply of British-manufactured components.

The SWP estimated the cost of such a structural adjustment to be in the region of £300 million, if its target of eliminating the sector's balance of payments deficit by 1984 was to be achieved. It suggested that the government had a crucial role to play in providing financial support for rationalization, in policing its inward investment guidelines, and in supporting and being seen to support the industry's negotiation of import restraints with Far Eastern producers. But clearly the major effort would have to come from British businesses learning to adopt Japanese methods and to achieve their volumes, and from the trade unions recognizing the necessity to accept redundancies (layoffs of workers). The tripartite form of the SWP was undoubtedly crucial in forging this degree of consensus on an appropriate industrial strategy for the sector. It represented for the first time the possibility of a radically different meso-corporatist model of sectoral governance (Cawson, 1985, 1986).

In March 1979, the British government accepted the SWP's plan and promised substantial financial assistance in the form of a special industry scheme that would allow some £80 million to be channelled to firms outside the existing regional development areas. However, the election of the Thatcher government, with its declared disavowal of industrial policy in June 1979, killed off the prospect of a concerted scheme. From that point on, sectoral governance reverted to the individual adjustment decisions of the firms, and the reliance on inward investment as a substitute for the ailing performance of the British industry was greatly strengthened.

The emergence of the VCR in the late 1970s coincided with the struggle in the industry to adapt to competition in its core product of color television. None of the indigenous firms had attempted to develop VCR technology, and few seemed interested in manufacturing VCRs under licence. The key actor was Thorn, the largest British CTV producer, and through its ownership of television rental chains it became the most important influence on the consumer market for VCRs. Despite strong pressure from Philips to support European (i.e., its own) technology, Thorn had signed an agreement with JVC to distribute its products under the Ferguson brand, which was attractive because it allowed for the eventual manufacturing of VCRs. In 1982 Thorn began production at a former hi-fi plant in Newhaven, in a joint venture with its partners JVC and Telefunken.

Because it had no domestic technological capability in VCRs (unlike Germany) or pretension (unlike France), there were few obstacles to the active pursuit of Japanese investment in video. The EC's voluntary restraint agreement of 1983 accelerated the pressure on Japanese firms to locate in Europe, and the British government entered into competition with other national governments and local development agencies to entice companies to come to Britain. Top government ministers, and even the Prime Minister, courted specific firms that had not opened EC plants, offering substantial subsidies. The result was no fewer than seven new entrants in 1985–87, bringing the total number of VCR plants in Britain to eleven and the total output to nearly a million units in 1986.

In France, as was argued above, the adoption of specific industrial policy goals for the sector through the grooming of Thomson as a "national champion" created a particular kind of interdependent relationship between the government and its protege. State actors could not be indifferent to Thomson's corporate strategy, but their capacity to control it proved to be limited, even though a formal mechanism was developed through the *contrat de plan*. The nationalization of the company by the Mitterrand government in 1981 paradoxically removed some of the constraints on Thomson's actions, especially after Laurent Fabius became industry minister in 1983 and articulated the government's new policy of requiring the nationalized companies to return a profit.

Thomson had added the CSF company to its already disparate structure in 1967, but it had never integrated its operations. CSF was locked into public defense contracting, and in 1976 entered the telecommunications market at the behest of the state. This aspect of Thomson's business was separately managed—and so not subject to control by Thomson-Brandt management—but the substantial losses incurred in telecommunications by Thomson-CSF drove the parent group into the red, which had repercussions on Thomson's consumer electronics business.

Thomson was in the late 1970s beginning to evolve a double strategy involving internationalization through investment in Germany and the Far East. Almost alone among French industry (the other was Rhône Poulenc), Thomson moved offshore by locating its audio production in Singapore. While clearly sanctioned by the Finance Ministry, this move attracted considerable criticism and an explicit call from the Planning Commission for the repatriation of these activities. This "Asian strategy" was reinforced by the negotiation of a link with JVC, through which Thomson would import Japanese VCRs for sale under the Thomson brand in France, thus effectively ending Thomson's commitment to developing an independent video technology (which was in any case weakened by its failure to develop a workable videodisc system). Thomson's strategy began to parallel that of Thorn-EMI in Britain, in accepting that it could not compete in product innovation with the Japanese; it would leave it to others to pioneer new markets, and then attempt to produce successful products under licence.

This stance not only attracted criticism within the French government but also was opposed from within Thomson itself. Abel Farnoux, head of Thomson's Videocolor tube subsidiary, had been pressing for Thomson to cooperate with Philips on the development of VCR technology and had supported Thomson's acquisition in Germany of two smaller firms, Saba and Nordmende, as well as Telefunken's tube factory in Ulm, which it later closed. The aim of these acquistions was to develop market share in Germany (which rose to 19 percent by 1982) that could serve as an important outlet for tubes from Videocolor's French factories. But in addition to market share, Thomson had acquired Saba's respected R&D laboratories at Villingen (in what was then West Germany), which Farnoux wanted to exploit as a resource for developing a European capability in new consumer products, in collaboration with Philips, which was seeking additional partners for Grundig for new-generation VCRs.

This ambivalence within Thomson persisted after Alain Gomez was appointed head of the newly nationalized firm, and Farnoux left to head the *Mission de la Filière Électronique*, from which position he continued to call for a "European alliance" between Thomson and Philips, with the blessing of the new Industry Minister, Pierre Chevènement, a socialist. The concept of the *filière* called for a new government agency charged with coordinating the electronics sector, which would have suggested a fundamental shift in the actual balance of power between the major firms and the state, thus implying considerable curbs on the autonomy of the firms. Chevènement's replacement by Fabius after the nationalized industry heads had appealed directly to President Mitterrand reflected the extent of opposition within the French government to the implications of the *filière* concept, and the willingness of the government from 1983 to underwrite Thomson's own judgment of its commercial interests.

This was in marked contrast to the position in 1981, when one of the first acts of the new socialist government had been to veto the proposed J3T deal among Thomson, Telefunken, Thorn-EMI, and JVC for the joint manufacture of a range of new video products. The government's objectives favored European links, and officials wished to see Thomson produce VCRs and audio equipment in France, and to this end supported Thomson's proposed takeover of Grundig, which had co-developed the V-2000 VCR with Philips.

Philips had a 24.5 percent stake in Grundig as well as an agreement that the remaining shares could not be disposed of by Gundig without Philips's consent. In negotiations between Thomson and Philips, the sticking point was apparently the refusal of Thomson to accept any binding commitment to the V-2000 format, which Gomez judged to be doomed. Even before the German Cartel Office ruling against the takeover, Thomson had been keeping its options open by negotiating with Telefunken, which would give it access to the J2T joint venture. Indeed, only three days after the ruling Thomson announced an agreed takeover of Telefunken, and the following month signed a wide-ranging technical cooperation agreement with JVC that would make Thomson the first licensee to produce VHS components outside Japan.

Despite the failure of the French government's attempts to foster a Thomson-Philips grouping, the specific outcome enabled it to realize at least some of its objectives. The absence of a French stake in VCR production had led to a spurt in import penetration of the French market in 1982, which lay behind the infamous "Poitiers measures" of October 1982 in which all VCR imports were channelled through an obscure customs post, ostensibly to prevent a flood of imports before a new tax on VCRs was to be introduced, but more plausibly part of a move to persuade the EC to take concerted action to restrain Japanese VCR exports. Thus Thomson ended up as the fully fledged VCR producer the French government wanted, even if the VCR was Japanese.

More importantly in terms of signaling a looser form of relationship between the state and major state-owned firms was the acceptance of the failure of the initial phase of expansionary macroeconomic policies signaled by the austerity package of deflationary measures introduced in the spring of 1983. The grand ambition of a planned and regulated French electronics sector as a major force in a regrouped European industry—a possible "Euro-*filière*"—gave way to a set of pragmatic policy concerns that brought governance in the French sector closer to the British pattern. Direct foreign investment by the Japanese was to be given more encouragement; the reality of the necessity for technical cooperation with the Japanese was recognized; and Thomson was encouraged to move from being the French champion to becoming a transnational with global ambitions in the manner of Philips.

There is thus an important element of convergence in the pattern of government–industry relations in British and French consumer electronics since the late 1970s. Technological change in the shape of the VCR undermined the relative insulation of a sector dominated by CTV and exposed both industries to the reality of Japanese competitive strengths. The major difference has been that the grooming of Thomson as a French national champion, while proving a failure from a narrowly parochial perspective, did at least weld together a group that had the option, in the mid-1980s, of becoming a player in the world market. By contrast, the continued fragmentation of the British firms left exit the most likely response to hardening market conditions. This contrast was symbolized in July 1987 when Thomson acquired the last major British consumer electronics manufacturer, Thorn-EMI-Ferguson.

Defensive Strategies and Sectoral Governance

The previous two sections have outlined in the form of an analytic narrative the pattern of response to Japanese competition that unfolded in the French and British consumer electronics industries. In this section we seek to account for the choice of defensive strategy adopted by the major actors and the factors governing the success of those strategies, in terms of differences in the modes of sectoral governance. In particular we will be concerned with the specific mix of state intervention and the organizational capacities of business associations and corporate hierarchies. The argument is that each kind of strategy carriers with it specific organizational requirements, which places different burdens on the collective actors involved. In this way we can begin to account for differences in outcome in the face of similar competitive pressures.

Following Ballance (1987), we can identify six types of strategic response to intensifying competition. A seventh response, which has featured strongly in the British case, in exit from the industry.

1. Rationalization is a strategy aimed at reducing costs by cutting back existing capacity, shedding labor and limiting wage increases, and reducing the range of products supplied to the market. Rationalization can be undertaken by single firms in isolation, as happened in 1982 when Philips began a program of plant closures, work force reduction, product streamlining, and the divestment of businesses excluded from its own definition of its core activities. In the 1980s Thomson shed its telecommunications and medical electronics businesses to concentrate on defense and consumer electronics.

Under some circumstances rationalization programs involve collective action by firms in the sector to achieve capacity reduction according to a coordinated plan, underwritten by state subsidy. Such a program, involving the elimination of subscale plants, was advocated in Britain in 1979 by the NEDO Sector Working Party for consumer electronics, but its introduction was thwarted by the election of an anti-interventionist government. As can be seen from the experience of rationalization programs in the steel industry (Rhodes, 1985) a very heavy burden is placed on the organizational capacity of the state and the industry association, and it is doubtful whether such a policy of coercive discrimination among firms could have been successful in Britain.

2. Diversification is most frequently an attempt to reduce dependence on slower-growing or maturing market segments by moving into related product areas, or introducing new and higher value-added products. The extent to which firms can adopt this strategy is crucially dependent on their innovative capacity, or organizational ability to capture synergies from complementary technologies. As we have seen, this is the area in which European firms have been at their weakest compared to the Japanese in the 1970s and 1980s. The crucial shift from CTV to VCR was attempted independently by only one company, Philips, and its failure to commercialize its own innovation led to a decisive shift toward a political strategy of demanding protectionism and a corporate strategy of increased interfirm collaboration (see below). All of the other European manufacturers sought to manage the transition to VCR through licensing or joint ventures with the Japanese. Few consumer electronics producers have even attempted to diversify into ralated product areas, such as telecommunications, semiconductors, or computers, and some of those that have, such as Thorn-EMI with its acquisition of INMOS, have had cause to regret the attempt. There has, however, been a diversification *into* consumer electronics by the Finnish conglomerate Nokia.

3. Offshore assembly became a major response of the U.S. consumer electronics industry when faced with Japanese competition, but its use by European firms has been limited. Compared to the United States, European tariff rules have inhibited its development, as has greater trade union pressure in Europe against exporting employment. Moreover, the relatively fragmented structure of the European industry reduces the extent of cost savings that can be achieved. Of the European firms analyzed in this chapter, Thomson and Philips made the most use of offshore assembly, mostly in audio products. In 1985 only 6 percent of Philips's assets were in Southeast Asia (Ballance, 1987:251). By contrast, the Japanese have employed this strategy extensively as competition from Southeast Asian countries began to be felt, but they have maintained employment levels and output of their domestic factories by a vigorous strategy of diversification.

4. Promoting "national champions" involves the development of an active industrial policy in which one or sometimes two major companies are given preferential treatment by the state, which may include R&D grants, production subsidies, tax write-offs, soft loans, as well as measures to boost demand for the company's products, often by preferential public purchasing. In Britain the major computer firm, ICL, was groomed as a national champion in the 1970s as part of the perception of the strategic significance of the sector as producing capital goods with major implications for the rest of the economy. Consumer electronics was not accorded such status in Britain, unlike in France where it was included among six priority sectors in the Fourth Plan.

The major French producer, Thomson, was protected at home by import quotas on goods from foreign manufacturers and by limits on foreign companies establishing factories in France, as well as by substantial subsidies. Its ability to respond to competitive pressures by increasing its share of the European market by a series of acquisitions in Germany was a direct result of Thomson's status as a national champion. Since Thomson was nationalized in 1981 it has been encouraged by the French government to become a major multinational producer—moving from national to international champion. Thomson's ability to sustain this program of acquisitions is crucially dependent on its status as a privileged supplier of defense electronics to the French government.

5. Protectionism takes many forms, including tariffs, quotas, and voluntary export-restraint agreements, and it serves multiple objectives, but principally that of slowing down the pace of contraction to allow for the development of responses at the level of the firm. In consumer electronics it has included industry-to-industry agreements, such as that in place since 1973 between BREMA and the EIAJ; the establishment of a high and common tariff level of 14 percent on consumer electronics products; bilateral quotas such as those restricting Japanese CTV exports into France; and the agreement between the European Commission and MITI to restrain exports of VCRs to Europe between 1984 and 1986. More recently, attention has shifted to the activities of the Japanese plants in Europe, with pressure from the European firms for minimum levels of local content, backed by antidumping measures taken against direct exporters of VCRs from Japan and Korea.

6. Interfirm collaboration can take a number of forms, including licensing agreements, pooled R&D, and joint ventures. It become an important part of the corporate strategy of European consumer electronics firms in the late 1970s and 1980s, and is now the most important means by which they seek to develop new products, such as high-definition television (HDTV), home automation, and interactive compact disc. In the 1970s, joint ventures such as those between GEC and Hitachi, between Rank and Toshiba, and among Thorn, Telefunken, and JVC reflected specific problems faced by the European partners in acquiring the requisite technology to remain in CTV production or enter VCR production; they also reflected problems faced by the Japanese partners in gaining access to European markets, either through political opposition in the case of Hitachi and Toshiba, or organizational weakness in the case of JVC.

More recent examples of interfirm collaboration reflect a number of different factors. The alliance between Philips and Sony for compact discs was designed to secure product standardization in an effort to prevent the struggle over rival formats that had proved damaging for both companies in the case of VCRs. In addition, the impulse toward interfirm collaboration arises from specific features of the tendency toward competition through innovation. Among factors listed by Teece and Pisano (1987) are discontinuities in technological trajectories, which require reference to sources of expertise outside the firm, increasing costs of innovation, the international diffusion of sources of innovation, and the increasing speed at which new technologies must be commercialized. New products and product systems, such as HDTV and home automation, involve the integration of expertise in such areas as telecommunications, computing, and semiconductor design with the existing expertise of the consumer electronics firms. As we have seen, the tendency of European manufacturers to rationalize into "core activities" has made them more dependent on interfirm collaboration than many of the major Japanese companies that are more diversified.

As is clear from the above discussion, the choice of strategy open to firms is constrained by the characteristics of the regime of sectoral governance, and in particular the role played by the state. In Britain, adjustment was largely left to the autonomous actions of the companies, and the principal response was the rationalization of production and the formation of joint-venture agreements to gain access to superior Japanese product and process technologies. State involvement in protectionism was indirect, and the more important effect of government policy was to attract direct foreign investment, which further reinforced the pattern of exit from the industry. With very few exceptions, British firms failed to diversify or reduce manufacturing costs through offshore assembly, and there was no attempt to foster a national champion in consumer electronics.

By contrast, sectoral governance in France was dominated by the relationship between the state and its national champion, with public policies fashioned to protect the interests of the domestic industry and facilitate its internationalization. Without such a regime it is difficult to see how Thomson could have managed the transformation from a medium-sized producer to the second force in European consumer electronics. Paradoxically, this transformation occurred at the same time that the sectoral regime which produced it was in the process of disintegration, with the acceleration of a process of "Europeanization" at both industry and government levels.

Internationalization and the Erosion of National Sectoral Boundaries

For the 1960s and early 1970s it makes some sense to analyze the European consumer electronics industry in terms of relatively discrete national sectors, with distinctive patterns of sectoral governance. National markets were supplied by national firms; there was relatively little intra-Europran trade in consumer electronics products; and national governments acted independently of each other in determining their trade policies. The only manufacturer crossing these boundaries was Philips, but its own structure reflected national segmentation in that it comprised a conglomeration of national "missions" loosely controlled by the parent company serving predominantly national markets.

By the mid-1980s the picture had changed dramatically. A series of rationalizations, mergers, and takeovers, and successive waves of inward investment, produced an industry that can best be analyzed by groupings of national capital rather than national boundaries. Essentially the industry is dominated by a grouping around Philips-Grundig, Thomson and its subsidiaries, and the Japanese manufacturers. With two key takeovers, of the ex-ITT subsidiary SEL and the Océanic Company in France in 1987, a fourth grouping has now emerged controlled by the Finnish firm Nokia. Together, these four groupings account for 80 percent of European CTV proudction: Philips-Grundig has 34 percent, Thomson 18 percent, and Nokia and the Japanese companies each have 14 percent. In VCRs, Philips-Grundig controls 37 percent of production, the Japanese roughly 45 percent, with Thomson and Nokia accounting for 12 percent and 4 percent, respectively.

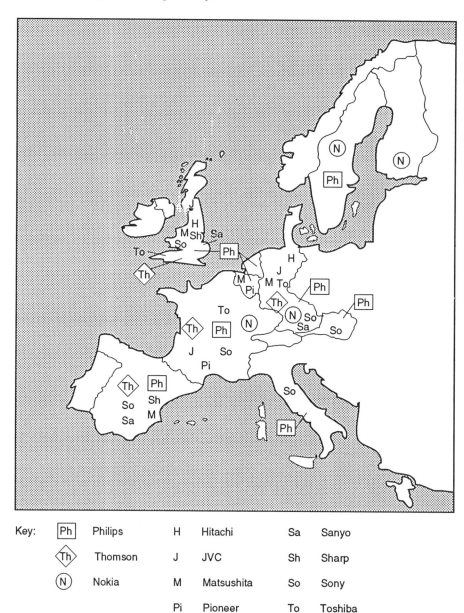

Key:

Ph	Philips	H	Hitachi	Sa	Sanyo
Th	Thomson	J	JVC	Sh	Sharp
N	Nokia	M	Matsushita	So	Sony
		Pi	Pioneer	To	Toshiba

Figure 9.2. Transnational Consumer Electronics Companies in Europe, 1988. (Transnational is defined as operating plants in more than one country.)

Figure 9.2 shows the extent to which the manufacturing activities of firms in the European consumer electronics industry cut across national boundaries. Philips has production facilities in nine countries; Thomson and Nokia in four each. Of the Japanese firms, Sony manufactures in six countries and Matsushita in four.

The implications of the trend toward transnational mergers and the consequences of successive waves of inward investment from the Far East are profound. First, the significance of national trade associations as defensive alliances of predominantly national capital has decreased as firms increasingly negotiate directly with national governments and, beyond them, the European Commission. Thus, the most significant aspect of government-industry relations has become the bilateral link between the corporation and the state agency; as the industry concentrates and internationalizes, the need for trade associations as intermediaries has diminished. Second, the locus of sectoral governance has shifted from national capitals to the supranational level as, increasingly, sectoral issues have been handled by the European Commission. The decisive shift took place with the negotiation in 1983 of the voluntary export restraint agreement between the Commission and MITI, but since then the European Commission has also taken an active role in pressing Far Eastern firms to become more integrated into the European economy by increasing their absorption of European components in the products they manufacture. The Commission, under pressure from European manufacturers, has also initiated a series of antidumping suits against Japanese companies regarding the use of electronic components as well as finished products.

The combined effects of protectionist measures and the increasing value of the Japanese yen, as well as the opportunities offered by the intention to complete the EC internal market by 1992, accelerated the process of direct foreign investment by Japanese firms since 1984. Table 9.6 shows the extent of these investments by 1987. Although Britain and Germany have absorbed the largest share, helped both by the size of their national markets and the relatively favorable policy regimes, France has succeeded in attracting significant investments, especially in car audio and compact disc players, ever since its hostile stance was dropped in the early 1980s. The initial reluctance of the French government to sanction the alliance between Thomson and JVC, which, as we have seen, Thomson circumvented by acquiring Telefunken, has given way to the encouragement of joint ventures involving technology transfer, such as that between Thomson and Toshiba to manufacture microwave ovens.

Internationalization at the level of corporate strategy has been paralleled by policy developments at the supranational level. An important part of EC policy in consumer electronics has been the encouragement of collaborative ventures between European firms in the development of new technology; these ventures emerged from the French-initiated Eureka program which was intended as a pan-European civilian equivalent to the U.S. Strategic Defense Initiative. One such program involves a group led by Philips to develop high-definition television; another, arising from an initiative of the British tripartite consumer electronics Economic Development Committee, aims to develop a set of

Table 9.6. Japanese Consumer Electronics Investments in Europe by Company (as of 1987)

Company	CTV	VCR	AUDIO	CD (1)	Tapes (2)	Microwave	Other
AIWA			UK	UK (P), France (P)			
Akai		France	France, Ireland				
Clarion							
Crown							
Fuji					Germany (V)		
Funai	UK	UK					
Hitachi	UK, Germany	UK, Germany	UK				
Hitachi-Maxell					UK (V)		France (VCR decks)
JVC	UK	UK, Germany			Germany (V)		
Kenwood			France, UK				
Matsushita	UK	Germany	Germany, Spain				Germany (VCR decks), Belgium (batteries)
Mitsubishi	UK	UK					
NEC		UK					
Pioneer			France, Belgium, Germany				
Primo	UK	UK					
Sanyo	Spain	Germany, Spain					
Sharp	Spain	UK	Spain			UK	
Sony	UK, Germany, Spain	Germany, Spain	Germany, Spain	France (P), Austria (D)	France (A + V), Italy (A)		UK (tubes)
TDK					Germany (V)		
Toshiba	UK	UK, Germany				UK, France	

SOURCE: *Journal of the Electronics Industry*, February 1988.

(1) P = Players; D = Discs

(2) A = Audio; V = Video

240

standards for the so-called smart house, or home bus, in which "intelligent" appliances will be linked to form a network. Both of these programes have been designed to exclude Japanese participation, and both are competing head-on with parallel Japanese developments.

The picture painted by the authors of such schemes of defensive collaboration by the European firms against Japanese competition may be seriously misleading as a guide to outcomes. *All* of the leading European manufacturers involved have various kinds of links with Japanese firms involving technology transfer, and privileged access to Japanese innovation may be a much more important prize for any one company than membership in a Eureka program. The technological lead established by the Japanese gives them the opportunity to drive a wedge between Philips and Thomson, whose previous record of collaboration has been far from encouraging. For example, the Japanese have been investing heavily in liquid crystal display (LCD) technology as a replacement for the cathode ray tube in television and computer monitors, and the leading firms have now displayed a 14-inch working prototype. It is not difficult to envisage a situation in which, say, Thomson is offered preferential licensing for such technology in exchange for support for the Japanese rather than the European standard for HDTV. It was precisely such an agreement among JVC, Thorn, Telefunken, and Thomson in VCR technology that effectively killed off the prospects for the Philips V-2000 system.

A further important trend concerns the reorganization of the Japanese subsidiaries in Europe in advance of the completion of the single market in 1992. These subsidiaries were initially tightly controlled from Japan, with very little horizontal coordination or communication between plants of the same companies in different countries. This situation has begun to change with the establishment of European headquarters by the leading Japanese firms Sony and Matsushita, and the allocation of specific European-wide functions to particular plants. In addition, for the first time some of the Japanese manufacturers have started to decentralize some of their R&D activities to Europe.

Conclusions

In the period from the mid-1970s to the mid-1980s we witnessed a transformation in the consumer electronics industries of both Britain and France. In 1975 these industries represented almost polar extremes in terms of government–industry relations: from the abstentionist market-dominated pattern in Britain to the interventionist state-dominated system in France. By 1988 the two industries had markedly different structures, but increasingly convergent patterns of sectoral governance. No longer does the French state seek to control the industry and channel it toward a goal of technological self-sufficiency; it would be more accurate to say that French industrial policy concerns for this sector consist almost entirely of underwriting the corporate strategy of the Thomson group. In Britain the role of government remains in essence the same—if the brief flirtation with meso-corporatism is discounted—but the structure of companies in the industry has changed almost beyond recognition. As one French participant in an Anglo-French industrial forum put it: "We came to talk to the British industry and found we were talking to the Japanese." Finally, it is unlikely that the process of rationalization in the European consumer electronics industry has run its course, given the continuing pressure on mature products such as CTV and VCR from the newly industrialized Far Eastern nations such as Korea and Taiwan, and the Japanese response involving product innovation on a scale that Philips alone among the European firms is able to match. What we are likely to witness in the next decade is the search for effective policy instruments at a European level—such as continued programs of interfirm collaboration—as well as mounting political pressure on Japanese companies in Europe to become more fully integrated into the European economy.

Acknowledgment

The research on which this chapter is based was supported by the Economic and Social Research Council under its Government-Industry Relations initiative.

References

Abegglen, James C., and George Stalk. (1985). *Kaisha: The Japanese Corporation*. New York: Basic Books.

Aoki, Masahiko (ed.). (1984). *The Economic Analysis of the Japanese Firm*. Amsterdam: North-Holland.

Ballance, Robert H. (1987). *International Industry and Business: Structural Change, Industrial Policy and Industry Strategies*. London: George Allen & Unwin.

Cawson, Alan (ed.). (1985). *Organized Interests and the State*. London: Sage Publications.

Cawson, Alan. (1986). *Corporatism and Political Theory*. Oxford: Basil Blackwell.

Crane, Rhonda. (1979). *The Politics of International Standards: France and the Color TV War*. Norwood, N. J.: Ablex.

Dore, R. P. (1986). *Structural Adjustment in Japan 1970–82*. Geneva: International Labour Organisation.

Dore, R. P. (1987). *Taking Japan Seriously*. London: Athlone Press.

EIAJ (1988). *Electronic Industries Association of Japan*. Tokyo: EIAJ.

Franko, Lawrence G. (1982). *The Threat of Japanese Multinationals: How the West Can Respond*. New York: John Wiley.

Kono, Toyohiro. (1984). *Strategy and Structure of Japanese Enterprises*. London: Macmillan.

Negishi, Takao. (1985). "New Roles, New Responses: The Future of the Japanese Electronics Industry." *Speaking of Japan*. 6(55), 21–26.

OTA. (1983). *International Competitiveness in Electronics*. Washington, D.C.: Congress of the United States, Office of Technology Assessment.

Rhodes, Martin. (1985). "Organized Interests and Industrial Crisis Management: Restructuring the Steel Industry in West Germany, Italy and France." In A. Cawson (ed.), *Organized Interests and the State*. London: Sage Publications.

Sako, Mari. (1989). "Neither Markets nor Hierarchies: A Comparative Study of the Printed Circuit Board Industry in Britain and Japan."

Shepherd, Geoffrey. (1982). "Japanese Exports and Europe's Problem Industries." In L. Tsoukalis and M. White (eds.), *Japan and Western Europe: Conflict and Cooperation.* London: Frances Pinter.

Teece, David J., and Gary Pisano. (1987). "Collaborative Arrangements and Technology Strategy." Berkeley: University of California, School of Business Administration.

Trevor, M. (1988). *Toshiba's New British Company.* London: Policy Studies Institute.

Watson Brown, Adam. (1987). "The Campaign for High Definition Television: A Case Study in Triad Power." *Euro-Asia Business Review,* 6(2), 3–11.

Zysman, John. (1983). *Governments, Markets and Growth,* Ithaca, N.Y.: Cornell University Press.

CHAPTER 10

Keeping the Shotgun Behind the Door

Governing the Securities Industry in
Canada, the United Kingdom,
and the United States

William D. Coleman

CAPITAL markets in the Anglo-American democracies of the United Kingdom, the United States, and Canada project a contradictory image. In one respect, they evoke a rampant capitalism: International competition is intense, firms are changing structures daily to meet this new global reality, and telecommunications technology has opened the way to a twenty-four-hour market day. The financial services sector has internationalized more quickly than virtually any other sector of the economy. The securities business, in particular, has grown rapidly and come to operate on a global scale barely within the reach of national policy makers. Yet few sectors in capitalist economies possess the extensive self-governing capacity that has developed in the investment business. Beginning in the nineteenth century with the institutionalization of stock exchanges, the securities industry has spawned a panoply of private arrangements for the management of its affairs that minimize intrusions by the state. These private arrangements have proven amazingly robust: Not only have they survived the great stock market crashes of the twentieth century but after renewed scrutiny and some reform they also appear to be the chosen mode of governance for financial markets during the 1990s. The same self-regulatory model seems to be emerging on the international plane, building on the national governing arrangements.

The securities industry embraces several kinds of market activity. First, it includes the creation of new debt or equity securities, an activity often termed *primary market operations,* or *investment banking.* Second, existing securities are purchased and resold on secondary markets, with firms acting as principals (taking positions in the name of the securities firms) or as market makers (standing ready to quote prices for purchases and sales of a given security) (OECD, 1987:8). A third activity involves the organizing and managing of groups of individual securities that are offered to the public and traded as single investment shares. These instruments are known variously as mutual funds, unit trusts, or investment trusts. Finally, a branch of the industry manages and provides advice on investment portfolios, whether held by private individuals or institutional investors such as pension funds or insurance companies.

Although each of these activities has grown significantly since 1960, the latter two represent the newer part of the sector and the first two the securities industry's core. This chapter focuses primarily on these core branches of the industry: underwriting and selling of new issues, and brokerage on secondary markets. These activities remain the most important in the sector and anchor the creation of mutual funds and portfolio management. Possessed of a long history, they also have the more elaborate self-governing arrangements that, in turn, have begun to serve as a model for the newer branches of the securities industry. Understanding these arrangements, then, is a necessary preliminary step to the analysis of the mutual funds and portfolio management subsectors.

This chapter argues that governance of the securities industry[1] has relied primarily on private institutions, both stock exchanges and interest associations, that have received a delegation of authority from the state. Operation of these institutions has drawn on strong community relationships and the willingness of individual firms to set standards of good business conduct. The state has maintained, to varying degrees depending on the country and on circumstances, an arms-length relationship with the sector. Strong state intervention has taken place only occasionally, usually reluctantly, with state officials normally eager to return to the norm of self-regulation. Although self-governance is the norm in each of the three countries under study, the specific terms and scope of the delegation of state authority vary. In the United States, where the state maintains the closest watch over the self-regulatory system, relationships among sectoral actors are the most formalized, interest associations are the best-resourced, and public lobbying is most prevalent. In the United Kingdom, where governments have relied primarily on statutory instruments promoting full disclosure and preventing fraud, informality has prevailed until very recently. The Bank of England acted as a quiet mediator between the City[2] and the Treasury, with formal interest associations playing a decidedly ancillary role. Community or clan networks were the primary means for aggregating and defining the interests of the industry. During the 1980s, the informal network mode of governance has given way to one that relies extensively on formal associative action. In Canada, the government has a well-defined role in exercising surveillance over the self-regulatory system, but this is not matched by the degree of formalization of relationships between industry and the state that is found in the United States.

By the beginning of the 1990s, structural differences in the governance regimes among these three countries had diminished significantly. The growing convergence in approaches to governance is largely a response to the internationalization of capital markets. Other major capitalist countries such as Germany and France are feeling strong pressure to change their regulatory regimes in ways that ensure compatibility with those in the Anglo-American democracies and Japan. Moreover, the pressures of internationalization have fostered the emergence of a nascent international governing system that is modeled on the private-interest government approach found in the Anglo-

American democracies. The internationalization and re-regulation of financial markets ultimately involve a diminution of national state sovereignty not only over financial policy, but also over other areas of economic policy. This loss of national power, in turn, raises critical questions about political economy theories on comparative state capacity.

This argument is developed in the following steps. First, the nature of the securities industry is reviewed, focusing on the character of business practices and the extent these have changed as a result of the internationalization occurring over the past two decades. Second, elements of self-regulation common to the three countries are presented, followed by a discussion of the specific institutions that have developed historically in each nation. The chapter concludes with a review of the emerging supranational governance regime and assesses briefly its likely impact on national sovereignty over economic policy-making. This assessment leads finally to the posing of questions about the adequacy of existing theories of comparative political economy.

The Securities Industry

The securities industry plays a key role in realizing two objectives of properly functioning capital markets. First, its firms facilitate saving and investment by providing the range of securities that borrowers may wish to issue and savers may wish to hold and do so in a way that offers a choice in meeting the requirements of each.[3] Their activities also contribute to the valuing of securities such that they reflect consistently the expected returns. Traditionally, attainment of these objectives has required the successful completion of three tasks: the underwriting of new debt or equity securities and their distribution in the primary market; dealing in already-issued securities in the sense of buying them for eventual resale; and brokering or acting as an agent in the purchase or sale of securities by a dealer or a private investor.

Generally speaking, debt instruments such as bonds and debentures tend to be sold over-the-counter, and equity issues are listed for sale on stock exchanges. But it also happens that equities are sold over-the-counter and bonds are listed on exchanges, particularly smaller exchanges in the United States. Secondary markets—those where the buying and selling of already-issued securities take place—also operate in these two arenas, the stock exchanges or over-the-counter.

Throughout the first half of this century, domestic capital markets tended to be highly protected, with each country devising its own set of restrictions on foreign firms and its own approach to regulation. Canada and the United States shared a similar pattern of specialization. Legislation (the Bank Act in Canada, the Glass-Steagall Banking Act in the United States) prohibited commercial banks from engaging in most of the more risky underwriting activity.[4] Consequently, firms specializing in corporate underwriting for primary markets— investment banks in the United States, investment dealers in Canada—played a key role. A separate set of firms, usually referred to as broker-dealers or simply brokers, acted as principals or agents in secondary markets.

In Britain, the primary market was not reserved by statute for a special category of firms, but informal rules and understandings kept these for merchant banks. Arrangements on British stock exchanges also differed from the North American practice. Members of an exchange could act as principals (jobbers) or as agents (brokers) but not as both—the so-called single capacity rule (Committee to Review the Functioning of Financial Institutions [Wilson Report], 1980:100–103). In addition, it was expected that at least two jobbers, and preferably more, would make markets in each security. Brokers therefore were to act only as agents for their clients and were remunerated on a commission basis. Hence, British practice differed from that in North America in two respects. North American firms could combine the jobber and broker roles and exchanges worked on a specialist system. In such a system, individual broker-dealer firms would specialize in making markets for a given set of securities; clients interested in that security would be directed to the given specialist on the trading floor.

These specialized national arrangements and various measures of market protection have largely disappeared with the development of international markets for securities; the operating procedures of stock exchanges and over-the-counter markets have converged significantly in the three countries. Several different developments have encouraged this internationalization. Since the late 1960s, institutional investors such as insurance companies and pension funds have become increasingly prominent in capital markets. These investors have sought to diversify their risks and increase their profitability by expanding their investment horizons beyond the domestic market (OECD, 1987:19). Financial institutions have made this expansion more attractive by introducing a variety of new financial products: note issuance facilities, Eurocommercial paper facilities, and several new instruments designed to accommodate better exchange-rate and interest-rate risks (Bryant, 1987:51–52). A further impetus to international markets came after the OPEC oil crisis in 1973 when the oil-producing nations decided to continue to denominate oil in dollars (Gilpin, 1987:328–36), thus adding to international liquidity. The entry of Japanese banks and investment firms following Japan's rise to the world's leading creditor nation in the 1980s added further to the international marketplace.

Finally, the breakdown of the Bretton Woods system of fixed exchange rates and the high inflation of the 1970s and early 1980s contributed indirectly to the growth of international markets. More variable exchange rates and high interest rates made banks increasingly unwilling to offer medium- to long-term loans. In response, larger corporations began to raise longer-term capital more frequently on securities markets. The less regulated international marketplace offered better terms than domestic markets, attracting the issues of bigger firms as well as the interest of large institutional investors. Each one of these changes has been hastened, in turn, by the steady advance of technology. Distance, unfamiliarity with other economic environments, and different procedures for trading securities have all been dampened through the use of new technology that can produce instantaneous information on trading conditions and electronic trading (OECD, 1987:19).

Together, these changes have spurred a rapid growth of international financial markets. Termed *Eurocurrency* and *Eurosecurities* markets,[5] these arrangements operated beyond the reach of domestic regulators and were based on an emerging wholesale banking network (Ingham, 1984:51; Kolko, 1988:105). Hence, these international markets have come increasingly to be dominated by multinational, highly capitalized firms. Some of these are long-standing securities firms that have expanded (usually through mergers), others are the securities affiliates of commercial banks, and still others are universal banks that have expanded well beyond their original domestic markets. All of the countries under study have facilitated the expansion of these global firms by easing restrictions on foreign participation in domestic capital markets over the past decade.

In summary, over the last two decades, highly protected, national capital markets have had to respond to the growth of international markets largely beyond state supervision. Internationalization has placed intense pressure on those long-standing domestic regulatory arrangements that inhibited competition, forcing a measure of deregulation. It has also fostered a greater interpenetration among banking systems and securities firms, and increased the connections between securities regulation and monetary and exchange rate policy, both at the domestic and international levels. Where previously a central bank governor or a banking supervisor might only take a passing interest in procedures in international capital markets, they now see very obvious connections between these markets and the viability of domestic banking systems. These new inter-dependencies have led to government-sponsored reviews; political authorities have suggested some changes as a result, and these have been implemented. Market deregulation, in short, has spawned more intensive state supervision and the outline of a supranational governance regime, yet self-regulatory private-interest governments have remained at the core of these revamped governing systems.

Industry Governance: Overview of the Self-Regulatory Model

During the twentieth century, governance arrangements in the securities industry have evolved away from market mechanisms supported by informal network ties toward an increasingly formalized self-regulatory system based on associative action involving an elaborate division of labor among firms, self-regulatory organizations (SROs), and state agencies. Already in the nineteenth century, small investors demanded protection against the consequences of their own imprudence (Moran, 1986). Their interests converged with those of companies that had established a reputation for probity and that sought some protection against new companies on the "fringe" that were prepared to use half-truths and outright lies to defraud the unknowing in their pursuit of a "quick buck." But, direct state or bureaucratic regulation was never touted very long or consistently as an instrument for ensuring ethical conduct. Moran (1990) has pointed out that the stock exchanges developed as significant centers of private regulation long before state bureaucratic intervention had become a significant factor in capitalist societies. Consequently, the exchanges fostered their own tradition of regulation, a tradition that relied heavily on moral suasion and informal networks. Relatively successful, the exchanges then acquired a virtual monopoly on expertise.

Thus, when pressure increased on the modern state to intervene more systematically in capital markets, the industry was able to stall by articulating a persuasive ideology that lauded the flexibility of a private, self-regulatory approach and that warned of the rigidity of state intervention. The state, it was said, was simply incapable of the swift, yet fine-tuned, intervention required. In the words of Louis Loss (1961:1361), an American specialist in securities law: "At best, however, direct regulation of a complex business through the machinery of government—even with the advantages which the administrative process offers over traditional enforcement by grand jury investigation and criminal prosecution—divides black from white with a buzz saw when the many variations of gray call for a surgeon's scalpel."

Over time, governments in Canada, Britain, and the United States accepted some variation of self-regulation that combines informal networks, associative action, and state regulation. In its White Paper of 1985, the Department of Trade and Industry (DTI, 1985:7) in Britain outlined the basic principles that are common to the three systems. "The aim is to see risk-taking fairly rewarded, to foster the spirit of enterprise but to reduce the scope for losses resulting from fraud or from the concealment of risk." The DTI also added the important *caveat emptor*: No regulatory system can or should relieve investors of their responsibility for exercising judgment and care in deciding how to invest. All three states provide a minimal statutory base outlining extensive rules of disclosure that must be followed in the issue of all new securities. The self-regulatory system is then constructed on top of this legal foundation.

The respective self-regulatory systems share the following principles.

1. *Firms must have a minimum financial base, and owners, partners, and employers must be knowledgeable.* Realization of this goal has entailed the creation of rules governing minimum capital requirements, minimum experience in the industry, proper accounting procedures, regular and surprise audits, and educational training for new employees.

2. *Business must be conducted in an ethical manner.* Achieving this goal requires rules that provide for essential minimal protection to investors from conflicts of interest, disclosure of all sources of remuneration, and protection against recommendations unsupported by evidence, and complete transmission of all information available to clients (Gower, 1984:54ff.). In particular, firms must avoid conflicts of interest by adopting a "best execution" principle—all instructions from clients should be executed to a client's best advantage—and a "subordination of interest" principle—the client's interests are paramount and clients are given priority in the execution of orders (DTI, 1985:20).

3. *Financial safeguards must exist to protect clients in the event of a collapse of those carrying on a securities business.* This objective implies first that securities firms segregate clients' money from that of the firm. Second, the industry must provide some sort of safety net in the form of a compensation

fund. Invariably, such funds are expensive and unpopular: The efficient and the honest feel that they are being asked to pay for losses incurred by the inefficient and the dishonest (Gower, 1984:63).

Development of the governance arrangements needed for addressing these objectives has taken place gradually, passing through three stages in each of the countries.[6] Any self-regulatory system combines informal network guidance, private associative action, and state bureaucratic regulation; at each of the three stages, one of these governing modes enjoys pride of place. In the first stage of *pure self-regulation*, informal networks provided the key governing mechanism. Rules were developed, applied, and enforced by the industry alone, acting on informal communal norms supported by stock exchanges and trade associations. Governance focused on developing minimum standards of operational capability, only slightly on business conduct, and not at all on financial safeguards. Industry associations and individual firms lobbied at this stage to limit the impact of disclosure and registration rules contained in companies and securities acts.

Pure self-regulation was replaced by a system of *negotiated self-regulation* where the industry voluntarily agreed to negotiate with the state the development, application, and enforcement of rules. In the process, private-interest government and associative action displaced informal networks as the key governance agents. Private industry associations became incorporated more formally into the policy formulation process but retained complete responsibility over implementation of the rules. These rules began to address more directly the issues of ethical business conduct and financial safeguards.

The negotiated system has given way in each country to *mandated self-regulation*. Under this arrangement, specific industry representatives are given a mandate to develop, apply, and enforce norms based on a formal delegation of state authority. Formal associative action displaces even further informal communal norms as a governing mechanism. But these associations, or self-regulatory organizations (SROs), come under more direct supervision by the state. Specifically, the state wishes to ensure that SROs promulgate and enforce fair and reasonable rules relating to the admission, discipline, suspension, and expulsion of members, that they possess the procedures and resources required for the effective monitoring and enforcement of the rules, that they maintain adequate independence from the sectional interests of members, and that they avoid rules that restrict market competition (Gower, 1984:54ff.). As technology shortens considerably the buying and selling times of securities, and as internationalization takes hold, the state is forced to assume a stronger supervisory role. By the end of the 1980s, state bureaucratic regulation was the most important governance mechanism, but it continued to rely heavily on private-interest governments and associative action in implementing policy.

The stages of development and these operational principles are common to the U.S., British, and Canadian securities industries, yet considerable scope remains for the use of different institutional arrangements. The manner of supervision of the SROs may differ depending on the industry's history and on macropolitical arrangements. The intrusiveness of the state can also vary, leaving more or less independence to SROs. The structures of the SROs themselves, the relationships they maintain with members, and the extent to which they embrace representatives of investors and the public—all of these may differ from country to country. What was clear by 1990, however, was that many of these historical differences have diminished in the face of the growth of international financial markets and of new linkages among domestic markets.

National Approaches to Self-Regulation

The United States

Of the three countries studied, self-regulation in the United States has evolved the most rapidly into a mature mandated system. It also involves the strongest degree of state intervention, the least reliance on communal norms, and the clearest demarcation between the public and private realms.

Pure self-regulation began with the gradual institutionalization of the stock exchanges during the nineteenth century. It expanded further following the movement by individual states to pass so-called blue sky legislation,[7] a process that started in Kansas in 1911. Introduction of these laws was preceded by over a decade of mounting criticism of the investment banking industry for manipulation and deception in the issuing and marketing of securities and for excessive industry concentration. In practice, however, the various laws were never really very effective: Exemptions ensured that securities outside the ligislation outnumbered those covered, state governments did not provide the funds and qualified personnel needed for enforcement, and they had difficulty regulating firms dealing across state lines (Levin, 1969:32).

These laws did force, however, a response by the industry and a renewed attempt to defend a pure self-regulatory approach. In August 1912, investment bankers split off from the American Bankers Association to form their own group, the Investment Bankers Association (IBA). The following year, the new association drew up a "creed" for its members that emphasized the need to improve protection for investors (Carosso, 1970:170) and entrusted its promotion to a Committee on Business Practice. The IBA mounted a campaign to improve the public image of the investment profession by stressing the moral and managerial responsibility of member firms. Behind this renewed pure approach, the association fought strenuously against the enactment of any investment laws deemed "unfriendly" or too restrictive. It aimed to secure as many exemptions from "blue sky" laws as was possible by stressing the capability of the industry to keep its own house in order.

This strategy foundered on the shoals of voluntarism. Although the IBA toughened its entrance requirements and succeeded in developing a more positive image for its own members, its roster in 1929 included only 650 of the approximately 3000 securities firms (Carosso, 1970:265). Those beyond its roster felt no compulsion to heed the advice of the association. Nor was the association capable of disciplining its own members. Throughout the 1920s, "IBA committees filed wholesome reports on the need for accurate, uniform disclosure. These same committees compiled model circulars, urged their immediate adoption by members, and bemoaned noncompliance. A laissez-faire attitude characterized enforcement of the recommendations" (Parrish, 1970:35). The ineffectiveness of pure self-regulation coupled with the holes that successive lobbying forays had punched into the states' formal, public regulation contributed to the speculative boom in the late 1920s and ultimately to the crash of capital markets that heralded the onset of the Great Depression.

The New Deal brought an end to the pure self-regulatory system. Following a series of well-publicized and damaging congressional investigations, Congress passed three separate laws that continue to shape industry governance to the present day. The Glass-Steagall Banking Act divided investment banking from commercial banking when it came to issuing most securities. Second, the Securities Act of 1933, following in the English disclosure tradition, required issuers of securities to disclose a detailed list of data on the company in a registration statement to be filed with the Federal Trade Commission (FTC). The FTC (and later the Securities and Exchange Commission [SEC] in its place) would then review the information and the prospectus before allowing the issue. Third, the Securities Exchange Act of 1934 extended federal government controls over trading in the stock exchanges, required the registration of the exchanges, and authorized a new body, the SEC, to regulate their operations and members.

But the Securities Exchange Act gave the SEC little direction on how to fulfill its mandate other than to use its discretion in drawing up specific rules (Seligman, 1982:99). A short stage of negotiated self-regulation followed with separate approaches to governance evolving depending on whether securities were to be listed on an exchange or sold over-the-counter. For listed securities, the SEC began negotiations with the New York Stock Exchange (NYSE) in an effort to strengthen the Exchange's own rules. After a protracted period of bargaining and the occurrence of further public scandals, the SEC gave the NYSE an official mandate to act as the self-regulatory body for listed securities under its still very limited supervision. The mandated stage of self-regulation had begun.

The movement to a mandated system worked differently for unlisted securities that did not have the established institutional mechanism of the stock exchange. The first move toward a system of self-regulation came from the IBA. Following passage of the National Industrial Recovery Act in 1933, the association formed a Special Code Committee that drew up a "fair competition" code designed to govern the conduct of investment bankers, their relations among themselves and with issuers and investors. Once approved by the National Recovery Administration (NRA), the code became binding on all investment bankers whether they had signed up or not (Carosso, 1970:387). When the U.S. Supreme Court declared the NRA unconstitutional, the Investment Bankers Conference Committee, the organization charged with implementing the code, entered into new negotiations with the SEC. Discussions culminated in the 1938 Maloney Act, a separate section added to the Securities Exchange Act, that permitted voluntary associations of broker-dealers to be formed and registered with the SEC to govern conduct in the over-the-counter securities markets. Only one national securities association, the National Association of Securities Dealers

(NASD), has ever registered with the SEC. Its registration became effective on August 7, 1939, making it an official self-regulatory organization. The IBA remained in existence as an independent trade association and lobby for the industry.

By 1940, then, both the NASD and the stock exchanges had received an official delegation of authority from the government to regulate their respective sectors. Both remained, however, private organizations funded by firms in their subsectors. In finally assuming this role, these organizations conformed to a philosophy of regulation articulated eloquently and passionately by the third chairman of the SEC, William O. Douglas. Douglas emphasized the common purpose of those charged with regulation and those subject to regulation: the preservation of capitalism itself. In the presence of such common objectives, business-government relations cease to be a subject of politics and become a matter for technicians. The commission's rules and regulations would evolve out of dialogue and rational discussion with those affected (De Bedts, 1964:167). "Self-enforcement and voluntary compliance by private bodies were preferable to formal decrees and courtroom forensics" (Parrish, 1970:182). Douglas added that the role of the state ideally would be a minimal one. In a now famous statement, he said: "Government would keep the shotgun, so to speak, behind the door, loaded, well-oiled, cleaned, ready for use but with the hope it would never have to be used" (Seligman, 1982:185).

Douglas identified the key factor in a successful, mandated self-regulatory system: a capable state agency willing to intervene when SROs fail to act against the dishonest or the unethical. After the departure of Douglas in 1939 for the U.S. Supreme Court, the SEC did not fulfill this role well and problems occurred regularly over the next thirty-five years. It was only in 1975 that amendments and new legislation produced the strengthened government oversight of the self-regulatory system that prevails today.

The powers of the SROs over their members were increased as were those of the SEC over the SROs. SROs were now compelled to submit proposed rule changes to the commission for specific approval, and more precise standards were laid down for their internal government (Moran, 1987a:209; Seligman, 1982:465). The SEC moved in July 1975 to adopt a uniform net capital rule that was imposed on the entire industry. Congress also passed the Securities Investors Protection Act that created an agency, the Securities Investor Protection Corporation (SIPC), to provide financial protection for investors. Funded by the industry but able to borrow up to $1 billion from the U.S. Treasury, the SIPC compensated for the inadequacies of a smaller discretionary fund administered by the NYSE (Seligman, 1982:465). This change also represented an enhancement of the government's presence in the industry.

Despite the increased supervisory powers of the SEC, policy-making in the securities field remains primarily consultative and cooperative, much as Douglas had wanted it to be. The SROs have grown into significant bureaucracies in their own right and, in recent years, have rationalized the inspection and compliance systems to minimize overlaps in jurisdiction (R. Hall, 1979:146–47). The NASD is the largest SRO in the United States. With a budget in excess of $126 million in 1987 and a staff of 150, the association regulates 6700 securities firms and their 450,000 registered employees. It also operates the NASDAQ computerized market system, in effect the second largest stock market in the United States and the third largest in the world. Elaborate disciplinary procedures are now in place at the stock exchanges as well. Complementing the actions of the SEC and the SROs are securities regulators that operate at the state level in the U.S. federal system. They administer laws affecting the registration of brokers, the structure of prospectuses, and consumer protection. The state regulators participate at the national level of decision making through their own interest association, the North American Securities Administrators Association (NASAA).

Joining the SROs and the SEC in the policy network responsible for the sector are numerous trade associations that serve as conventional policy advocates rather than private-interest governments. The most important of these is the Securities Industry Association (SIA), which was created in 1972 following a merger of the IBA and the Association of Stock Exchange Firms. It acts as the trade association for the industry as a whole, employing sixty-five full-time staff and running thirty-two national committees (SIA, 1987). Also active in the policy community are various other groups that represent investors' interests: the National Association of OTC Companies, the United Shareholders Association, the Council of Institutional Investors, the Alliance for Capital Access (junk bond issuers), and the National Venture Capital Association.

Governance in the U.S. industry appears to be a joint project of these several actors. The SEC is by no means the captive of the industry—it has considerable expertise and power in its own right. Nor is it the "bureaucratic blight" so feared by the industry during the New Deal. It tends to consult closely with the several industry actors on policy matters. The SROs retain considerable responsibility for implementing policy. In fact, the system remains perhaps too cooperative; several critics suggest that the SEC has acted to protect the industry against the development of a national market system for listed securities advocated by Congress as early as 1975 (Seligman, 1985). Nevertheless, the state's primacy over private-interest governments and informal networks is strongest in the U.S.; perhaps as a consequence, voluntary interest associations like the Securities Industry Association are more confrontational and more publicity conscious in their lobbying than analogous associations in Canada and Britain.

The United Kingdom

The British self-regulatory system has differed from that in the United States by virtue of less intrusive state involvement, less bureaucratization, and more reliance on communal norms in promoting good business conduct. Movement toward a mandated approach to self-regulation only began in the 1980s, but once engaged, it quickly served to diminish significantly the differences between the U.S. and British systems.

A system akin to pure self-regulation persisted in Britain until 1944 and even then changed to a negotiated style only very slowly. Ingham's (1984) analysis suggests that pure self-regulation rested on a kind of unwritten understanding among the financial industry (the City), the Bank of England, and the Treasury. Leading elites in each of these spheres came from the south of England, possessed a similar class background, and attended the Clarendon public schools (Ingham, 1984:151). Their close relationship had its origins in the preindustrial era when the Bank of England managed the state's debts by means of loans raised in the City. They shared in the "Treasury view" of the state's role: noninterference in the economic affairs of private individuals implemented through a negative and parsimonious approach toward government spending. Together, these elites promoted an open economy and a strong currency and opposed strenuously political initiatives designed to construct a "nationalist" economic or industrial policy (Ingham, 1984:152; Hall, 1986).

This orientation also implied that the City would enjoy complete autonomy to play out its role as the world's commercial and banking center. As part of this understanding and in the context of the disclosure principles of successive versions of the Companies Acts, the London Stock Exchange was left free to regulate the investment industry as it saw fit. The Exchange did not set up a highly bureaucratic system of discipline and enforcement, preferring to rely on suasion and the informal norms of the City to produce good business conduct.

During this pure self-regulatory stage and even for a long time during the negotiated stage, formal associative action had a small place in this system. The Bank of England traditionally combined the functions of central banker, representative of the City in government, and informal overseer of the conduct of financial institutions (Moran, 1981). With respect to securities, the Bank of England believed strongly in private self-regulation. As the financial industry became more complex, the bank then began to encourage trade associations to act as self-regulators, seeing them as an alternative to state bureaucratic control.

The gradual transition to a system of negotiated self-regulation involved increased interchange between these associations and the Bank of England, with the bank continuing to act as an intermediary with other parts of the state. Two sets of laws provided the framework for this transition. The long-standing Companies Acts laid down minimal conduct rules covering such things such as capital structure, disclosure, and the duties of directors. The Prevention of Fraud (Investments) Act, particularly after amendments introduced in 1958, made it an offense to deal in securities without being a member of the Stock Exchange, or a recognized association of dealers in securities, or without possessing an individual exemption from the act or a license from the Department of Trade. By the mid-1970s, there were over 400 exempt institutions (mainly banks and insurance companies) and five recognized associations (see Wilson Report: chapter 22). Nonetheless, the Stock Exchange remained the key self-regulatory organization. It had gradually formalized its rules, drawn up a Code of Dealing, and developed investigatory procedures. Of its 1000 permanent staff in 1978, 100 were concerned primarily with regulation. The Exchange had also created the Stock Exchange Compensation Fund, a discretionary, nonstatutory, open-ended fund for compensating investors in the event of fraud. The Exchange began to require members to take out fidelity insurance against staff dishonesty (Wilson Report: chapter 22).

A series of controversial takeovers in the 1960s and several insolvencies of securities firms in the early 1970s suggested the self-regulatory system was no longer working effectively. The City reacted by drawing on the guidance of the Bank of England to set up two private, nonstatutory bodies to oversee the regulatory system. These bodies, the Council for the Securities Industry (CSI) and the Panel on Takeovers and Mergers, drew together the executives of relevant interest associations and other City institutions to create a slightly more formalized variant of the traditional informal consultative system that prevailed in the securities industry.

If the CSI and the Panel on Takeovers and Mergers were to succeed, ethical, informal communal norms had to remain strong, yet the rapid internationalization and expansion of the sector in the late 1970s weakened community ties. Speaking of the panel, the Wilson Report (p. 307) noted this problem. "Their authority rests on the acceptance of Panel and executive rulings by the general financial community and by the associations which make up its membership. The main sanction available is public censure, which derives its power from its effect on the reputation of the individual concerned and is therefore of less force in cases involving those without standing in the financial community." The specific event that sparked movement toward a mandated system was the introduction in 1976 of Statutory Instrument 98 (Moran, 1986:8). This measure, the Restrictive Trade Practices (Services) Order, extended the scope of restrictive practices legislation to cover services. Immediately the securities industry was in difficulty. The Stock Exchange's rule book contained two restrictive practices that were the cornerstone of its entire modus operandi: the requirement that members charge a minimum commission on bargains transacted and the single capacity principle. An intense lobbying effort to exempt the Stock Exchange from the order failed and it began to prepare to defend itself in the Restrictive Practices Court.

If this had been the United States, the matter probably would have been resolved in the courts. Circumstances conspired, however, to produce a more typically British solution to the dilemma. The DTI had appointed Professor L. C. B. Gower to review the system of investor protection following losses suffered by small investors in a series of collapses of high-risk investments in 1980. Gower (1981) published a discussion document raising a number of telling questions about the existing system of regulation. Within the City itself, a reform tendency had developed that wished to break down barriers to entry to the British securities industry and to end the minimum commissions (Moran, 1986:16). Many British firms saw integration with large multinational firms as increasingly necessary if they were to compete beyond their national borders. When Cecil Parkinson, the Secretary of State for Trade and Industry, met with the chairman of the Stock Exchange in July 1983 to discuss the growing crisis, circumstances were conducive to a private accommodation.[8] The Exchange agreed to virtually all the changes demanded by the Office of Fair Trading, and the government agreed to introduce legislation exempting the Stock Exchange from restrictive practices legislation. The 1983 agreement opened the door to what has come to be called the "City Revolution."

Questions remained, however, about the character of the revamped self-regulatory system. In the first part of his report published in 1984, Professor Gower (1984: chapters 2, 3) argued that the state must assume a formal regulatory role in the industry. Although SROs such as the Stock Exchange and associations would continue to occupy themselves with day-to-day enforcement and discipline, these would have to be overseen by the Department of Trade and Industry or a new independent agency. Gower (1984:11) noted that without such a state presence, the old restrictive practices would continue.

Such a suggestion did not sit well with the financial industry and its centuries-long tradition of freedom from state intervention. On May 23, 1984, the governor of the Bank of England put together a group of senior City figures to advise him on how SROs should be structured. The report of this advisory group was never published, but its advice materialized in the Department of Trade and Industry's White Paper of January 1985. Instead of giving supervisory powers over the SROs to an independent government agency or to DTI itself, the White Paper proposed that the Secretary of State for Trade and Industry delegate them to *private* agencies on the grounds that such agencies would be better suited to a "practitioner-based" system of self-regulation.[9] Unlike the SEC in the United States and the provincial securities commissions in Canada, the new Securities Investments Board (SIB), created in the 1986 Financial Services Act, was a private, not a public, body. It is financed by a levy on the industry, with its chairman being appointed by the Secretary of State for Trade and Industry with the agreement of the Governor of the Bank of England. The members of the board, in contrast, are appointed by the governor with the agreement of the Secretary of State.

The SIB, in turn, has authorized the creation of five SROs. For our purposes, the most important of these was The Securities Association, subsequently renamed The Securities and Futures Authority (TSFA) following a merger with another SRO. This association drew its staff largely from the regulatory arm of the London Stock Exchange and was charged with overseeing all firms dealing in shares and securities. The role of the Stock Exchange has been cut back to that of managing and supervising a securities exchange. The functions of the SIB parallel those exercised by the SEC and the Canadian securities commissions.[10] It participates in the development of the rules to be used by the SROs, themselves private associations, funded by the subscriptions of members. Membership in an SRO is compulsory, their rules have the force of law, and the composition of their governing bodies is prescribed by statute (Moran, 1987b:6–7). In these respects, the TSFA is analogous to the NASD and the stock exchanges in the United States.

Creation of private-interest governments has contributed, in turn, to an enhanced role for voluntary industry associations. In 1988, two associations, the Accepting Houses Committee and the Issuing House Associations, combined their efforts to form the British Merchant Banking and Securities Houses Association (BMBSHA). Although analogous to the SIA in the United States, the BMBSHA is less directly confrontational and appears to take more of a direct role in policy formulation. Less direct state intervention appears to foster less adversarial trade association activity.

What has changed then is that an organization has received a formal delegation of state authority to oversee the financial services industry. Under the previous negotiated arrangements, no such delegation had taken place. The fragmentation and the independence of controlling institutions in the old system have given way to a more hierarchical approach with clearly defined lines of authority. Informal communal approaches to governance have yielded to formal associative action backed by state power. What is curious, of course, is that the delegation of authority has not been matched by any rigorous mechanism of accountability. Parliament's ability to monitor the use of its delegated authority is very weak. In the words of Moran (1987b:24), the "SIB will, through delegated powers, enjoy many of the coercive powers of the state.... Yet it will be largely controlled by the markets located in the City; paid for by the markets; its governing body drawn from the elite of the financial services industry; and its staff largely recruited from the City, at City salaries."

Canada

Governance of the Canadian securities industry shares some properties with both the British and the American systems. From Britain, Canada inherited the disclosure tradition of the Companies Acts with governments following this British lead beginning even before Confederation (Williamson, 1960:8–10). Canadian governments and securities firms also were predisposed to use informal communal suasion as a disciplinary mechanism and have continued to work with informal committees for discussions of crucial issues even to the present day. Yet Canada adapted this British approach by borrowing liberally from the United States, beginning with "blue sky" legislation and later with the creation of government agencies for supervising self-regulatory organizations. Its trajectory from pure through negotiated to mandated self-regulation also more closely resembles that of the United States than that of Britain. Finally, like the U.S. industry, the Canadian sector has historically been more autonomous from other financial services sectors than its British counterpart. To these properties, Canada adds one of its own: Regulation is decentralized with provincial-level agencies possessed of constitutional responsibility for the securities industry. There is no national supervisory body, whether public like the SEC or private like the SIB.

Prior to 1928, a pure self-regulatory system existed in Canada. Stock exchanges located in Montreal, Toronto, Winnipeg, Calgary, and Vancouver maintained a limited watch over listed securities. Surveillance of the unlisted markets was even more primitive. The Bond Dealers Association of Canada was founded in 1916 and had established a Vigilance Committee by 1923. The association changed its name to the Investment Bankers Association of Canada (IBAC) in 1924 and the name of the Vigilance Committee to the Business Conduct Committee in 1928. Irrespective of the names involved, the association and its committees contented themselves with reporting on the need for greater vigilance at successive annual meetings. In practice, the association exercised no discipline over its members.

Interest in American "blue sky" legislation set the stage for the transition to a negotiated self-regulatory system. Prior to 1920, three of the western provinces enacted legislation similar to that pioneered in Kansas, but Ontario did not pass analogous legislation until 1928.[11] The Ontario Security Frauds Prevention Act of that year contained a series of antifraud provisions and a requirement that brokers and sales persons be registered. When it was revised slightly in 1930, the act became a model for all provinces except New Brunswick (Williamson, 1960:21). The new law contained the first formal recognition of stock exchanges as agents of self-regulation.

The 1930 version of the law also allowed for the possibility of a government board to watch over the affairs of the securities industry. Created in 1931, the board assumed its present name, the Ontario Securities Commission (OSC), in 1933. In 1932, the OSC moved to improve its supervision of the bond industry by enlisting the support of the IBAC.[12] The first commissioner, Colonel George Drew, approached the association to consider instituting both an examination for its members and some sort of voluntary audit system. The latter suggestion gave rise to considerable debate within the association; its members understood that agreeing to such procedures would change the organization in a fundamental way. Commissioner Drew also indicated that he would have to consider seriously direct state regulation if no changes were made. Faced with this unpalatable alternative, the association (now called the Investment Dealers Association of Canada [IDA]) acquiesced. At its annual meeting in 1937, the IDA toughened its entrance requirements by requiring an audited financial statement of all new members, legislated that all firms maintain a minimum net capital of $10,000, and instituted a compulsory audit system whereby each member would submit a financial statement annually to auditors chosen by the association.

In short, by 1938, the IDA had negotiated arrangements that allowed it to regulate the over-the-counter securities industry in place of the government. These arrangements were not formalized in any legal sense. Since the association was willing to self-regulate, the government saw no reason to involve itself with the conduct of IDA members.

The minimal mandated system involving the stock exchanges and the negotiated arrangements for the IDA lasted a short six years. During the early 1940s, Ontario added to its already growing reputation as a haven for fraudulent stock promoters (Dey and Makuch, 1979:1419). A royal commission inquiry into the mining industry returned a stinging indictment of existing securities laws. In response, the Ontario government introduced a new Securities Act in 1945, which, after amendments in 1947, completed the institutionalization of a fully mandated system for the industry. It formally delegated more authority for regulating business conduct to the stock exchanges and, for the first time, to the IDA.

Since 1947, the IDA and the stock exchanges have gradually had this mandate expanded: the IDA generally taking the initiative itself in advance of legislation while the exchanges have responded to legislative direction. The IDA has tightened up further its membership entry requirements, raised the minimum net capital rule, and expanded and professionalized its audit system. In 1948, it appointed its first Director of Education, who developed an "Elementary Course in Investment Banking." This initiative was the first step toward the eventual creation in 1971 of the Canadian Securities Institute (CSIT). A joint project of the IDA and the stock exchanges, the CSIT offers courses that are now compulsory for everyone entering the industry. These same organizations established in 1969 an investor protection fund that indicated industry's willingness to assume open-ended and contingent member liability for failures of securities firms.

The mandated system was not finally formalized until 1966 when various amendments to the Securities Act followed still another stock manipulation involving the mining industry. The new act outlined for the first time in detail the relationship that should exist between the Toronto Stock Exchange (TSE) and the government of Ontario through the OSC. Analogous then to the SEC and to the SIB, the OSC acquired at this stage the powers to regulate the internal affairs of the TSE. The IDA, in contrast, acted on its own to revise its structures and is thus subject to much less direct government supervision. It expanded its professional staff, created in 1976 for the first time in its history a board of directors, added four "public directors" in 1982, and placed its finances on firmer ground by instituting an underwriting levy on all transactions. Its ability to react swiftly and thus to avoid greater direct government supervision gives it a unique status in the context of this study. On the one hand, it is definitely an SRO, overseeing the over-the-counter securities markets. On the other hand, it remains a private-interest association with an elaborate public affairs program and acts as an advocate for the industry in the halls of government.

This self-regulatory system absorbed further sweeping changes in the 1980s. Following the American lead, commission rates that securities dealers can charge their clients were deregulated. New rules now allow commercial banks and trust and insurance companies to offer investment services through subsidiaries and foreign investment firms to acquire full ownership of Canadian companies. Both the new subsidiaries of Canadian financial institutions and the foreign firms have been accepted into the IDA and have purchased seats on the stock exchanges.

Summary

Governance arrangements for the securities industries in Canada, the United States, and Britain have become increasingly similar over time (see also Moran, 1991), yet some differences remain. Figure 10.1 summarizes the situations in each of the three countries as of 1990. Three spheres of activity may be distinguished: a public or official governmental sphere, an "official" private sphere where private organizations receive a formal delegation of state authority, and a wholly private sphere. Relationships among industry bodies may be direct and regulatory, where one body supervises closely the activities of another; or they may be indirect, where a body has titular responsibility for another but

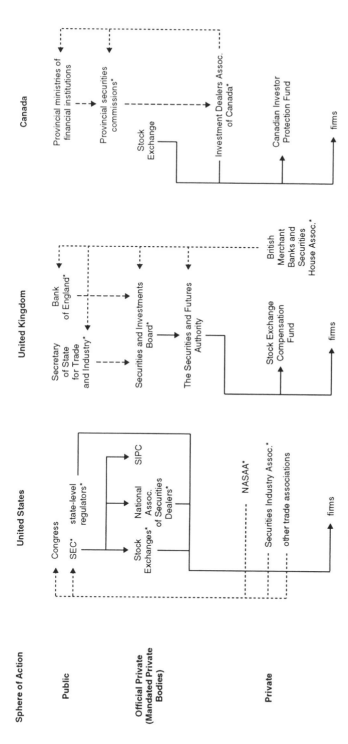

Figure 10.1 Summary Description of Governance Arrangements in the Securities Sector, 1990.

KEY: ———— direct regulatory relationship.
——— formal titular responsibility but informal governance.
········· lobbying or advocacy relationship.

its supervisory powers are not extensive nor described in a statute. Supervision draws on informal communal norms and private consultation. Figure 10.1 notes that firms in all three systems engage in collective associative action as well. Finally, in each policy community one can isolate those organizations that participate directly in the industry's policy network. The policy network embraces the organizations that formulate and implement policy in a given sector.[13]

Figure 10.1 illustrates first of all how the three systems have converged in form. In each country there is a two-tiered structure overseeing the activities of firms. The first tier contains the self-regulatory organizations, or private-interest governments, that supervise directly the firms' behavior; the second tier is composed of organizations that watch over the SROs, ensuring that they do not become the captives of their clientele or obstacles to competition and industry development. A second similarity pertains to the SROs themselves— whether stock exchanges or associations, all occupy, wholly or partially, the "official private" sphere. Third, each of the systems has generated over the past two decades an industry-supported fund to compensate investors in the event of the failure of securities firms. Finally, the presence of the formal two-tiered structure plus the compensation fund indicates that informal networks have now a minimal place in the governance arrangements. They remain more important in the operation of the markets themselves.

Figure 10.1 also highlights several differences among the three systems. First, there is variation in the degree of state intrusion. The second-tier supervisory bodies in Canada and the United States are placed in the public domain whereas their counterpart in Britain, the SIB, occupies the "Official Private" sphere. Public supervision in Britain by the Secretary of State for Trade and Industry and the Bank of England tends to be indirect and more informal in character. The U.S. system involves the greatest state intervention. The SEC is a very large bureaucratic organization; the provincial securities commissions in Canada are much smaller and tend to work more informally. Similarly, the investors protection fund falls in the "Official Private" sphere in the United States, but occupies the private domain in Britain and Canada. Second, the British system has begun to amalgamate supervision of listed and unlisted securities under one SRO—The Securities and Futures Association. In Canada and the United States, these functions remain separate with the stock exchanges continuing to play an important supervisory role.

Third, the Canadian system differs from the other two in one key respect: The Investment Dealers Association of Canada (IDA) is involved as both an SRO and a trade association and is increasingly joined by the Canadian Bankers' Association, as the securities affiliates of the chartered banks have become active. In the United States and Britain, the lobbying and self-regulatory roles are functionally differentiated with the NASD and TSFA performing as self-regulators and the SIA and the BMBSHA as policy advocates.

Finally, if the U.S. system shows the most state intervention, the British and Canadian systems continue to work in some areas on the basis of informal communal ties. This policy style is certainly that preferred by the Bank of

England and is the choice of provincial ministers responsible for financial institutions in Canada and of the provincial securities commissions in dealing with the IDA. The Canadian securities commissions also rely on these kinds of relationships in overseeing the investor protection fund; if the analogous fund remains private in the UK, one might expect that the SIB would develop similarly informal relations with it as well.

Internationalization and National Sovereignty

Although it is true that securities have been bought and sold over national borders for a long time, internationalization has taken on several new aspects since the early 1960s. First, U.S. balance of payments deficits in the 1960s led to the accumulation of large holdings of U.S. dollars overseas. Late in the decade, when demands arose for long-term loans of ten to fifteen years, many of these demands were met through the issuance of *Eurobonds*, which drew from this dollar pool (Thomas, 1989). These securities were underwritten and sold in various markets simultaneously and handled by international banking groups. By the mid-1980s, Eurobonds were being issued at a rate of over $100 billion per year. Second, the past two decades have also seen the emergence of *Euro-equities*, stocks for a company that are issued outside its domestic market and distributed internationally. Largely organized by international investment bankers based in Europe or Japan, these issues have been used by multinational companies wishing to tap several capital markets. Third, facilitated by technology and the general expansion of international trade, domestically issued bonds and equities have come increasingly to the attention of foreign investors. The largest Japanese and U.S. investment banking houses, and the German universal banks, now have branch organizations in each of the major financial centers: New York, London, Tokyo, Paris, Frankfurt, Luxembourg, and Toronto. Each of these changes has had an impact on governance arrangements.

Governance of the Eurobond markets is moving presently from the pure self-regulatory to the negotiated self-regulatory stage. Pure self-regulation began in 1968 when nineteen of the most active investment houses formed a steering committee to study the creation of an association designed "to introduce greater stability and order in the market" (AIBD, 1989:7). In February 1969, the committee's efforts resulted in the creation of the Association of International Bond Dealers (AIBD) that over the next nineteen years sought to establish uniform market practices and to initiate contact with various monetary authorities having an interest in the development of an orderly international bond market. Following passage of the new British Financial Services Act in 1986, the AIBD entered into negotiations with British authorities over being recognized as an international securities SRO under the act. Approval was received in April 1988, thereby giving AIBD an official mandate to act as a recognized investment exchange. It would not be correct to say that AIBD has reached the mandated stage of self-regulation because there is no overarching international state body that confers such a mandate. Rather, the combination of strong informal networks among the international houses plus the introduction of a formalized exchange through associative action has moved governance from a purely private to a kind of "official private" status.

A similar path has been followed for Euro-equities. About a year before the major deregulatory changes in London, called the "Big Bang," the London Stock Exchange introduced a screen-based system for international equities (SEAQ International) (Thomas, 1989:204). Following passage of the Financial Services Act, the international investment houses based in London took advantage of the new law to set up a new exchange, the International Stock Exchange of the United Kingdom and the Republic of Ireland (Thomas, 1989:36). With some success, London has encouraged the listing of international equities on this exchange and the new exchange has taken over the operation of SEAQ International. Firms with seats on the exchange are regulated by The Securities and Futures Association (TFSA), the general British SRO for investment bankers. Governance of international equities has moved, therefore, toward the national self-regulatory model with one important caveat. Not all international equities are listed on the London exchange and some trading takes place in other financial centers.

Governance of the third category of international securities, namely domestic securities issued domestically but also traded internationally, still rests primarily with national self-regulatory systems. Issues posed by international trading in these securities have occasioned increasing bilateral contacts among national securities regulators and among SROs, and given life to two worldwide organizations, the International Organization of Securities Commissions (IOSCO) and the International Council of Securities Dealers and Self-Regulatory Organizations (ICSDSRO).

Bilateral contacts have developed most extensively between the SEC and the provincial securities commisions in Canada and between the SEC and the SIB in Britain. Agreements on increasing information sharing and on cooperation in enforcement and prosecution are now in place. The SEC and the Canadians are working presently toward a system of reciprocal registration. More broadly, as part of the Single Market program, the EEC has sought to put in place directives covering investment services and stock exchange listings. Progress here has been slow and difficult.

On the broader international plane, implementation of arrangements among nation-states is increasingly the concern of IOSCO. Founded in 1975, this organization assumed increasing importance in the late 1980s. Its members are state agencies responsible for supervising securities SROs; the SEC, the Ontario and Quebec securities commissions, and the SIB are all members. The SROs, it is useful to add, founded their own organization, ICSDSRO, in December 1988. It is still early to say whether this replication of the state regulator/self-regulator division on the international plane will be a lasting one. The IDA and NASD were founding members of the ICSDSRO, as was FIMBRA, the SRO organization for brokers in Britain.

The eventual success of IOSCO depends largely on the efforts of its Technical Committee, which has taken on the more difficult topics related to harmonization. At its annual meeting in the fall of 1989, the Technical Committee offered a proposal for uniform capital requirements for multinational securities firms. It appeared initially that the recommendations would be accepted by members but, at the last moment, Germany withdrew its assent.

The reasons behind this disagreement, and some of those in the EEC, are crucial and indicate a key problem that must be addressed before international governance can proceed further. Securities activities in countries like Germany with universal banking systems are conducted simply as one of the ongoing activities of the bank. Hence, regulation and supervision of securities trans-actions come under the jurisdiction of banking and not separate securities regulators. The question of capital requirements for securities activities is part of the larger question of capital requirements for banks. In the Anglo-American nations and in Japan, though it is true that banks can now engage to varying degrees in securities activities, they must do so through affiliates or subsidiaries that concern themselves only with securities and are separated from the banks by "firewalls." These affiliates are regulated, in turn, through the types of self-regulatory systems described in this chapter.

Therefore, state regulators and SROs in these countries have tended to perceive the question of capital requirements in terms of these dedicated securities firms; these securities regulators do not regulate capital adequacy of the parent bank or bank holding company. Germany perceives this regulatory issue as crucial to the competitive future of its securities industry and even its industrial development (Henzler, 1989). If international regulatory systems are designed to fit the bank-affiliate model rather than the universal bank model, German banks fear their in-house securities facilities will not be competitive. Not surprisingly, the same issue has arisen in the European Community as it has moved to harmonize bank regulation (Arnold, 1989).

Conclusions

The fact that attempts to develop governance arrangements on an international scale have finally come face to face with fundamental differences in the structures of national financial systems suggests in itself how far internationalization has developed in the financial arena. If sovereignty refers to the final assertion of authority within a given territory and the ability to control transborder move-ments of people, goods, and capital (Krasner, 1988:86), then nation-states have lost sovereignty over financial policy. Removal of capital and credit controls and the evolution of international financial markets increase greatly the free movement of capital across national borders. The degrees of freedom for any given state in the use of financial policy instruments have declined proportionately; changes in financial policy increasingly can be realized only through coordination among individual states on the international plane.

Therefore, some of the received wisdom in comparative political economy about the relationship between the structure of the financial system and the conduct of industrial policy must be questioned. Zysman (1983) distinguishes among three types of financial systems: capital markets-based (U.S., Britain), credit-based (France), and negotiated credit-based (Germany). The internationalization of financial markets has removed many of the instruments used in credit-based systems from the hands of national policymakers. Credit controls, exchange controls, and interest rate ceilings—all crucial policy instruments in a credit-based system—have largely disappeared in the advanced capital nations. The French state's desire to steer the economy (*dirigisme*) is now more constrained than ever before.

In addition, as we have just seen, moves to develop an international governance regime have begun to bring pressure on the German universal banking system whose particular structure was seen by Zysman to be crucial to the conduct of its bank-led industrial policy. The capital markets-based model in operation in the United States and Britain, with its presumed separation of banking and industry and its reliance on markets for the allocation of credit and the pricing of loans, is closest to the model that has developed in the international sphere. As it expands, this model increasingly limits national state actors to the use of company-led rather than state-led industrial policies. Consequently, the differences in approach to industrial policy found across advanced capitalist nation-states are likely to diminish further. In this respect, the internationalization of financial markets is raising fundamental questions about the traditional understanding of the role of the nation-state in theories of political economy.

Notes

Research supported by the Social Sciences and Humanities Research Council of Canada, Research Grant 410-88-0629.

1. Unless otherwise noted, the term "securities industry" will be used henceforth to refer to the underwriting and brokerage subsectors of the industry only.

2. I use the term "City" here in the British sense, which refers to a geographically fixed spatial unit in London and to a wide range of activities generally and loosely classified as financial (Ingham, 1984:42). Somewhat analogous terms in the United States and Canada would be "Wall Street" and "Bay Street," respectively.

3. The Organization for Economic Cooperation and Development (OECD) (1987:103) defines a security broadly: "an interest, or instrument evidencing such interest, commonly known as a 'security', including any share or stock, debt security, bond or debenture, and further including any note, treasury stock, evidence of indebtedness, certificate of interest or participation in any profit-sharing agreement, collateral-trust certificate, pre-organization certificate or subscription, transferable share, investment contract, voting-trust certificate, certificate of deposit for a security, equipment-trust certificate, fractional undivided interest in oil, gas or other mineral rights, or a certificate of interest or participation in temporary or interim certificate for, receipt for, guarantee of, or warrant or right to subscribe, purchase or otherwise acquire or sell, convert, exchange or otherwise dispose of the foregoing."

4. In both countries, banks were allowed to underwrite certain "exempt" securities, usually government issues.

5. The prefix *Euro-* in the front of a currency (Eurodollars) or a security (Eurobond) refers to that currency or security being bought and sold in international markets, rather than in the domestic system from which it originated.

6. These three stages conform to the pattern traced by Boddewyn (1985) in his

discussion of self-regulation in the advertising industry and are adapted from that article. I develop them further in a detailed analysis of the evolution of self-regulation in the Canadian securities industry (Coleman, 1989).

7. The term "blue sky" law originated in Kansas. When Kansas passed the first state securities law in 1911, it was intended to check stock swindlers so brazen they "would sell building lots in the blue sky" (Seligman, 1982:44).

8. For more details on the agreement, see Moran (1986:11–12).

9. The White Paper actually argued that the state delegate its powers to two private agencies, one to regulate the marketing of pre-packaged collective investments in unit trusts and linked life policies, and the other to regulate the rest of the industry. Professor Gower (1985:9–10) opposed this proposal strongly in the second part of his report, and his views on the virtues of a single agency eventually prevailed.

10. The SIB and the Canadian commissions do not have all the responsibilities of the SEC, however. In particular, the SEC administers all of the disclosure provisions of the Securities Act while the Companies Acts in Britain and Canada are administered by the Department of Trade and Industry and the federal and provincial departments of corporate affairs, respectively.

11. The discussion that follows will focus on the Ontario case only. There are three reasons for this. First, the Toronto Stock Exchange is the leading exchange in Canada with over 80 percent of the business in the country. Toronto is also the country's financial center. Finally, other provinces have tended (until very recently) to emulate Ontario's actions.

12. The following discussion is based on Coleman (1989)

13. For elaboration on this concept, see Atkinson and Coleman (1989).

References

Arnold, Wolfgang. (1989, September). "Trennbank- order Universalbanksystem: Wohin führt die EG-Bankrechtsharmonisierung?" *Börsen-Zeitung*, p. 14.

Association of International Bond Dealers (1989). *The Association of International Bond Dealers January 1989*. Zurich: AIBD.

Atkinson, Michael M., and William D. Coleman. (1989). "Strong States and Weak States: Sectoral Policy Networks in Advanced Capitalist Economies." *British Journal of Political Science*, 19, 47–65.

Boddewyn, J. J. (1985). "Advertising Self-Regulation: Organization Structures in Belgium, Canada, France and the United Kingdom." In W. Streeck and P. C. Schmitter (eds.), *Private Interest Government: Beyond Market and State*. Beverly Hills, Calif.: Sage Publications.

Bryant, Ralph C. (1987). *International Financial Intermediation*. Washington, D.C.: The Brookings Institution.

Canadian Securities Institute. (1986). *The Canadian Securities Course*. Toronto: CSIT.

Carosso, Vincent P. (1970). *Investment Banking in America: A History*. Cambridge, Mass.: Harvard University Press.

Coleman, William D. (1989, Winter). "Self-Regulation in the Canadian Securities Industry: A Case Study of the Investment Dealers Association of Canada." *Canadian Public Administration*.

Committee to Review the Functioning of Financial Institutions (Wilson Report). (1980). *Report*, Cmnd 7937. London: HMSO.

De Bedts, Ralph F. (1964). *The New Deal's SEC: The Formative Years*. New York: Columbia University Press.

Department of Trade and Industry (DTI). (1985). *Financial Services in the United Kingdom,* Cmnd 9432. London: HMSO.

Dey, Peter, and Stanley Makuch. (1979). "Government Supervision of Self-Regulatory Organizations in the Canadian Securities Industry." In *Proposals for a Securities Market Law for Canada, Vol. 3: Background Papers.* Ottawa: Supply and Services Canada.

Gilpin, Robert. (1987). *The Political Economy of International Relations.* Princeton, N.J.: Princeton University Press.

Gower, L. C. B. (1981). *Review of Investor Protection: A Discussion Document.* London: HMSO.

Gower, L. C. B. (1984). *Review of Investor Protection, Report: Part I.* London: HMSO.

Gower, L. C. B. (1985). *Review of Investor Protection, Report: Part II.* London: HMSO.

Hall, Peter A. (1986). *Governing the Economy: The Politics of State Intervention in Britain and France.* New York: Oxford University Press.

Hall, Robert C. (1979). "The Semantics of Securities Industry Deregulation." In Lawrence G. Goldberg, and Lawrence J. White (eds.), *The Deregulation of the Banking and Securities Industries.* Lexington, Mass.: Lexington Books.

Henzler, Herbert. (1989, October 6). "Neue Beschränkungen für das Kreditgewerbe würden dem Industriestandort Bundesrepublik schaden." *Die Zeit,* pp. 12–30.

Ingham, Geoffrey. (1984). *Capitalism Divided? The City and Industry in British Social Development.* London: Macmillan.

Kolko, Joyce. (1988). *Restructuring the World Economy.* New York: Pantheon.

Krasner, Stephen. (1988). "Sovereignty: An Institutional Perspective." *Comparative Political Studies,* 21, 66–94.

Levin, David Saul. (1969). "Regulating the Securities Industry: The Evolution of a Government Policy" (Unpublished Ph.D Dissertation, Columbia University).

Loss, Louis. (1961). *Securities Regulation* (2nd ed.; 3 vols). Boston: Little, Brown.

Moran, Michael. (1981). "Finance Capital and Pressure Group Politics in Britain." *British Journal of Political Science,* 11(4), 381–404.

Moran, Michael. (1986). "Corporatism Resurrected: Economic Interests and Institutional Change in the City of London." Manchester Working Papers, No. 3. Manchester, UK: Victoria University of Manchester.

Moran, Michael. (1987a). "An Outpost of Corporatism: The Franchise State on Wall Street." *Government and Opposition,* 22(2), 206–23.

Moran, Michael. (1987b). "Thatcherism and the Constitution: The case of financial regulation in the 1980s." Mimeograph.

Moran, Michael. (1990). "Deregulating Britain, Deregulating America: The Case of the Securities Industry." In Colin Crouch and Ronald Dore (eds.), *Corporatism and Accountability: Organized Interests in British Public Life* (pp. 103–24). Oxford: The Clarendon Press.

Moran, Michael. (1991). *The Politics of the Financial Services Revolution: The USA, UK and Japan.* London: Macmillan.

National Association of Security Dealers. (1987). *1986 Annual Report.* Washington, D.C.: NASD.

OECD. (1987). *International Trade in Services: Securities.* Paris: OECD.

Parrish, Michael. (1970). *Securities Regulation and the New Deal.* New Haven, Conn.: Yale University Press.

Securities Industry Association (SIA). (1987). *Annual Report 1986.* New York: SIA.

Seligman, Joel. (1982). *The Transformation of Wall Street: A History of the Securities and Exchange Commission and Modern Corporate Finance.* Boston: Houghton Mifflin.

Seligman, Joel. (1985). *The SEC and the Future of Finance.* New York: Praeger.

Thomas, W. A. (1989). *The Securities Market.* New York: Philip Allan.

Williamson, J. Peter. (1960). *Securities Regulation in Canada.* Toronto: University of Toronto Press.

Zysman, John. (1983). *Governments, Markets and Growth: Financial Systems and the Politics of Industrial Change.* Ithaca, N.Y.: Cornell University Press.

CHAPTER 11

Countries and Sectors

Concluding Remarks on Performance, Convergence, and Competitiveness

J. Rogers Hollingsworth
and Wolfgang Streeck

O UR concluding chapter will attempt to draw together some of the insights of the sectoral case studies in this volume and place them in comparative perspective. We will begin by exploring the *relationship between sectoral and national factors* in the creation of industrial order, examining how they account for the diversity in economic governance regimes that the chapters in this book have uncovered. Next, we will turn to the differences in the *institutionalized performance standards* and in the actual economic *performance* of sectors and their governance regimes, and their relationship to the increasing *internationalization* of sectoral economies. Following this, we will discuss the prospects for *institutional convergence under competitive pressures in international markets.* In particular, we will address the possibility that internationalization may amount to *deregulation* of sectoral regimes, with national or local governance mechanisms being increasingly superseded by an institutionally "thin," neoclassical order governing the "world market."

The Character of Industrial Regimes: Country and Sector

Markets and corporate hierarchies, the two core institutions of both capitalism and economic theory, are but *elements of larger systems of social-industrial order* that also include, at a minimum, *communities* of shared cultural identity, *associations* representing common structurally based interests, and *state agencies* protecting and creating socially generated obligations and exercising public power with the ultimate backing of legitimate force (Streeck and Schmitter, 1985; Campbell, Hollingsworth, and Lindberg, 1991). Regimes of economic governance differ in the way in which these, and possibly other, elements are configured—in particular, the way in which market and corporate hierarchy relations are embedded in community structures, moderated by associational bargains, and conceded, protected, facilitated, promoted, subsidized, privileged, prescribed, or, for that matter, outlawed by the state. The resulting institutional configuration governs economic transactions by, among other things, generating and sanctioning motivations for gainful exchange, setting prices, standardizing products, providing and maintaining durable relations between traders, enforcing contracts, ensuring hierarchical compliance, arranging for cooperation in the face of competition, and extracting contributions to the generation and maintenance of collective resources without which the rational pursuit of self-interest would be self-defeating or yield less than optimal results.

Regimes of economic governance vary with *spatial-territorial location* as well as between *functional-economic sectors*. Variation by territory occurs because social institutions are rooted in local, regional, or national political communities and their shared beliefs, experiences, and traditions. While localities and regions always were, and continue to be, important bases for distinctive institutional orders (Sabel, 1989), comparative social research has focused primarily on the *nation* as its principal unit of analysis. This is because in the modern period, crucial resources for institution-building—especially formal law and physical force—have come to be vested in the nation-state. Typically, as regimes of economic governance are configured and reconfigured, actors advance their interests by having recourse to "power resources" (Korpi, 1978) derived from their participation in national politics, from nationally shared cultural values, and from already existing nationally sanctioned institutional constraints and opportunities.

In addition, regimes of governance are shaped by *sectoral properties*, in particular the contingencies of *technology* on the one hand and *products and product markets* on the other. Products may be customized (printed circuit boards, ships) or standardized (television sets, steel); they may be homogeneous (milk) or heterogeneous (fine chemicals); perishable (milk) or easy to keep (steel), and so forth. Similarly, acquiring up-to-date technology may require large and lumpy investment in some sectors (automobiles, chemicals) and relatively little in others (machine tools). Also, technologies may be operated by unskilled (printed circuit board) or skilled labor (shipbuilding), or by manual (steel) or nonmanual workers (securities). It is important to note that all of these conditions may change, and that much of what happens in the politics of industrial sectors has to do with adjustment of governance structures to such changes.

A sector's technological and economic contingencies influence its *industrial organization*. By defining the pertinent economies of scale and scope—the extent to which newcomers face barriers to access, the trade-offs that firms confront between capital and labor intensity, the requisite composition of their labor force, etc., technological and market conditions affect, among other things, an industry's rate of concentration, the vertical integration of its member firms, the scope of their product range, and the extent to which they may rely on internal labor markets. Unlike what transaction cost economics and much of mainstream organization theory suggest, however, industrial organization in the technical sense of a specific combination between corporate hierarchies and market exchanges is only part of a sector's regime of governance. Technology and economics also affect the inclination and ability of capital and labor in a sector to engage in associative action, separately or together; the extent to which firms and workers may benefit from involvement in dense, communal "networks" of privileged, preferential trading relations; and their interests and capacities in relation to the state and the public sphere in general.

While identical technologies and market conditions do make for similarities in the industrial organization and the governance of sectors across countries, historically they have left room for significant national differences. *Just as sectoral differences in technology and market conditions give rise to differences in industrial order within countries, national differences produce different governance regimes within sectors* (Campbell, Hollingsworth, and Lindberg, 1991; Aoki, 1988). A important example is the different organization of the financial sector in the Anglo-American countries (Coleman, this volume) and, for example, Germany and Japan with their universal bank systems. Also, vertical integration and contracting practices in the printed circuit board industries of Japan and the United Kingdom differ regardless of basically identical technologies and market conditions (Sako, this volume); and the role of the state, the influence of shareholders, and the significance of market pressures in the governance of the Japanese steel industry are quite unlike what they are in the United States (O'Brien, this volume).

Similarly, while American machine tools are, or used to be, produced by large vertically integrated firms, German machine-tool producers are typically small or medium-sized (Herrigel, this volume); and German chemical firms tend to be more research-intensive than their competitors, their product range being more differentiated (Grant and Paterson, this volume).

Differences in governance within sectors are often recognizable as national differences in that they follow a similar logic across sectors. To this extent, they can be traced back to contextual, or "societal" (Maurice, Sellier, and Silvestre, 1984), effects that modify the impact of sectoral contingencies—just as these modify the sectoral manifestation of national properties. The impact of the national context makes itself felt in at least three ways:

1. Through *identical rules of behavior* created and enforced at national level that penetrate all sectors of a national economy regardless of technical and economic conditions. An example would be a country's antitrust law, or the influence national company law grants to shareholders over the operation of a business (Cornish, 1979; Bork, 1978; see the contrast among the American case and the Japanese, German, and Swedish cases, as documented in various chapters in this volume).

2. Through *identical factual conditions* facing all economic actors in a given country. Such conditions may be created by distinct nationwide institutions that affect, for example, the procurement of vital production inputs for all economic sectors. Thus, national differences in the organization of capital markets—as among the United States, Japan, and Germany—may require or generate nationally typical cross-sectoral practices in the governance of financial transactions. Similarly, nationwide systems of general and, perhaps more important, vocational education create similar constraints and opportunities for employers in all sectors of a national economy—see, for example, the role of the German vocational training system in automobiles, chemicals, and machine tools (Dankbaar; Grant and Paterson; Herrigel, this volume). A third example would be a national pattern of craft trade unionism standing in the way of long-term job tenure with high internal labor market flexibility.

3. Through *identical cultural and political resources* defining the constraints and opportunities under which individual and collective actors operate. Such resources determine, among other things, the extent of "trust" on which actors can draw; the degree to which socially imposed obligations can be invoked to regulate economic transactions; the acceptability and feasibility of formalization of exchange relationships; a governance regime's preference and capacity for standardization of transactions, and so forth.

The material in this volume allows us to identify a number of national differences that seem to generate consistent *cross-national variations* in the governance of sectors:

1. The degree and mode of *state intervention* in a sector seems to be determined almost exclusively by national factors, with only marginal impact of sectoral technologies and economics. There are some indications that sectors with small firms (see the chapters on the dairy, printed circuit board, and machine-tool industries in this volume) may attract direct state intervention more regularly than sectors with large, internationalized firms, like automobiles[1] and chemicals. A counter example, of course, is offered by shipbuilding, which in Japan, Germany, and Sweden received strong state support long before the "socially compatible" and heavily subsidized "management of decline" in the 1970s and 1980s (Stråth, this volume).[2] In any case, however, differences among countries appear vastly more significant. The American state stands out as a vigilant enforcer of antitrust rules, intensely devoted to protecting, and indeed permanently re-creating, the "self-regulating" "free" market against associative collective action and communal networks (Campbell, Hollingsworth, and Lindberg, 1991; Hollingsworth, 1991). At the same time, especially but not exclusively where "national security" interests are at stake, it is also capable of deep and highly bureaucratic regulation. While the British state shares the basic American commitment to the moral primacy and economic superiority of "the market," formal-legal regulation, in the spirit of nineteenth-century liberalism, is generally eschewed (cf. Coleman on the securities industry, this volume).

At the other end of the spectrum, the French state is known to be extremely interventionist, and in the two French sectors that were studied for this volume (consumer electronics and the automobile industry), it certainly lived up to its reputation. But while its state-centeredness sets the French system apart from the two market-centered Anglo-Saxon countries, it shares especially with the United States a fundamental discomfort with collective action outside the state proper (Hayward, 1986; Suleiman, 1974; Keeler, 1987; Hall, 1986).

Germany and Japan, on the other hand, appear as *facilitating* or *enabling states* that contribute to economic governance by encouraging—and even compelling—sectoral interests to organize and govern themselves. What seems to distinguish these countries from the three others is the presence *between state and market* of institutional and organizational resources, underwritten by, but not necessarily incorporated in, the state, that provide their sectors with *additional facilities* to govern their transactions.[3] Indeed, while direct state intervention seems to play a larger role in Japan than in Germany—see O'Brien (this volume) on the Japanese steel industry—in both countries the presence of strong potential agents of intermediary self-regulation may make direct state intervention dispensable (Okimoto, 1989; Johnson, 1982; Johnson et al., 1989; Katzenstein, 1989). This would explain the apparent paradox that countries like the United States and Britain, for all their emphasis on free markets, periodically have to go through surprising bouts of etatism unthinkable in postwar Germany or, perhaps less so, Japan[4] (Atkinson and Coleman, 1989; Rabin, 1986).

   2. Like state intervention, *trade associations* are most likely to play a prominent role in sectors with small firms.[5] Again, however, differences in the character of the national state appear of greater importance than do sectoral factors (Schneiberg and Hollingsworth, 1990). The trade association is a powerful player in the Japanese printed circuit board industry where it is backed and encouraged by an enabling state; in laissez-faire Britain, the association looks pathetic by comparison. In machine tools, the small firms that constitute the industry in Germany depend greatly on their association. In the United States, machine tool manufacturers are typically not small, and as one would expect, associations are much less developed and significant. Indeed, it could be argued on the basis of Herrigel's chapter that American machine tool companies are large (and specialized) precisely because the American antitrust regime has made it impossible for them to survive *as small* (and generalist) *firms*, so that it may in fact be the absence of associations that accounts for the pattern of industrial organization, rather than vice versa (see Hollingsworth, 1991).

   Large companies are less likely to need associations than small ones since they may either be able to survive on their own or able to cooperate without the help of a formal organization (see the chapters on shipbuilding and consumer electronics, this volume). Again, however, the prevailing pattern of state activity modifies the impact of industrial organization. In the German chemical industry, the close historical links between firms and the public educational system have traditionally been operated through a strong industry federation. More recently, the German state's environmental policy activism—combined with a general inclination of German regulatory agencies to press industries into some form of negotiated self-regulation—seems to have confirmed the importance of that federation. Environmental policy is of much lower significance for the British state, and the chemical industry association is weak (Grant and Paterson, this volume; Allen, 1989).[6]

   National patterns of industrial relations and collective bargaining also influence the position of associations, adding a further national characteristic to the composition of sectoral governance systems (Schneiberg and Hollingsworth, 1990). In no country does the automobile industry form strong trade associations: Firms are large and few in number to begin with; foreign ownership is frequent (Opel and Ford in Germany, Ford in the United Kingdom); and in some countries (France, the United Kingdom, to some extent Germany) part of the industry was for a long time owned by the government. Even Germany conforms to the general pattern in that the trade association of its automobile industry is one of the weakest of its manufacturing sector (Streeck, 1989). However, Germany does have centralized, industrywide collective bargaining and a large, inclusive industrial union representing not just the automotive but the entire metalworking industry. As a result, automakers are active and leading members in the general employer association of the metal sector.

Similarly, industrywide collective bargaining ultimately led to the merger of the German Chemical Industry Association with the sector's employer association. In Britain, by comparison, the final disintegration of decline of industrywide bargaining in the metalworking sector was brought about by the withdrawal of British Leyland from the sector's employer association (see the chapters by Grant and Paterson and by Dankbaar, this volume).

3. Trust-based preferential trading relations, in spite of the technocratic-mathematical connotations of the term that is now commonly applied to them, are the least tangible mechanisms of economic governance. Japanese sectors are always suspect of being wired with invisible "networks"; so are, to a lesser extent, German sectors. In a very general sense, any trading relation where the personal identity of the trading partner—and, in particular, favorable past experience with the partner's performance—plays a role seems to qualify as a network relationship.[7] It is important to note that experientially based information on a trader's good faith is not the same as a common culture; it can be used for calculating the risks and costs of a planned transaction regardless of the presence or absence of a shared value system or social identity. While the latter may well result from repeated satisfactory exchanges (Blau, 1964), it does not have to in order for a "network" to crystallize and reproduce.

"Networks," then, may or may not be underwritten by culturally shared value orientations. To the extent that they reflect no more than the transaction cost advantages of repeated dealings with certified bona fide traders, they are likely to be present even in the most anomic of societies,[8] if only as a statistical probability that traders will prefer to treat with traders with which they have successfully treated before. Technological and economic sectoral differences may more or less encourage this.

For example, while automobile or shipbuilding firms have traditionally never traded with one another, chemical companies always had to for both technical and economic reasons, and from early times, on a global scale. It is likely that the resulting "trust" relationships, and the opportunities offered by frequent interaction, account for the chemical industry's infamous ability to build national and international cartels (Grant and Paterson, this volume). Similarly, the technology of printed circuit board making allows for a high degree of customization, which encourages dense, preferential relations between producers and customers, in principle even in an "arms-length" country like Britain (Sako, this volume).

How much trust can actually be generated by successful commercial transactions, and how much networks can support customization, joint development, and reduction in costs is a different matter and depends on exogenous conditions.

One way in which networks can be made to work beyond what "weak ties" (Granovetter, 1973) between rational individuals can sustain is through *pre-existing cultural-communal bonds*, often associated with common ethnicity or a traditional social structure of informally enforced social obligations. Thus, in a country like Japan or in certain regional economies—see the already mythical "industrial districts" in Italy (Beccattini, 1990; Brusco, 1982)—it seems to be primarily through such mechanisms that network participants receive important additional reassurance reinforcing, validating, and sometimes substituting for information gathered through direct personal experience that trading partners will not defect; that "trust" will not be abused; and that conscientious performance of contractual obligations will not depend exclusively on the other side's shifting perception of self-interest.

Alternatively, market-generated and individually based (and even individually owned) trust my be reinforced and underwritten by formal and politically generated, as opposed to traditionally inherited, institutions like associations, collective bargaining, and state regulation. *Reconstructing community through politics* may be the only way for societies that have irrevocably moved beyond traditionalism fully to exploit the transactional economies of networks. In such societies, networks of privileged trading are likely to be maintained and activated through purposely designed instruments of collective action—like associations or government agencies—which, in turn, tap into the integrative dynamics of successful exchanges to develop their own organizational capacities.

Empirical research is therefore more likely to find networks to be present and effective where there is also a facilitating state or association. Herrigel's analysis of the machine tool industry in Baden-Württemberg (this volume) is a case in point. Also pertinent is Coleman's study of the securities industry (this volume)—a sector that would appear to be a particularly privileged site for network governance given its need for "trust" and the close cultural bonds both among traders and between traders and their customers. Coleman shows, however, that the industry's growth during the twentieth century, with its accompanying and inevitable increase in the number and diversity of market participants, required a continuous upgrading of self-regulatory networks through formal associative action under continuous and growing, albeit indirect, government intervention. In the process, self-governance moved from a voluntary through a negotiated to, more recently, a legally mandated stage—with industry associations turning into "private-interest governments" (Streeck and Schmitter, 1985) utilizing but also mandating network-like relationships among firms so as to increase their effectiveness as self-regulatory mechanisms.[9]

Networks, then, *especially where they work, are more than just networks.* Tendencies at the microlevel of social exchange toward privileged trading with previous partners are universal and occur in all settings: markets, hierarchies, associations, communities, and states. But to contribute significantly to the governance of economic relations, privileged trading must be insured and reinforced by institutions, from contract law to trade unions, which often happen to be nationally based. Different countries may thus be more or less able to utilize the social cohesion, generated by repeated successful exchanges, for the construction of sectoral industrial orders; in the limiting case, they may consider emerging networks as possible threats to the free market or to political liberty and try to dismantle them under antitrust and conspiracy law. It is only if "embedded" in a favorable macroinstitutional context that the microdynamics of exchange between individual actors can contribute to the governance of economic sectors.

4. States, associations, and networks regulate *market* competition and support as well as circumscribe the functioning of corporate *hierarchies*. Hierarchies are more important in some sectors than in others, reflecting transaction cost advantages of vertical integration under certain economic and technological conditions. But within sectors, the extent to which actors are allowed to, or must, rely on hierarchical means of coordination differs greatly by country. An instructive example is the German machine tool industry, which appears to have found hierarchical coordination dispensable, given the rich availability of associative governance in its country.

Moreover, hierarchies function differently in different countries. The Japanese style of informal, diffuse, collective, group, or, again, network-based organizational decision making in large companies, and its difference from American "macho-management," has often been noted (Aoki, 1988). Less attention has been paid to the impact of co-determination on large German firms (see, however, the chapters by Dankbaar and Stråth, this volume), where hierarchical authority is both constrained and legitimated, not by informal understandings and cultural obligations, but by legally based participation rights of an associatively organized work force.[10]

As far as *markets* are concerned, relations between producers and their customers would seem to be generally more market like in sectors that produce consumer goods (automobiles, yogurt, television sets) than in sectors producing investment goods (shipbuilding, chemicals, and machine tools). Once again, however, national differences are pervasive. Relational, or obligational, contracting with customers and, for example, cooperation in product design occur more frequently in the Japanese printed circuit board and the German machine tool industries than in their respective British and American counterparts. Similarly, early successful efforts at product customization have enabled German auto manufacturers to produce tailor-made automobiles for individual consumers in a way quite unknown in the British or French markets.

More importantly, firms in different countries are exposed to different product market pressures, reflecting different ways in which markets are defined and circumscribed by other mechanisms of governance. As in the growth period of the Japanese steel industry or the transition period of the French consumer electronics industry (O'Brien and Cawson, this volume), state agencies may intervene to suspend the imperatives of short-term profitability in the pursuit of longer-term objectives like technological leadership, progress toward which is not properly indicated by current operating returns. As the chapters in this volume demonstrate, markets are not only social constructs but would as "pure" markets neither function nor exist.

For example, a frequent pattern seems to be that of sectoral trade associations defining the arenas and rules of competition among sectoral producers, often converting price competition into competition over quality or innovation (e.g., machine tools and chemicals in Germany, or printed circuit board and steel in Japan). Such collective definition of arenas of competition must not be confused with elimination of competition. The latter is as likely to be brought about by free markets themselves, with their tendency toward industrial concentration requiring from time to time a restoration of competition by political intervention—for example, through antitrust action or government support for small firms. Also, as Herrigel's study (this volume) shows, the alternative to associationally instituted quality competition is not necessarily unregulated competition. In the American case, it was a highly competitive market regime that eliminated "generalists" and favored large, vertically integrated producers with high economies of scale, ultimately replacing market relations along the production chain with hierarchical authority and creating a need for continued antitrust intervention by the state.

National differences are perhaps most pronounced in the governance of labor markets and employment relationships, and in the way in which "pure" markets are institutionally modified if the commodity at stake is labor power. Since comparative industrial relations is a relatively well-studied subject (Bean, 1985; Poole, 1986), the chapters in this volume focus primarily on other aspects of sectoral governance. Still, they do suggest that nationally different institutionalized constraints and opportunities for firms in labor markets may have important consequences for the behavior of firms in other arenas, including strategic decision making with respect to product markets and products.

As Stråth's chapter (this volume) illustrates, Japanese shipbuilding firms operated under a strong *labor constraint* that forced them to expand their presence in other markets and sectors, so as to be able to keep their commitment to lifetime employment for their core labor force. Rather than releasing "redundant" workers, Japanese firms retrained and redeployed them, thereby confirming and renewing the paternalistic bonds with their work forces that serve them so well in their labor process.

Similarly, institutionalized pressures on German automakers to upgrade the skill level of their employees and win the support of a strong works council seem to have significantly contributed to their strategic decision in the 1970s to move upmarket toward higher value-added, more innovative, and more customized production (Dankbaar, this volume; Streeck, 1989). These and other observations suggest that, as with government intervention and regulation, the "right" kind of labor constraint may serve to suspend or counterbalance managerial preferences for short-term allocative efficiency and profitability *in a way that ultimately contributes to a firm's international competitiveness.*

National-sectoral regimes of economic governance *evolve over time* and constitute *historically grown social facts* for each new generation of traders. At any given point, economic actors are confronted with a legacy of local social institutions that are not of their making; not subject to their choosing; not in principle amenable to contractual reordering; and whose functional and evolutionary logic is different from that of a market or a formal-organizational hierarchy. At the center of this logic is the ability of governance regimes to impose *socially constructed collective obligations* on individuals, if necessary against their resistance.[11] It is only in the limiting case of a completely "deregulated" market regime—which interestingly constitutes the normal, and indeed the only theorizable, case in standard economics—that institutional constraints and obligations are entirely and timelessly at the disposal of market participants. At that stage, they arguably cease to be constraints and obligations—just as the order that generates them ceases to be one that exists outside of the shifting volitions of its members.

In the real world, the "givenness" of an industrial order is visible in its ability to *socialize* its subjects into distinctive identities. While individuals "belonging to" a particular order may undertake to remake it—for example, in line with perceived imperatives of efficiency and "economizing"—in doing so they are forced to observe its present modus operandi and the constraints it imposes on them (in other words, to accept its "path-dependency"). This implies a fundamental paradox for actors who expect their interests to benefit from liberation of markets and hierarchies from the encumbrance of other social or political institutions. To transform an existing governance regime in the ideal image of neoclassical economics, actors have to acquire and deploy cultural, social, and political power resources of a more-than-just-economic kind. Also, if successfully instituted, the resulting new order would, in violation of its own basic principles, have to be continuously watched over and enforced by strong noneconomic mechanisms of governance, among them very likely a strong state.[12]

The omnipresence in economic action of logics other than those of markets and hierarchies is indicated by the fact that even multinational companies continue to retain local-national properties that make it easy to identify their "home base."[13] According to Michael Porter (1990), both the structure and the organizational culture of a multinational firm represent a product of an interaction between sectoral contingencies and the institutional environment of its country of origin. Multinationalization does not diminish the importance of the latter, as illustrated by the distinctively "German" characteristics of organizations like Bayer Leverkusen, Hoechst, and BASF; the "Japanese" makeup of Honda, Toyota, Sony, Mitsubishi, and others; and the identifiable "Americanness" of companies like Ford of Europe. This seems to confirm the idea, implicit in the extended concept of economic governance put forward in this volume, that the markets-and-hierarchies logic of industrial organization is by itself not sufficiently instructive for economic actors to organize their transactions satisfactorily. To close the Gestalt of a "sector" or "firm" and to know how to "do business," traders must be able to draw on additional *social rather than economic* instructions. The persistence of national traits in multinational enterprises thus tends to confirm the idea that *purely economically driven economic behavior is underdetermined*, leaving fundamental gaps in the orientations of actors that must be filled by rules generated and enforced by more-than-economic social institutions. In the present period, most such institutions are still nationally distinct.[14]

Industrial Order and Economic Performance in an
Internationalized Economy

Sectoral analysis within and across countries suggests that the relationship between institutional arrangements and economic performance is far more complex than the neoclassical economic literature indicates. To begin with, there are alternative *standards of good economic performance* that firms within sectors may adopt, and there is apparently no "natural" rank-order between them. The type of performance that companies seek differs not only from sector to sector within countries but also between countries within sectors. For example, Traxler and Unger (this volume) demonstrate that the relative priority of *allocative, dynamic, and distributional efficiency* varies substantially among the dairy industries of the United Kingdom, Germany, and Austria. Similarly, according to O'Brien (this volume), the performance of firms in the American steel industry is typically evaluated in terms of their profitability, while the most important performance criterion for Japanese steel firms was for a long time their advancement toward technological leadership and their share in the world market.[15]

The chapters in this volume suggest that countries have a tendency to favor "typical" performance standards across sectors. For example, while there is some sectoral variation in the type of economic performance that American companies pursue, large American manufacturing firms tend to place strong emphasis on allocative efficiency and to give high priority to maximizing short-term rates of return on capital invested. As a consequence, American corporations work to maintain an environment in which capital and labor have freedom to move between firms and sectors. Or, put the other way around, given the high mobility and the resulting "unreliability" of production factors in the American economy—which may reflect a nontraditional, highly modern type of social structure—the pursuit of short-term profitability at the expense of other possible economic objectives would appear to be a rational response of firms to their environment.

On the other hand, countries whose institutional arrangements reflect or impose communitarian and political obligations and commitments, resulting in lower factor mobility, tend to give less priority to short-term maximization of profit. For example, Japanese and German firms in a number of sectors—and indeed their sectoral governance arrangements *in toto*—often seem to be oriented toward maximizing the pursuit of what Leibenstein (1976, 1978) has called X-efficiency (see Sako, this volume). In contrast to allocative efficiency, however, there are no readily available quantifiable measures for X-efficiency. X-efficiency involves complex social processes leading to long-term improvement in the skill levels of employees, and to better communication among actors engaged in producing, processing, and consuming goods and services. Investments designed to enhance X-efficiency tend to improve product quality and innovativeness in product development, and to contribute to the ability of firms to shift from one product to another in response to changing marketing conditions. Lower factor mobility and, perhaps, lower productivity may thus coincide with higher process flexibility and product innovativeness.

National sectoral regimes can be conceived as institutionalized constraints and opportunities for companies strategically selecting their performance standards in line with what their environment permits, rewards, and forbids. Different industrial orders favor different performance standards,[16] which out of the wide range of possible economic objectives that a sectoral regime emphasizes—allocative efficiency, high employment, use of high-skilled as opposed to unskilled labor, high wages, an equitable distribution of returns, a high long-term share in the world market, etc.—is not a foregone conclusion. Unlike in the simple world of economics, there is in real economies no preestablished universal standard toward which economically rational actors will "economize." Performance standards are, and have to be, socially selected and may differ in time and space. In particular, even under capitalism, "profitability" as an objective of economic activity remains less than determinative and unable to instruct economic behavior unless supplemented by additional criteria establishing, for example, whether profits are to be sought in the short or in the long term; what, at a given point in the product and business cycle, can be regarded as an "adequate" level of profit; or how long and in what conditions profitability can, or has to, be neglected in pursuit of partly or temporally conflicting objectives.

Whether or not an industrial order can sustain its chosen performance standard depends not on the latter's intrinsic economic "rationality" but on the system's environment and external relations. Interestingly, it is on this fact that standard economics today seems to place its strongest hope for an unambiguous, "objective" criterion of economic performance. More specifically, the hope seems to be that global competition in an integrated world market will ultimately replace the variety of national definitions of good economic performance with a general standard of universal *competitiveness*. Economists may grudgingly have come to accept that a country may for a long time be able to hold on to a non-neoclassical, and less than "allocatively efficient," institutional order, presumably employing "politics" of all kinds to suspend the "economizing pressures" of "the market" at the cost of a reduction in overall welfare. However, as national sectors are no longer isolated from international competition, market forces may be expected eventually to undermine and destroy "artificial" regimes that try to distort the "laws" of the marketplace. Internationalization of sectors, by introducing *competition over the performance of performance standards*, would thus adjudicate—and indeed lay to rest once and for all—heretic claims that a unionized economy with a low wage spread, high wages, and high employment stability may be "efficient"; that government support for selected industries may contribute to economic growth; and that firms with co-determination of workers and long-term "captive" investors may perform better than firms with unmitigated managerial prerogative that operate in a highly flexible capital market.

Again, however, sociological and historical analysis raises a number of caveats. First, the world market is no less an "instituted," socially constructed, and politically contested order than are national markets. Only in the limiting case, if ever, will its institutional structure and operation follow strictly neoclassical prescriptions. Even to the extent that it does, this is not "naturally" so, but is the result of collective political choice among nations in the arena of international politics. Powerful countries may create trade regimes that favor their industries and firms by rewarding their strengths and neutralizing their weaknesses and even force competitor nations to reorganize their domestic institutions in the image of the "hegemonic" country. In this respect, the construction of international economic regimes for trade, investment, and production is exactly analogous to domestic regime building in that both, by defining the cultural, social, and political rules under which economic transactions may take place, determine which firms with which strategies and capacities will have competitive advantage over others (Keohane, 1984; Krasner, 1983; Ruggie, 1983; Haggard and Simmons, 1987; Keeley, 1990; Gilpin, 1987).

Second, even under an international free trade regime where national markets are easily accessible to nonnational traders, there is no guarantee that this will favor firms whose domestic systems of industrial order are primarily based on markets and corporate hierarchies (McKeown, 1983). Indeed, the chapters in this volume offer strong evidence that institutionally rich domestic regimes capable of overriding or supplementing the logic of markets and hierarchies may help "their" firms prevail over competitors based in institutionally impoverished, neoclassical, market and hierarchy-driven governance systems. Examples are the competitive advantages that German firms draw from the German vocational training system—under which their workplace-based training activities are to a large extent institutionally governed rather than market-driven (Streeck et al., 1987); the positive impact of co-determination on the ability of large German companies to run advanced human resource policies (Streeck, 1984); and the positive consequences of the institutional suspension of the profit motive in the Japanese steel industry for its competitiveness at the international level (O'Brien, this volume).[17]

Not all of a country's sectors compete and perform equally well internationally. Countries typically succeed in some sectors but not in all. At the same time, they rarely have isolated sectors that perform well at the global level. National success tends to occur with clusters of sectors that are complementary or similar to one another. Moreover, firms within successful sectors are often concentrated within specific regions of countries where they are covered by similar governance arrangements allowing them, among other things, to utilize similar skills and to rely on the same kind of educational and research institutions. Spatial proximity also enables companies to have rich communication with their competitors and feedback from their suppliers and customers (Porter, 1990). Whether or not a country excels in a particular sector seems to depend on whether its national (or regional) institutions define, favor, or prescribe performance criteria for firms that happen to match current requirements of success in international competition. The same criteria, if imposed on firms in other sectors whose international environment is different, may well be counterproductive. It is also possible that institutionalized performance criteria that enhance the competitiveness of a company in one period may, as environmental conditions change, detract from it in the next.

The often superior world market performance of firms governed by non-laissez-faire domestic institutional arrangements poses a puzzle for countries with market-driven economies as they attempt to design the world economy in the image of their own domestic practices.[18] In general, the effect of domestic institutions on the international performance of a company's sector or economy seems often paradoxical, difficult to predict, and unintended. For example, a demanding industrial relations and training regime that drives up the costs of labor may, as shown by the German case, increase rather than reduce the competitiveness of a national economy by forcing its firms into a pattern of quality-competitive and highly customized production.

Similarly, the presence of seven automobile producers in Japan, and of five in Germany, was for a long time regarded as a liability for the two industries in international competition; this was based on the assumption that fragmentation on the supply side would prevent companies from attaining necessary economies of scale. It was only in the 1970s that the fierce competition in the German and Japanese domestic automarkets and the diverse and "oversized" design capacities associated with industrial "fragmentation" were recognized as sources of international competitive advantage. Also, when after World War II the German machine tool industry re-created its traditional, quasi-artisanal structure and its long-standing arrangements of associational governance, there was no way of predicting that fragmentation of product markets and the emergence of microelectronics in the 1980s would turn a pattern of industrial organization and institutional governance inherited from the nineteenth century into a source of worldwide competitive advantage.

As noneconomic domestic institutions are increasingly recognized as important sources of success and failure in world markets, economic competition turns into social system competition, and competitive pressures for economic rationalization become pressures for general social change. A country whose system of industrial order—under given "terms of trade" (i.e., given institutionalized criteria of success and failure in the international "market")—provides firms in a particular sector with competitive advantage is likely to turn into a principal location for production in that sector.[19] As a result, its share in global sectoral output and capacity will increase. The country will also be able to retain its system or governance, including its preferred performance standards.

Conversely, a country whose industrial order disadvantages firms under given conditions of international competition will either experience sectoral deindustrialization,[20] or will have to rebuild its institutions and adjust its performance preferences. The latter will as a rule be accompanied by redistribution of political power and economic advantage, between as well as within sectors.[21] Competition between industrial orders may thus cut deeply into a country's social and political fabric[22] and may raise fundamental questions about the *democratic sovereignty* of political entities that cover a significantly smaller territory than the market in which their citizens must operate.[23]

Competition, Selection, Convergence

Economic functionalism would expect that under a given international trade regime, national systems of sectoral governance that create competitive disadvantage for the firms under their control[24] will be reconfigured on an institutional "model" of "best practice." There are, however, a number of reasons why such *convergence*[25] may fail to occur:

1. While some industrial orders may be capable of restructuring toward a given high-performance "model," others may not. To the extent that the evolution of an institutional configuration is *path-dependent*—that is, conditioned by its historically grown structure—the number of developmental trajectories on which a system can embark is limited. Inability to copy a more "efficient" mode of governance may condemn a country to permanent competitive disadvantage in specific sectors—unless it can develop a functionally equivalent arrangement (see below) that fits its existing structure and raises its sectoral performance to a competitive level. Without change, a country may face the prospect that certain productions that are disadvantaged by its mode of governance will move to other countries. For example, one may argue that the present labor market regime in the United States—with its erratic school-to-work transition, a widespread preference for narrowly specialized job definitions, on average very short job tenure, and an almost complete absence of systematic workplace-based training—is both deeply culturally rooted and therefore unchangeable, *and* incompatible with the requirements of advanced manufacturing. Assuming that this was the case, one would *ceteris paribus* expect the deindustrialization of the U.S. economy to continue.[26]

2. Convergence also fails to occur if sectors under noncompetitive modes of governance manage to reorient themselves toward a market niche whose performance requirements match their institutional endowment. To the extent that the new niche allows for a satisfactory level of output and investment, *specialization* may thus offer a viable *alternative to convergence*. If a country cannot give its firms the institutional support required to compete successfully for product quality and diversity, its industries may instead move downmarket toward price-competitive, standardized production. Conversely, firms that are forced to operate under a "rigid" high-wage labor market regime that is resistant to convergence on more "flexibility," lower wages, and a wider wage spread may as an alternative to emigration move upmarket so as to earn the margins they need to pay their expensive workers. The result may be very different modes of governance coexisting in different national divisions of the same sector.[27]

3. A country's "dominant coalition" may be willing to pay a price for the preservation of a noncompetitive industry by granting it *protection from foreign competition*. The price of protection is, of course, paid by consumers who are deprived of access to less expensive or superior products, and by producers in other sectors who may lose their export markets as a consequence of other countries' retaliation. Treating a sector as "infrastructure" (Traxler and Unger, this volume) and paying for its preservation is not necessarily against a country's general interest, even though this involves a less than optimally efficient allocation of resources and serves the special interest of sectoral producers. A prominent example of a sector whose state-sponsored industrial order shields it against competitive pressures—and that is for this purpose isolated from international convergence pressures—is European agriculture. It is arguable that even with

complete convergence on the industrialized, market-driven "best practice" represented by, perhaps, the United States, European agriculture could never successfully compete with American agriculture. It is also arguable that given the unpredictability of international trade policy, tendencies to employ trade restrictions for political purposes, and wide currency fluctuations, high publicly administered and guaranteed prices of domestic produce may be a reasonable insurance premium for a country to pay. Convergence on a superior mode of governance may thus fail to come about in spite of strong market pressures for "economizing."

4. Even in a free-trade international environment, a less competitive country may avoid convergence on a best practice governance mode by *forcing its superior foreign competitors to converge on its own institutional pattern.* If domestic change—for whatever reasons—is not feasible, if specialization is impossible, and if the costs and opportunity costs of protectionism are unacceptable, then a country may employ its international power to intervene in a competitor's domestic structure so as to undo its institutional advantages or impose on it the same handicaps that it itself faces. If successful, the country may in this way protect its "way of life" from "unfair competition." *Reverse convergence* of this kind is not as infrequent as it might appear—take the successful effort of the post–New Deal United States after 1945 to install free trade unions and collective bargaining in other countries, especially Japan and Germany, in part to saddle them with the same social costs that America had to accept. A similar and more exclusively economically motivated case would be the current Structural Impediments Talks between the United States and Japan, in which the United States tries to persuade the Japanese government, among other things, to dismantle the *keiretsu* business networks and a range of capital market practices that may have been an important source of Japan competitive advantage.[28] Reverse convergence—or *convergence on second-best practice*—may be demanded as a precondition for "free trade" where access to the market of a larger country is made conditional on the smaller country accepting foreign intervention in what effectively ceases to be its "domestic affairs."[29]

5. Convergence on a universal pattern of "best practice" can also be avoided if a country manages to develop institutional arrangements that, while *structurally different* from the leading model, *perform equally well* under existing terms of international competition. Indeed *functional equivalence* may be more frequent than outright convergence since institutional arrangements, in order to be stable and efficient, have to "fit" their larger societal contexts, which differ by country. A functionally equivalent arrangement would not upset its institutional context as much as, perhaps, a structural transplant. At the same time, confidence in the capacity of different structures to produce equivalent economic outcomes seems to decline with internationalization and competition, as national arrangements that in the past were regarded as equivalent are increasingly discovered to have survived only under the protection of, now dissolving, institutional mechanisms of market segmentation.

For example, while for a time the "societal effect" theory associated with the Aix-en-Provence school of industrial sociology tended to treat different national patterns of work organization in manufacturing as equivalent, they now regard them as sources of competitive advantage and disadvantage (Maurice, Sellier, and Silvestre, 1982). Note that the development of functionally equivalent regime structures may in a given case be as impossible as convergence on best practice for the same reasons of institutional path-dependency. Note also that protectionism, specialization, and reverse convergence can be employed to avoid the need, not just for copying a leading model, but also for devising functionally equivalent solutions.

6. Another reason why convergence on a model configuration of markets, "networks," corporate hierarchies, associations, and state authority may not be empirically observable is that the reconfiguration of an institutional order in line with given economic performance requirements is likely to be a protracted process. While in standard economics adjustment occurs instantly and without delay, empirical analysis must allow for *historical time*. Above all, this is because social institutions are less economically accountable than, ideally, business. Since they serve a diversity of functions, their performance cannot be unambiguously judged; there is for an industrial order no equivalent to what profitability is for an individual firm. Also, under a less than competitive regime, some firms may still be doing well, giving rise to hopes that things may get better without fundamental change. And declining industrial performance can always be attributed to a large number of noninstitutional factors, such as the business cycle, macroeconomic mismanagement, or simple bad luck—which may further delay institutional reform.[30]

Institutional inertia and delayed adjustment may also result from the agonizing difficulty of the *strategic choices* that have to be made. In principle, a country whose institutions perform unsatisfactorily in a given sector can always try to change the rules of the international trade regime so that they better match its capabilities[31]; or it may try to isolate itself from international pressures by protectionism. Exploring these strategies and ruling them out will typically require time. But even when domestic institutional reform is accepted as inevitable, there still remains the choice between adaptation of the leading "model" or development of an indigenous functional equivalent. While the former may run up against formidable and unpredictable contextual constraints,[32] the result of the latter is uncertain. Given the long feedback time required for evaluating the effects of institutional reforms and the opportunities this creates for opponents of change and proponents of alternative strategies, institutional responses to governance deficits can be expected to be systematically, and not just contingently, long-drawn processes.

7. Best-practice convergence is further impeded by *uncertainty* as to what exactly "best practice" is. For example, there was always wide variation in "Fordist" production regimes not only between but even within countries—consider the different "corporate cultures" of Ford and General Motors. Similarly, the way different Japanese auto manufacturers organize production is far from identical, leaving those trying to adopt "the Japanese way" wondering what it is. Moreover, leading regimes may evolve over time, so that what is "best practice" may significantly change while others are trying to emulate it. Also, since the economic effects of institutional structures cannot be easily measured and decomposed, no one can say unambiguously how much of a difference quality circles really make, or whether enterprise unionism is a central or a peripheral element of the "Japanese mode of production." In other words, there is an endemic uncertainty as to which out of a number of more or less fluid institutional provisions that together constitute an industrial order are actually the ones responsible for a regime's superior performance.[33] This allows for claims and counterclaims by proponents of different institutional reforms that are typically not adjudicable within the time in which decisions have to be made.

8. Pressures for institutional convergence are also mediated by *shifting performance requirements*, making the "best-practice" point of convergence a *moving target of uncertain location*. In the historical time needed for performance pressures to move divergent sectoral-industrial orders toward convergence, the technological and economic conditions that would have favored one sectoral order over another may themselves change. Such change can be expected to proceed only slowly, gradually and inconspicuously, and to be fully understandable only with hindsight—which is another way of saying that institutional adjustment takes place in an historical setting where the horizon is open and all that can be said about the future is that it lies ahead.

Taking unpredictable shifts in the point of institutional equilibrium into account, even a simple economistic, "best-practice" model of competition-driven convergence would be fully compatible with high observed institutional diversity, where progress toward convergence would be continually reversed by surprising changes in its required direction. For example, while present economic and technological conditions seem to favor governance arrangements that engender and support highly diversified and quality-competitive production (Streeck, 1991), there is no guarantee that this will not give way at some later time to a situation that calls for some other, as yet unknown, producton pattern. The present capacity of institutionally embedded, or governed, "diversified quality producers" to outcompete "mass producers" by making smaller batches of more customized products at not excessively higher prices is, to an important extent, an offshoot of the discovery, some three decades ago, of microelectronic technology in the U.S. weapons and space program. That discovery was largely exogenous to the dynamics of institutional evolution at both the national and the international level (and in any case had the quite unanticipated consequence that it placed the very country where it occurred at a disadvantage relative to countries that had less successfully and less completely adapted to the performance requirements of mechanized mass production—countries whose "lagging" institutions happened to be more congenial to the new technology's potential to narrow the price differential between standardized and customized products). Just as no one would have predicted microelectronics elevating "outmoded," pre-Fordist production regimes to the place of "best practice," no one knows what today's ongoing and as yet hidden technological, economic, political, and institutional changes may imply for the direction of convergence pressures in the next several decades.

Taking seriously the inherent dynamic and constitutive unpredictability of performance criteria and institutional "best-practice" convergence points, the most important property of a competitive institutional system may be a *general capacity to respond to a wide variety of continuously shifting performance pressures.* "Best practice," in this sense, would be almost the opposite of structural adjustment and dedication to a historically dominant set of performance criteria. Rather, it would consist in the preservation of a *rich "requisite variety" of self-reorganizing responses to newly emerging opportunities and constraints.* The essence of such a system would consist of its observable configuration at any given point in time, not in the underlying *reflexive intelligence* that has created and may undo that configuration—that is, in what the system, in any of its contingent structural incorporations, is *not* (Streeck, 1991).

It is important to emphasize that under any given set of competitive performance pressures, core capacities of a high requisite variety governance regime are liable to appear expendable or "redundant." This is due, among other things, to the inevitable tendency of actors to take present contingent conditions as constant; develop apparently experience-tested orthodoxies; and "economize" by devoting all available resources to the most urgent task. For this reason, *an institutional system's reflexive intelligence is difficult to build and maintain if the system is governed exclusively by rational-economic considerations.* This holds even if the pressures that place a premium on reflexive intelligence are economic in kind. Ultimately, competitive superiority in an unpredictable and rapidly changing environment requires a *culturally rather than instrumentally* based "higher-order rationality" that prevents actors from being excessively "economistic"; that obliges them not to dedicate "redundant" resources irreversibly to specific purposes; and that makes them adhere to a *logic of efficient nonallocation.*

To the extent, then, that the competitive economic performance of institutional arrangements depends on their requisite variety, the problem of convergence would have to be fundamentally redefined. If best practice consists in "cultural" preservation of potential structural alternatives of as yet unknown use, the *economic performance of an institutional governance system would depend on its successful refusal to become totally controlled by economic performance criteria.*[34] The problem of competitive survival may therefore not at all be to converge on some contingent "best practice." Rather, it may be to ensure that noneconomic values and institutions ramain resistant against the "satanic mill" (Polanyi, 1944/1957) of market-driven economic-instrumental rationalization. The difficulty, of course, is that such resistance cannot be successfully mobilized *for economic purposes and from economic motivations alone.*

Internationalization of Governance?

One way in which cross-national convergence of sectoral governance may be advanced is by international or supranational regime formation in response to *internationalization of sectoral economies.* While internationalization usually refers to growth of *product markets* and *product market competition* beyond national boundaries, there are other distinct but equally important aspects of the process, such as the following:

1. internationalization of *products*, as in the case of the "world car" of the 1960s and 1970s;

2. internationalization of *supplier relations* and *production chains*, with firms engaging in "global sourcing" and entering in international "strategic alliances" in marketing, production, or research;

3. internationalization of *finance markets*, as a result of which firms may obtain credit globally and outside the purview of national regulatory agencies. Being able to move their capital rapidly from one nation to another, investors may drive up the price they extract from firms, labor, and national governments for their cooperation in "job creation";

4. internationalization of *labor markets* due to higher mobility of labor between countries, which may undermine the control of national unions and governments over labor standards;

5. internationalization of *industrial organization*, where large firms locate their subsidiaries worldwide and in the process become multinational enterprises whose "corporate culture" may or not begin to cut across national boundaries.

The different dimensions of internationalization do not necessarily develop concurrently. In both form and extent, internationalization may vary vastly between sectors and countries. National dairy industries seem to be almost entirely unaffected (Traxler and Unger, this volume)—or only indirectly in that growing competition in other sectors may cut the resources that national governments give to support low-productivity domestic agriculture.[35] By comparison, the chemical industry has been highly international from its inception (Grant and Paterson, this volume). Similarly, whereas printed circuit board production is still largely local (Sako, this volume), internationalization of the machine tool industry varies strongly among countries, with French or American producers exporting a much lower share of their product than, for example, Swiss, Swedish, and German producers (Herrigel, this volume).

Internationalization of product markets, products, production chains, factor markets, and industrial organization gives rise to "networks" of relations among sectoral actors across national borders. As these become sufficiently dense and stable, they may serve as a basis for an emerging international governance regime distinct from the national regimes preceding it. In the limiting—as it were, "federalist"—case, this new regime will eventually become strong enough to "harmonize," unify, supersede, and absorb its constituent national regimes, resulting in *integrated supranational governance* for the sector as a whole. Rather than market pressure or, as in older theories of "convergence," technology, the driving force behind this would be a new layer of (international) institutions obliging previously "sovereign" national systems, and the actors within them, to submit to uniform and more encompassing regulation.

This event, however, is far from predetermined. Most international regimes exist on top of strong and heterogenous national regimes that do not seem likely to wither away soon. Basically, this is because markets and hierarchies are easier to internationalize than other governance mechanisms, especially those associated with public power. While internationalization of markets and hierarchies can erode the *effective sovereignty* of national states over sectoral economies, it does not by itself restore at a higher level the authority historically vested in national governments and create supranational public institutions with the authority to set and enforce common standards. As a consequence, economic relations that have outgrown national regulation are typically internationally governed by private, market or network-like arrangements embedded in—and partly shaped by—complex and dynamic relations between fragmented national and weak international industrial orders. This is why internationalization and international regime formation are today so often associated with *deregulation* (i.e., with "freer," more "self-regulating" markets than were typically allowed to exist under national auspices).

As integration of sectoral markets and hierarchies is not necessarily accompanied by integration of other institutions, it is bound to complicate the study of sectoral regimes of economic governance. Instead of assuming as a matter of course that economic internationalization will ultimately somehow result in global regime consolidation, empirical analysis has to be attentive to a wide range of interaction effects between international and national regimes, as well as among the latter, affecting the way in which internationalized markets and hierarchies are embedded in sectoral institutional orders. Three types of interactions seem to be of particular importance (Streeck, 1992b):

1. *Horizontal interaction among diverse national regimes in an internationalized economy.* In most internationalized sectors, national regimes of governance continue to figure prominently as sources of competitive advantage and disadvantage for "their" firms in the international arena. Although the chemical industry is highly internationalized (Grant and Paterson, this volume), the German vocational training system and the close traditional links in Germany between the industry and the universities are still important determinants of competitive outcomes on a global scale. Similarly, the competitive position of firms in the globalized consumer electronics industry of the 1990s is significantly influenced by nationally specific factors like the Japanese social system of production and the capacity of French "industrial policy" in the 1980s to convert its "national" into a "European champion" (Cawson, this volume).

More generally, separate national industrial orders in internationalized sectors tend to be subject to what may be called *regime competition*. Very little is known about the dynamics of this. What seems clear, however, is that in addition to more or less successful efforts to emulate international models of "best practice," competition may as such fundamentally change the political capacities and the internal makeup of national governance.

For example, as economic internationalization enables producers and mobile production factors to move between regimes and pick the one most convenient to them, the balance of power inside national industrial orders may tilt against less mobile parties, making it difficult to sustain and enforce social obligations like high taxes or a mandate on employers to share their managerial prerogative with their work forces. In this way, regime competition may make regimes more voluntaristic and contractual—in other words, deregulate them. (This, essentially, is meant when internationalization is described as undermining the "sovereignty" of national systems.) Deregulation and emulation of best practice may not always be the same, or only after fundamental and potentially painful adjustment of domestic performance criteria or of the international rules of the game.[36]

2. *Upward delegation of governance from national regimes to an emergent international regime.* As sectors internationalize, national actors may find it to their advantage to overcome their fragmentation by reorganizing into integrated supranational actors and submitting to supranational rules and regulations. This process, too, is uneven and contradictory, and may have a wide range of outcomes. Private traders in commodities and corporate property rights seem to require not much more than an internationally compatible civil law to start building international markets and hierarchies. Community relations, by comparison, are less easy to transfer to an international level, although they may newly emerge from specialized networks of mutually beneficial trading relationships. Associations, to the extent that they require state facilitation for their full development, may also have difficulties developing governing properties in an international setting. As a result, emergent international regimes are likely to be dominated by private arrangements among large firms, as in the chemical, financial, or consumer electronics sectors (see the chapters by Grant and Paterson; Coleman; and Cawson, respectively, this volume), with a strong role for informal networks and relatively little associational intermediation.

A critical question in the construction of supranational governance concerns the role of states and statelike agencies. National states, in response to the pressures of regime competition and the "tyranny of external effects" resulting from economic internationalization under nationally fragmented governance, may try to defend their "sovereignty" by collective action through international organizations. However, limiting the functions of supranational governance to the protection of national governance is difficult. Building a capacity for public intervention at the supranational level to compensate for its erosion at the national level may require national states to submit themselves to the authority of a new supranational sovereign, thereby formalizing the very loss of sovereignty they are trying to reverse. National states may not be willing to pay that price, nor may they have to, as long as they can use their remaining sovereignty to resist absorption into a unified supranational order. The result may be unabated regime competition in the public sphere of internationalized sectors—or, more likely, an uneasy coexistence among competing national and international states and quasi-states, permanent haggling over jurisdiction, and continuous oscillation between nationalism and internationalism in sectors whose markets, corporate hierarchies, and private networks may be increasingly integrated and unified.

An outcome like this would appear especially likely under national governments that pursue economic deregulation as a policy objective in its own right, and may hope to use a deregulated international regime to advance their domestic agenda. From their perspective, the dialectics of *sacrificing sovereignty in order to restore it*[37] would seem to make particularly little sense as such sacrifice would contribute to an unwelcome reassertion of public control over private markets. As the policy of the Thatcher government on European integration has shown, insistence on national sovereignty in an internationalized economy can be an extremely effective instrument for the political creation of a "self-regulating" market—just as neoliberal disengagement of public policy from the economy may be at least as effective in protecting state sovereignty as its transfer from national to international governments.

Whatever the relative role of national and supranational governance in an internationalized sectoral economy, national governments will always try to ensure that international regimes are compatible with their domestic practices and thereby confer competitive advantage on firms based in their countries.[38] Sometimes countries can rely on sheer economic, political or military power to shape the international regime to their image and to the benefit of their corporations. But it seems also true that countries have *ceteris paribus* more influence on how internationalized sectors are governed if they prefer private over public regimes, and favor freedom for markets and hierarchies over political interference. As again the Thatcher experience has shown, all that these countries may have to do is stick to "negative politics" and refuse to contribute to supranational public institution-building.[39]

3. *Downward authoritative modification of national regimes by supranational governance.* International regimes may acquire the authority to homogenize the national regimes comprised by them.[40] While this is the purest form of institutionally *mandated* convergence, and ideally suited to contain regime competition, it presupposes the growth of a powerful statelike international organization—which may be unlikely as long as such growth is controlled by the nation-states affected by it. More frequent seems to be *imposed* convergence under a common regime administered by a hegemonic country. An example would be the successful effort of the United States in the postwar period to build a free-trade regime among democratically organized nation-states with similar labor-inclusive "settlements" between capital and a moderate labor movement modeled on the New Deal and ensuring that firms from all countries had approximately the same social costs to bear as American firms.[41] The breakdown of this regime was accompanied by rising diversity, especially in the 1970s and 1980s, among the industrial relations systems of the three leading trading nations—Germany, Japan, and the United States.

How much homogeneity among their constituent countries international regimes require is not well understood. Nor are the conditions under which an international order may radiate into the national orders covered by it and change them. To the extent that international economic regimes do acquire formal jurisdiction over national public policies, their authority tends to be limited to the opening of national borders for international trade. In some cases, what has been referred to as "market-making" may even involve a measure of hierarchical intervention in national systems, to rearrange their rules so as to make them compatible with those of other countries so as to facilitate traffic of products, production factors, and property rights across borders.

Beyond this, however, there appears to be no guarantee that international regimes will develop a capacity to "harmonize" national standards, overcome regime fragmentation, and contain regime competition. In fact, as we have pointed out, such fragmentation and competition may be preserved or instituted on purpose in order to promote convergence in a "liberal," free-market direction, perhaps even in the name of a desirable diversity of national political institutions.[42] Whether and to what extent the institutionalization of a "self-regulating" international market will nevertheless ultimately require national actors, and in particular national states, to cede growing chunks of authority and sovereignty to supranational authorities—whether, in other words, there actually is such a thing as a logic of "spillover" from economic to political integration (Haas, 1958; Lindberg and Scheingold, 1970)—is a question that is presently being explored in the politics of the European Community. Here, the struggle over the "Social Dimension of the Internal Market" is essentially about the problem of whether market-making is possible in the long term without state-building; whether the former may in fact be pursued in the service of the latter; how far international regime formation can advance under conditions of fragmented sovereignty and competing political authority; and what the economic and social consequences may be of a potential supersession of public national by private international governance.

While the jury on this is still out, earlier assumptions that an integrated European economy can only be a "mixed," "managed," or "bargained" economy with strong integrated public governance are no longer being taken for granted after the experience of the 1980s (Streeck and Schmitter, 1991). That experience shows, in short, that the absence of an affirmative state at the supranational level, *whatever dysfunctions it may also have*, offers the advantage to nationalist governments that it is relatively compatible with national state sovereignty vis-à-vis other states, and to conservative governments and their business clientele in particular that it is supportive of neoliberal projects of general political disengagement from the economy.

Moreover, it would seem that the beneficiaries of a primarily "negative" mode of integration and regime formation have not only the interest but also the political power effectively to arrest whatever spillover automatism may in addition be at work in internationalized sectors and economies. In such circumstances, it seems premature at best to base predictions of supranational institutional development on assumed "functional needs" for the effective deregulation of national regimes through internationalization to be compensated by supranational re-regulation. While national states are not generally faring well in an age of internationalization, under given conditions their role and status may be maximized if internationalized sectors are governed primarily by private networks and if states make it their sovereign policy to spin off control over domestic economies to the "free play of market forces."

In several of the chapters in this volume (Cawson; Coleman; Grant and Paterson; Traxler and Unger, among others), the European Community figures prominently as an example of an emerging agent of strong, statelike, supranational public governance. Assessments differ as to its actual and potential impact on both economic actors and national regimes, and on the difference it makes, or will eventually make, for economic governance. Even in the strongest possible case, however, it is important to remember that the jurisdiction of the European Community extends only to part of the world economy. Today's global economy links Western Europe, internally integrated or not, to many other areas, in particular Japan and the United States.

For the German chemical industry, for example, Europe is no more than a segment, albeit an important one, in an effectively global marketplace and production system (Grant and Paterson, this volume). The same holds even more for large European financial institutions.

Finally, whatever may happen in Europe itself, there is no indication at all that the larger relationships that make up the world economy will any time soon be brought under the purview of anything only faintly resembling a supranational government. Even if the European Community were to grow institutionally beyond any reasonable expectation, the coincidence of internationalization of economic relations with privatization of governance in networks and corporate hierarchies, and the attrition this is likely to cause on public capacities for the correction of markets and the domestication of hierarchies, will continue to be a core problem for the governance of advanced capitalism.

Notes

1. Where state ownership of key manufacturers in Europe—a holdover from the age of extended land wars (France, Germany) and from 1970s-style industrial-*cum*-social policy (Britain)—has either disappeared (in Britain and, for all practical purposes, in Germany) or is on its way out (France).

2. To the extent that the direct role of the state in large-firm sectors has declined in the past decade, this may have to do with declining "effective sovereignty" of national states in an internationalizing economy—a theme we will address in the last part of this chapter.

3. A sector in which the apparent reluctance of Anglo-American states to employ "corporatist" self-regulation for public purposes is overridden by sectoral contingencies is the securities industry (Coleman, this volume). Here, the presence of strong networks among a powerful elite (investment bankers), the high technical complexity of the trade, the need for judgment and discretion, and a compelling self-interest among market participants in projecting an image of trustworthiness to potential customers forced and allowed governments to leave regulation to collective action of the industry itself.

4. For example, mandatory incomes policies. France and the United States have since their formative periods (which, of course, took place simultaneously under the influence of similar political ideas) shared deep-seated suspecions against "factions" and organized intermediary powers. Compare today the very low level of unionization and the indistinct role of political parties in the two countries. Britain is a special case in that older traditions of collective action have survived and prospered there in a pattern of "collective *laissez-faire*," without ever organically connecting with the constitution

of the state. Apart from sectoral exceptions, intermediary organizations thus were never in a situation in which they could have been turned into resources of public policy.

5. See Traxler and Unger (this volume), who show that trade associations are well developed in the dairy industries of most countries. This includes Britain where the Milk Marketing Board stands out as a rare example of a genuinely corporatist arrangement in that country. Note, however, that the other type of industrial association, labor unions, tends to be much better organized in sectors with large firms.

6. It must be added, of course, that there are three large chemical companies in Germany and not just one; and that the number of small chemical firms is much larger in Germany.

7. In other words, any transaction that is only marginally more personal and "particularistic" than a spot market contract. This would appear to entail the danger of the concept becoming all-encompassing.

8. *Nota bene* that Macauley (1963) discovered preferential and "relational" contracting among, of all occupational groups, traveling salesmen in, of all countries, the United States—and *not* in Japan, the favorite place of the "network" industry.

9. That networks exist primarily inside other, more "classical" social formations should not come as a surprise. According to Granovetter (1985), networks are present in both markets and corporate hierarchies, making them work better by compensating for their respective shortcomings. In Granovetter's world (where there are neither states nor associations), markets and hierarchies actually seem to dissolve into "networks," and it is difficult to conceive of anything social that is *not* one.

10. Both Japanese and German corporate decision making has been described as taking an inordinately long time by American standards, while also often resulting in qualitatively better decisions (Aoki, 1988; Katzenstein, 1989; Streeck, 1984).

11. As Coleman (this volume) points out, to the extent that the "deregulations" of financial markets in the 1980s involved the construction of a new, globalized industrial order, it was inevitably accompanied by far-reaching re-regulation.

12. This is the theme of Andrew Gamble's book on Thatcherism. *The Free Economy and the State* (1988).

13. The only example in this volume of a multinational corporation that seems to be abandoning its home base may be the Britain chemical company ICI. But this apparent cosmopolitanism may itself be a national trait, given the historical footlooseness of British capital and the notorious inhospitability of the British institutional environment to manufacturing industry. Also, a move from Britain to the United States is not one over a very long distance.

14. This is not to say that a company could not try to construct a worldwide, nationally indistinct "corporate culture" or could not succeed at it. The important point is, however, that the result would have to be a "culture" (i.e., would have to be morally in addition to economically based). Whether this is possible without alignment to a localized social and political community is an interesting empirical question.

15. Also see the different performance criteria of firms in the securities industry, depending on whether they are investment banks only or universal banks. How the industry is organized, in turn, depends entirely on the national regulatory regime. To the extent that international regulation mandates a particular performance standard, it may create competitive disadvantages for companies from one country in relation to companies from another (Coleman, this volume).

16. A particularly good example is the securities industry (Coleman, this volume) where national regulatory regimes give different priority to such criteria as profitability

and high returns on the one hand, and prudence and long-term stability on the other (Coleman, this volume).

17. Also see the important advantages the French consumer electronics industry derived from a traditional, etatistic industrial policy in the 1980s. As Cawson (this volume) points out, comparing the French to the British case, it is largely because of deep government intervention that there still is a significant French presence in the sector. The case is particularly interesting since it demonstrates the potential effectiveness of nonmarket national governance in an industry undergoing rapid internationalization in a highly competitive world market.

18. See Coleman (this volume) on the "deregulation" of the international capital market, in the image of traditionally Anglo-American sectoral regimes, and the potential incompatibility of the emerging international regimes with French and German practices.

19. However, it will attract inward investment only to the extent that foreign companies feel confident about their ability to operate in the country's institutional environment. See the almost complete absence of Japanese manufacturing in Germany.

20. See the shipbuilding industries in Germany and Sweden, or the automobile and consumer electronics industry in Britain.

21. An example is the effective takeover of consumer electronics production (and, in part, of automobile production) in Britain by Japanese firms, with the attendant changes in government industrial policy and, very importantly, industrial relations.

22. For example, a national capital market regime that makes a country's banking system subservient to the government's industrial policy objectives may have to be "liberalized" and "deregulated," with potentially major political and social consequences, if under new international conditions it can no longer attract enough capital for successful performance (see Coleman, this volume).

23. We will return to this theme in the final section of this chapter.

24. That is, in a "free" world market, regimes of governance that detract from the allocative efficiency of companies.

25. *Nota bene* that in comparison to the 1950s and 1960s (see Kerr, et al., 1960), expectations of institutional "convergence" among industrial societies today are only rarely based on assumptions of common, endogenous evolutionary tendencies. Usually these were located in the constraints imposed on social organization by modern technology. Today, technological determinism seems to have been superseded by a form of economic determinism, reflecting the vastly increased expansion and integration of the world market.

26. For more examples of production emigrating from an unfavorable regime, see the decline of the British consumer electronics and automobile industries (Cawson and Dankbaar, this volume). Certain models of "best practice" may be more suitable than others to being emulated, and national systems seem to differ in their ability or willingness to "converge" on foreign practices. While Japanese "lean production" is claimed to be universally applicable (Womack, Jones, and Roos, 1990), there have been no attempts to re-create German work organization or co-determination outside Germany, probably bacause of the dependence of these factors on supportive societal institutions outside the individual plant or enterprise. Moreover, while the United States and Britain seem to find it easy to accommodate Japanese "transplants" and even remodel parts of their own social system of production in their perceived image (for a strong note of caution, however, see Milkman, 1991), the few Japanese plants in Germany are said to have extremely poor labor relations.

27. Of course, as the products sold in the two market segments cease to compete with one another, we would eventually have to speak of two different sectors. While Hyundai and Daimler Benz are usually regarded as belonging to the same industry, they may in fact not really be competitors.

28. The Japanese response is to suggest upgrading American instead of downgrading Japanese competitiveness. Realization of their proposals, however (e.g., elimination of the federal deficit, a higher savings rate, better education, and a more long-term orientation of American firms), would appear to require institutional changes vastly beyond the reach of any American government.

29. The underlying general problem, of course, is that of the allowable range of domestic regime diversity for countries subject to a common international regime—in this case, one of "free trade." For more on this, see below.

30. This was what happened in British industrial relations from the early 1960s on, when the incompatibility of "free collective bargaining" under "voluntaristic" rules with the postwar political commitment to full employment and a basic social wage began to become visible. Reform was tried not before the early 1970s, only to be rejected under highly divisive domestic conflict.

31. This applies even to small countries that can attempt to mobilize majorities in international organizations in favor of their interests.

32. As, for example, the introduction of flexible job allocation and redeployment between direct and indirect production functions in an environment of powerful craft unionism.

33. This problem is not just a methodological one for studies like ours, but also, as it were, an ethnomethodological problem for practitioners in the real world.

34. In other words, greed does not pay, or greed alone is not enough.

35. Also, countries may be forced to open their agricultural product markets by threats of retaliation against revenue-generating export sectors.

36. The possibility of a regulatory "downward spiral" as a consequence of regime competition, and of a Gresham's law-type replacement of high performance by low performance regimes, has recently been discussed with respect to the European Community (Mayes, Hager, and Streeck, in press).

37. Or of sacrificing national for supranational sovereignty, or external sovereignty in relation to other states for internal sovereignty over the economy.

38. See the example, reported by Coleman (this volume), of the potentially negative effects of a deregulated—or only privately regulated—international securities market on countries with a universal bank system and more traditional prudential standards.

39. Another possibility is that a country may force accelerated internationalization and deregulation on an international scale by deregulating its own industry (see Coleman, this volume, on the securities sector).

40. Which is what is called "harmonization" in European Community jargon.

41. By comparison, the possible outcomes of the Structural Impediments Initiative for the American and Japanese political economies could be characterized as *negotiated convergence*.

42. See the recent rise in the European Community of the concept of "subsidiarity." In some interpretations, subsidiarity refers to a general principle to accomplish common policies through diverse national regimes, interfering with the latter only to the extent that they are unable to comply with—narrowly defined—common standards. However, subsidiarity is also invoked to legitimize abstention from supranational standard-setting and a policy of *laissez-faire* in relation to national standards.

References

Allen, Christopher S. (1989). "Political Consequences of Change: The Chemical Industry." In Peter Katzenstein (ed.), *Industry and Politics in West Germany: Toward the Third Republic* (pp. 157–84). Ithaca, N.Y.: Cornell University Press.

Aoki, Masahiko. (1988). *Information, Incentives and Bargaining in the Japanese Economy.* Cambridge: Cambridge University Press.

Atkinson, Michael, and William D. Coleman. (1989). "Strong States and Weak States: Sectoral Policy Networks in Advanced Capitalist Economics." *British Journal of Political Science*, 19, 47–65

Bean, Roy. (1985). *Comparative Industrial Relations: An Introduction to Cross-National Perspectives*, London: Croom Helm.

Becattini, Giacomo. (1990). "The Marshallian Industrial District as a Socio-Economic Notion." In Frank Pyke, Giacomo Becattini, and Werner Sengenberger (eds.), *Industrial Districts and Inter-firm Cooperation in Italy* (pp. 37–51). Geneva: International Institute for Labor Studies.

Blau, Peter M. (1964). *Exchange and Power in Social Life.* New York: John Wiley.

Bork, Robert H. (1978). *The Antitrust Paradox: A Policy at War with Itself.* New York: Basic Books.

Brusco, Sebastiano. (1982). "The Emilian Model: Production Decentralization and Social Integration." *Cambridge Journal of Economics*, 6, 167–84.

Campbell, John, Rogers Hollingsworth, and Leon Lindberg. (1991). *The Governance of the American Economy.* Cambridge and New York: Cambridge University Press.

Cornish, William R. (1979). "Legal Control over Cartels and Monopolization, 1880–1914: A Comparison." In Norbert Horn and Jürgen Kocka (eds.), *Law and the Formation of the Big Enterprises in the Nineteenth and Early Twentieth Centuries: Studies in the History of Industrialization in Germany, France, Great Britain and the United States* (pp. 280–303). Gottingen: Vandenhoeck and Ruprecht.

Gamble, Andrew. (1988). *The Free Economy and the State: The Politics of Thatcherism.* Durham, N.C.: Duke University Press.

Gilpin, Robert. (1987). *The Political Economy of Industrial Relations.* Princeton, N.J.: Princeton University Press.

Granovetter, Mark. (1973). "The Strength of Weak Ties." *American Journal of Sociology* 78, 1360–80.

Granovetter, Mark. (1985). "Economic Action and Social Structure: The Problem of Embeddedness." *American Journal of Sociology* 91, 481–510.

Hass, Ernst B. (1958). *The Uniting of Europe: Political, Social and Economic Forces 1950–1957.* London: Stevens and Son.

Haggard, Stephan, and Beth A. Simmons. (1987). "Theories of International Regimes." *International Organization*, 41, 491–517.

Hall, Peter A. (1986). *Governing the Economy: The Politics of State Intervention in Britain and France.* New York: Oxford University Press.

Hayward, Jack. (1986). *The State and the Market Economy: Industrial Patriotism and Economic Intervention in France.* Brighton, UK: Wheatsheaf Books.

Hollingsworth, J. Rogers. (1991). "Die Logik der Koordination des verabeitenden Gewerbes in Amerika." *Kölner Zeitschrift für Soziologie und Sozialpsychologie*, 43, 18–43.

Johnson, Chalmers. (1982). *MITI and the Japanese Miracle: The Growth of Industrial Policy, 1925–1975.* Stanford, Calif.: Stanford University Press.

Johnson, Chalmers et al. (eds.). (1989). *Politics and Productivity: The Real Story of Why Japan Works.* New York: Harper Business.

Katzenstein, Peter (ed.). (1989). *Industry and Politics in West Germany: Toward the Third Republic.* Ithaca, N.Y.: Cornell University Press.

Keeler, John S. (1987). *The Politics of Neocorporatism in France.* New York: Oxford University Press.

Keeley, James F. (1990). "The Latest Wave: A Critical Review of the Regime Literature." In David G. Haglund and Michael K. Hawes (eds.), *World Politics: Power, Interdependence and Dependence* (pp. 553–69). Toronto: Harcourt Brace Jovanovich.

Keohane, Robert O. (1984). *After Hegemony: Cooperation and Discord in the World Political Economy.* Princeton, N.J.: Princeton University Press.

Kerr, Clark, John T. Dunlop, Frederick Harbison, and C. A. Myers. (1960). *Industrialism and Industrial Man.* Cambridge, Mass.: Harvard University Press.

Korpi, Walter. (1978). *The Working Class Under Welfare Capitalism: Work, Unions and Politics in Sweden.* London: Routledge & Kegan Paul.

Krasner, Stephen D. (ed.). (1983). *International Regimes.* Ithaca, N.Y.: Cornell University Press.

Leibenstein, Harvey. (1976). *Beyond Economic Man: A New Foundation in Microeconomics.* Cambridge, Mass.: Harvard University Press.

Leibenstein, Harvey. (1978). *General X-Efficiency Theory and Economic Development.* New York: Oxford University Press.

Lindberg, Leon N., and Stewart A. Scheingold. (1970). *Europe's Would-Be Polity: Patterns of Change in the European Community*, Englewood Cliffs, N.J.: Prentice Hall.

Maurice, Marc, Francois Sellier, and Jean-Jacques Silvestre. (1982). *The Social Foundations of Industrial Power: A Comparison of France and Germany.* Cambridge, Mass.: MIT Press.

Maurice, Marc, Francois Sellier, and Jean-Jacques Silvestre. (1984). "Rules, Contexts and Actors: Observations Based on a Comparison Between France and West Germany." *British Journal of Industrial Relations*, 22, 346–63.

McKeown, Timothy. (1983). "Hegemonic Stability Theory and 19th-century Tariff Levels in Europe." *International Organization*, 37, 73–91.

Macauley, Stewart. (1963). "Non-Contractual Relations in Business: A Preliminary Study." *American Sociological Review*, 28(1), 55–67.

Mayes, David, Wolfgang Hager, and Wolfgang Streeck. (in press). *Public Interest and Market Pressures: Problems Posed by Europe 1992.* London: MacMillan.

Milkman, Ruth. (1991). *Japan's California Factories: Labor Relations and Economic Globalization.* Los Angeles: University of California, Institute of Industrial Relations.

Okimoto, Daniel I. (1989). *Between MITI and the Market: Japanese Industrial Policy for High Technology.* Stanford, Calif.: Stanford University Press.

Polanyi, Karl. (1957). *The Great Transformation: The Political and Economic Origins of Our Time.* Boston: Beacon Press. (Original work published 1944).

Poole, M. (1986). *Industrial Relations: Origins and Patterns of National Diversity.* London: Routledge & Keagan Paul.

Porter, Micheal E. (1990). *The Competitive Advantage of Nations.* New York: Free Press.

Rabin, Robert L. (1986). "Federal Regulation in Historical Perspective." *Stanford Law Review*, 38, 1189–1326.

Ruggie, John Gerard. (1983). "International Regimes, Transactions, and Change: Embedded Liberalism in the Postwar Economic Order." In Stephen Krasner (ed.), *International Regimes.* (pp. 423–88). Ithaca, N.Y.: Cornell University Press.

Sabel, Charles F. (1989). "Flexible Specialization and the Re-emergence of Regional Economies." In Paul Q. Hirst and Jonathan Zeitlin (eds.), *Reversing Industrial Decline: Industrial Structure and Policy in Britain and Her Competitors* (pp. 17–70). Oxford: Berg.

Scheniberg, Mark, and J. Rogers Hollingsworth. (1990). "Can Transaction Cost Economics Explain Trade Associations?" In Masahiko Aoki, Bo Gustaffason, and Oliver Williamson (eds.), *The Firm as a Nexus of Treaties* (pp. 199–232). London and Beverly Hills: Sage Publications.

Streeck, Wolfgang. (1984). "Co-Determination: The Fourth Decade." In B. Wilpert and A. Sorge (eds.), *International Perspectives on Organizational Democracy: International Yearbook of Organizational Democracy, Vol. 2* (pp. 391–422). London: John Wiley.

Streeck, Wolfgang. (1989). "Successful Adjustment to Turbulent Markets: The Automobile Industry." In Peter J. Katzenstein (ed.), *Industry and Politics in West Germany: Towards the Third Republic* (pp. 113–56). Ithaca, N.Y.: Cornell University Press.

Streeck, Wolfgang. (1991). "On the Institutional Conditions of Diversified Quality Production." In E. Matzner and W. Streeck (eds.), *Beyond Keynesianism: The Socio-Economics of Production and Employment* (pp. 21–61). London: Edward Elgar.

Streeck, Wolfgang. (1992a). *Social Institutions and Economic Performance: Studies of Industrial Relations in Advanced Capitalist Economies.* London and Beverley Hills: Sage Publications.

Streeck, Wolfgang. (1992b). *European Social Policy: Between Market-Making and State-Building.* Unpublished manuscript.

Streeck, Wolfgang, Josef Hilbert, Karl-Heinz van Kevelaer, Friederike Maier, and Hajo Weber. (1987). *The Role of the Social Partners in Vocational Training and Further Training in the Federal Republic of Germany.* Berlin: European Centre for the Development of Vocational Training (CEDEFOP).

Streeck, Wolfgang, and Philippe C. Schmitter. (1985). "Community, Market, State—and Associations? The Prospective Contribution of Interest Governance to Social Order." In W. Streeck and P. Schmitter. (eds.), *Private Interest Government: Beyond Market and State.* Beverly Hills and London: Sage Publications.

Streeck, Wolfgang, and Philippe C. Schmitter. (1991). "From National Corporatism to Transnational Pluralism: Organized Interests in the Single European Market." *Politics and Society,* 19(2), 133–64.

Suleiman, Ezra N. (1974). *Politics, Power, and Bureaucracy in France: The Notaires and the State.* Princeton, N.J.: Princeton University Press.

Womack, James P., Daniel T. Jones, and Daniel Roos. (1990). *The Machine That Changed the World.* New York: Rawson Associates.

Zeitlin, Jonathan. (1992). "Industrial Districts and Local Regeneration: Overview and Comment." In F. Pyke and W. Sengenberger (eds), *Industrial Districts and Local Regeneration.* Geneva: International Institute for Labour Studies.

CONTRIBUTORS

Alan Cawson is Professor of Politics at the University of Sussex. He has written extensively on corporatist theory, including *Corporatism and Political Theory* (1986). Since 1985 he has been researching the political economy of the electronics industry, and is coauthor of *Hostile Brothers: Competition and Closure in the European Electronics Industry* (1990).

William D. Coleman is Professor of political Science at McMaster University, Hamilton, Ontario, Canada. He has written three books: *The Independence Movement in Quebec, 1945–1980* (1984), *Business and Politics: A Study in Collective Action* (1985), and (with Michael M. Atkinson) *The State, Business, and Industrial Change in Canada* (1989). His current work focuses on political institutions, financial policy, and changes in financial markets.

Ben Dankbaar is Director of Research in Technology and Labour at Maastricht Economic Research Institute on Innovation and Technology (MERIT) in Maastricht, the Netherlands. Between 1976 and 1982, he was a lecturer at the Economic Seminar of the Faculty of Social Sciences of the University of Amsterdam, after which he moved to Berlin where, until the end of 1987, he participated in several research projects at the Wissenschaftszentrum Berlin and the VDI-Technologiezentrum. Since then he has been working at MERIT.

Wyn Grant is Professor and Chairman of the Department of Politics and International Studies at the University of Warwick. He is the author of numerous books and articles on comparative political economy and continues to do research on issues related to economic and industrial policy.

Gary Herrigel is Assistant Professor of Political Science at the University of Chicago. He is the author of a number of scholarly articles on the political economy of twentieth century Germany and the forthcoming book *Industrial Orders in Twentieth Century Germany.*

J. Rogers Hollingsworth is Professor of Sociology and History and Chairperson, Program in Comparative History, University of Wisconsin, Madison. He is the author or editor of numerous books and articles on comparative political economy.

Patricia O'Brien is an Associate Professor at the Harvard Business School. The author of several articles and cases, she has focused her research on the comparative differences in Japanese and American business systems. She is presently writing a business history book, *Managers and the Market: Rethinking American Steel*, analyzing the competitive decline of the American steel industry.

William Paterson is Salvesen Professor of European Institutions and Director of the Europa Institute, the University of Edinburgh and Chairman of the University Association for Contemporary European Studies. He has written widely on Germany politics and is presently studying Germany's role in the "new Europe."

Mari Sako is a Lecturer in the Department of Industrial Relations at the London School of Economics and political Science. She was previously a research associate at the Technical Change Centre and at Imperial College, London. She is the author of *Prices, Quality and Trust: Inter-firm Relations in Britain and Japan* (1992) and the coauthor with Ronald P. Dore of *How Japanese Learn to Work* (1989).

Philippe C. Schmitter is Professor of Political Science at Stanford University and has conducted research on comparative politics and regional integration in both Latin America and Western Europe, with special emphasis on the politics of organized interests. He is the coauthor of *Transitions from Authoritarian Rule: Prospects for Democracy* (4 vols.) and is currently completing a book on *The Organization of Business Interests* with Wolfgang Streeck. At Stanford, he served at the director of the Center for European Studies from its foundation in 1986 until early 1992. He has been the recipient of numerous professional awards and fellowships, including a Guggenheim in 1978, and has been vice-president of the American Political Science Association.

Wolfgang Streeck is Professor of Sociology and Industrial Relations at the University of Wisconsin, Madison. He is the author or editor of the following books: *Social Institutions and Economic Performance: Studies in Industrial Relations in Advanced Capitalist Economies* (1992); *Beyond Keynesianism: The Socio-Economics of Production and Employment*, with Egon Matzner (1991); *Industrial Relations in West Germany: The Case of the Car Industry* (1984); *Private Interest Government: Beyond Market and State*, with Philippe C. Schmitter (1985).

Bo Stråth is Professor of History, Gothenburg University. Most of his published research has focussed on comparative modernization processes in Western Europe. He is the author of several books and many articles.

Franz Traxler is currently Professor of Industrial Sociology at the Faculty of Social and Economic Sciences, University of Vienna. His published research has focused on industrial relations, economic governance, and the organization of collective action.

Brigitte Unger is Assistant Professor of Economics at the University of Economics, Vienna. She was a Joseph-Schumpeter fellow at Harvard University in 1989–90 and Erwin Schroedinger fellow at Stanford University 1990–91. Her fields of specialization are comparative social science, institutional economics, and open macroeconomics; she has published a number of papers in these areas.

Index